SCREAM FROM THE SHADOWS

Scream from the Shadows

THE WOMEN'S LIBERATION MOVEMENT IN JAPAN

Setsu Shigematsu

University of Minnesota Press

Minneapolis

London

Portions of chapter 5 were published in "The Japanese Women's Liberation Movement and the United Red Army: A Radical Feminist Response to Political Violence," *Feminist Media Studies* 12, no. 2 (2012).

Published by the University of Minnesota Press
111 Third Avenue South, Suite 290
Minneapolis, MN 55401-2520
http://www.upress.umn.edu

Library of Congress Cataloging-in-Publication Data

Shigematsu, Setsu.
   Scream from the shadows : the women's liberation movement in Japan / Setsu Shigematsu.
   Includes bibliographical references and index.
   ISBN 978-0-8166-6758-1 (hc : alk. paper)
   ISBN 978-0-8166-6759-8 (pb : alk. paper)
   1. Feminism—Japan.   2. Women—Japan.   3. Women—Japan—Social conditions.   I. Title.
   HQ1762.S493 2012
   305.42'0952—dc23

                                                     2011044784

Printed in the United States of America on acid-free paper

The University of Minnesota is an equal-opportunity educator and employer.

20 19 18 17 16 15 14 13 12   10 9 8 7 6 5 4 3 2 1

To the *ribu* activists and
all those who have given their lives to
the struggle for collective liberation

CONTENTS

Preface: Feminism and Violence in the Womb of Empire   ix

Introduction: *Ūman Ribu* as Solidarity and Difference   xv

I. GENEALOGIES AND VIOLATIONS

1 Origins of the Other/*Onna*
The Violence of Motherhood and the Birth of Ribu   3

2 Lineages of the Left
Death and Reincarnation of a Revolutionary Ideal   33

II. MOVEMENTS AND MEDIUMS

3 The Liberation of Sex, *Onna,* and Eros
The Movement and the Politics of Collective Subjectivity   65

4 *Ribu* and Tanaka Mitsu
The Icon, the Center, and Its Contradictions   103

III. BETWEEN FEMINISM AND VIOLENCE

5 *Ribu*'s Response to the United Red Army
Feminist Ethics and the Politics of Violence   139

Epilogue: Lessons from the Legacy   171

Acknowledgments   181

Notes   189

Index   255

Feminism and Violence
in the Womb of Empire

After more than a decade-long U.S.-led globalized war *of* terror that has punctuated the onset of the twenty-first century, what are the conditions of possibility for feminist politics in this age of Empire? What have been the interventions as well as the fault lines of feminism(s) in such times? This book begins by posing questions about the interrelationship of feminism, imperialism, and violence to delve into the frequently disavowed conditions of violence that make many feminisms possible. To pose such questions at this historical moment seems particularly urgent given the ways that certain feminist discourses have been rallied in the name of U.S.-led multinational crusades to protect women's liberty and freedom in places like Afghanistan. The patriotic support of liberal feminist institutions (such as the Feminist Majority Foundation) have endorsed the invasions of other nations as a means to liberate women.[1] If notions such as women's liberation can be invoked to help cosmeticize imperialist warfare, then how should we reassert the imperatives and strategies for women's liberation today?

More than forty years ago, a women's liberation movement—called *ūman ribu*—was born in Japan amid conditions of violence, radicalism, and imperialist aggression. The movement was catalyzed by the forces of capitalist modernity and infused with anti-imperialist politics directed against what was deemed to constitute a U.S.–Japanese neo-imperialist postwar/Cold War reformation. Given the broader imperialist conditions that constitute feminisms through and across the borders of the United States and Japan, one of the tasks at hand for feminists located in the centers of Empire is to self-reflexively and critically analyze the different kinds of violence within the subject of feminism and the feminist subject as a means of confronting and potentially more effectively disrupting the systemic forms of violence that constitute our conditions of existence.

In recent decades, the hypervisibility of women who have authorized and sanctioned massive forms of imperialist state violence has been notable. On the global stage, Madeleine Albright's (in)famous public statement that the death of 500,000 Iraqi children, even prior to the official invasion, was "worth it" was followed by the prominence of Condoleezza Rice, and now Hillary Rodham Clinton, as the advocates of U.S. foreign policy.[2] These stateswomen serve as the most visible apogees of the convergence of liberal feminism and imperial power. Given how liberal feminist political goals for women's equality has largely enabled the rise of such elite women and has created the institutional space for women, myself included, to enter and occupy positions in the U.S. academy, I am disturbed by the relative hesitation, if not reluctance, of feminists to theorize the capacities, complicities, and desires for power, domination, and violence *in women*.

Informing this book's trajectory is a concern about the capacity of feminist subjects—including feminist-identified scholars and activists and those sympathetic to and informed by feminist politics—to engage with the questions, manifestations, and modalities of violence constitutive of our political horizon. Haunting the writing and completion of this book are thus unresolved questions that arise through a confrontation with the ways in which hegemonic (liberal and radical) feminist paradigms and particular kinds of feminist discourses have contributed to U.S. domestic and imperialist state violence.[3]

After the Abu Ghraib torture scandal and the sensational images of U.S. Army Private Lynndie England and her compatriots engaging in sexualized racial violence, feminist authors such as Barbara Ehrenreich declared that the era of naïve feminism has seen its own demise.[4] In contrast to the sensationalization of women's use of violence as a gender aberration, feminist scholars like Jacinda Read have argued that the popularization of the role of vigilante women in the mass media is an aftereffect of the infusion of second wave feminism into mass culture.[5] The valorization of gun-toting women getting even or outdoing men has become a staple part of popular culture. While some feminists may desire such forms of women's empowerment, the attempt to blame women's violence on the emergence of feminism is a perilous endeavor.[6] The origins of violence do not lie exclusively within the bounds of feminism; however, the empowerment of women perhaps has enabled the production of new kinds of violent female subjects. Liberal feminist tenets have constituted the political foundations that have enabled the entry of women, even those who do not identify as liberal feminists, into many professions, including the military, policing, and prisons. This may account for why feminist critiques that rigorously problematize women's relationality with violence have remained, until recently, rather reticent, lest such criticism bolster discrimination against women and undermine the work of multiple generations of feminists.[7]

The contributions of the legacy of "second wave feminism," as well as the problems with this dominant periodization, are well documented.[8] Feminist activism from the 1960s through the 1970s enabled a fundamental shift in our political understandings of violence against women, producing significant legal and sociocultural changes that contributed tremendously to the politicization and criminalization of domestic violence, sexual assault, and rape. These particular forms of violence against women have been rendered highly visible, and their criminalization and prosecution have relied on a legal system that reinforces liberal notions of the individual and punishment as its formula for justice. This feminist legacy is also implicated in the endorsement of policing and imprisonment as the primary apparatuses that have exponentially increased and expanded domestic state violence.[9] These penal regimes are imbricated with the history of racist practices and state-sanctioned violence in the forms of physical, psychological, and sexual violence against inmates regardless of gender or sexual orientation.[10] Accommodation to such forms of state violence through policing and prisons is one example of how many feminists have been complicit in perpetuating cycles of systemic violence.[11]

As a feminist scholar, my work in no way attempts to minimize the historical-material conditions of women's symbolic and systemic subordination. My own intellectual and political identity formation and life work is predicated on commonly held feminist tenets about the history of modern sex and gender subordination as constitutively intersecting with race and class, and I am committed to a "women-centered" praxis in terms of my own research and activism. Nevertheless, I am interested in interrogating how feminist subjects have both resisted and been implicated in the expansion of empires, national ideologies, state violence, and interpersonal and microlevels of normalized violence. Cognizant of such contradictions, how is more effective insurgency possible in the womb of Empire and at its extremities?

While recognizing the paradigm-shifting contributions of feminist movements, it is imperative to problematize how certain feminist discourses have rendered paramount (if not unassailable) the victimhood of women as one of its universalizing discursive tendencies. Although feminist gains have significantly empowered certain groups of women, particularly those racialized as white and middle-class, the feminization of poverty on a global scale and the wages of war continue to disproportionately impact women and children.[12]

Such conditions, at the very least, point to the limits of feminist politics to effectively prevent and transform these conditions. While this suggests how much feminist work remains to be done, I wish to emphasize that a delimited focus on the concept of women's victimhood may prevent us from taking seriously the problem of women's complicity and agency in the perpetuation of violence against other women, children, and men and how these circuits are maintained and reproduced geopolitically through gendered and racialized economies. Arguably, the relative feminist muteness about violence among women (intrafemale/woman on woman) might be symptomatic of a problematic desire and discursive tendency to posit women as the perpetual victims of patriarchy and sexism, obscuring or eclipsing differences of power and how such a discourse has sanctioned violence against men, particularly men of color.[13] I suggest that universalizing discourses of women's victimhood may function to obscure and forestall an adequate theorization of women's differential power, agency, and shifting investments in perpetuating systems of violence against the other. This underrecognized condition of women's ontologies in and of violence remains a shadow subject of feminism and a vexing problematic for those concerned with the future efficacy of feminist politics.

This book initiates a modest attempt to address the condition of Japanese women engaging in violence against other women and children and men. I raise questions about how adequately feminism has theorized this phenomenon or whether it has remained a taboo subject in feminist studies. Japanese feminists have long examined women's complicities in Japanese imperialism. Through my study of the Japanese women's liberation movement, I not only pay attention to its legible forms of liberation, antisexist practices, and counterhegemonic resistance but also tarry with the contradictions, repressive tendencies, and power dynamics among feminist activists to better understand the workings, limits, and impasses of our own notions of liberation, resistance, and radicalism.

At this historical juncture, I am most interested in examining what remains compelling and relevant about *ūman ribu* for contemporary politics. Given the global dimensions of the war *of* terror in the present context, what lessons and interventions were not learned adequately from the politics of the early 1970s? When *ūman ribu* emerged in the early 1970s, counterviolence was an active horizon of contestation and deemed, among certain political radicals, as necessary to liberate people from the capitalist-imperialist state. In the early 1970s, the state violently suppressed political radicalism and revolutionary movements across the United States and Japan. How was the state able to hegemonize its monopoly over political violence, and how were liberals and leftists implicated in conceding this hegemony?

Activists of *ūman ribu* sought to examine how Japanese women were constituted by the conditions of a violent society, a society that largely disavowed its complicity in the violence being done to others, especially other peoples of Asia during Japan's imperial past and in its ongoing neo-imperialist formations. By closely examining the political genealogy, formation, and fissures of the Japanese women's liberation movement, this study offers an opportunity to reflect on the blind spots within our contemporary and dominant understandings of feminism across their liberal, socialist, Marxist, radical, Euro-American, postcolonial, and women-of-color discursive configurations. It offers a nuanced understanding of how dominant forms of feminist inquiry may have minimized and repressed different forms of violence within and among feminist subjects through less visible forms of violence, including silencing, repression, and gatekeeping of what and who counts as a proper feminist subject.

Ūman ribu offered an important intervention in how we approach violence expressed by women. *Ūman ribu* activists sought solidarity with women who killed their children, and they supported the female leader of a notoriously "violent" far left sect known as the United Red Army. Through its political approach to violence expressed by women, I suggest, *ūman ribu* provides insights into an alternative feminist epistemology of violence that locates violence in the female body and the feminine subject. Through an inquiry into this movement and its productive politicization of women's relationship with violence—as potentially violent subjects—we can rethink feminism's relationship to political violence and women's relationality with the politics of violence.

An examination of feminism's relationality to violence suggests the need for a new feminist analytics of violence as well as the possibility for an alternative feminist ethics of violence. Such analyses would involve an examination of how feminisms and feminists have been structured by and within systems, ontologies, and epistemologies of violence and domination (be they class, race, sexual) and entangled with other dominant ideological systems such as liberalism and its continual domesticating calls to moderation, reason, and nonviolence as the proper norm.

My representation of the movement may unsettle and disturb how some feminists and *ūman ribu* activists desire to represent their legacy and contributions. The movement was of course heterogeneous and complex and, at moments, troubled by its own contradictions. The lessons of this movement's legacy have remained in the shadows and include its complex relationship to violence. I chose to grapple with this difficult and undertheorized issue precisely because of the urgency of critically theorizing the multifarious modalities of violence in a time of perpetual war. Although some may question or be wary of its possible effects or implications, such a feminist inquiry is vital as we face the perilous conditions of feminism along with its complicities with state violence in all its spectacular and muted forms. Given my supposition about the ontologies of women's violence as an aporia of feminist thought, I turn to the title of the book—*Scream from the Shadows*. The polyvalence of the scream marks an eruption, evoking a spectrum of sensation from ecstasy to terror and rage. As we turn the pages, let us reckon with the shadows that follow us and our relationality to the sound of their screams.

Ūman Ribu as Solidarity and Difference

In 1970, a new women's liberation movement, known as *ūman ribu* (woman lib), erupted across Japan. This grassroots feminist movement was catalyzed by the 1960s uprisings in the wake of the anti–Vietnam War movement, student movements, and New Left radicalism. This book forwards an analysis of the historical significance of *ūman ribu* and its politics, philosophy, legacy, and lessons for the future. As part of the crest of social movements that arose internationally during the 1960s and 1970s, *ūman ribu* can be understood as a particular incarnation of radical feminism, born from the cross-fertilizations of genealogies of resistance both domestic and international.

A study of *ūman ribu* offers a vital contribution to understanding the gendered formations of Japanese modernity, imperialism, and the limits of postwar liberal democracy and its complex leftist history. *Ūman ribu* activists forwarded an incisive critique of Japanese national imperialism and how its dynamics of discrimination shaped Japanese leftist culture. Beyond assessing *ūman ribu* within the framework of the nation-state, a close examination of its historical and political formation illuminates the international and transpacific dimensions of the feminist and liberation movements of this era.

The study of any non-Euro-American, or non-Western, feminist formation must, at the outset, take into account the implications of the constructed global divisions of West and East, first and third worlds, north and south, and their racialized and gendered significance. This framework is further complicated by Japan's complex rivalry with Western "civilization," its history as an imperialist power, and its colonial legacy that articulates through the *ūman ribu* movement in multiple ways. This project is therefore necessarily positioned within and against the centuries-long orientalizing gaze that sees the non-West as subordinate, inferior, feminized, and colored, yet it remains mindful of the racialized and first-world geopolitical status of the nation-state designated Japan.[1]

My project, as an interpretive analysis of this feminist movement, seeks to unsettle Euro-American epistemic hegemonies and imperializing power-knowledge formations, constituting a critical counterdiscourse that exposes the domesticating implications of certain master narratives that would seek to render resistant subjects marginal. While some may argue that the numerical size of *ūman ribu*, approximating a few thousand participants during the early 1970s, was marginal compared to the massive memberships of existing Japanese women's movements, the importance of its historic interventions and its critique of modern society and the Japanese left cannot be adequately measured by a sociological enumeration of its participants.[2] *Ūman ribu* not only was a past social movement but also constituted a political identity and a living philosophy. Its political interventions and contradictions remain as relevant lessons for our present political condition.

Many *ūman ribu* activists were variously involved in the New Left and the anti–Vietnam War and student movements of the late 1960s, and they learned many difficult, painful, and productive lessons from those formative experiences. Most *ribu* participants were college-educated young intellectuals, largely women in their twenties and thirties. They had come of age in the education system that had undergone democratic reforms during the U.S. occupation, and thus they witnessed the limits of Japan's democracy and experienced the contradictions of inequalities within a capitalist state. As women who were predominantly ethnic-majority Japanese and largely from the postwar Japanese middle and lower-middle classes, they occupied a positionality that was relatively privileged yet discontent. In sync with the student rebellions and middle-class dissent erupting across cities around the world, the women of *ribu* identified with this larger wave of revolt. As a network of urban-based autonomous groups, *ribu* groups did not seek to establish a hierarchical organization or appoint a formal representative or leader, which characterized the new organizing style of the late-1960s movements.[3]

Its break from the existing constellation of progressive and leftist movements was based on its emphasis on the "liberation of sex" and the "liberation of *onna*." *Ribu* adopted and politicized the term *onna*, a term for women that was imbued with sexualized connotations. Linguist Orie Endo states that *onna* "contains a strong and negative sexual connotation" and can be considered disrespectful, taboo, and "dirty."[4] *Ribu* activist Sayama Sachi writes that precisely because *onna* emphasized a "sexual being, with many desires" and had a negative connation during the 1960s, *ribu*'s deliberate use of this term was similar to the reclamation of the term "queer" by lesbian, gay, bisexual, and transgender (LGBT) movements.[5] The liberation of sex was a key concept and slogan but did not imply an open-ended advocacy of free sex. Rather, *ribu*'s discourse emphasized a notion of the liberation of sex that focused on a critique of the modern family system as the foundational unit of Japanese national imperialism that reproduced discrimination. This link between the family system and Japanese imperialism characterized *ribu*'s discourse as a feminist critique that deciphered the interlocking logics of capitalism and imperialism and its reproduction through the regulation of gender roles in the family system.

Within the broader histories of competing imperialisms, colonialism, Eurocentrism, and orientalism, such geographies of power cannot be elided or undone through the invocation of the rubric transnational or transnational feminism. While the rubric of transnational feminism has proven useful as a means to critique the globalizing impulses of certain feminist discourses and "Western cultural imperialism,"[6] what remains to be elaborated is the political trajectory and discursive effects of any given method and the need to further examine transnationalism.

While it has been necessary to critique how area studies methods have served to reinforce the interests of dominant nations, the postarea studies' paradigmatic shift to the transnational has not been without its own attendant problems.[7] Transnationalism has been rightly criticized for the way it privileges first-world and (middle- to upper-) class mobilities and subjectivities who can appropriate, consume, and represent difference and otherness.[8] Transnational mobility across and beyond the boundaries of the nation-state does not necessitate or imply reciprocal forms of exchange, critique, and collaboration or dismantle imperialist formations. The political open-endedness of transnationalism (like the endless possibilities of globalization) enables both its capacious lure and the potential space for change. Even as we recognize postarea studies imperatives and other formations of postnationalism, I emphasize a close analysis of the conditions of possibility that frequently traverse indices of the local-global, domestic, and international.

In terms of conceiving a *transdisciplinary* method that produces a critical historiography and a genealogy of internationalist or transnational liberation and feminist movements, this introduction proceeds with an elaboration of my argument for a translocational politics. The kind of transdisciplinary and translocational approach I take cautiously grapples with material specificities while recognizing that any claim to materiality is nonetheless constantly open to reiteration and appropriation. Even as we trace genealogies and lines of connection and identification, it is imperative to acknowledge, preserve, and mark differences and recognize how terms such as women, liberation, and feminism shift and morph across various historical and semantic contexts and intersections of time and space.[9] Theorizing transnational feminist movements involves an ongoing contestation over who and what defines the feminist subject and the meaning of liberation. An analysis of *ūman ribu* contributes to an understanding of the transnational circuits of feminist discourses and, perhaps more significantly, how this movement's formation in an East Asian and Japanese context illuminates the limits of dominant paradigms of second wave feminism as integral to the master narratives emanating from Euro-American-centric globalizing feminism. How we approach or assess *ūman ribu*, as a "non-Western," East Asian radical feminist movement requires a recalibration of existing methodologies to account for local and linguistic, racial and regional specificities as well as translational troubles and nontranslatable differences.

Translational Troubles

Throughout the book, I use the terms *ūman ribu* (woman lib) and *ribu* (lib) to refer to the movement, its activists, its discourse, and its praxis. Those women who identified themselves as *ribu* and considered themselves part of the movement are referred to as *ribu* women and *ribu* activists. *Ribu* activists reappropriated and politicized the word *onna*, and this nomenclature was used by the women of the movement as their markers of political identification. Although differing views and priorities, as well as conflicts and debates, existed among the activists within the movement, akin to many other feminist and liberation movements, *ūman ribu*'s relative coherence as a social movement was based on a definable set of core political critiques and premises, which aimed specifically at the liberation of *onna* and sex as key to human liberation. The significance and praxis of these core premises are further elaborated throughout the book.

Ūman ribu is an abbreviated transliteration of women's liberation (*ūmenzu riberashion*). It is written in *katakana* (ウーマン リブ), the phonetic alphabet used to mark emphasis and foreign words. To be more precise, it is the phoneticization of the Japanese-English phrase "woman lib" *(sic)* versus the "correct" English phrase "women's lib." This is a minute example of the translational trouble involved in assessing translocational difference, signified by this Japanese-English phrase.[10] Given that several other Japanese terms for women's liberation existed (such as *fujin kaihō* and *josei kaihō*), the movement's adoption and adaptation of this new name signified its distinction from existing Japanese women's movements and a desire to signal its connection to women's liberation across national borders. My (re)invocation of *ūman ribu* thus underscores a relationship of internationalist feminist solidarity and difference alongside other women's liberation movements across the first and third worlds. *Ūman ribu* activists, on the one hand, identified with U.S.-based women's lib and its feminist movements of the 1970s, and on the other hand, reached out to women in other Asian nations, expressive of a Pan-Asian feminist solidarity.[11] Insofar as *ūman ribu*'s politics were infused by the broader anti-imperialist trajectory of the Japanese left and New Left, its feminist postcolonial consciousness was directed toward other Asian women as a potential nexus of solidarity in opposition to the reformation of neo-imperial–colonial relations.

Across the Japanese context, *ribu* and *feminizumu* (feminism) are not synonymous. *Ūman ribu* and *ribu* are associated with the movement era of the late 1960s and 1970s, with the direct-action political style and grassroots activism that characterized its organizing models. Unlike, for example, in the United States where *women's lib* and *feminism* were often used interchangeably during the 1970s, in Japan, the usage and meanings of *ribu* and *feminizumu* have been historically and semantically distinct, at times signifying a contentious relation.[12] It was not until the late 1970s that the transliterated term *feminizumu* was more widely used as a direct translation of "feminism" and, in contrast to the more activist and grassroots connotations of *ūman ribu*, *feminizumu* signified more explicitly a "foreign" concept and became associated with academic feminism and the establishment of women's studies that began in the 1980s.[13] Thus, in addition to marking *ribu*'s own distinct politics within a transnational context of feminist movements, I designate *ribu* by its own name to mark its difference from *feminizumu* in Japan and to signify that these terms are typically used and understood differently among *ribu* women and feminists in a Japanese context.

Ribu as Radical Feminism

While I mark *ribu*'s specificity, I also recognize that this movement most closely approximates what has been categorized and designated as radical feminism in other contexts. *Ūman ribu* has been referred to as a version of radical feminism by Machiko Matsui (1990), Ichiyo Muto (1997), and others, even though it did not refer to itself as such.[14] Therefore, my deliberate use of the terms *ribu* and *ūman ribu* instead of *feminism* marks this contextual and linguistic specificity. Through my examination of *ribu* as a radical feminist movement, I elaborate its synchronicities and solidarities with other liberation movements and feminist politics and attend to its departures and differences. I redeploy these terms to mark the intricacies of solidarity and difference signified by this appellation.

My use of the term *radical feminism* in characterizing *ribu* follows what Imelda Whelehan has defined, in contrast to liberal feminism and socialist feminism, as a version of feminism that generally has the following traits.[15] First, it is a feminist discourse that demands comprehensive political, economic, and cultural transformation, in contrast to the more limited aims of attaining women's equality or advancing the recognition of women's rights within the existing sociopolitical system. Second, in terms of its genealogy, many radical feminists were "defectors from the New Left"; therefore, much of radical feminist theory was forged in direct reaction to the theories, organizational structures, and political style of the male-dominated New Left.[16] Third, in terms of its political style, radical feminism's language is more confrontational and militant than its liberal and socialist feminist predecessors, with its militancy taken to be an expression of the rage of women against male dominance, "a rage which became channeled into numerous acts of militancy and direct action against patriarchy."[17]

Like other radical feminist discourses, *ribu*'s politics were not defined or circumscribed by the goal of achieving equality between men and women, nor did its discourse promote the importance of women's rights as central to *ribu*'s conception of liberation. Instead, *ribu* activists collectively forwarded a comprehensive critique of the political-economic-social system as fundamentally male-centric *(dansei-chūshin)* and discriminatory. They sought to politicize sex discrimination *(sei sabetsu)* and male-centrism *(dansei-chūshin shugi)*, denouncing them for their oppression of both women and men. At the core of their politics, *ribu* activists emphasized that sex and sex-based discrimination were fundamental to human oppression, and this tenet characterized their discourse, with lesser attention to ethnic and class distinctions. They also used the terms male supremacy *(dansei shijō shugi)* and patriarchy *(kafuchōsei)* but to a lesser extent than sex discrimination and male-centrism (which was an analytic concept similar to "masculinist").

During the 1970s, *ribu* activists engaged in myriad activities on multiple fronts. They protested many forms of sex discrimination and formed women-only organizing groups and women-centered collectives and communes. Some of their most significant and sustained campaigns were directed against the state's attempts to restrict access to abortion, emphasizing instead "the creation of a society" where "women could decide" whether "they wanted to give birth."[18] Many *ribu* activists formed communes where women raised their children together to resist the family system.[19] They protested against the legal discrimination against unwed mothers *(mikon no haha)*, which exemplified the male-centered structure of the family system. The *ribu* movement's critique of the family system, as a patriarchal and patrilineal system, was rooted in a deeper critique of Japanese national imperialism. *Ribu* activists, furthermore, criticized how Japanese women were complicit in imperialism, taking account of Japan's colonial legacy in Asia. They also organized in solidarity with women who killed their children (known as *kogoroshi no onna*), which was a phenomenon that peaked in the early 1970s. Many *ribu* women were informed by Marxism and anti-imperialism. But rather than conceive of women's liberation as the outcome of class revolution, they articulated a new post-Marxist woman's theory *(onna no ronri/onna no shishō)* which made sex discrimination and women's perspective central. This emphasis constituted an epistemic turn between sex and political subjectivity, re-articulating the meaning of women's liberation by reconceiving of the sexed-body and sexual subjectivity as integral to revolution. Revolution was to be understood as a living and lived practice in which the subject struggled to transform society and the self and the self's relationship with the other—not a future utopia.

Solidarity and Differences

Despite its similarity with radical feminism in the United States, my approach illuminates the solidarities and underscores the differences in how feminist movements conceive of liberation. The differences between *ūman ribu* and U.S. radical feminism were particularly salient around the issues of abortion and reproductive technologies (discussed in chapter 3) and *ribu*'s approach to other violent, abjected women, such as women who killed their children *(kogoroshi no onna)* and political fugitives. Throughout the book, I explore the various contested origins and genealogies that shaped this movement's formation, attending closely to its local conditions of emergence.

One significant site of *ribu*'s transnational identification during the 1970s was the women's lib movement in the United States. The transnational communication about the U.S. women's liberation movement, via the mass media, functioned as circuits of potential political identification.[20] The U.S.-based women's lib movement and the dissemination of its texts provided affirmative signals for the incipient movement that had already begun to coalesce in Japan. The dissemination of information about the U.S. women's lib movement abetted and encouraged *ūman ribu*'s own formation and self-definition; however, it was neither the exclusive origin of the movement nor its terminus. Rather, it served as a point of inspiration and a productive interlocutor that enabled *ribu* activists to compare and define their movement through articulating their solidarities with and critiques of its U.S. counterpart(s). From the beginning of the movement, *ribu* women expressed that they felt their movement would be different from the lib movement in the United States.[21] Such a transnational circulation of information and exchange enabled the possibility for recognition and identification; however, this potential economy of recognition and identification should not be conflated with or equated with what constitutes the most determinative conditions of *ribu*'s formation.

The degree to which the U.S.-based women's lib movement played a role in the formation of *ribu* remains a contentious and vexed topic. On the one hand, many who are antagonistic to feminism in Japan have attempted to belittle its organic emergence as an import or imitation despite an almost century-long history of diverse Japanese feminist formations. Many *ribu* activists identified with this genealogy of feminist movements that began to emerge in Japan at the beginning of the twentieth century. Historians Sharon Sievers (1983) and Vera Mackie (2003) provided impressive accounts of the diverse feminist movements that have critiqued Japanese modernity, capitalism, and patriarchy and the *ie* (family) system.[22] *Ribu* women read and identified with earlier Japanese feminists, anarchists, and intellectuals such as Takamure Itsue, Kanno Sugako, and Hiratsuka Raichō.

On the other hand, given the enduring orientalist and Western-imperialist pretensions that imagine Japanese women (and other non-Western women) as behind in their development compared to their more liberated Western counterparts, the assumption that Japanese women need to learn from their Western feminist "sisters" typically colors any recognition of *ribu*'s connection with U.S.-based feminism.[23] As Chizuko Ueno stated, "Since feminism is frequently criticized at the local level as a Western import, feminists are under continuous pressure to distinguish themselves from Western feminists" and must always "define themselves negatively or oppositionally in order to establish a distinctly indigenous feminist identity."[24] This problematic schema reifies the constructs of the East and West, for it is a paradigm that fails to account for modernity as a hybridized and global process and project that fundamentally produced nonsymmetrical power relations. The processes of identification with the West are necessarily underwritten by nonsymmetrical power relations negotiated and mediated through economies of desire, resistance, aggression, and critique.[25]

Lest it seem that the United States appear as a privileged or conspicuous site of influence or comparison, we must recall the American Occupation of Japan from 1945 to 1952 and the continued U.S. political and military presence in the archipelago and region. Under the Occupation, Japan and

Okinawa became key U.S. military outposts in its wars against communism in Asia.

Japan's positionality regionally and globally emerged after the Asia–Pacific War(s), enmeshed in the competing imperialisms of the Cold War era, as part of a neo-imperialist alliance with the United States as its subordinate partner. As part of Pax Americana's global Cold War operations, Japan served as a launchpad and supply base for U.S. military interventions and thus played a vital and supportive role in the United States' wars in Korea and Vietnam. During the Occupation, America's anticommunist reverse-course policy and the war in Korea had already begun to contradict the postwar constitutional values of "peace and democracy." U.S. embeddedness in Japanese postwar politics and its continued militarized colonization of Okinawa constituted the fundamental grounds of both leftist and citizens' movements' opposition to this U.S.–Japan political–military–security alliance. Despite massive popular opposition, the U.S.–Japan Mutual Cooperation and Security Treaty was ratified and reimposed in 1960. To recall the language of the New Left at this juncture, the United States and Japan had formed a new imperialist alliance, called *nichi-bei teikokushugi*—Japanese–American imperialism, with democratic Japanese consent appearing to mask the violent facade of U.S. militarized imperial power.[26] In the context of competing imperialisms and ongoing Cold War conflicts across Asia and around the globe, this book elaborates how *ūman ribu* imagined liberation as the struggle against and beyond the binary confines of competing empires of capitalism and communism and conceived of itself as part of the ongoing multitude of liberation struggles organizing across the globe.

It is important to recognize how *ribu* forwarded an unprecedented political critique of the gendering of Japanese postwar society and the Japanese left, its past imperialist nationalism, and its ongoing neo-imperial and neo-colonial formations, vis-à-vis Asia, Korea, and Okinawa.[27] One of *ribu*'s discourses and campaigns denounced the comfort women system and ongoing sexual exploitation of Korean sex workers, denouncing Japanese men's and Japanese women's complicity in this sexualized violence. In this context, *ūman ribu* provides a particularly interesting political formation due to its non-Western first-world status and relative "in-betweenness." Its racialized position as ethnic-majority Japanese women vis-à-vis other "minority" women in Japan, such as Okinawans, Ainu, *burakumin*, *Zainichi*-resident Koreans in Japan, and other postcolonial Asian subjects, positions *ribu* women as relative "whites" within a national context but nonwhite relative to other white women in a global economy of race. Given *ribu*'s relative positionality between whites and colored women and its in-betweenness as an ethnic yet marginal majority on the basis of its politics compared to other Japanese women's movements, what can we learn and decipher about how these women negotiated their relative power?

Ūman ribu's emergence marked the generation of a movement that identified with other social movements in Japan, such as disabled citizens' movements and ethnic minority movements; however, cross-ethnic solidarity with Ainu, resident Koreans, Okinawans, and *burakumin* liberation movements within Japan was not central to its politics. The historical specificities of the formation of *ūman ribu,* with its political subject known as *onna,* constituted a correlated movement of political consciousness with other liberationist discourses that emerged domestically and in different contexts in other parts of the world.

Genealogies of Resistance and Translocational Politics

While Japan and Japanese language provide a specific textual context and content, this book emphasizes how the crossings and collisions of the domestic and international and the cross-fertilizations of local and diasporic conditions generated *ūman ribu* as a movement whose origins lie within and beyond the place called Japan. This project seeks to problematize extant comparativist frameworks that assume self-same unity between national and linguistic entities and identities and, rather, attends to the imbrications and interpenetration of local, linguistic, transcultural, and transnational forces.[28] My project forwards a methodology for a translocational politics that moves beyond the national and linguistic boundaries of Japan and Japanese and offers a theorization of translocationality as a political practice of intercultural mediation and translation.

Within this context of theorizing the conditions of shared and interconnected genealogies of resistance, the importance of the (racialized) labor of translation as a political practice of intercultural mediation cannot be overstated. This project not only is unambiguously a labor of translation and mediation across different linguistic and cultural contexts but also advocates a *politics of translocation* between hierarchies of knowledge forms that contends with their constitutive antagonisms. Through such practices of translation and mediation that account for troubled translations and the nontranslatable, we can unsettle and contest existing hierarchies of racialized and gendered knowledge production. My invocation of translocationality attends to the importance of the local conditions of emergence, which nevertheless continually intersect, converge, and collide with transnational imperialist formations, and resistance to those formations as the eruptive and determinative forces that reconfigure political movements.

My project therefore emphasizes *ūman ribu*'s solidarity with many other genealogies of resistance, including its critical relationship to the Japanese New Left, anti–Vietnam War and student movements, existing women's movements in Japan, as well as its relations with U.S. feminist and other liberation movements. At this historical juncture, the diasporic crossings of Black Power ideology, as one strand of U.S.-based third world liberation, also identified with Asian procommunist forces (particularly Maoist China and North Vietnam), creating a network of transpacific anti–U.S. imperialist movements that also fertilized the rise of *ribu*.[29] One of *ribu*'s leading theorists and activists, Tanaka Mitsu, inspired by the Black Power movement declaration that Black is beautiful, declared that *onna* is beautiful. This declaration captures solidarity and difference but also entails a whole set of uneven transpositions and nonequivalences that invite further analysis and raise questions about political coalition.[30]

As part of my theorization of translocational politics, I emphasize a notion of genealogy over historiography. I do not purport to offer a comprehensive, encyclopedic representation of the entire movement history. All knowledge is situated, limited, and invested, though it perhaps often obscures its own bias. My analysis and approach is guided by my own investments and concerns. I ask, what are the lessons to be gleaned by tracing *ribu*'s political genealogies, fissures, and contradictions, and how might these lessons be apt when we consider the formations and fragmentation of other radical political movements in other contexts? What elements ought to be excavated through careful examination of its archive, and how might its archive illuminate or contrast with what *ūman ribu* has become today?

I am interested in deploying a genealogical method not only to track *ribu*'s cross-fertilizations with other political movements domestically and internationally but also to emphasize the importance of alternative, nonlinear temporalities, when assessing *ribu* and other liberation movements, as a means of preserving, theorizing, and working through their political relevance. *Ribu*'s history did not unfold in a linear manner, nor was its dissemination and revolt unidirectional.

While it can be argued from a sociological perspective that *ūman ribu*'s most cohesive, vibrant, and visible period as a social movement spanned from 1970 to 1975, with a few hundred participants at its early gatherings and its largest events drawing a few thousand, in this book, I argue that *ribu*'s historical significance and relevance spans temporally beyond this time frame.[31]

Rather than reproducing a developmental narrative, I am interested in excavating the political meaning and relevance of the movement today, thus traversing the linear temporality of forty-plus years and, instead, suggesting the vital power of alternative temporalities that privilege and seek out antagonisms, that bear radical forms of creativity and abolition over reformism, investedness over putative objectivity and disciplinary limitations. I advocate for the continued imperative of the scholarly and political work of tracing and working through the unfinished genealogies of liberation and decolonization that we must preserve, rearticulate, and renew. This unfinished and incomplete state makes possible the translocational relevance through time, recognizing that the passing of time in no way guarantees progress or sublation, a more sophisticated form of politics, or transcendence from the violence of politics.

Included in this conception of translocational politics is a recognition of its multiplicity of origins and points of connection, within and beyond the nation and its "Japaneseness" and within and beyond subjects marked as women, *onna*, and feminist, offering an oeuvre, a circuit, and multiple portals to genealogies of resistance and subjects in the past, present, and future. How did *ūman ribu* posit *onna* as a potential revolutionary subject and therefore as a subject not simply synonymous or equivalent with woman/women but translatable and translocational (in other contexts) as a feminized subject of resistance? I therefore underscore that it is not anything culturally or linguistically essential about *onna* but rather how the revolutionary potential of any subject is iterated and mobilized within a specific circuit of forces, which is necessarily contingent and contextual. By interrogating and adhering to the specificities of *ūman ribu* and *onna*, I recognize how translational troubles and the nontranslatable may serve as reminders of epistemological otherness and excess and are not always reducible or subsumable to master narratives (be they liberalism, progress, multiculturalism, or globalization). Rather, an analysis of *ūman ribu*'s solidarities and differences offers a lens that both mirrors and illuminates many of the limitations of dominant paradigms of second wave feminism, particularly the ideology of liberal feminism. *Ūman ribu*'s distinct version of radical feminism provides a way beyond the delimitation of the individualism foundational to liberal feminism that has facilitated the assimilation of select groups of women into positions of privilege, power, and violence. Through a transdisciplinary analysis of *ūman ribu* that recognizes its own limitations and translational troubles, this study forwards a project of critical translocationality that is transnational but maintains the imperative to critique the persistence of nationalist claims to sovereign power over life and death, the biopolitical, and its structuring and institutionalizing forces.

One of my objectives is to demonstrate how the *ribu* movement offers us new forms of knowledge across multiple contexts and temporalities, with relevance when we situate such knowledges within genealogies of ongoing and unfinished resistance movements. *Ūman ribu* thus possesses multiple and contested origins, and my book is just one form of approaching and articulating its significance.

Movements and Contested Origins—Tanaka Mitsu

One of these contested origins and points of difference was Tanaka Mitsu (1943–). Feminist scholar Akiyama Yōko wrote that one cannot speak about the *ribu* movement without mentioning Tanaka Mitsu.[32] Tanaka was one of the many origins of the movement and points of collision; she was an originary force that shaped the movement in profound and distinct ways. She is recognized by those outside the movement as its iconic figure and a highly influential theorist and activist of the movement.

At the genesis of the movement, Tanaka offered one of the most creative and sustained philosophical exegeses of liberation. This study analyzes Tanaka not only as a thinker of *ribu* but also as a thinker who has made an important contribution to contemporary feminist philosophy. Tanaka's contribution offers an alternative feminist paradigm of ontology and identification, subjectivity, and violence. My project critically examines Tanaka's philosophical contribution as a feminist theorist in a transnational context and her role in the movement. Although she is recognized as *ribu*'s iconic figure and more attention has been devoted to her than to any other woman of *ribu,* Tanaka's contribution as feminist philosopher and the problems of her leadership have yet to be adequately assessed. One of the primary objectives of this book is to introduce Tanaka as a feminist philosopher and to examine her unique contributions as a theorist of women's liberation while remaining critical and cautious of her iconic status within Japan.

Tanaka's role in the movement was pivotal in determining the ways in which *ribu* became a distinct articulation of radical feminism, particularly in terms of a feminist conception of violence as political. My reading of the movement is shaped by my interest in how Tanaka's role, leadership, and discourse symbolized and constituted *ribu*'s difference as a radical feminist movement. My attention to Tanaka is thus purposeful and deliberate but admittedly reinscribes a limit and (re)produces her iconicity as a point of contested origin. Some *ribu* women have pointed out that the creation of Tanaka as "the star" of the movement is antithetical to the politics of *ribu*. The historical production of the persona of Tanaka Mitsu—as the icon of women's liberation—remains one of the most provocative, ironic, and contradictory historical effects of *ūman ribu* and its canonization.

From the inception of the movement, the struggle over self-representation, especially across the various fora of the mass media, alternative media, and leftist publications, was an arena of power struggle that *ribu* women strategically engaged.[33] Like many other social movements, *ribu* produced its own alternative media, known as *mini-komi* (mini-communications), referring to newsletters, journals, pamphlets, zines, and, later, its own video documentaries. This practice of producing one's own alternative media as a means of self-determination was at the core of the movement's attempt to articulate a new kind of feminine political subject with her own conception of liberation. The material of *ribu*'s multifaceted alternative media offers an enormous body of texts that have yet to be thoroughly explored and assessed.

A primary method of my investigation involved a close reading and analysis of several hundred Japanese language sources, focusing on the massive body of literature and alternative media produced by members of the *ribu* movement, including published, private, and unpublished sources. I also examine documented responses to *ūman ribu* from the New Left and press coverage in mainstream and alternative media, including newspapers, magazines, and Japanese intellectual journals, from the 1960s to the present. I also critically engage with both English and Japanese secondary commentary on *ūman ribu* written by academics, historians, sociologists, feminists, and social critics.

My sustained and close engagement with the literature and women of the movement eschews a method of analysis that relies solely on close literary or textual analysis. My fieldwork, which was conducted intensively from 1999 to 2001, involved extensive interviews and discussions with over twenty *ribu* activists and feminist intellectuals, primarily those who are based in the Tokyo and Kansai regions.[34] During my fieldwork, I participated in several *ribu* gatherings, retreats, and study circles. Over the last ten years, I have continued conversations, face-to-face interactions, and correspondence with several core *ribu* activists, including Miki Sōko, Saeki Yōko, Tanaka Mitsu, Yonezu Tomoko, Sayama Sachi, and Watanabe Fumie, to name several of my main interlocutors. In this vein, my approach to *ribu* has been profoundly shaped by my encounters and relationships with women of the movement and Japanese feminist intellectuals. Insofar as my study has centered on *ribu* women from the Tokyo and Kansai regions, and in particular the figure of

Tanaka Mitsu, my work, at one level, is limited regionally: it does not constitute a nationwide scope of analysis or offer a complete coverage of every detail of the movement. It nonetheless provides a point of departure for later studies and critiques. Other scholars have already begun important studies of other aspects of the movement, such as its connection with the emergence of the lesbian movement and its diffusion into popular culture.[35]

Chapter Summaries

Each section and chapter unfolds a different dimension of *ribu*'s multifaceted constitution. Part I, "Genealogies and Violations," traces the genealogies of resistance that gave birth to *ūman ribu,* that are at once part of the multiplicity of modernities and therefore international, but with more detailed attention to their embedded domestic, localizable, linguistic conditions. Part I elaborates *ribu*'s genealogical positioning at the crossroads of a rich heritage of women's movements in Japan that were entangled with complex genealogies of the Left. The Japanese Left involved a complicated legacy of leftist, communist, and Marxist disputes that gave rise to Japan's New Left during the 1960s.

From an international perspective, *ūman ribu* was an extension of the crest of progressive and radical social movements that arose internationally during the 1960s. *Ribu* emerged at the intersections of a transnational protest against U.S. imperialism across Asia and as part of the rise of what has been dominantly narrated as "second wave" feminism in the First World. This framework has been adopted and reproduced among feminist scholars in Japan, who have largely located and defined *ūman ribu* as the beginning of second wave feminism in Japan.[36]

In "Women's Postwar History," Fujieda Mioko writes that there were four main factors that constitute the context of the rise of women's liberation movements across industrialized countries. These movements shared the following conditions: (1) the existence and expansion of a middle class characteristic of industrialized countries; (2) the increased radicalism prevalent worldwide in the 1960s and the prominence of New Left movements; (3) the inflexible structure of the past women's movements; and (4) the expansion of information networks, particularly women's information networks.[37] All of these conditions were pertinent to the case of Japan. The inflexibility of the existing array of women's movements combined with the internal fracturing of the Left and New Left comprised the conditions that impelled the rise of a new movement. An understanding of these particular domestic conditions is imperative to recognizing how *ribu* is distinct from other versions of feminism in Japan and elsewhere. Thus, while we can understand the synchronicity of these conditions across many industrialized nation, naming the explosion of radical feminism as part of second wave feminism recenters Euro-American feminist movements as the origin and arbiter of the "waves" of feminism by centering struggles for white women's suffrage movement as the first wave.[38]

While there were important moments of identification and disidentification with Euro-American feminists and movements, in Part I, I demonstrate that it was not the rise of North American or European feminisms that were most determinative in *ribu*'s political formation. Such an assumption would facilely assume that any foreign (Western) movement could and would be mirrored, imitated, and adopted rather than taking the time to understand the domestic and local conditions that were fomenting the emergence and crystallization of this political movement in Japan.

Chapter 1, "Origins of the Other/*Onna:* The Violence of Motherhood and the Birth of *Ribu*," examines the significance of *ribu*'s departure from the existing constellation of women's movements in Japan and how its feminist politics were distinct from other versions of radical feminism in a transnational context. In chapter 1, I explore how *ribu*'s self-formation involved a rupture from existing women's organizations in Japan and an embryonic link to the anti-imperialist women's left. "Origins of the Other/*Onna*" examines how *ribu* broke away from the women's movements that were largely based on the identities of women as "housewife," "mother," and "citizen." *Ribu*'s criticism and political refusal of the acceptable identities and regulated trajectory for women, as wife-to-mother within the hetero-coupling of the family system—what *ribu* activists called the "one-wife-one-husband" system—constituted a fundamental fissure from existing women's movements. Chapter 1 also explicates the semantic and political significance of the term *onna* and why *ribu* women chose to reclaim and identify using this word. This chapter not only elaborates how *ribu* refused the identity and prescriptive telos of wife-to-mother but demonstrates how many *ribu* activists instead formed communes with other women to raise their children and simultaneously declared their solidarity with mothers who killed their children (*kogoroshi no onna*). In purposely organizing to support and declare solidarity with such violent and criminalized women, *ribu*'s praxis as a radical feminist movement offered a complex and counterhegemonic response to how womanhood and motherhood in Japan were bound by the ideology of Japan's nationalist family system. *Ribu*'s identification with criminalized and abjected women/*onna*—such as sex workers, unmarried mothers (*mikon no haha*), mothers who killed their children, and women fugitives—was part of its radical feminist politics and arguably marked the radical potential and revolutionary impulse of its feminist politics.

Chapter 2, "Lineages of the Left: Death and Reincarnation of a Revolutionary Ideal," elaborates the formation of the New Left, which in turn catalyzed new kinds of student and anti–Vietnam War protests that exploded in the late 1960s. In chapter 2, I demonstrate that *ribu*'s direct predecessors comprised a complex genealogy of the Japanese left and the New Left and the local intersections of the radical student movements and anti–Vietnam War protests, whose politics constituted the turbulent terrain from which *ribu* emerged and departed. The anti-imperialist politics that also infused the New Left, radical student movements, and anti–Vietnam War protests constituted the larger crucible that gave rise to *ribu* and informed its politics as a fundamentally antiestablishment movement that rejected the validity of governmental politics, and its liberal democratic parliamentary system, as the only legitimate arena of politics. A knowledge of the history of post-1960s leftist politics is imperative to understand the decentralized and antihierarchical politics of *ribu* as well as its relation to the ultraleftist and revolutionary underground sect, the United Red Army *(Rengo Sekigun)* during the early 1970s. This chapter also demonstrates how *ribu* was very much a successor to what has been called the neo–New Left, namely, the movements of the late 1960s called Beheiren and the Zenkyōtō student movement. An understanding of the diverse political genealogies that gave birth to *ribu* is necessary in order to recognize how *ribu* as an incarnation of an anti-imperialist radical feminism offers an important critique of the Japanese New Left and its Marxist notions of revolution. Insofar as the political genealogy of the Japanese New Left was both a domestic and internationalist formation, *ūman ribu*'s political significance must likewise be read in a context that is forged through the convergences and conflicts of the local and the international.

Part II, "Movements and Mediums," analyzes the emergence, dynamics, and organizing principles of *ūman ribu* during the first half of the 1970s, which constituted *ribu*'s most vibrant, cohesive, and interventionist formation. I focus on this eruptive moment to emphasize how its multidirectional and centrifugal dynamics necessarily resulted in the movement's diffusion rather than its consolidation into a unified institution or single organization. Chapters 3 and 4 explore the dynamics between the collectivity of *ribu* as a social movement and the intersubjective and interpersonal economies that constituted its collective subjectivity. By highlighting several of its key activists who were formative mediums of the movement during the 1970s, these chapters analyze the internal characteristics of the movement and explore the contradictions of *ribu*'s counterhegemonic practices and the limitations of its multifaceted activism.

Chapter 3, "The Liberation of Sex, *Onna,* and Eros: The Movement and the Politics of Collective Subjectivity," theorizes what I call *ribu*'s political ontology. The symbiotic relationship between the movement's core concepts, its organizing principles, and the collectivity of its subjects comprise *ribu*'s political ontology. Chapter 3 elaborates how the liberation of sex formed the core organizing logic of the movement and how it manifested through its *onna*-centered (women-centered) organizing principles and *ribu*'s representative campaigns around abortion and unmarried mothers. By examining the logic of *ribu*'s collaborations with other social movements, such as disabled citizens' movements, I demonstrate how *ribu*'s expansive notion of the liberation of sex provided a coherent, yet centrifugal, organizing logic that guided its coalitional politics. This chapter maps out *ribu*'s main events during the 1970s, such as its *ribu* summer camps *(ribu gasshuku), ribu* conferences, and "Witch Concerts" as windows into *ribu*'s *onna*-centered style of politics. By introducing and highlighting the roles of several of its key activists, I track how *ribu* activism around abortion would rearticulate decades later in the continued struggle for reproductive freedom. By tracing the emergence of key lesbian activists, whose political roots were grounded in *ūman ribu,* we can gain an appreciation for the tensions and contradictions involved in liberating women from heterosexist investments.

Chapter 4, "*Ribu* and Tanaka Mitsu: The Icon, the Center, and Its Contradictions," provides a critical historiography and examination of Tanaka's relationship to the *ribu* movement. In this chapter, I analyze Tanaka's position as a formative medium of a collective movement who is recognized by many as the one who decisively shaped the movement's unfolding. This chapter offers a critical assessment of Tanaka's productive and contradictory relationship to the movement. Some have pointed to Tanaka's contradictory position as the de facto leader of a movement that purported to have no leader. In this connection, I examine how, like many other radical social movements, *ribu*'s antihierarchical organizing ideals generated a set of contradictions and problems that were not worked through or resolved, indicative of the constraints of counterhegemonic movements. I offer a critical analysis of how Tanaka, as a leading philosopher-activist, becomes problematically constructed as the symbolic figure of the *ribu* era, as is depicted by filmic documentaries such as *Ripples of Change.*[39] My discussion underscores how we must critically assess the production of historiographies, feminist and otherwise, that reinscribe developmental narratives that too easily conflate social movements with the production of their iconic figures, even as we seek to produce alternative histories as part of the ongoing contest over representation.

Part III, "Between Feminism and Violence," most explicitly interrogates the relationality between feminism and violence. Chapter 5, "*Ribu*'s Response to the United Red Army: Feminist Ethics and the Politics of Violence," analyzes *ribu*'s relationship with the underground revolutionary sect, the United Red Army (URA). The URA was considered by many to be the most militant and violent revolutionary sect of the Japanese New Left. The events surrounding the URA in 1972 became a turning point for Japanese leftist radicalism because of the way political violence was deployed in the name of revolutionary purposes.

Among *ribu*'s various campaigns, in this chapter, I focus on how many *ribu* activists in Tokyo supported the women of the URA during their detention and trial in the early 1970s. Through this analysis, I argue that this movement's complex response offers an illuminating approach to political violence and its contradictions and constitutes what I describe as a *feminist praxis of critical solidarity*. My chapter on *ūman ribu* and the URA constitutes one attempt to rethink dominant conceptions of political violence as an issue that remains relevant to contemporary politics.

The second part of this chapter elaborates Tanaka's philosophy of ontology, which I argue offers a unique and critical contribution to contemporary feminist philosophy, particularly in relation to dominant conceptions of violence and nonviolence. In sharp contrast to models of individual choice, equality, women's and citizens' rights, and nonviolence, Tanaka's philosophy of being entails a compelling theorization of subjectivity revolving around her concepts of contradiction, violence, contingency, relationality, and eros. Chapter 5 elaborates how Tanaka's response to the misguided execution of revolutionary violence was not to condemn violence categorically but to expose how its dominant conceptions reinforce the erasure of state violence and the disavowal of one's own relationship to the violence enacted against the other.

In my Epilogue, "Lessons from the Legacy," I reflect on a few of the lessons we can take from the legacy of *ribu* as a way to inform and transform the future of feminism and other political movements. *Ūman ribu*'s formation and canonization remains foundational to understanding the subsequent trajectories, characteristics, and contentions across feminist formations in Japan and beyond. I discuss the establishment of women's studies and the institutionalization of academic feminism and how this history has been marked by antagonisms and tension. By tracking the establishment of women's studies and the incorporation of liberal feminism into the state apparatus during the 1980s and 1990s, we can appreciate why many *ribu* women do not identify with feminism *(feminizumu)* in the Japanese context. The rise of state liberal feminism as a sign of progress has occurred along the resurgence of right-wing nationalism. How do we account for the implementation of such feminist reforms in the wake of *ribu*'s legacy? Since the mid-1990s, a veritable *ribu* renaissance has occurred, evidenced by the number of *ribu* retrospective publications and collections. Here, I account for how the reiterations of *ribu* in a transnational context and the production of feminist icons have come to signify in neoliberal times. In closing, I discuss the difficulties of sustaining feminist relations and leftist formations when there is a lack of accountability of how power can be used and abused across cultures of the left. Part III, "Between Feminism and Violence" will hopefully provide us with greater clarity of our current political horizon and its impasses.

As a final note, understanding the legacy of *ūman ribu* deepens our critical appreciation of radical liberation movements and their power to change and shape history, subjectivity, and knowledge. Equally important in this endeavor is our analysis of their inevitable contradictions, limits, achievements, and failures. My meditation on *ribu* offers one approach to work through a movement's complex assemblage of alternative knowledges, subjectivities, contradictions, and practices. This work represents a way to enter into dialogue about *ribu*'s historical significance and current relevance. My desire is that it will initiate more debate and dialogue regarding the potentialities of intersecting genealogies of resistance and translocational politics across the ongoing and future horizons of liberation struggles.

I

GENEALOGIES AND VIOLATIONS

Origins of the Other/*Onna*

The Violence of Motherhood
and the Birth of *Ribu*

Declarations like the "scream from the womb" and the "truth spoken by the vagina" were emblematic of the discourse that distinguished *ūman ribu* (woman lib) from its political predecessors. *Ūman ribu* was conceived from the cross-fertilization of multiple political and intellectual genealogies that catalyzed a new social movement.

This chapter traces the political genealogy of *ūman ribu* by mapping the points of divergence, (dis)continuities, and fault lines that distinguished it from other women's movements in Japan. *Ribu*'s relationship to mainstream Japanese women's movements was highly critical, involving a deliberate distance and break from the existing constellation of political organizations such as housewife associations, women's democratic leagues, and mothers' peace movements.[1] *Ribu* activists were thoroughly critical of the modern family system and political movements that were premised on the identities of wives and mothers. The extent of *ūman ribu*'s critique and rejection of the legitimacy of the family system marked a decisive break from both existing women's movements and the left. In the course of tracing these fissures, I outline why *ūman ribu* can be defined as a specific form of radical feminism in contradistinction to other women's movements. *Ribu*'s discourse exposed how the overwhelming majority of postwar women's organizations failed to offer a critique of the interconnections between Japanese imperialism, discrimination, and the family system. *Ribu* activists thus distinguished themselves as a radical feminist movement through their critical denunciation of the modern family system as a foundational reproductive mechanism of a discriminatory society.

"Origins of the Other/*Onna*" thus examines *ribu*'s critical relation to other

Japanese women's movements as well as how *ribu*'s discourse about the liberation of *onna* was an extension of this critique. In contrast to other Japanese words for woman, such as *fujin* (lady) or *josei* (the generic term for woman), *ribu*'s deliberate use of *onna* signaled the politicization of what was widely considered a pejorative term, with sexual or lower-class connotations. *Ribu*'s reclamation of *onna* was linked with its rejection of the legitimacy of the gender-conforming roles of *shufu* (housewife) and *haha* (mother) that were rooted in the family system. *Ribu* activists critiqued the family system as a microcosm of Japan's male-centered *(dansei-chūshin)* discriminatory capitalist order. *Ribu*'s politics around giving birth and abortion expressed the movement's aims to liberate sex from the confines of this order. Many *ribu* women rejected the marriage system and instead created communes where they lived together with their children to express their rejection of the family system.

In stark contrast to the feminine identities of *fujin* (lady) and *shufu* (housewife), *ribu* allied itself with criminalized women. In the early 1970s, *ribu* activists declared their solidarity with mothers who killed their children—known as *kogoroshi no onna* (child-killing *onna*)—symbolizing a bold repudiation of the prescribed roles for women. *Ribu*'s collective response to these "violent mothers" demonstrates how the movement articulated a distinct conception of the relationship between women and violence that recognizes the potential power of *onna* to engage in a mutiny against an oppressive system.[2] By critically engaging with *kogoroshi no onna* who symbolized, at once, the violence and violation of motherhood *(bosei)* and the potential violence within mothers, *ribu* activists forwarded an alternative feminist conception of violence. The final part of this chapter focuses on how one of the movement's leading activists and theorists, Tanaka Mitsu, elaborated a distinct theory about women, abortion, and violence that remains a compelling contribution to feminist thought.

The Contradictions of Postwar Equality, Peace, and Democracy

After the catastrophic culmination of a series of Japan's wars and inter-imperialist conflict across Asia, World War II ended in August 1945. During the U.S. Occupation (1945–52), Japan's political system was dismantled and reformed under the command of General Douglas MacArthur. As scholars have noted, "The transformation of the Japanese national polity from a wartime belligerent nation to a demilitarized and peaceful one was a highly gendered process."[3]

The governmental regulation of the Japanese family began in the twentieth century through the establishment of the Civil Codes that enforced family law based on a patriarchal *(ie)* household.[4] Postwar revisions to the Civil Code sought to promote greater equality between the sexes in regard to marital property, divorce, and child custody. Postwar reforms enacted significant constitutional and legal changes that granted women the right to vote and codified their formal equality under the law.[5] The first paragraph of Article 14 of the postwar constitution declares, "All of the people are equal under law and there shall be no discrimination in political, economic or social relations because of race, creed, sex, social status or family origin."[6] The postwar political system enabled women's formal entry into the public arena of parliamentary politics and governmental offices. Women's formal political participation had been barred since 1900 because of the repressive enactment of the Public Peace Police Law (Chian Keisatsu Hō), which aimed to repress the burgeoning popular rights movements and leftist activities at the turn of the century.[7]

Granting women suffrage and formal political representation was an epoch-shifting change. The top-down imposition of the postwar constitution and the reform of the Civil Codes points to the contradictory process of issuing democratic decrees under the rule of a U.S. military occupation. Although Japanese women had been agitating for suffrage and political rights long before the Occupation, the strategic "publicizing [of] Japanese women's liberation and their improved status" was a key part of the Occupation's propaganda that has created the enduring image of the United States as an agent of women's liberation.[8] The assumption that women's liberation and antipatriarchal rebellion originated from the United States or the "West" is often based on a lack of historical knowledge about the ways in which gendered and racialized subordination was integral to Western modernity. In their overview of the research on women's history in Japan, historians Wakita Haruko, Narita Ryūichi, Anne Walthall, and Hitomi Tonomura emphasized that it was the spread of "civilization" and "modernity" that effectively homogenized and demoted women's status.[9] One of the most influential historians of the 1970s, Murakami Nobuhiko, argues that modernity was the most effective force that spread gender inequality through all sectors of society.[10] The lack of such historical knowledge about the regulatory and homogenizing effects of modernity has contributed to the idealization of the West as the model of enlightenment and progress.[11]

Women's activism and the documentation of feminist activity in Japan long preceded the U.S. Occupation. Many historians consider leading women of the popular rights movement, such as Kishida Toshiko (1861–1901), the forerunners of Japan's feminist legacy.[12] Sharon Sievers, Vera Mackie, and

Mikiso Hane provide rich accounts of Japanese feminists who were active since the dawn of the twentieth century, with the formation of the *Seitō* (Blue Stockings) movement and the legacy of Japan's anti-imperialist and anarchist women martyrs.[13] *Ribu* women were conscious of and often cited this Japanese legacy, referring to the lives and works of feminist intellectuals such as Hiratsuka Raichō (1886–1971), the founder of *Seitō;* Takamure Itsue (1894–1964), the first feminist women's historian and poet; and anarchists such as Kanno Sugako (1881–1911).[14] *Ribu* activists and intellectuals often cited and looked to this legacy of feminist and revolutionary women who defied gender norms. The rise of Japanese imperialism, as a reaction to Western imperialism, had resulted in the conscription and constriction of Japanese subjects to support the expansion of the empire, which in turn incited rebellion and subsequent repression. Despite the official end of the Japanese Empire, many existing governmental institutions, such as the education system, the family registration system, and the emperor, were reformed and utilized for political purposes in the postwar.

While recognizing the significance of such reforms, it is important to note how the postwar state produced a new modern family system and continued to regulate proper gender roles through legal and bureaucratic means. The Civil Code and the legal regulation of the family unit through the family registration system *(koseki seidō)* functioned as a key mechanism in the biopolitics of the modern nation-state. The family registration system, established in 1872, continued to function as the key bureaucratic and regulatory device through which the state documented the population's birth, movement, and reproduction since the end of the nineteenth century.[15] The family registration *(koseki)* has served as the official document that provides proof of one's birth and records one's place of residence, marital status, and death. Despite the postwar reforms of the Civil Code and family registration system, legal scholars have documented how a patriarchal family model underlies the family registration system and have argued that it serves to maintain hierarchy and discrimination in modern Japanese society.[16]

The contradictions produced through the imbrications of constitutional and legal equality, along with the limited reforms of the Civil Code and family registration system, converged with the promotion of a postwar reformation of the ideology of "good wife and wise mother" *(ryōsāi kenbo)*. Official state-sanctioned discourses created the concept of *ryōsāi kenbo,* which prescribed and idealized the role of good wives and wise mothers. This gender ideology was not only influential as a remnant from the prewar and wartime periods; in the postwar, the state and corporations worked together to reform and promote a new version of this model.[17] Historian Andrew Gordon described the way in which the state, corporations, and women's movements worked together in the postwar to erect and sediment a gendered division of labor that promoted and rationalized women's place as managers of the home. Describing the changes of *ryōsai kenbo,* Kathleen Uno writes that in the postwar, "a transmuted vision of women that often emphasized their difference from men as homebound wives and mothers continued to influence state policies toward welfare, education, employment, sexuality, and reproduction at least until the late 1980s."[18]

In the immediate postwar period, women's organizations were reorganized, constituting a diverse political spectrum from the left to the right. Throughout the postwar period, there were substantive political differences among women's organizations in the same way that there were substantive differences among other political groups. However, these differences are often left unmarked because of an assumed homogeneity among women that facilely renders "women's movements" equivalent or commensurate, when in fact their political trajectories may be not only divergent but antithetical. Vera Mackie argues against the tendency to "seek to push all of women's political activities into a false coherent 'women's movement.'"[19] Furthermore, Chizuko Ueno argues against assuming that women's organizations ought to be considered feminist simply because women are the agents of a movement and engage in political activity to increase their own interests.[20] By examining *ūman ribu*'s criticisms of other women's movements, we can appreciate how this liberation movement originated as a version of radical feminism, distinguishing itself from previous suffrage and labor movements and from liberal feminism that broadly promoted women's equal rights with men. Although the contest over what constitutes feminism remains an ongoing endeavor, *ribu*'s version of feminism aligns closely with what has been defined as radical feminism, which centers and privileges sexual discrimination and emphasizes the need for cultural change.[21]

The wide spectrum of women's movements in the postwar provides a context to understand how *ūman ribu* formed as a Japanese women's movement that largely defined itself through a dialectical dynamic of critical negation and self-affirmation. Postwar women's organizations ranged from the established left, comprising the Japanese Communist Party (JCP), the Japan Socialist Party (JSP), and various labor unions and workers movements. They included women's divisions of political parties and also right-wing and patriotic associations, which had ties to the wartime organizations and were explicitly nationalistic.[22] Various women's democratic organizations were linked with the U.S. Occupation government and the subsequent Japanese government. Grassroots and community-based women's movements also re-emerged around a variety of issues forming women's cooperatives, agricultural and consumer collectives, and various women's religious, literary, and cultural organizations.

"Peace and democracy" became keywords that characterized the political ideals of a large number of postwar women's movements. Many democratic women's organizations were established and maintained close relations to the governmental apparatus. In 1945, the New Japan Women's League (Shin Nihon Fujin Dōmei) was established to enlighten women about the meaning of democracy and their responsibilities as citizens.[23] The next year, the Women's Democratic Club (Fujin Minshu Kurabu) was established and was initially affiliated closely with the Occupation government.[24] An important change in the structure of postwar women's movements was that many leaders of women's movements were brought into the government apparatus as part of the Occupation's democratization efforts.[25] For example, in 1948, Yamakawa Kikue, a prominent prewar socialist intellectual, established the Democratic Women's Association (Minshu Fujin Kyōkai). That same year, she was made the director of the Women's and Minors' Bureau, a division established by the Ministry of Labor. All of these democratic women's organizations participated in the massive movement to stop the renewal of the U.S.–Japan Mutual Cooperation and Security Treaty (Anpo) in 1960 aiming to protect Japan's new democracy.[26] Motivated by a sense of their duties and rights as citizens of Japan, these political groups were organized by a belief in the validity of Japan's liberal democracy. Some of the bourgeois leadership of former women's movements justified the top-down legislative ruling that gave women the right to vote as fully warranted on the basis of "women's cooperation with the state during wartime."[27] By doing so, women's political participation was grounded on a contradictory logic that legitimated their new democratic rights on the basis of their wartime contributions to the state while at the same time assuming that their political participation would be characterized by an antiwar/propeace stance.[28]

In contrast to such established women's democratic organizations, as a post–New Left political movement, many *ribu* activists came of age at a time when the legitimacy of parliamentary democracy had already been severely compromised during the 1960 Anpo struggle. Like many leftist activists of the era, *ribu* women refused to privilege the concept of citizenship as the basis of their politics. *Ribu* activists referred to Japan's postwar democracy as the facade or mask *(tatemae)* of Japan's authoritarian state *(kenishugi kokka)*. In describing the political context of *ribu*'s formation, *ribu* intellectual Mizoguchi Ayeko writes that by 1969, the very basis of any "peace and democracy" had been thoroughly destroyed, evidenced by the "U.S.–Japan joint declaration to place Asia under a system of military control," which combined with the "relentless violence of state authority demonstrated by members of the riot police."[29] This break from an investment in Japan's formal system of liberal democracy was a post-1960 New Left political stance from which *ribu* emerged.

Despite legal declarations of equality, as a founding principle of postwar democracy, the material realities of gender, class, and ethnic stratification pointed to substantive inequalities in material conditions. From 1955 to 1970, the number of women in the workforce doubled from five to ten million; however, there remained a significant discrepancy in how women workers were treated.[30] Postwar reforms allowed women to access the same education as men, but they were not treated equally in the workplace. Although the Labor Standards Act passed in 1947 prohibited unequal wages, employers continued to treat women workers with separate standards.[31] Kazuko Tanaka describes how the underlying assumption of employers was that women's proper place was in the home, and workplace policies reinforced this ideology.[32] Women who graduated from four-year universities were subjected to unequal pay and promotion, and women who reentered the workforce after marriage were designated as part-time workers and received low wages.[33] As women gained greater access to education in the postwar, the disparity between equality under the law and their lived experience prompted some women to question the rigid enforcement of a gender-based division of labor.

By categorically framing *ūman ribu* within a chronology of women's movements in Japan, some narratives have overlooked the historical and political significance of *ribu*'s deliberate departure from existing women's political organizations.[34] *Ribu* activists were thoroughly critical of the modern family system and the limits of Japan's postwar democracy. *Ūman ribu* took issue with how mainstream women's organizations were based on women's roles as wives and mothers, consumers and citizens. Insofar as *ūman ribu* denounced the ideology of *ryōsai kenbo* as an integral part of the family system, this thorough rejection marked its break from mainstream women's movements.

The largest and most visible women's organizations, such as Shufuren and Chifuren, had ties with the postwar government and were premised on women's roles as wives *(shufu)* and mothers *(haha)*.[35] For example, Shufuren, commonly translated as Housewives Association, was formed in 1948.[36] The term *shufu* (housewife) refers to a married woman who takes on the responsibility of domestic work.[37] Shufuren aimed to "stabilize living conditions" and "rationalize consumption"[38] and to "link government directly with [its members'] lives." It adopted the slogan "Succeed and see hope as house-wives."[39] Given Shufuren's stance and close working relationship with the government, it is not surprising that one of the pioneering activists and theorists of *ūman ribu,* Tanaka Mitsu, publicly declared Shufuren as a *"hanmenkyōshi"* for *ribu*—a teacher or model of what *not* to become—in one of the nation's largest daily newspapers, *Asahi Shinbun.*[40] This hostile language and stance toward Shufuren and marriage are examples of the antagonistic style of Tanaka's discourse, which was highly influenced by the radicalism of the pe-riod. Another *Asahi* article published *ribu*'s denunciation of marriage, "The one husband one wife system is nonsense," as one of its headlines. *Ribu*'s initial process of self-formation hence involved the rejection and critique of mainstream women's groups like Shufuren.[41]

Mainstream women's organizations, such as Chifuren, were massive. By 1951, six million women were registered as part of these regional women's as-sociations, which is indicative of the extensive basis of mainstream women's organizations.[42] Chifuren's objectives were to promote the status of women, develop healthy youth, reform family and social life, and "encourage mutual coordination and cooperation among the regional women's associations for the purpose of establishing world peace."[43] Many of these larger associations organized to campaign for the ruling party during election time and received state funding. The close ties to the government and investment in women's roles as good housewives and wise mothers formed the basis of the interlock-ing relationship between the Japanese family and state capitalism that *ūman ribu* criticized as the reproductive unit of a discriminatory social system.

In contrast to the vast size of these mainstream women's organizations, *ribu* was much smaller, if not numerically marginal. *Ribu*'s largest meetings drew two to three thousand participants, and the regular circulation of *ribu* journals and newspapers during the 1970s remained under three thousand.[44] The movement was composed predominantly of urban middle-class and lower middle-class, educated, ethnic Japanese women, the majority of whom were in their twenties and thirties. It is important to note that expanding membership or recruitment was not one of *ribu*'s primary political objec-tives, which is another factor that distinguishes it from most other politi-cal organizations. As was the case with certain radical feminist cells in the United States during the 1970s, *ribu* cells operated as small, discrete, and autonomous groups that forged coalitions with other *ribu* cells for specific actions, events, and campaigns.[45] The quality of its politics, not expansion or organizational establishment, was prioritized. This turn away from empha-sizing the size of the movement and its critical stance toward the state was also indicative of its post–New Left formation and is further elaborated in chapter 2. As a post–New Left movement, a critique of capitalism also characterized *ribu*'s discourse at the outset of the movement.

The published dialogues of the first major *ribu* gathering in Tokyo on November 14, 1970, contained many of the key concepts of *ribu*'s feminist discourse. This meeting drew approximately two hundred participants and lasted for about seven hours, indicative of the sense of urgency of the moment and the priority given to long debates and discussions. Men were officially excluded from the meeting. The following quote outlines how capitalism and women's confinement to the home were recognized as two major systemic factors that produced the *ribu* movement.

> *Ribu* has arisen in capitalist nations out of historical necessity. The way modern civilization has provided women with the latitude to think about issues, but at the same time has shut women up inside their homes, and uses the home as the basis to reproduce this system as a capitalist society, is the reason this [movement] erupts. . . . I think the liberation of the self is about the liberation of the self that cannot be contained; I think this liberation of the self is for *onna* (woman) as an *onna* (woman).[46]

What is notable here is how the rise of *ribu* is explained as an inevitable outcome of the contradictions produced through modernization and capitalism, with an emphasis on the liberation of *onna*. At this first major *ribu* gathering, a participant stated: "The women's movements *(fujin undō)* until now have never thoroughly taken up the issue of sexual desire *(seiyoku)*. On this point, I think that there is a new significance in this movement."[47] By underscoring this shift that made sex and sexuality a central political issue, this speaker pointed to how *ribu* would focus on articulating how sex and sexual discrimination were foundational to the reproduction of capitalism. At the same time, another participant declared that the scope of the problems at hand could not be "resolved as an individual problem" but required a "confrontation with the entirety of the society."[48] Therefore, while sex and sexual discrimination were focal points of the movement, *ribu* would forward a broader systemic analysis of how controlling sex was vital to reproducing a discriminatory capitalist society.

Iijima Aiko: What Is Left of Mother's Peace?

Ūman ribu's simultaneous rejection of existing women's movements and the establishment left was prefigured by the communist and socialist activist Iijima Aiko (1932–2005). Iijima was a pivotal leftist intellectual who can be considered one of the forerunners of *ribu*. From the age of fourteen, Iijima was

interested in antiestablishment politics. She became an official member of the
JCP at age seventeen. She married Ōta Ryū in 1952, the man who is considered
the founder of Japanese Trotskyism. She worked different jobs to support her
husband, who was a professional revolutionary with no income.[49] She spent
most of her life working as an organizer for the Japan Socialist Party.[50] Having
experienced what she describes as "the oppression of her sex" in her marriage,
Iijima decided to leave Ōta in 1963, ending a seventeen-year relationship.[51]

The *ribu* intellectuals who edited the massive three-volume *The Documents of the History of Women's Lib in Japan* locate *ribu*'s lineage in direct
connection with Iijima's group. Under the subtitle "The Dawn of *Ribu:* From
Fujin Movements to *Ribu*," the history of *ūman ribu* begins with the Committee of Asian Women (Ajia Fujin Kaigi) that Iijima established in 1969.[52]
The full name of the organization, Asian Women's Committee Who Fight
Discrimination=Aggression (Shinryaku=Sabetsu Ajia Fujin Kaigi), underscored
the emphasis on discrimination and a Pan-Asian political consciousness.

In the late 1960s, Iijima began to publicly question the peace politics of
existing women's movements, such as the Mother's Convention *(haha oya
taikai)*.[53] The role and concept of motherhood *(haha)* became the rallying
point for many women's groups from the mid-1950s until the late 1960s, with
the historic Mother's Convention that began in 1955. The Mother's Convention was one of the more successful forums for bringing together disparate
women's groups to agree upon the following aims: protecting children, the
defense of women's lives and rights, and the defense of peace.[54] The Mother's
Convention initially drew over two thousand attendees, bringing together a
politically diverse coalition of women's organizations, including Shufuren,
the Women's Democratic Club (Fujin Minshu Kurabu), the Christian Temperance Union (Kirisutokyō Kyofukai), the Japanese Association to Protect
Children (Nihon Kodomo o Mamoru Kai), the Japan Teachers Union, the
Federation of Women's Organizations (Fudanren, of which Hiratsuka Raichō
served as the president), and many other women's groups. In 1960, the national
meeting of the Mother's Convention drew thirteen thousand women, indicative of the broad appeal of this postwar pairing of "mother" and "peace."

This antiwar and propeace discourse was linked to the postwar reconstruction of motherhood as being innately nurturing and peace loving. In
October 1969, while still associated with Nihon Fujin Kaigi (the women's
organization affiliated with the Japan Socialist Party), Iijima wrote a position
paper that outlined her critique of the Mother's Convention:

> Since the postwar reform, "mother" is now defined as desiring peace and as
> protector of life. We need to question the ways that the system and [postwar]
> reform have both manipulated "motherhood" as much as possible.[55]

Iijima's criticism points to how *ryōsai kenbo* was transformed in the postwar and how this reformed peaceful image could be dangerously deceptive. Iijima questioned the meaning of the "peace" that the mother's movement advocated, because this peace and prosperity at home was at the expense of military aggression and economic domination against other peoples of Asia.[56] Despite Japan's supportive role in the U.S. wars in Korea and Vietnam, the majority of postwar women's movements heralded a banner of antiwar and peace in the face of the ongoing colonization of Okinawa by the U.S. military and Japan's complicity therein. Iijima criticized how Japan's "peace and democracy" was being maintained at the cost of "sacrificing Okinawa."[57] This attention to the occupied condition of Okinawa was articulated among the diverse yet interconnected political concerns of the *ribu* movement. However, insofar as *ribu* activists initially focused on the liberation of their sex, sustained alliances or solidarity with Okinawan women did not become a focal organizing point for *ribu* activism.

Leftist women like Iijima, who were firmly grounded in Marxist theories of capitalism and imperialist expansion, sought an alternative model to counter the tendency of postwar women's organizations to maintain a "victim's consciousness" about Japan's imperialist past and instead departed from a self-understanding of their complicity in the violence and aggression being waged against other Asians, particularly in Vietnam.[58] Iijima writes in this regard:

> Since we know that, more than anything, without Okinawa as a front line base, and without the Japanese mainland as the supply base, this war of aggression could not continue. As we enjoy this prosperity and silently recognize this condition, I have begun to sense that in fact we have become the terrible accessories to the murder of the Vietnamese people.[59]

Iijima's articulation of her connectedness, via silent complicity, with the "murder of the Vietnamese" expresses how women's and mothers' peace movements needed to face their relationship and potential connection to the ongoing war in Vietnam that the Japanese state was supporting. This kind of critique unsettled the existing assumption about women's relative desire for peace, which needed to be rigorously interrogated. Iijima's discourse anticipated *ribu*'s declaration that "the greatest victims and the greatest accomplices are women *(josei)*."[60] This bold assertion was the title of one of the *ribu* movement's earliest manifestos, written in August 1970, that underscored the complex ontologies of women as victim-accomplices.

In 1970, Iijima worked with other politically active women to organize a conference that would set a new direction for women's leftist politics. This conference, and the group that Iijima would establish, reflected an attempt for Japanese women to confront their own imperialist legacy and political responsibility to other Asian women of the nations that Japan had colonized. After much discussion and debate, to demonstrate their solidarity with other Asian women, Iijima and cofounding member Yōko Matsuoka decided to call the conference Asian Women's Committee Who Fight Discrimination=Aggression.[61] To make explicit their intention to fight against Japanese aggression toward other Asian peoples, Iijima determined to take an explicitly Pan-Asian stance in contrast to reinscribing a political position based on one's national identity. This notion of "Asian women" *(ajia fujin)* was race based and regional, referring to a racialized solidarity that stood against the geopolitics of imperialism.

The Embryonic Stage of Radical Feminism

This historic conference was held at Hosei University in Tokyo, August 22 and 23, 1970, and was one example of how such leftist women's organizing was an embryonic political space from which *ribu* emerged as a radical feminist movement. Iijima's political trajectory constituted one of the anti-imperialist legacies that informed *ribu*'s feminist investment in Pan-Asian solidarity.[62] The conference was a major forum for women on the left, with over a thousand women attending each day. A large range of leftist women's groups attended the conference, such as the women of Shibokusa, the representative of the Women's Committee of Sanrizuka, as well as women from New Left sects and student movements.[63] Asian women from Taiwan, Malaysia, and China, who lived in Japan and were fighting against Japan's discriminatory immigration laws, were also key speakers and participants at the conference.[64]

In theorizing the purpose of this conference, Iijima made three important points that delineated their group's differences from former women's movement paradigms, laying the groundwork for *ribu*'s version of radical feminism. First, she called for a theory of women's liberation that was not subsumed under class liberation. This signaled a shift from a class-based politics to a reconception of women's liberation as a specific form of identity politics based on the notion that women constituted a group that suffered from discrimination.[65] Sex and gender discrimination was rearticulated as a fundamental systemic oppression and no longer a secondary effect of capitalism.

On the one hand, Iijima's group argued that discrimination against women was to be regarded as coequal with the discrimination against outcast *burakumin,* Okinawans, and *Zainichi* (Koreans residents in Japan). The reconceptualization of women as a group that suffered from a common form of discrimination was a central theme of the *ribu* movement from its outset. This claim that Japanese women comprise a group that is equally discriminated against as other "minorities" in Japan was representative of the larger political framework of discrimination versus equality. Such a claim was problematic because it did not attend to differences of class, sexuality, racial, and ethnic differences and was analogous with the ways in which feminists elsewhere have represented "women" in a universalizing manner, disregarding other significant differences among women.[66]

This understanding of women, on the other hand, was complicated by Iijima's determination that their organization should take an Asian perspective, declaring that U.S. imperialist aggression should be interpreted as aggression against Asian women, with whom they needed to declare solidarity. By recognizing their own subject position as women complicit in a Japanese–U.S. neo-imperialist formation, Iijima stated that it was imperative to learn about how other Asians struggle against oppressive conditions, placing the burden to forge an anti-imperialist praxis on Japanese women, given their position of relative power. This leftist political formation became an important point of connection that linked *ribu* to a longer anti-imperialist and antistate legacy that gave *ūman ribu* its internationalist and Pan-Asian political consciousness.

For Iijima, the problem of discrimination against women was to be approached as an issue of self-transformation, emphasizing the importance of autonomous action. This critique of the discrimination against women, however, did not imply that *ribu* women were demanding to be equal with men—on the contrary, they recognized the need to dismantle the system so that men could also be liberated from the domination of the system.

From *Fujin* to *Onna*

Having been involved with the established Left during the 1960s until *ribu*'s inception, Iijima and her group comprised the closest genealogical link between the women of the established Left and *ribu*. By offering both a critique of the dominant logic of postwar women's movements and the limits of Marxist theory, Iijima had already begun the labor of breaking new ground, thus clearing a politico-theoretical space for *ribu*. In 1970, Iijima forwarded an unprecedented critique of the male-centered, gendered condition of the Left in a manifesto called, "What Is Discrimination for *Onna*?" In this well-known position paper, Iijima stated that the "laboring class," "labor unions," and "theory" were men's domains. She went so far as to declare that "theory was a man," marking the emergence of a radical feminist critique from within the Japanese left.[67] In contrast to existing Marxist theories of class liberation, or human liberation, Iijima insisted on the need to attend to the specificity of the historical oppression of women, which could not be reduced to "class domination."[68] Iijima wished to emphasize that her group was not advocating "women's right to work" but was fighting discrimination as a structure of aggression.[69] This emphasis on discrimination against women was deeply inflected by a critique of Japanese imperialism.

By the fall of 1970, Iijima had significantly shifted from her previous Marxist position to conclude that "the originary structure" of human oppression was the "discrimination of sex."[70] In so doing, Iijima outlined a position that formed the basis of *ribu*'s formation and departure and was cited and read by many Japanese *ribu* activists. Iijima also had a significant amount of interaction with Tanaka Mitsu leading up to the conference and stated in an interview that she had once received a "love letter" from Tanaka.[71]

According to Iijima, her group members did not consider themselves to be part of *ribu* but worked alongside of *ribu* in various campaigns.[72] Throughout the early 1970s, the Committee of Asian Women organized coordinated protests with *ribu* women against Japanese sex tourism in South Korea as well as joint efforts to protest the government's attempted revisions to the Eugenic Protection Law. Iijima's group thus maintained a working relationship with *ribu* while retaining its own distinct identity. The reason Iijima herself did not ultimately identify as *ribu* illuminates the point of departure that made *ribu* distinct from other women's liberation movements. Looking back at her relationship with *ribu*, Iijima stated that in spite of the fact that she wrote and spoke about the liberation of *onna*, in the final analysis, she could not self-identify as an *onna*. The name of Iijima's group deployed the conventional and more respectable term for women, *fujin*. Inoue Teruko and many others have emphatically stated that the change from *fujin* to *onna* was not simply a change in terminology but a substantive element of *ribu*'s criticism of the fundamental premises of existing women's movements.[73] Because the term *fujin* implied, at this historical juncture, a lady with its middle- to upper-class connotations and *shufu* meant housewife or homemaker, *ribu* rejected both these terms with their respective moorings in class divisions and the family system.[74]

In the Japanese context, the semantic distinctions between the terms *fujin*, *josei*, and *onna*, which are all translated as "women" and/or "woman," must be given careful attention, as they often signal political differences. *Ribu* activists deliberately chose and reappropriated *onna*, a term for woman that can be used in a pejorative manner with sexual or lower-class connotations. As noted by Kano Masanao, the term *onna* approximated a discriminatory word *(sabetsu go)*. It signified the raw and total being that had to be liberated. According to linguistics scholar Orie Endo, its strong sexual implications made it a term that could "be substituted for many sexually related terms, such as mistress or prostitute," and this was considered disrespectful, taboo, even "dirty."[75] *Ribu* activists concur that the use of the word *onna* was deliberate and clearly marked a distinction from the existing *"fujin* movements" and the common phrase *"josei mondai"* (women's problems/issues).[76] In this connection, Iijima stated that she felt more comfortable with the terms *josei* and *fujin* because *onna* was too base and crude a term for her. The willingness to identify as *onna* became a kind of code or standard of *ribu*, what Verta Taylor and Nancy Whittier have called a "boundary marker," that differentiated the women who identified as *ribu* from other leftist women.[77] The subject *onna* and the concept of the liberation of sex constituted the core of *ribu*'s formation. *Ribu*'s concept of the liberation of sex and how it articulated through its political campaigns is elaborated in chapter 3.

Ūman ribu thus sought to expose how terms such as *fujin, shufu, josei,* and *onna* regulated women and their proper forms of femininity and domesticity. Hence, at its first public protest, *ribu*'s placards questioned, "What is femininity?" and "Mother, are you really happy with your married life?" That such questions were posed at an antiwar rally signaled *ribu*'s clear intention to politicize gender and sex norms that were not integral to the political discourse of the Left.

The photo from *Asahi Shinbun* illustrates how the slogan "Liberate *onna*" (おんな) marked *ribu*'s first demonstration on Antiwar Day. Another placard

This first demonstration by *ūman ribu* in the Ginza district of Tokyo calls for *"Onna*'s Liberation" as part of antiwar protests on October 21, 1970. Photograph from *Asahi Shinbun.*

stated, "A housewife and a prostitute are both raccoons in the same den."
Ribu questioned how women's sexuality was devalued and controlled by a
male-centered society *(dansei-chūshin shakai)*, dividing women into good
housewives and dirty prostitutes. Although there were changes in the dominant family formation from the modernization of the *ie* system to the rise of
the postwar nuclear family model, *ribu* activists referred to the *ie* system *(ie
seidō)* as the target of their antipatriarchal critique.[78]

From *Josei* to *Onna*

From the outset of the movement, some of *ribu*'s earliest manifestos deployed
the term *josei,* which was, and remains, the most generic modern term for
women. For example, one of the earliest *ribu* groups that formed in April 1970
called itself the Committee to Contact and Prepare for Women's Liberation
(Josei Kaihō Junbi Renraku Kaigi). Four months later, the members of this
group started another group called Group of Fighting Women (Gurūpu
Tatakau Onna), indicative of a decisive and meaningful shift from *josei* to
onna.[79] The rejection of the term *shufu* and the shift from *fujin* and *josei* to
onna constituted a deliberate attempt to produce a cognitive and symbolic
disjuncture.[80] *Ribu* purposely selected and reclaimed *onna* as a means to mark
its departure and critique of the gendered ideologies that had hitherto prescribed the standards for respectable women who reproduced the status quo.
Like other movements that reappropriated existing derogatory terms, *ribu*'s
gesture simultaneously involved an interrogation and a rearticulation that
positivized its meaning. At *ribu*'s first public street demonstration in October
1970, the women chanted *"onna kaihō—zettai shori"* which means, "liberate
onna—we will definitely win." Thus, the *ribu* movement constituted a new
women's movement that transformed *onna* into a new politicized subject.

In "Liberation from the Toilet," the most well-known manifesto of the
movement, Tanaka Mitsu connects the "chaste" status of the Japanese wife
to the violation of those euphemistically referred to as the "comfort women."
The comfort women were women who served in military brothels known as
"comfort stations." A vast number of these women were often deceived and
forced to act as "sex slaves" as part of the militarized brothel system during
Japan's imperial invasion of Asia. This famous *ribu* manifesto declared: "The
chastity of the wives of the military nation and the dirtied pussies of the
'comfort women' are both two extremes of a structure of consciousness that
denies sex."[81] The shocking effect of the explicit, sexual, and vulgar language
was characteristic of *ribu*'s performative and discursive style that sought to
shatter the legitimacy and lauded value of the housewife by connecting her

to the violence done to comfort women. In this manner, *ūman ribu* made connections between the status of Japanese wives and Japanese imperialism by recalling the sexual violation of the comfort women.

Even more pertinent than the stunning effect of such rhetoric was *ribu*'s intention to bring the female body into discourse, as expressed in the opening lines of this chapter. *Ribu* women spoke a new political discourse from the subject position of *onna* as a means to politicize sex and center the body of *onna* as a political expression. Moreover, *ribu*'s articulation of sex shifts away from conceiving of sex as "personal politics" but rather underscores the conditions of state-sanctioned sexual aggression and its connections with militarism and economic domination. *Ribu*'s discourse was thus performative across multiple registers. By seeking to disrupt who spoke, about what topic, and in what manner, *ribu*'s practice entailed the combined effect of a new subject speaking about the sexual violations of Japanese imperialism against other colonized Asian women and how the respectable status of Japanese housewives and mothers depended on this structure of violent colonization. In making such connections, *ribu* sought to destabilize the idealized status of the peace-loving Japanese mother as it had been (re)constructed in the postwar. This articulation of the conjuncture of Japanese imperialism and Asian women's sexuality demonstrates how *ūman ribu*'s radical feminism was informed by a broader anti-imperialist critique.

Not only did *ribu* question and critique the state-sanctioned institution of motherhood, but some *ribu* activists sought to mock and shatter its idealization.[82] For example, in 1972, *ribu* activists in Tokyo organized a Mother's Day demonstration and rally under a banner that read, "Mother's Day, what a laugh!" The *ribu* movement was fundamentally critical of how motherhood and maternal love *(bosei ai)* had been deployed as a nationalist ideological device, especially during wartime Japan, and how modern society regulated women's natural procreative capacities through the patriarchal and a predominantly patrilineal nationalist family system.[83] Its demonstrations heralded slogans that advocated "Let's fix the world: Overthrow patriarchal authority." *Ribu* pamphlets declared, "Let's smash a Mother's Day that robs the *onna* from motherhood *(bosei)*." Such aggressive language, again, was characteristic of the radicalism and "male language" *(otoko kotoba)* used by many *ribu* activists.[84]

Ribu Communes

Ribu denounced the system that only legitimated giving birth within the confines of the marriage system. Instead, many *ribu* activists practiced and supported the politics of giving birth outside the family system. They did so in part by refusing to enter the marriage system and establishing communes where women lived with each other to raise their children. *Ribu* communes were integral to the movement and formed across the country from Sapporo, Hokkaido, in northern Japan to Tokyo and the central Honshu region of Kansai. As Nishimura Mitsuko points out in her recent study of *ribu* communes, these collectives were highly practical and ideological. By living together, the women could organize and support each other while they refused to comply with the marriage–family system as a core principle of their feminist politics.[85]

A well-known *ribu* commune in Tokyo, called Tokyo Komu-unu, was established in August 1972 and took its name by abbreviating and combining the words for giving birth and commune (*ko umi* and *komyūn*).[86] Four *ribu* women lived together with four children as part of the commune "to search for a new kind of relationality between *onna* and children." These *ribu* activists sought to redefine and create new conditions for raising children that rejected the "sacrificial mother" paradigm that placed all the responsibility on the birth mother. *Ribu* women theorized the meaning of their new communal formations in their own alternative zines and journals. *Ribu* activist Takeda Miyuki writes, "The *onna* who gave birth is not necessarily the mother; even if you don't give birth, you can still raise a child."[87] While this statement may seem banal in the twenty-first century, the ideological work of delinking motherhood from the family system was itself a radical break. Given the extent to which bloodlines and family lineage have been constitutive of Japan's social structure and systems of discrimination, the disruption of the ideological and state regulation of motherhood was a stark violation of this patriarchal basis of power. As they lived together from 1972 to 1975, these women organized several "baby-stroller demonstrations" (see photo) against department stores, Japan Railway, and museums, protesting their policies against the use of strollers. Such a prohibition represented the sociocultural norm that mothers and their infants should remain in the home. The inclusion of children and infants as part of this demonstration characterized the politicization of the family system.

Ribu activists critiqued the state-sanctioned concept of motherhood and instead articulated and affirmed *onna* as a politicized subject who possessed birth-giving power. *Ribu* rallied around the subjects of "unwed mothers" (*mikon no haha*) and conceived the term *hikon no haha*, which literally means "antimarriage mothers," or "negation of marriage mothers." The creation of new language alongside the adoption of the term *onna* marked *ribu*'s understanding of the politicality of language. *Ribu* activists sought to expose

Demonstration to protest revisions to the Eugenic Protection Law. The banner reads: "A society where humans can live. We want to live! We want to give birth!!" Tokyo, June 11, 1972. Photograph from *Asahi Shinbun*.

how motherhood was only legitimate through its confinement to the hetero-marriage–family system, which they explicitly critiqued as the monogamous "one-husband and one-wife" system *(ippu-ippu seidō)*. By denaturalizing how motherhood had been normativized as apolitical, they politicized and

Tokyo Komu-unu, a *ribu* commune of women and children established in August 1972.
This photograph was reprinted in the Ribu Shinjuku Center Document Collection,
pamphlet edition; the photograph collection was distributed in May 1975.

questioned the freedom of giving birth. *Ribu* thus decoupled the legitimacy
of giving birth from the marriage system and emphasized the need to create
the socioeconomic and cultural conditions under which women could freely
determine whether or not to give birth. *Ribu*'s slogan regarding women's
procreative capacities called for "the creation of a society where we want to
give birth," a position that emphasizes women's procreative capacities and
differs significantly from the "abortion-as-women's right" approach of many
liberal and radical feminists in the United States.[88]

   Ribu women and their children would face many forms of discrimination, ostracism, and economic disadvantage for refusing to legally marry and
have their children within the confines of the family system that was documented in the family registration system *(koseki)*. Going against family expectations and the compulsory normative telos of marriage-to-motherhood,
ribu's politics permeated the most intimate spaces and relationships with
lovers, partners, and children. Despite the daily forms of disadvantage and
discrimination they would face, forty years later, *ribu* women continue living
this politics.[89] For example, Saeki Yōko, who edited the first anthology of
ribu writings published in 1972, *Onna's Thought (Onna no shisō),* refused to

legally marry and register her daughter as part of the family system under the father's name on the basis of her critique of the politics of the family system. Despite the way *ribu* activists fundamentally critiqued the family system, some *ribu* women were already married at the time the movement began, and other women married in spite of their critical stance toward the family system. Although not all *ribu*-identified women refused to marry or chose to annul their marriages, this critical stance toward the family system constituted one of the core perspectives that distinguished *ūman ribu* from its predecessors.

Ribu and Mothers Who Kill Their Children

In May 1971, in a pamphlet called "Love Letter to My Mother," the Group of Fighting Women begin with the question: "What is the meaning of the word 'solidarity' when we say, we are *ribu* who seek solidarity with women who kill their children?"[90] These *ribu* activists in Tokyo deliberately chose Mother's Day to announce their solidarity with mothers who killed their children.[91] In tandem with advocating birth outside the marriage system and declaring a desire to create a new kind of relationship between *onna* and her children, *ribu* activists called for an alliance with mothers who killed their children, although they did not advocate such acts of violence. This unusual stance toward such gendered violence further distinguished *ribu*'s distinct incarnation of radical feminism.

In the early 1970s, the mass media represented child killing *(kogoroshi)* as an alarming social crisis.[92] In 1970, there were nearly four hundred reported cases of child killing.[93] These figures peaked until 1974, nearing six hundred cases that year.[94] As Tama Yasuko points out in her detailed study, newspaper reporting created its own distinct narrative about child killing, placing the blame on mothers.[95] Even when fathers killed their children, the stories implied that the fathers were also victimized due to absent mothers who had left them with the children. When mothers killed their children, these stories became the basis for a cause of alarm about "bad mothers" *(dame na haha)* who lacked motherhood *(bosei)*.[96] Because child killing could no longer be excused as a way to circumvent starvation as it had in former generations, these acts of violence by women against their children were deemed to be unnecessary, unnatural, and therefore an aberration.

Many women of *ribu* attempted an intervention vis-à-vis this crisis in the early 1970s, creating a different discourse about this criminalized category of Japanese women. *Ribu* activists rearticulated the meaning of these acts not as aberrations but as signs of the extreme conditions of how women were alienated from their sex and evidence of women's violent capacity to revolt against the system. On May 8, 1971, *ribu* women in Tokyo held demonstrations and meetings to call for women to unite in solidarity with mothers who killed their children. In June 1971, in Hokkaido, the most northern prefecture, a *ribu* cell called Metropolitan organized a rally to declare its solidarity with these "violent mothers." *Ribu* groups collected data and statistics on these incidents. They conducted research interrogating the living conditions in which these incidents occurred. Instead of separating themselves from these cases of infanticide, *ribu* activists sought to understand and connect with these women, writing them letters and visiting them in prison. Activists such as Sayama Sachi, Aida Fumi, and Mori Setsuko attended such court hearings and created reports about what transpired. Activists such as Takeda Miyuki, who were part of the Group of Fighting Women and Komu-unu, invested themselves in writing letters to these mothers and visited them in prison.[97] They wrote pamphlets and held teach-ins on the theme of women who kill their children.[98]

Ribu writings made consistent reference to the phenomenon of *kogoroshi no onna,* and the documents of the movement indicate the extent to which child killing was part of the consciousness and activism of the movement. *Ribu* activists grasped such actions not only as an indicator of the misery of women's lives but also as a sign to question what it meant to live as a woman as well as an opportunity to reflect on their own relationship to such violence and their own potential for such violence as *onna*. In the words of veteran *ribu* activist Yonezu Tomoko, *ribu*'s alliance with mothers who killed their children had the following significance:

> Our solidarity was not just expressed in words, we tried to contact these women and communicate with them to understand them. Even though we recognized that killing a child is wrong, we didn't want to place the blame on that one mother, rather, the blame could be placed on me as well, for allowing and perpetuating such a society. Even though there is no way I could feel the extent of the pain these women felt, the meaning of our solidarity included how we wanted to reflect on what these women experienced and what were the conditions that allowed this to happen.[99]

Ribu's declaration of solidarity with mothers who killed their children powerfully demonstrates the extent of their repudiation of the "good wife, wise mother" *(ryōsai-kenbo)* ideal. The rising dominance of the nuclear family formation overwhelmingly placed the burden of child rearing on the mother, yet a woman's desire and capacity to have a child without a husband was deemed illegitimate. Under state regulation, the very naturalness of a woman's procreative capacity was restricted by the family registration system. The family registration system enforced the regulation of patrilineality by rendering the children of women without a husband "illegitimate" *(hichakushutsushi)*.[100] This male-centered social regulation of women's reproductive capacities and labor through the imposition of the family registration system institutionalized and formalized this control over the presumed naturalness of motherhood *(bosei)* that was only legitimized by the name of the father. The presumed naturalness of a woman's procreative capacity is thus doubly inscribed as a social duty and potential danger to the social order.

Tanaka Mitsu on *Ribu,* Child Killing, and Abortion

Within the *ribu* movement, Tanaka Mitsu's discourse on the relationship between child killing and abortion was particularly distinctive. Tanaka's role as one of the leading activists and theorists of *ūman ribu* is taken up in detail and analyzed in chapter 4. Tanaka's highly personalized treatise on women's liberation, *To Women with Spirit: A Disorderly Theory of Women's Liberation (Inochi no onna-tachi e: torimidashi ūman ribu ron)*, was written and published in 1972.[101] Tanaka devotes Part 4 of the book to the relationship between "*Onna* who kill their children and *ribu*." The significant presence of *onna* who kill their children *(kogoroshi no onna)* as a recurring motif throughout the work provides a frequent reminder of women's capacity for violence, which is an integral aspect of Tanaka's disorderly theory of liberation.[102]

Tanaka's approach to child killing refrains from casting it in moralistic terms or absolute values of good or evil. Rather, she speaks of it as a cruel consequence of an oppressive social system, a grave and tragic sign for collective mourning. Child killing is a signal of the unnatural negation of life that should be understood structurally and historically. According to Tanaka, women were not simply participants in a system that reproduced a violent social structure. For Tanaka, violence was also inherent to the specificity of woman's body and being, to the particularity of her sex. Tanaka wrote metaphorically of "the revival of the womb" that gave birth to both *kogoroshi no onna* and the women of *ribu*. This revival of the womb refers to the transformation of the womb from a site of negation and control to a site of resistance and revenge. Tanaka writes,

> It is precisely the emergence of child killing *onna* that signals the mutation
> of the womb from being an object to being a womb that thinks for itself,
> that screams and stamps its revenge in the blood of its own child. *Ribu*

and the children who are killed are both two extreme examples of
branches that share the same root.[103]

Women who kill their children and *ribu* women share the same originary process, referring to the historical (r)evolution of the womb's mutation from an
object to a subject. Tanaka connects child killing to the liberation of sex, saying that this is part of the revenge of the womb, a sign of the violent revival of
the hitherto repressed power of women's sex.[104] Therefore, women were not
outside or separate from violence; rather, violence was to be located *within*
women. For Tanaka, the womb was not only the symbolic and material site
of the creation of new life but also the origin of violence. Tanaka conceived
of the womb as the place that carried the grudge (怨) of women's historicity
and her oppression, and this grudge bore possibilities that were both violent and creative. By locating this origin of violence within a woman's body,
within her womb, the specificity of femininity bears the forces of creation
and destruction, of life and death. It was the expression of this grudge, located in the womb, that gave birth both to *ribu* and to women who kill their
children. Tanaka's naming of this shared origin articulated a genealogy of
defiant women who pose a danger to the system and violation of the "good
wife, wise mother" ideal. Both *ribu* women and child-killing mothers, in different ways, revolted against the system that dictated that marriage and children must be a woman's reason for living.[105] Instead of negating their sex and
their ability to procreate, the women of *ribu* expressed their defiance of the
system—not by killing their children but by deliberately having their children
outside of the modern family system.

Tanaka interpreted child killing as an extreme act of defiance that un-
masks the myth of maternal love by revealing the violent nature of women
that has remained repressed. This expression of violence from the womb
was an alarm. Child killing was therefore also understood as an expression
of a woman's will to power, of her power to destroy life. Tanaka writes,
"Child killing mothers have screamed out that the king is naked, and *ribu* is
none other than a collective that attempts to make this message into a movement."[106] According to Tanaka, the abject and violent figure of the child-
killing mother was the symbolic subject that prefigured the collective movement of *ribu*.

Tanaka's views on abortion were deeply influenced by her close relationship with Yonezu Tomoko, a pivotal and central *ribu* activist with a disability, who was born with a partial spinal cord paralysis. As Tanaka meditated
on the conditions of those women who killed their children, she related the
act of abortion to child killing.[107] In the postwar period, abortion remained

a criminal act, following from the laws instituted in 1880.[108] However, as a means of population control, the Eugenic Protection Law was revised in 1948 to include a clause that allowed women access to abortion "for economic reasons."[109] Although abortion was still deemed a criminal act, this loophole was used liberally by women to legally access abortion with their physician's consent. Japan's abortion policy history and *ribu*'s politics around abortion are further elaborated in chapter 3.

While most women were able to abort their unwanted children by using this legal provision, in Tanaka's discourse, abortion remained a violent act.[110] For Tanaka, *kogoroshi* and abortion ought to be recognized on a continuum of violence; abortion and child killing were both acts of murder. According to Tanaka, *kogoroshi no onna* were those unfortunate enough to have missed the option to kill an unwanted child before she or he was born.[111] Tanaka criticized the (in)justice of a system that legitimized the abortion of a child at seven or eight months yet criminalized a woman who could not get an abortion in time to stop the birth of an unwanted child and, in desperation, killed her child after she or he was born. By arguing for the contiguity of abortion and child killing, she wanted to point to the dubious common sense that meted out the severest condemnation for women who killed their children after birth, in contradistinction to those "wise mothers" who aborted their children, yet failed to question the state sanctioning of abortion as a means of population control.

Tanaka expresses her views about abortion, murder, child killing, and self-recognition in the following terms: "In a society *where we do not want to give birth*, abortion is nothing more than another name for child killing."[112] Further, "To undergo an abortion under objective conditions, that is, when the self subjectively selects an abortion, I would want to make myself conscious of that self, that self that is a murderer."[113] Tanaka avoids morally condemning both women who abort and women who kill their children; rather, she argues that women should recognize their own inherent capacity for violence in their act of aborting their children. According to Tanaka, to abort a child is a murderous act not committed as a free choice but rather situated in a social system produced through population control and the selective criminalization of gendered bodies.[114]

Tanaka speaks of the multiple origins of the violence that culminates in child killing. The crux of her argument interprets this act of violence as constituted by conditions of violence that extend beyond the individual woman, the child, and the actual moment of violence when a woman kills her child. Tanaka argues that child killing is a violent response to a violent system "that does not allow a woman herself to live."[115] It was the culmination of the

calculating logic of the capitalist system that valued profit and productivity over the value of giving birth and human relationships. According to the
logic of this heterosexist system, a woman could validate her existence only
by becoming a man's wife and giving birth to his children. A woman's womb
had thereby been reduced to a mechanism to reproduce the labor force within
a male-centered nuclear family structure. A woman therefore was not free
to give birth or to raise her children outside the family system; instead, her
natural sexual capacities had to be restricted in order to bind her to a man.
Her sexual nature was confined and regulated through this cooptation by a
capitalist system that abstracts the value of her procreative power through a
calculus of productivity and profitability. Women who killed their children
were part of a society that did not value the complexity, creative power, and
chaotic potential of *onna*'s sex.

In *To Women with Spirit,* Tanaka describes child killing as "the most extreme form of expression of the oppressed."[116] But how can a woman who
kills her child be recognized as oppressed? Tanaka's approach to this form of
violence critically suspends the assumption of a mother's criminality and/or
insanity to further interrogate the causes of such violence. For such women,
their domesticated identity as mother, the sole responsible caretaker of the
child, became a condition that, perhaps only momentarily, added to their
sense of oppression. As an extreme expression of their condition, women
began to destroy what was supposed to be their source of fulfillment. It was
the breakdown of the social order, marking the extremity of a woman's alien-
ation from her sex. Mothers who kill their children are those who take life
(and their lives) into their own hands and express the power to kill that even
the oppressed possess. These acts of violence express both the power and the
desperation of the oppressed.

Toward an Alternative Feminist Epistemology of Violence

In regard to violence and abortion, Tanaka's *ribu* discourse was distinct from
that of many other feminist movements in the United States and elsewhere
that emphasized women's rights to abortion without linking abortion to
women's capacity for violence and the violent conditions of the larger society. *Ribu* women's critical embrace of mothers who kill their children as one
of their own political issues constitutes a distinguishing characteristic that
differentiates *ūman ribu* from other versions of feminism, particularly those
that abide by liberal notions of citizenship and the law. *Ribu* activist Tanaka
writes, "A society that makes a woman kill her child is obviously a society

that does not allow a woman to live." Here it is clear that *ribu* women argued that the responsibility for child killing was not to be individualized—singling out an "individual before the law"—but was to be placed collectively on a society that makes a woman kill her child.[117] *Ribu* rejected the hegemonic common sense that attempted to individualize this social phenomenon by saying that such women were "bad mothers," mentally ill, or amoral. *Ūman ribu*'s rejection of a discourse of rights or advancement within the current system was a radical departure from the models of liberal feminism that promoted the professionalization of women and their economic independence. Instead, *ribu* forwarded a protofeminist abolitionist politics that radically questions and critiques the assumptions of the individual and validity of the logic of the law.[118]

As an extension of their adamant rejection of the prescription that women remain good wives and peaceful mothers, *ribu* activists also eschewed the idealization of nonviolence. *Ribu* activists were able to confront and respond to the violence around them and the violence expressed by women—even when it took the extreme form of killing one's child, and in so doing forwarded an alternative feminist epistemology of violence. Some *ribu* activists interpreted mothers who kill their children as a mutiny against the system, by revolting against the dominant masculinist ideology and institutionalization that regulated women's sex and reproductive freedom within the confines of the national family system.

Ribu activists' solidarity with these criminalized Japanese women contrasts starkly with their rejection of a vast array of women's movements that were broadly based on the acceptable identities of wives, mothers, consumers, and citizens. Insofar as *ribu* activists selectively identified with certain groups of stigmatized Japanese women for political reasons—such as sex workers, unmarried mothers, and other criminalized and fugitive women—this movement rejected prioritizing an appeal to a wide range of women. *Ribu*'s attempted solidarity with women who kill their children evinced its philosophical and political radicalism. Rather than attempt to appeal to the common sense of civil society, *ribu* aligned itself with these criminalized women, refusing to alter or compromise its political critique to make it more palatable. These *ribu* activists insisted on breaking away from the common sense of civil society about what is criminal and denounced the logic of a system that did not value the lives of those who were deemed nonproductive members of society, referring to "women, children, the elderly, the disabled." *Ribu*'s radical feminist politics went against the grain of the majority as they sought to live their politics in the day to day.

The *ribu* movement's solidarity with mothers who killed their children distinguishes it from other feminist discourses that categorically condemn violence as a masculinist modality and promote nonviolence as a feminine principle of being. Although some *ribu* activists espoused a politics of antiviolence and/or nonviolence, many *ribu* activists maintained a complex approach to violence, and their solidarity with mothers who killed their children represents a significantly alternative feminist conception of violence and feminine ontology. This stance (which is further elaborated in chapter 5) distinguishes it from more common feminist commitments to nonviolence and pacifism, which are often assumed as the ultimate ethical stance. *Ribu's* stance toward these women *(kogoroshi no onna)* is suggestive of what might constitute an alternative *feminist ethics of violence* that is not based on an ethics of nonviolence.[119] Such a feminist ethics of violence would not idealize violence, its use, or its consequences, but it would depart from an understanding of women's inherent capacity for violence and women's ontological and historical constitution in systems of violence and domination. Such an alternative feminist ethics of violence would need to continually interrogate what would constitute ethical conditions for the use of violence and how and when violence is a legitimate form of self-defense on an interpersonal and collective basis.[120]

Some *ribu* activists advocated and practiced martial arts as a form of liberation and self-defense, as did feminists elsewhere, although some other feminists might consider martial arts a violent and masculinist practice. For example, one of the ongoing projects of the Ribu Shinjuku Center in Tokyo was the practice of self-defense. An English-language pamphlet states:

> If we don't have enough power to strike the other, we don't have a choice
> of whether to strike or not. We want to be able to defend ourselves, and
> at the same time have the choice of "not to strike the other." So, we are
> practicing the art of Shorinji Kenpo, a method of self-defense based on
> the concepts of centering and the knowledge of weak points.[121]

It is notable that the power to strike the other was not something prohibited or beyond contemplation. Rather, what was emphasized was the option to strike or not to strike the other. The choice to *not* strike was based on the assumption that a woman has that ability and capacity to strike, and the choice constituted the condition of a liberated ontology for *ūman ribu*. The movement's capacity to work with such expressions of violence in conjunction with its desire to re-create relations with children formed a productive tension at the core of its radical feminist politics. The political implications of a feminist ethics of violence are addressed further in chapter 5.

Conclusion

As an extension of a series of breaks from and fissures within existing political movements, the rise of *ūman ribu* marked the eruption of a new political movement that focused on sex discrimination and reclaimed the term *onna*. *Ribu*'s iconoclastic critiques were aimed at rupturing the confines of the nationalist family system and at deliberately violating the good wife, wise mother ideal. If we understand how *ribu* sought to explode the (in)coherency of the postwar idealized image of the peace-loving mother, then it becomes possible to appreciate the context of *ribu*'s strategic political solidarity with child-killing *onna*. This move was motivated not only by these broader social determinants of the peaceful postwar maternal image and the good wife, wise mother regulatory ideal: for *ribu* activists, their meditations on the child-killing *onna* expressed the significance of the potential power of women's capacity for violence and *onna*'s constitution in and through a history of violence that was passed on through generations. If these *onna* who killed their children were the criminalized figures who prefigured the *ribu* movement, then the path that led to *ribu*'s painful birthing was stamped with the blood of both unborn and murdered children. Rather than turn away from such spectacles of maternal violence, *ribu* reflected on the conditions of *onna*'s oppression and her need for liberation through such unsettling confrontations. By reflecting on the constitutive violence that permeated the subjectivity of *onna*, in terms of her potential for violence within larger conditions of structural and historical violence, *ribu* would be able to critically confront the masculinism of the New Left's revolutionary ideals. These leftist revolutionary fantasies and attendant violent tragedies are the subjects of the following chapter.

CHAPTER TWO

Lineages of the Left

Death and Reincarnation
of a Revolutionary Ideal

Ūman ribu was an offspring of a complicated leftist genealogy. An understanding of the political genealogy of the New Left in Japan is crucial to assess *ribu*'s political significance as a postwar social movement that offered a critique of the Japanese state and the Japanese left.[1] Reading the margins of Japanese leftist history, it is striking how the watershed events between 1960 and 1972—such as the 1960 Anpo (U.S.–Japan Mutual Cooperation and Security Treaty) protests, the beginning of the Zenkyōtō student movement (1968–71), and the subsequent breakdown of the New Left in 1972—have each been marked by the death of a young leftist woman revolutionary. The 1960 Anpo involved massive protests against the renewal of the U.S.–Japan Mutual Cooperation and Security Treaty.[2] It was punctuated with the death of Kanba Michiko (1937–60). The beginning of the Zenkyōtō student movement in 1968 was foreshadowed by the death of Tokoro Mitsuko (1939–68), a student activist at the University of Tokyo. The 1972 murder of Kaneko Michiyo (1948–72) of the United Red Army epitomized the tragic cost of a misconceived revolutionary plan. By tracing how these three deaths marked the turbulent years of Japan's New Left, we can see how the deep contradictions and violent repression of the 1960s and 1970s gave rise to the *ribu* movement.

1960 Anpo

The renewal of the U.S.–Japan Mutual Cooperation and Security Treaty in 1960 was a defining moment in Japanese political history. The 1960 Anpo crisis has been described as the greatest mass movement in Japanese political history that shook the foundations of Japan's democratic system.[3] The U.S.–Japan Mutual Cooperation and Security Treaty was imposed as part of the conditions that

ended the formal U.S. Occupation of Japan (1945–52). Opposition to the renewal of the treaty came from a vast array of political perspectives, ranging
from pacifist citizens' groups to nationalist right-wing politicians, who saw the
treaty as representing Japan's continued subservience to U.S. interests, as well
as from the established Left.[4] The major organizations that comprised the establishment left were the Japanese Communist Party (JCP), the Japan Socialist
Party (JSP), and Sōhyō (the General Council of Trade Unions).

The postwar student movement was one of the political bases from
which *ribu* emerged. The largest student movement organization was called
Zengakuren and was founded in 1948. During its first decade, Zengakuren
(All-Japan Federation of Student Self-Government Associations) was led by
students who were members of the Communist Party. Zengakuren organized
militant anti-imperialist demonstrations against the U.S. Occupation's Red
Purge (1949–50), the presence and expansion of U.S. military bases, and the
Korean War.[5] However, through the 1950s, communist students became critical of and dissatisfied with the JCP's authoritarian attempts to interfere in
student politics. On many occasions, JCP authorities tried to suppress and
discipline student communists. The conflicts within the left were heightened
during the 1960 Anpo crisis.

During the multitude of demonstrations leading up to the renewal, millions of Japanese mobilized in the form of various protests and strikes. In
spite of the massive protests across the nation, the government's intention to
force the renewal through parliament regardless of public sentiment exposed
the hollowness of Japan's parliamentary democracy. The use of five hundred
riot police to forcefully remove opposing Diet members during the delibera-
tion processes nullified the validity of parliamentary politics.[6] The inability to
stop the renewal exposed the lack of any effective political opposition to the
government.[7] Despite the massive outpouring of oppositional sentiment and
millions of protesters expressing their disdain with the government's actions,
the treaty was automatically renewed on June 18, 1960.

After the dismal results of 1960 Anpo and the debacle of parliamentary
politics, the meaning of democracy was seriously called into question. For
many, the new democratic political system proved to be a failure, rendering the state rhetoric of peace and democracy a facade. The hollowness of
this postwar democracy instigated the pursuit of political activity outside the
boundaries of the parliamentary party system.

The killing of Kanba Michiko remains one of the symbolic and commemorated tragedies of 1960 Anpo. Kanba was a University of Tokyo coed and a
communist-oriented student activist leader who was killed during the demonstrations in front of the Diet on June 15, 1960.[8] According to the autopsy
reports, she was strangled to death, which implicated the police, who com-

Anpo demonstrations in front of the Japanese National Diet on June 18, 1960. Photograph from *Asahi Shinbun*.

monly used stranglehold tactics with their batons to remove protestors. The response to Kanba's death was profound and immense not simply because someone had been killed by the police but because Kanba was an exceptional young woman who had entered the University of Tokyo, the most prestigious institution of higher learning.

Kanba's death crystallized sentiment against the nondemocratic actions

Kanba Michiko (1937–60), Tokyo University student activist killed on June 15, 1960, during demonstrations against the renewal of the U.S.–Japan Mutual Cooperation and Security Treaty (Anpo).

of the government, and she became a symbol of the cost of resistance to state violence. On June 19, hundreds of thousands of protestors outside the Diet were mourning both Kanba's death and the defeat of democracy.[9] Kanba's death was the apposite symbol of the death of democracy, for her life represented an ideal image of the new democratic hope, a woman who had risen to the pinnacle of the educated elite and was killed for exercising her right to protest against the state. In the same way that her life and political right to protest were violently extinguished in their youth, the hope many people had invested in postwar democracy was also shattered by the actions of the state.

The irony of Kanba's life becoming visible through her death also demonstrated the limits of the postwar system of political reforms that enabled women to legally enter the political process but failed to provide a reformation of the culture needed to sustain the lives of women who actively sought a role in the political process. Analogously, although Kanba had merited entrance to Todai (the University of Tokyo), the campus provided no restrooms for women, who comprised 15 percent of the student population. This disregard for women's most basic necessities captured the male-centered campus climate of the times.

Kanba not only had entered the most prestigious university in the nation but also had become a Bund leader.[10] Bund was an organization of student communists, formed in 1958, that had broken away from the JCP. The JCP refused to support any group that did not adhere to its party line and therefore alienated those on the left who were involved in independent and autonomous struggles.[11] The established Left's adherence to hierarchical bureaucratic structure and its loyalty to parliamentary politics were also seen as conservative by leftists who were critical of the system of parliamentary democracy. The rigid organizational hierarchy of the JCP along with its sudden and extreme shifts in postwar policy caused multiple splits and divisions and resulted in many anti-JCP Marxist and communist offshoots from the late 1950s through the late 1960s.[12]

Bund had spearheaded the struggle against the treaty renewal over the course of a fifteen-month campaign.[13] Bund's interpretation of the meaning of the security treaty was significantly more radical than the interpretations put forth by most other participants in the antitreaty movement. Bund insisted that the new security treaty was a clear sign of the resurgence of Japanese imperialism, and thus blocking the treaty was necessary to stop Japanese imperialism. During the Anpo crisis, the infighting between leftist groups climaxed. During the struggle, the JCP appeared to be more invested in repressing and destroying the anti-JCP Bund than in blocking the renewal of the treaty. This became clear when the JCP and the JSP tried to physically block and prevent other groups from helping anti-JCP students who had been injured by the riot police during the demonstrations. Kanba's death was commemorated for decades, but as Wesley Sasaki-Uemura writes, "Despite the outpouring of sentiment for Kanba, the Japan Communist Party and Japan Socialist Party leadership still branded her a Trotskyist because of her Bund affiliation."[14] Insofar as Kanba's death also pointed to the fractiousness within the Japanese Left, her death would foreshadow how many on the left would fail to value their own but prize the party line, theory, abstraction, and even death over lived-experience. The actions of the established Left during the Anpo struggle starkly revealed its authoritarian structure and its betrayal of the students, whom they did not consider worthy of protection from state violence. The established Left's investment in its authority as part of the parliamentary governing system became even more reason for the emergent New Left to completely reject the validity of parliamentary democracy.

This focus on state violence and anti-imperialism would continue to characterize the student movement through the 1960s and was an integral part of the heritage of student politics that shaped the *ribu* generation. Kanba's death also makes visible her relative vulnerability as a woman in this form of protest, as her presence as a woman may have provoked the wrath of the police.[15] Her specific vulnerability as a woman against the police and the different dangers she faced, however, were not sufficiently addressed within the political culture of the left as an integral question of what *forms of resistance* the struggle should take. Rather than serve as a warning of the limits of this form of confrontation with the state, this ritual of street protest would become the chosen method of protest throughout the next decade.

The New Left and Anti-Imperialism

Zengakuren became a very different organization after 1960 Anpo. By 1960, there was already a sense of disillusionment with world communism for many leftist students. After the failed struggle against the treaty, Bund broke into several factions, and the remaining Bund factions continued to emphasize having the "correct tactics."[16] The New Left emerged during the 1960s as these rebel offshoots from the established Left. It was a heterogeneous and explosive constellation of Marxist and revolution-oriented political sects that argued over the interpretation of revolution and the correct tactics to pursue it. The sect movement became the dominant style of the student movement until the late 1960s. New Left sects such as Front (1962), Kakumaru (1963), and Chūkaku (1963) were formed in the early 1960s.[17] Chūkaku inherited Bund's tradition of mass-action-oriented tactics, whereas Kakumaru emphasized the importance of possessing the correct revolutionary ideology and executing its own program. Kakumaru also thought that rival political groups had to be subordinated or eliminated, if necessary, through violent means. These violent revolutionary tactics, along with state repression, would contribute to the (self-)destruction of many New Left sects.

In addition to these sects, the New Left was composed of student action committees, community action groups, concerned intellectuals, and worker initiative groups, with a mass base in the tens of thousands.[18] In contrast to the established Left's stance of maintaining "peace" and "order," and its efforts to expand its voter base, the New Left sought a different arena of authentic and meaningful political action. For example, the Kaihō faction formed in 1965 and based itself on the theories of Rosa Luxembourg, advocating spontaneity and the "liberation of sensibility."[19] The necessity of struggling against Japanese imperialism meant waging battles against state power. Direct action against the state became the recognized modus operandi of the New Left, which took the form of street battles with the riot police. In October 1967, the New Left spearheaded a series of demonstrations to protest Japan's support of the Vietnam War. These demonstrations later were interpreted as evidence of the New Left's decision to engage in "revolutionary violence" as a means to bring attention to the violence in Vietnam. Beginning in 1967, street battles increased.[20]

Born in the era of the Cold War, and coming of age amid the violence of Vietnam, the women of *ribu* were politicized in the face of the violent state repression of the antiwar and student rebellions. As part of a post-Anpo generation, *ribu* activists no longer trusted parliamentary politics and its version of democracy. *Ūman ribu* formed when the New Left was in its last phase of radicalism, immediately following the climax of the student movement rebellions. Street battles against the riot police, urban guerrilla attacks against police stations, and nationwide student uprisings were part of the tumultuous process that gave birth to *ribu*. The government expanded its paramilitary police forces, and throughout the late 1960s, the riot police regularly initiated assaults against student activists who protested against U.S. imperialism.[21] In 1969, in conjunction with the October 21 International Antiwar Day demonstrations, the police arrested over fourteen thousand demonstrators and activists.[22] Like their New Left predecessors, the women of *ribu* no longer looked to either governmental institutions or the established Left as viable agents of social change. The women of *ribu* witnessed how the state attempted to enforce Japan's putative "peace and democracy" through the massive expansion and violent tactics of the riot police to quell domestic protest.[23] Following the New Left's rejection of the dominant postwar ideology of peace and democracy, some *ribu* activists also engaged in extraparliamentary forms of direct democracy and saw extralegal means as a legitimate form of political expression. As Ehara Yumiko has noted, many *ribu* women learned how to organize and execute political actions through their involvement in New Left politics.[24] By gaining a knowledge of Marxist theories as tools of political analysis, the women of *ribu* deployed those same methods of analyses against the New Left. Although *ribu* has been understood as a separatist movement, it initially attempted to critically engage the New Left by forwarding a vital analysis of its gender politics and its limited concept of revolutionary praxis.

Anti–Vietnam War Movement and Beheiren

From the mid-1960s, the U.S. invasion of Vietnam sparked a new wave of protests against Japan's supportive role in what was seen as an unjust war. The rise and expansion of the anti–Vietnam War movement forged new forms of political organizing, creating solidarities across national, regional, and racial divides. Japan's alignment with and specific geopolitical positioning as part of Pax Americana set the stage for antiwar and anti-imperialist protests on multiple fronts. The expression of this resistance ranged from citizens' groups who raised awareness and monetary support for the Vietnamese victims of war to support groups for AWOL American soldiers based in Japan. While there was a significant constituency of the antiwar movement that advocated an antiwar and propeace stance, at this historical juncture, the New Left emerged with an unequivocal critique of U.S. imperialism.

For the New Left, American imperialism, specifically as manifested in its wars in Korea and Vietnam and its continuous military occupation of Okinawa and other areas of mainland Japan, fundamentally determined the political horizon of resistance and rebellion in postwar Japan.[25] Articulated as part of an international struggle against U.S. imperialism, the New Left involved itself in the anti–Vietnam War movement, which in turn infused other ongoing local protests such as Sanrizuka, the farmers' rebellion against the building of Narita airport, which became a symbol of the struggle of the people against the actions of an authoritarian state.[26]

Immediately after the United States began bombing North Vietnam in 1965, a new kind of urban-based citizens' movement emerged.[27] In 1965, a new anti–Vietnam War citizen's movement called Beheiren (*Betonamu ni heiwa o! Shimin Rengo*) was formed. Beheiren is commonly translated as the Citizen's Alliance for Peace in Vietnam. Organized specifically in opposition to American and Japanese participation in the Vietnam War and as a response to the factionalism of the existing New Left, Beheiren embodied a new style of progressive politics.[28]

Many of *ribu*'s characteristics and idiosyncrasies can be accounted for as learned from its intimate relations with the New Left, Beheiren, and the student movement known as Zenkyōtō. Both Beheiren and Zenkyōtō have been referred to as the neo–New Left. Although *ribu* women asserted a searing critique of what they declared to be the masculinist, male-centered (*dansei-*

chūshin) tendencies of the New Left and student movements, both Beheiren and Zenkyōtō, in many aspects, provided models of the decentralized approach to organizing movements that would influence *ribu*. By reconceiving the relationship between the subject and revolutionary practice, in many ways, Beheiren and Zenkyōtō shaped *ribu*'s approach and principles of movement organizing.

Beheiren served as a vehicle for political organizing that sought to stimulate social change without seeking to consolidate political power. This style of organizing provided a positive model for *ribu*. In sharp contrast to the top-down bureaucratic structure of existing political organizations and the ideological orthodoxy and theoretical formalism of the New Left sects, Beheiren refused to promote any specific ideology and rejected any attempts to form a national organization, as would *ribu*. Beheiren was antihierarchical and sought to privilege flexibility and spontaneity. In principle, Beheiren allowed anyone who agreed with three basic slogans to form their own local Beheiren group: "Peace for Vietnam," "Vietnam for the Vietnamese," and "Stop the Government of Japan from Cooperating in the Vietnam War."

Furthermore, Beheiren sought to deprivilege theory and emphasized action as the essential political mode of expression. Beheiren's first principle was, "When you advocate something, you must be the first to do it." Its charismatic chairman, Oda Makoto, said, "Let's junk radicalism based on words."[29] Unlike existing political organizations and sects that required loyalty to the party line, Beheiren emphasized the importance of a flexible movement and promoted nonviolent action to help stop the war in Vietnam. Although it initially maintained a position of nonviolent action, by 1967 it had developed an underground network to smuggle U.S. military deserters out of Japan and into neutral nations, openly defying state law and authority.[30] *Ribu*'s political style was similar in many respects. When deemed necessary, some *ribu* activists openly defied state law and authority and went so far as to support criminalized women and revolutionaries.

Beheiren articulated a different style of politics in tandem with the various actions local groups carried out. For example, by pointing to how the Japanese political economy was supported by the war, the slogan "the Vietnam within ourselves" characterized the move to personalize politics by realizing one's own position and complicity in the system. In response to one's complicity, Beheiren advocated that it was through action that people could transform themselves from "passive functionaries to active human beings." In this manner, Beheiren attempted to ground political meaning in direct and immediate action. Thus, in response to the many versions of Marxist or social revolution that relegated "liberation" to a distant future, Beheiren conceptualized liberation as part of the process of action. Liberation was a practice to remake one's subjectivity, emphasizing the temporality of the present-continuous in contrast to the future tense. Beheiren's organizational practices and its personalized, action-oriented approach to social transformation was one model that influenced *ribu*'s politics.

Tokoro Mitsuko and Feminine Sacrifice: From Zenkyōtō to *Ribu*

Zenkyōtō was the mass movement that evolved out of the university struggles of 1968 and 1969, among which Nihon University and the University of Tokyo protests became the best known.[31] Zenkyōtō was an abbreviation for Zengaku kyōtō kaigi, often translated as the All-University Joint-Struggle Committee.[32] On the margins of Zenkyōtō's legacy are two deaths that symbolize the internal tensions of the movement: the premature death of Tokoro Mitsuko in 1968 and the famous and spectacular suicide of Yukio Mishima in November 1970. The significance of and difference between these two deaths point to the internal contradictions and oppositional logics within the New Left that induced the formation of *ribu*.

The death of Tokoro Mitsuko has been described as marking the beginning of Zenkyōtō. Tokoro was a graduate student at the University of Tokyo who was politicized during the 1960 Anpo struggles.[33] After participating in the anti–Vietnam War struggles, she collapsed from exhaustion and died soon thereafter from an undiagnosed illness in January 1968, at the age of twenty-nine.[34] The main spokesman of the Zenkyōtō movement, Yamamoto Yoshitaka, writes, "The University of Tokyo struggle began on the day of Tokoro Mitsuko's funeral."[35]

Ribu women have repeatedly marked Tokoro's place within the lineage of intellectuals whose ideas fertilized and shaped the Zenkyōtō movement. In "The Origins of Zenkyōtō Thought," Guy Yasko writes that Tokoro's ideas would become the "theoretical axes" of Zenkyōtō and that the movement "inherited her approach to life."[36] Thus, rather than seeing Zenkyōtō as "exclusively male," in this connection, Yasko suggests that "it is perhaps more accurate to say that the history of women's thought and struggle were essential ingredients in Zenkyōtō."[37]

In 1966, Tokoro published an essay in the journal *Shisō no kagaku* (Science of Thought) titled "The Organization to Come" ("Yokan sareru soshiki ni yosete").[38] In it she elaborated her thoughts about subjectivity, coexistence, and social change; her critique of science and economic rationalism; and the importance of a nonhierarchical organizing structure. Tokoro's ideal vision for a nonhierarchical organization called for a "fluid structure."[39]

Tokoro criticized what she saw as the manner of measuring social change, which privileged assessing change in terms of quantity over quality.[40] The "economic imperative towards greater efficiency" had become the dominant logic of established political organizations.[41] She instead saw the *process* of change as extremely important and the need to foster internal debate among an organization's members was vital to building trust. Her emphasis on the importance of debate became one of Zenkyōtō's hallmarks. Tokoro writes, "Within an organization, it is vital to continually foster trust by recognizing the totality of the other's existence, to train each other and build up each other's subjectivity."[42]

Through her readings of Takamure Itsue, Simone de Beauvoir, Morisaki Kazue, and Simone Weil, Tokoro criticized what she interpreted as "male thought," arguing that "the rationalistic, male logic of science obscured the multiplicity of existence."[43] In her essay "How Does *Onna* Desire to Exist?" she contrasts "women's theory" *(josei no ronri)* with patriarchal and scientific systems of order and control, suggesting a different time–space of the symbiotic relationality of the mother and child.[44] Iijima Aiko and Inoue Teruko read Tokoro as a theorist who distinctly called for a "woman's theory" *(onna no ronri)* as an alternative to the dominance of the "logic of productivity."[45] This concept of the logic of productivity became a target of *ribu*'s anti-capitalist criticism. One of *ribu*'s incisive interventions entailed its gendered critique of how the logic of productivity infected the New Left.[46] Tokoro's critique of science, which was linked to the rejection of the dominant values of a capitalist postindustrial society and its rationalist *(gōrishugi)* economic thought, also became a benchmark of the movement. Even though Tokoro offered an important critique of science and modern thought, as a decentralized movement, many Zenkyōtō activists failed to take seriously Tokoro's feminist analysis. Ironically, Tokoro believed that the unknown disease that took her life was a result of the scientific experiments she conducted in the laboratories at the University of Tokyo.[47]

Although Tokoro envisioned and articulated what became the organizing principles and theoretical axes of Zenkyōtō, her contribution was overshadowed by the spectacular images of male students confronting university administrators and the riot police. At its peak, the Zenkyōtō movement involved over 165 university campuses, comprising over 40 percent of all universities in Japan.[48] Students barricaded and occupied campuses, destroyed university property, and effectively disrupted the management of academic institutions.

Despite the ultimate failure of Zenkyōtō to dismantle the university (as an apparatus of the capitalist class system), many of Zenkyōtō's organizational principles and characteristics provided the template for *ribu*'s ideal vision of politics. Many *ribu* women took seriously Tokoro's work, particularly the essay "The Organization to Come."[49] Through their movement, many *ribu* activists, to a much greater degree than Zenkyōtō, were able to grasp Tokoro's critique of science and embody her vision for a fluid movement. In doing so, *ribu* has been described, by scholars such as Ichiyo Muto, as "Zenkyōtō's successor."[50]

Zenkyōtō's ideal was to be a flexible movement, as Tokoro had emphasized. It attempted to accommodate the subject's freedom by stressing the importance of doing what one could, where and when one desired.[51] Zenkyōtō's goal was to have an organization without hierarchy and to build a movement based on the decisions and actions of the students involved, as opposed to establishing any formal leadership or structure.[52] Characteristic of Zenkyōtō's nonsect style of movement was the rejection of the organizational or group discipline so crucial to the sects.[53] Like Beheiren, Zenkyōtō was not a monolithic organization but a network of nonaligned student groups that was able to organize students who did not want to participate in the sectarian struggles of the New Left. Among nonsect-affiliated students, the New Left sects were largely seen as dogmatic, exclusivist, competitive, and destructive.[54] This refusal of formal group organization and discipline would also characterize *ribu*'s nonorganizational structure. Inheriting Zenkyōtō's non-hierarchical organizational style, in like fashion, *ribu* refused to appoint a formal leader or to establish a headquarters. *Ribu* even went further than this in that it never attempted to form a *zen-onna rengo,* that is, an all-*onna* alliance or nationwide *onna*-alliance, indicating that "unity," or strength in numbers, was not its main purpose.[55]

Ribu was not based simply on an identity politics defined by the category of women or *josei* (the most generic term for woman) but rather on a specific form of political identification, with its key symbiotic concepts being the liberation of *onna* and the liberation of sex. This rejection of any attempt to form an all-*onna* alliance *(zen-onna rengo)* is an indication of *ribu*'s disinterest in expansion for the sake of expansion; in other words, it did not base its political success on the quantity of its members. Again, Tokoro's rejection of quantity over quality is evident in *ribu*'s political style. *Ribu* rejected a national or nationwide formal organization from the outset; therefore, the assumption that *ribu* failed to establish an organization such as NOW (National Organization of Women) neglects the point that *ribu* activists rejected the idea of creating a centralized organization, precisely because it emphasized that each *ribu* cell needed to determine what its own struggle for liberation would entail. The *ribu* movement was thus deliberately decentralized and antihierarchical, which reflected its rejection of established forms of authority.

Thus, while it is often summarily stated that the women of *ribu* broke away from the New Left and Zenkyōtō because of their sexism, *ribu*'s critical engagement went beyond a simple rejection of sexism and a sexist division of labor. *Ribu*'s relationship with the New Left and Zenkyōtō was more intimate and its criticism of its masculinist tendencies was more comprehensive than a simple rejection of women's designated roles. Women were typically placed at the rear of the marches or put in charge of first aid at the demonstrations; they were asked to prepare food or perform other supportive labor. *Ribu* activists criticized how a sexist logic produced the common sense of the leftist culture, producing a typology of leftist women ranging from the theoretically sophisticated "Rosa Luxembourg" types to the beautiful Madonnas and "cute comrades." It extended to what some leftist men would refer to as those who were also disrespected and passed around like "public toilets" for men to "relieve themselves."[56]

Many of the women of *ribu* were of the Zenkyōtō generation and came of age after the Anpo protests, during the anti–Vietnam War movement. The students of Zenkyōtō and many of the women of *ribu* were part of a countercultural generation whose criticism of society and the establishment *(taisei)* was more comprehensive in scope than those of previous generations. Unlike many existing forms of political organization, both Zenkyōtō and *ribu* were interested in reconceiving and rearticulating what constituted a legitimate site of politics and what kind of politics was possible for those who are privileged and complicit in the reproduction of a hierarchical, exploitative, and violent society. The politics of this generation produced a new arena of contestation. This entailed the establishment of one's subjectivity as a site where one could express and demonstrate one's relative autonomy through critique and opposition to the system.

Ribu would depart from this understanding of the political as beginning from the horizon of one's day-to-day existence, stressing the concept of everydayness *(nichijōsei)*. This was a feminist reincarnation of Zenkyōtō's location of politics. Zenkyōtō's was distinct from previous student movements in that it stressed autonomy *(jiritsu)* and the importance of struggling within the horizon of one's day-to-day existence rather than insisting on a "correct" revolutionary strategy or on direct confrontation with the state.[57] According to Guy Yasko,

> Instead of grand slogans and direct confrontation with the state, Zenkyōtō activism centered around local issues. This localism was at once more

modest and even more ambitious than earlier militants. Zenkyōtō
militants attempted to make revolution in their own immediate
surroundings.[58]

Ribu would further Zenkyōtō's understanding one's day-to-day existence
and pursue a vigorous embodiment of the politics of daily living that would
reach beyond the gates of the campus and penetrate into the mundane and
gendered practices of domestic life, one's relationship to one's family, and
how one confronted the self and related to the other. The movement sought
to question the common sense of daily living and the way one's subjectivity
and political consciousness were constituted by one's daily existence.

In contrast to Beheiren, which emphasized action over words, as a student
movement, Zenkyōtō privileged intellectual and philosophical debate and
became known for its endless debates *(eien no ronsō)* and existentialist soul
searching. Zenkyōtō's self-reflectiveness emphasized what became a hallmark
of Zenkyōtō—the process of self-denial *(jiko hitei)* and self-criticism *(jiko
hihan)*.[59] The process of self-denial and self-criticism was meant to make the
self conscious of one's own privileges and complicities in the system and thus
allow one to formulate a more individualized notion of revolutionary activity. Yamamoto Yoshitaka, a University of Tokyo student leader, theorized the
centrality of this concept:

> Without continually engaging in *"jiko-hitei"* (self-negation), as the
> practice of struggle to dismantle the social system, there will be no way
> to transcend the contradiction of including ourselves as part of human
> liberation.[60]

The inevitability of class contradiction for the theorists of Zenkyōtō necessitated a different notion of politics that would nevertheless validate engaging
in politics beginning with a confrontation with the self.[61] Zenkyōtō's concern with the complex positionality of the subject attempted to allow for the
necessity of contradiction and desire. The process of self-criticism and the
recognition of one's privilege and complicity were supposed to enable a new
approach to political activity that recognized the inevitability of contradiction and desire without insisting on adherence to one correct political ideology. However, according to Yasko, this process of *jiko hihan* (self-criticism)
focused too much on the negation of one's privilege and became, in effect,
an overemphasis on one's criminality, so much so that it was ultimately one's
criminality that would link the self to other struggles.[62]

Like Zenkyōtō, *ribu* also valued the process of self-reflection and self-
criticism; however, it arrived at a conclusion very different from self-denial or
self-negation. The women of *ribu* would criticize the theory of self-negation

(jiko hitei), saying that its impossibility of realization became the root of the *zassetsu*, the sense of failure and breakdown felt by many of those who participated in Zenkyōtō.[63] Given that most *ribu* women were educated, middle-class and lower middle-class Japanese women, they recognized that theirs was a position of relative privilege. This critique of their own imperial privilege was informed by this context of leftist self-critique. *Ūman ribu*'s discourse was thus marked with a self-reflexive critique of Japanese women's historical complicity as imperial subjects, which required a recognition of how one's present privilege was accrued through an imperialist history of power and domination. *Ribu* women's confrontation with Japan's past and ongoing imperial conditions foregrounded their critique of the gendered sexual violence of imperialism and how Japanese women were complicit in this history.

As part of the heritage of the New Left, many *ribu* activists emerged with a clear critique of the violence of U.S. imperialism and Japan's strategic geopolitical positioning as part of what was called Japanese–U.S. imperialism *(nichi-bei teikokushugi)*. Insofar as *ribu* departed from this critique of the intersections of a U.S. and Japanese neo-imperial formation, *ribu* was distinct from other versions of first-world feminism that failed to confront the history of imperialism.[64] As one *ribu* woman put it, in more colloquial terms, this meant that the Japanese were "yellow Yankees."[65] In other words, the Japanese were acting not only in compliance with and on behalf of Yankee interests but also on behalf of their own neo-imperial interests. For the New Left and *ribu*, the anti–Vietnam War movement was not simply an antiwar movement but conceived as an anti-imperialist movement that was part of a worldwide liberation struggle. In contrast to the existing women's peace and antiwar movements, many *ribu* activists were informed by a distinctly anti-imperialist politics, which constitutes a significant political distinction that is too often overlooked when postwar women's movements are presumed to be antiwar/propeace movements. Even more than reiterating a leftist critique of U.S. and Japanese imperialism, it was *ribu*'s confrontational stance with the gendered violence of imperialism that distinguished its critique from that of other leftist groups.

For example, *ribu* activists criticized how Japanese women were not blindly led into war but were rather part of the violence of imperialism by cooperating with the war effort, by going to the colonies, and by structurally benefiting from it without sufficiently questioning its costs to others. In doing so, *ribu* created a new discourse that criticized Japanese women's positionality and ethical responsibility to other colonized women in a language that was often explicit and graphic. The following quotation is from a *ribu* manifesto distributed at the Thirtieth Zengakuren Convention in 1972. The manifesto expresses how some *ribu* women articulated their positionality in relation to the violence done to the colonized woman.

> I am a Japanese woman who made Korean women die from insanity. Ninety percent of Japan's military comfort women were Korean women. Japanese women [who were comfort women] could be saved from a death of insanity through thinking that their service was for "the sake of the nation." . . . But Korean women were penetrated and could not help but find themselves going insane. As for the comfort women, didn't they have to perform this sex service always in the face of death? Korean women and Japanese women, however, were placed in this extreme opposition. As part of a race of Japanese oppressors, the women of Japan were opposed to Korean women. I am not a comfort woman. But as a woman who has been marked *(oshitsukeraru)* by the universal essence *(fuhenteki honshitsu)* of women's sex, which is symbolized by the comfort woman— how far I am from the comfort woman. Am I not on the side of those Japanese women who forced these Korean women to suffer this kind of insane death? I no longer want to add to the misery of my woman's sex by being an accomplice in killing other women. I've had enough. It is not out of sympathy or empathy for those who are oppressed, but from my very own pain . . . it is the problem of the race of the oppressors—the Japanese.[66]

Rather than take this imperial history for granted, as that which she must passively accept, this *ribu* woman traces back through time to confront the violence enacted against the other colonized women's sex, a remembrance of a violent past that she allows to haunt her present. Through the production of a self-critical anti-imperialist discourse, this *ribu* woman creates a logic and a language that connects her to the violence done to the Korean comfort women.

This writer's words mark *ribu*'s confrontation with how nation opposes women against women and how imperialism establishes and enforces relations of violence between Japanese and other Asian women. The woman who wrote this text is twenty-four years old. Although this military sex slave system was formally abolished almost thirty years before this writing, the passage is striking in how the author chooses to articulate her own subject position and her political desire in relation to the colonized women she does not know and may never meet. Even though this writer states that she too is marked by the universal essence of "women's sex," she simultaneously recognizes that she was never forced to occupy the same position and bears witness to the structures of imperialism, nationalism and ethnicity, class and race that place women in extreme opposition—in positions of life and death. In doing so, she practices a form of transnational feminist identification that does not erase these incommensurate differences in power and experience. When this *ribu* woman says that she no longer wants to add to "the misery of my woman's sex" by being an accomplice in the killing of other women, "the misery of my woman's sex" signifies that which potentially links them because they share in this common essence of women's sex.

This discourse also points to the radical incommensurability between the experiences of those who are protected as Japanese women and those colonized women who are killed despite that they potentially share in what is called the universal essence of women's sex.[67] The "misery of my woman's sex" is named as one of the effects of the violence done to the comfort women, positing the possibility that "the *ribu* woman's sex" may also be brought into relation with the sex of the comfort women as something that does not make them the same but provides the possibility for identification across national, ethnic, and temporal differences. However, this commonality does not become the basis for her sympathy or empathy. Rather, it is a notion of complicity that becomes the vehicle for this *ribu* woman's identification. Thus, this discourse raises the possibility of "sex" as a form of political identity and desire that seeks to transcend national and ethnic difference as articulated from the position of a Japanese woman's complicity in imperial violence.

Ribu also spoke out against the ongoing sexualized violence against the women of Okinawa and the colonization of the bodies of Okinawan sex workers by the men of the U.S. military.[68]

> "Okinawa is our problem." As for our relationship with Okinawan women, due to the history and the way that the state has divided us, we cannot say that we are the same women as the Okinawan women. . . . Because we are women of the mainland, we are the women who belong to the class of oppressors. . . . We cannot be liberated until Okinawa is liberated. . . . Okinawa functions as the mainland's protective wall. The prostitutes that are being raped by American soldiers serve as Okinawa's protective wall. And in the sex that is sold by the Okinawan prostitutes, we can see the naked colors of Japanese imperialism that we must destroy.[69]

This critique of the gendered violence of imperialism and militarized colonialism as a structure of Japan's modernity distinguished *ribu* from other women's groups who took an antiwar/propeace stance, but it did not confront the fact of Japanese women's complicity in the violence done to other women, whether it be the military comfort women, the women of Okinawa, or other Asian women. Chapter 3 explores how this politics translated into *ribu*'s collective actions.

Although *ribu* women understood their position as complicit in structures of violence, they simultaneously recognized their need for a practice that would not only negate their privilege as Japanese women but also would liberate them from the confines of the system's regulation of proper feminine identity. In contrast to Zenkyōtō's formulation of the denial of the self through oppositional movement, *ribu* sought to affirm a new self and bring into being a new kind of feminine subjectivity through oppositional practice.[70] Zenkyōtō's mode of self-reflectiveness set a precedent for *ribu*'s existential inquiry into the meaning of liberation for women. Departing from Zenkyōtō's question, "What does it mean to live as a human?," *ribu* declared, "Our struggle as women begins by asking the fundamental question: What does it mean to live as an *onna*? Or are we even living as *onna*?" Although *ribu* has been interpreted as taking an antitheoretical stance, one of *ribu*'s sustained endeavors was its philosophical inquiry into the relationship between *onna*'s subjective experience and the formation of a revolutionary subject.[71] *Ribu* activists sought to know and act upon the political implications of the existential condition of *onna*'s sexual difference and examined the ontological status of *onna,* given her history and the unarticulated historicity of the suppression of her sex. This philosophical inquiry was an expansion of what Tokoro had begun in terms of *josei no ronri* (woman's theory) and what Saeki Yōko and others would later call *Onna no Shisō—onna*'s thought.

Tokoro's philosophical contribution, which might be described as constituting the more flexible and nonhierarchical aspects of Zenkyōtō, has often been eclipsed by the more spectacular clashes with the riot police. Spectacular televised clashes with the riot police in January 1969 at the University of Tokyo during the takeover of Yasuda Hall have become the symbolic images of Zenkyōtō's resistance.[72] Despite Zenkyōtō's nonhierarchical principles, the images of Zenkyōtō that remain are of barricaded university campuses and helmeted young men, ready to engage in battle with the riot police. The photograph on the next page captures Zenkyōtō spokesman Yamamoto Yoshitaka in the middle of the second row, standing shoulder to shoulder with his helmeted male comrades during the takeover of the University of Tokyo's Yasuda Hall.[73]

The gendered coding of this image is striking. The young men who stand guard beneath the phallic symbol of Yasuda Hall's clock tower had taken over the campus with the purpose of dismantling the hierarchical university system. Several men in the front row stand grasping these long bamboo shafts. These shafts were used for demonstration flags and as symbolic weapons against authority. These shafts, wooden staves, and metal pipes, called *gebabō,* were

Zenkyōtō struggle at Tokyo University. Yamamoto Yoshitaka stands in the top row, third from left, with other male activists in front of the clock tower of Yasuda Hall. Photograph from *Chisei no hanran* (Revolt of the Intellect), Zen'eisha, 1969.

used against the riot police and in the inter- and intrasectarian fighting. For many New Leftists, whether or not someone could take up the *gebabō* and engage in battle became the measure of one's revolutionary intent and commitment.[74] Thus, by the late 1960s, even beyond confronting the riot police in the street, as Kanba had fatally done, leftist protest was symbolized in the phallic object of the *gebabō*.

As *ribu* activist Mori Setsuko recalls, it was during those moments that she was being trained by male student activists on how to use the *gebabō* that she began questioning this path to revolution. As she was being taught how to use the *gebabō* to fight and beat the enemy, she felt that beating members of the riot police was not the way to prove herself or her desire for revolutionary change. She believed there must be other immediate actions and alternative practices that were integral to achieving liberation. This experience training with the *gebabō* is what led her to begin a women-centered movement to achieve liberation.[75]

Tokoro's lack of visibility in relationship to Zenkyōtō and relatively unacknowledged theoretical contributions are symptomatic of the sacrificial feminine role that women performed in the New Left. If Tokoro had lived, could she have become an icon of Zenkyōtō? Would Zenkyōtō have taken a different path? Or did her premature death enable her valorization because she did not live to critique what the movement became? Tokoro's apparent ardent devotion and early death render her a model of an "ideal revolutionary woman." Guy Yasko describes her as a devoted political activist, so much so that

> no one could boast a finer movement résumé. As a veteran of some of the most important struggles in the peace and socialist movements, Tokoro occupied an ideal position for reflecting on the nature of the movements to come. Had she lived, Tokoro would certainly have entered the spotlight with Yamamoto, Saishu Satoru, and the rest.[76]

But it was precisely this idealized notion of a revolutionary woman—who was a model of feminine sacrifice—that *ribu* would reject and criticize as a leftist male fantasy. By reifying resistance to the form of the *gebabō,* this phallic form of confronting state violence with counterviolence became the measurable, visible, and chosen form of revolutionary action. Consequently, the overvaluation of this kind of resistance had the negative effect of devaluing the life-affirming forms of alternative existence that *ribu* sought that were not reducible to capitalist or quantifiable economies.

Zenkyōtō's existence was relatively brief, from 1968 to 1971, largely because its campus strikes and protests were crushed by the riot police and also because, from the outset, it organized on a temporary and provisional basis rather than establishing a permanent organization.[77] Moreover, given Zenkyōtō's militant rejection of status quo values, it was assumed that it was natural for the movement to fail to gain general support and thus experience temporary failure.[78] Zenkyōtō ventured further than Beheiren in terms of its break from the form of a citizens' movement based on its rejection of the legitimacy of citizenship.[79] Explicating the philosophy of Zenkyōtō, Takada Motomu states that the outright rejection of postwar democracy led to the practice of "direct democracy" and the refusal of the notion of "the rights of citizenship."[80] Following from Zenkyōtō's search for a valid political subject, *ribu* also rejected the model of the citizen *(shimin).* Although all *ribu* activists were not categorically against the use of violence as a legitimate means of political resistance, as evidenced in the following section, *ribu* would criticize the way that violence had become a valorized form of political expression in the culture of the New Left.

Masculinism and the Idealization of Violence

In the fall of 1970, the right-wing writer and intellectual Mishima Yukio committed *hara-kiri,* the ritual of disembowelment.[81] He performed this death ritual to protest what he considered to be a betrayal of the Japanese imperial system. By killing himself in this manner, Mishima demonstrated the ecstatic heights of his political determination and desire for a reinvigoration of the Japanese emperor system. The figure of Mishima would continue to haunt some men of the New Left, demonstrating how political identifications cross over from the left to right and how the excess of desire infuses revolutionary fantasies. It was *ribu*'s recognition of the power and dangers of the idealization of violence as part of a gendered revolutionary fantasy that constituted a breaking point that would lead to the New Left's self-destruction and *ribu*'s formation.

Mishima had addressed the students of Zenkyōtō at the University of Tokyo in 1969. After the riot police violently removed the defeated students who had taken over the University of Tokyo campus, Mishima criticized the students for not believing in their cause enough to die for it.[82] For many men of the left, Mishima's hardened resolve to commit ritualistic suicide and his ability to carry through with it came as a blow to their egos. Tanaka Mitsu writes that the men of the left "responded to the incident with a kind of envy, because Mishima had outdone them by committing an act that they wished they could do."[83] For some, Mishima's death drive, his willingness to sacrifice himself in such a violent manner for his political cause, epitomized the authenticity of his political determination. But it was precisely this privileging of the use of violent rituals as a sign of authenticity that *ribu* activists criticized as the masculinist and militaristic tendencies within the New Left.

As militancy and militarism mounted, many men of the New Left felt compelled to prove their political loyalty to each other by displaying their determination to sacrifice their own lives or the lives of others. Certain performances and concrete actions became the evidence of one's revolutionary intent. Among sects such as Kakumaru, Chūkaku, Kaihō, and the United Red Army, to beat, to injure, and finally to kill or be killed for the sake of "justice" became the way of the revolution. From 1969 to 1972, the rise of incidents of intrasectarian violence and killing peaked, especially among the Chūkaku, Kaihō, and Kakumaru sects. Over three thousand reported injuries and at least twenty-five reported murders resulted from this intrasectarian fighting called *uchigeba* (meaning "internal violence" or "violent conflict within an organization"). Frederick Wheeler writes that these violent conflicts "stem from basic theoretical differences and competition for the support of students."[84] Even though these sects were all anticapitalist, rivalry and competition among them came to characterize their relationship to each other. Throughout the 1970s, Kaihō had killed over twenty Kakumaru members, and Kakumaru had killed many of Chūkaku's leaders and members. In turn, Chūkaku killed to avenge these murders, generating a cycle of internecine violence and killing.

Leftist students fighting each other at the University of Tokyo, November 12, 1968.
Photograph from *Asahi Shinbun*.

This desire to be able to measure or quantify one's revolutionary intent
or action was caught up in the "logic of productivity." Even though the New
Left was anticapitalist, Tanaka saw that the logic of productivity, which she
defined as a masculinist logic, had thoroughly infected its mode of organizing and its definition of what counted toward revolution. Like Tokoro, *ribu*
women criticized how the organizing of the New Left depended on quantified ways of measuring one's revolutionary intent. Similar to Tokoro, Tanaka
criticized how the logic of productivity sought to rationalize, quantify, and
hierarchize the value of human life according to its productivity, as a product of Western rationalism and the dominant logic of capitalism. Tanaka
forwarded a gendered analysis of the connections between the left's idealization of abstraction and the logic of productivity. That the New Left sects
were competing with each other to increase their numbers, and at the same
time were killing each other over this competition, was symptomatic of three
things. First, it characterized a quantitative measurement of the success of a
movement by measuring its numbers, which Tanaka attributed to the logic of
productivity. The competition to achieve revolution through demonstrating
one's force through numbers and battles with the riot police was a form of
quantifying revolutionary action. These measures of proving one's revolu-

tionary intent, however, often turned inward and were negatively directed toward one's own kind. Second, even though the conflicts were often over gaining members or theoretical differences between sect leaders, violence was chosen as a means to respond to the conflict. To use violence against the other sects was a means to evince the seriousness of the battle at hand between the other sects. Third, the use of violence to destroy, injure, and kill other leftist activists, as opposed to striking out against right-wing forces and the state, was symptomatic of a self-destructive dynamic of the New Left that became valorized as a means to prove one's revolutionary intent. In the United Red Army, one's willingness to torture and kill one's *own* comrades became evidence of one's commitment to the revolution. It was a kind of death drive that became obsessed with killing the newfound "counterrevolutionary enemy" that resembled the self within one's own ranks.

Within the ranks of the New Left, the women of *ribu* criticized how the men's struggle and the men's theory defined what counted toward the revolution, stating, "Within the men's revolution, the 'raw body of *onna*' *(nama no mi no onna)* is nowhere to be found."[85] According to *ribu* discourse, this raw body of *onna* was a conception of a feminine subject that had been repressed and not allowed to live. The *ribu* movement therefore sought to recover *onna* as a revolutionary subject, seeking to speak of and through her embodied position. Because this feminine subject had been repressed, woman in her current state of being was not living freely or living fully as *onna*. *Onna*'s life was being negated under the dominant logic of productivity.

Even though *ribu* was not categorically against the use of violence per se, *ribu* activists thoroughly rejected the way the use of violence had become idealized in the New Left as *the* privileged mode of political engagement. *Ribu* women often referred to the common practice among New Left men of bragging and testing each other by saying, "Hey, were you there during the fight against X, Y, or Z, on such and such a day?" This form of testing and competing with each other was the way to prove their masculinity and revolutionary intent. They were "man enough" if they could prove themselves in the battles against the riot police and against other leftist men. The men who fled from violence were deemed cowardly, unmanly, and not devoted enough to the revolution. The New Left created its own masculinized standards of revolutionary intent but often failed to live up to them.[86] Because the New Left failed to recognize its own masculinism, *ribu* women sarcastically referred to the New Left's inability to face its own failures in gendered terms as men fearful of their own impotence. Among the militant and increasingly militarized organizations of the New Left, the men who were unable to prove themselves in street battles against the riot police could not keep their honor, which

Tanaka criticized as the the facade or mask *(tatemae)* of their masculinism that limited their revolutionary praxis.

The way that killing and enacting violence had become idealized in the New Left was, for *ribu* activists, a convergence of the logic of productivity *(seisan no ronri)* and a tendency toward abstraction, which were both considered masculinist ways of ordering and controlling the natural world, in contradistinction to what Tokoro and others would theorize as feminine ontological principles. Although abstraction was not rejected or resisted in its entirety, what *ribu* criticized was a kind of abstraction that negated, repressed, and devalued nature, the body, the fluidity of desire, eros and multiplicity and contradiction, all of which for *ribu* women constituted elements of a feminine ontology that had been controlled, suppressed, and abjected through the dominant ordering of society.[87]

The *ribu* women saw that the logical extension of this practice of self-negation was the tendency toward self-destruction. This willingness to sacrifice and destroy oneself for the sake of justice was what *ribu* activists identified as a historical repetition of a masculine mode of constituting a homosocial identity through displaying loyalty toward one's male counterparts. It was a male-centered social formation that allowed men (and women) to prove themselves by cutting themselves off from other men, women, and children. The ef-

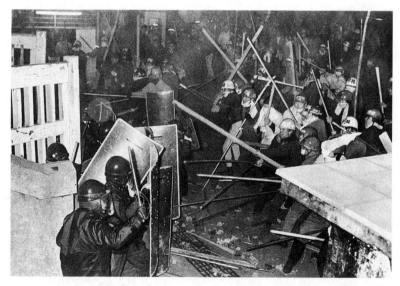

Students confront the riot police at Kyoto University, March 1, 1969. Photograph from *Asahi Shinbun*.

fect was the complete negation of an embodied relationality that *ribu* sought
to privilege.

This not only derived from a masculinist consciousness, through the logic
of production and desire for abstraction that cut off women and children and
all those who were not considered productive, but was, moreover, a misogynist logic. In this connection, Tanaka writes,

> The assumption that men=human and that men=society is at the heart of
> the logic of productivity. In contrast to the logic of productivity, which is
> based on western rationality, women's intuitive logic has until now been
> discriminated as worthless and discarded. Within man's system, women
> have typically only been an excessive existence. . . . The logic of productiv-
> ity of this society abhors a woman's menstruation, and if it were neces-
> sary, it would, no doubt, not hesitate to obliterate an *onna*'s existence.[88]

Tanaka thus connects the logic of productivity to women's menstruation in
order to show how, according to this logic, such feminine excess is "valueless"
and something to be eliminated. This connection is also indicative of *ribu*'s
insistence on bringing the female body and sexuality into the language of
politics. In her essay "The Ideas from the Body," *ribu* activist Iwatsuki Sumie
also writes about menstrual blood and questions why "'menstrual blood' is
rendered a 'dirty thing' and why *onna* is also 'dirty'?"[89] Speaking from the excess of the body and the womb, *ribu* brought into language the body of *onna*.
In contradistinction to the excessive flows of sexual desire and women's procreative capacities, the logic of productivity (as a logic of capital) continually
seeks to quantify and abstract value.

The New Left's destruction is often attributed to state repression, but
alongside state repression, many *ribu* women experienced its destructive
drive. Miyaoka Maki's experience within the New Left exemplifies this critical intimacy and repressive violence. She became a member of the Chūkaku
sect when she was a university student in Tokyo in the late 1960s.[90] Even
before entering Chūkaku, she recalls being able to clearly see the sexist discrimination in the New Left's division of labor, where "men gave the orders
and women performed the supportive labor in the shadows."[91] Miyaoka observed that women in the New Left had become accustomed to following the
men's directives without any debate and thus were being mobilized without
asserting their own subjectivity.[92]

Miyaoka believed that the political relationship between men and women
was crucial in any revolutionary struggle. As a member of Chūkaku, Miyaoka
felt it was vital for her to try to change the sect's gender politics by continually trying to raise the issue of "discrimination against and oppression of

onna" and the "politics of the relations between men and women."[93] She felt
certain that "if Chūkaku did not problematize the relationship between men
and women," there would be "no future to the revolution that they were trying to achieve, and all of Chūkaku's sweat and blood would be in vain."[94] As
demonstrated in Miyaoka's criticism, it was precisely at this historical juncture that sexism and gender politics coalesced into a coherent, marginalized,
though militant, political discourse from within the ranks of leftist women.

Miyaoka experienced how male leaders established their dominance in the
New Left through debating about revolutionary theory. After she was given
permission by a senior male comrade to raise her issues to a committee of
Chūkaku leaders, Miyaoka was most disappointed in the response of other
Chūkaku women. When she raised the problem of sexist discrimination, the
other women responded in exactly the same way as the men, leaving Miyaoka
shocked at how thoroughly the women had been assimilated into the male-
dominated culture of the New Left. She was stunned at how these women
had been "totally robbed of their subjectivity by men," extending her understanding of subjectivity *(shutaisei)* to speak of it as a site of struggle between
the sexes.[95] Through *ribu*'s discourse, subjectivity itself was no longer gender
neutral but became a site of contestation and sexual difference.

Miyaoka could also see the limits of the New Left's revolutionary tactics. Miyaoka recalls challenging one man by asking, "What is revolutionary
about men who struggle by fighting against the riot police, but don't have
any critical thinking about marriage or the family?"[96] One of the New Left's
masculinist tendencies became manifest in the way the "fight against imperialism" was executed through designated days of protest, when the organized
forces of the New Left would engage in street battles against the riot police.
These confrontational revolutionary tactics required that one be willing and
able to withstand the onslaughts of the thoroughly armed riot police. Because one's ability to battle in the street became the way to express one's
political authenticity, women were either measured by this same standard or
seen as in need of extra protection. The commemorated death of Kanba in
1960 signals how death can be seen as a sign of sacrifice and can slip into a
potentially dangerous idealization of political martyrdom.

During a demonstration at Nihon University in Tokyo, Miyaoka witnessed
a student being brutalized by a group of right-wing students. Miyaoka entered the fray and was beaten by the riot police. After suffering head injuries
from her beating, she had to be hospitalized. She was told by the doctor, "You
better be ready . . . because you might die from this."[97] When a male Chūkaku
comrade came to visit her, he said while laughing, "When I saw you enter
the demonstration, I thought, oh no, not a woman."[98] In spite of her efforts

within Chūkaku, she finally realized that the other Chūkaku officers would likely never properly recognize her existence as a woman *(onna)*, whether she was dead or alive. As she was lying on the hospital bed, she decided that if she was going to die, she did not want to die for the cause that had been defined by men.

Miyaoka's experience in the New Left made her critical of the extent to which women were captivated by their own fantasies of male power. Although she had tried to raise the problem of discrimination, she sensed that she had come up against what she describes as the "authoritarian wall" of Chūkaku's central committee. Even though she was ordered to write a "self-criticism," and in spite of the possibility that she could be eliminated as someone trying to disrupt the organization, she refused to retract her position.

In 1971, Miyaoka tried to intervene at the Thirtieth Zengakuren Convention, a mass gathering organized by Zengakuren. Miyaoka circulated a manifesto at the convention stating that the sexist discrimination within the revolutionary New Left was the "final fortress of bourgeois chauvinism."[99] Miyaoka's manifesto denounces how the men of Zengakuren have "suppressed women with the violence of sexist discrimination" and mockingly suggests that "without an understanding of their own sexism, calling themselves revolutionary was actually an anti-revolutionary act." Miyaoka's manifesto critiqued the pervasiveness of sexism that permeated the student movements. Miyaoka theorized the treatment of women as a fundamental form of violent oppression and discrimination. At this historical juncture, those like Miyaoka denounced "sexist discrimination" *(sei sabetsu)* in militant terms as a form of violent oppression, constituting the emergence of a radical feminist discourse from within the New Left. Miyaoka forcefully urged women activists to rid themselves of men who "try to direct us [women] how to fight," declaring that "we have no need for men who think that we should follow their struggle." She speaks of the men at hand as the enemy, stating that "authority always bears a man's face." The recognition of "men" as a class of oppressors marked the eruption of a radical feminist discourse, constituting *ribu*'s oppositional formation from within the New Left.

In *ribu*'s first anthology, *Onna's Thought*, published in 1972, Miyaoka wrote and published the story of her experiences in the New Left. She included an account of how she had survived a beating by the members of Chūkaku's rival sect, Kakumaru. By referring to Kakumaru as a "group that despised women," she put her life at risk.[100] Precisely at the time Miyaoka was openly denouncing the practices of the male-dominated New Left, Kakumaru and Chūkaku were beating and killing those members who were deemed to be counter-revolutionaries. Many New Left men and women regarded her activities as counterrevolutionary attempts to "destroy the organization."[101] Miyaoka concludes her criticism of the New Left by stating that in the end, Chūkaku tried to bury her criticisms and set about to destroy her life. The threats to her life and the violence that Miyaoka experienced were direct factors that induced *ribu*'s painful parturition.[102] The will to destroy and annihilate the voices of criticism within its own ranks was a tendency that *ribu* women directly experienced or observed. This silencing of feminist criticism and the exclusion of *ribu*'s presence from the official histories of the New Left would characterize an incapacity and unwillingness to seriously respond to the gender politics that *ribu* insisted on exposing.[103]

Given their understanding of the ongoing liberation struggles throughout the world, the women of *ribu* sometimes looked to other resistance struggles beyond their immediate political context. One *ribu* pamphlet raised the example of the black liberation struggle in the United States.

> By calling white cops "pigs," blacks struggling in America began to constitute their own identity by confirming their distance from white-centered society in their daily lives. This being the beginning of the process to constitute their subjectivity, who then should women be calling the pigs? . . . First, we have to strike these so-called male revolutionaries whose consciousness is desensitized to their own form of existence. We have to realize that if we don't strike our most familiar and direct oppressors, we can never "overthrow Japanese imperialism." Those men who possess such facile thoughts as, "Since we are fighting side by side, we are of the same-mind," are the pigs among us. To say more, the pigs in our house are the men who think that this is "women's liberation," the men who want to erect their own illusions about what is a "revolutionary."[104]

When women of the left began to identify this new intimate enemy, this moment of disidentification with Japanese leftist men became a decisive point of collision. Conversely, this moment of cross-racial identification with black liberation in the United States became a pivotal moment of departure. The discovery of a new "intimate enemy" forced the women to recognize that they had to redefine their relationship to the revolution from the specificity of their own subject position.

Many women within the Left began to sense that to live as women, they would have to define their own meaning of revolution, but first, they had to confront an "enemy" who was closest at hand. This discovery of the enemy at hand was another way that *ribu* resembled the New Left, but *ribu* chose another means to deal with its enemies. Rather than possessing the correct revolutionary theory or tactic, *ribu* valued the concepts of relationality, eros, and the encounter *(deai)*. The expression and theorization of these concepts was evident throughout the writings of the movement, published in journals such as *Onna Erosu*. As reflected in the theme of the inaugural issue of *Onna Erosu*, in principle, the *ribu* women rejected the modern family system as an extension of discrimination and sought to create new kinds of human relations outside and beyond these dominant logics. *Ribu* valued an ideal of relationality free from the dominant logic of productivity, capitalism, and patriarchy that rationalized, quantified, and hierarchized the value of human relations. The *ribu* movement did not aim to eliminate, injure, or annihilate the other but rather to create different conditions for the encounter with the other. The point of liberation was to create better conditions that would enable the self to encounter the other more freely. For *ribu* activists, identifying the other through the prescribed roles and categories that modernity had constructed prevented the subject from being free to encounter the other.

The New Left's idealization of revolutionary theory and the correct tactics, including revolutionary violence, would, from *ribu*'s perspective, prevent an authentic encounter *(deai)* between the self and the other. The dynamics of the New Left had, in effect, generated a masculinist fantasy of the "ideal revolutionary woman" and the "ideal revolutionary man" who desired the other to be without contradiction. Within the culture of the New Left, acting like the ideal revolutionary woman required women to deny the political significance of their own sexual difference and live according to the revolutionary standards prescribed by men.

For many women of the left, the attempt to fight alongside men was a self-negating and painful experience, a process through which they came to sense the deceitfulness of such men's male-centered theories of revolution. Many women who stayed in the New Left sects as they grew more militant and militaristic would consequently have to prove themselves according to standards of behavior that were largely determined by men. This was the tragic fate of Kaneko Michiyo.

The most disturbing display of leftist violence led to the breakdown of the revolutionary left. In 1972, it was revealed that the United Red Army had tortured and killed twelve of its own sect members as part of a process of an internal purge during their period of training to engage in revolutionary violence against the state. Among these twelve young men and women was Kaneko, a twenty-three-year-old woman who was eight months pregnant. The disclosure of the purge was a devastating blow even for those who advocated revolutionary violence.

The 1972 murder of Kaneko represented the overburdened meaning of the United Red Army killings (which is more fully elaborated in chapter 5).

Kaneko's corpse—heavy with an unborn child—signified not only the self-destructive drive of the New Left but also how the mainstream corporate logic of productivity had infected the politics of the New Left. In the United Red Army, if the bodies of those within their own sect were not deemed by the leaders to be fully devoted and useful to the revolutionary cause, their lives were cut off. Within the United Red Army, the expression of traditional femininity or sexual and erotic desire was deemed "counterrevolutionary."[105] This extreme definition of revolution cuts off and kills all who were not seen as productive enough, or "pure" and "perfect revolutionaries." In theorizing the lynching incident, a *ribu* woman named Kazu writes,

> In this extreme reality of the New Left, *onna* is killed off. No matter what sect it is, there is no change in that essence. And not being able to go along with that, *ribu* started with the affirmation of *onna* and thus far has been able to cling to the relationality between those who are in the struggle.[106]

This killing of *onna* as the excess of a masculinist definition of revolution was theorized by *ribu* women as the extreme outcome of the idealization of abstraction and violent death. For *ribu* women, in order for *onna* to live, she had to create a space and a way to live on by forging her own road to liberation that would neither kill her in the process nor require her to sacrifice her desire to live on with the other. For *ribu,* revolution was to be sought, grounded, and experienced somewhere in between a present-tense desire for the imperfect other and in a better relationality to come. In contrast to the call for self-negation that led to self-destruction, the *ribu* movement began by recognizing the need for *onna* to affirm-her-self and criticize her positionality, forming the contradictory core dynamic of the *ribu* movement. This contradictory dynamic constituted the core of *ribu*'s collective subjectivity as a movement, which is elaborated in chapter 3.

Having been strained by having to be more productive for the revolution, but never being productive enough, the shattering of the fantasy of the ideal revolutionary woman was the final phase of the violent gestation process that gave birth to *ribu*. The combination of feminine sacrifice under the unbearable weight of abstraction and death would lead to the negation of *onna*. Not willing to become idealized as feminine revolutionary sacrifices or to be killed for not living up to a revolutionary ideal, the *ribu* women instead sought to affirm the imperfect *onna* as a new incarnation of a revolutionary embodiment.

MOVEMENTS AND MEDIUMS

CHAPTER THREE

The Liberation of Sex, *Onna,* and Eros

The Movement and the Politics of Collective Subjectivity

Ribu refers to a social movement, a political identity, and a living philosophy and spans multiple temporalities. From its rupturing moment of emergence in 1970 to its rearticulations four decades later, its dynamic constitution has been forged through a collective contestatory process. This chapter elaborates how *ribu* emerged as a social movement by focusing on the work of several of its key activists who shaped *ribu*'s central concepts and were part of the movement's core organizing groups during the first half of the 1970s. These central concepts—the liberation of sex, *onna,* and eros—marked the beginning of a new movement.[1] The symbiotic relationships among *ribu*'s core concepts, the collectivity of its subjects, and its organizing principles comprise *ribu*'s dynamic movement formation. *Ribu* is both a collective and a subjective identity, and its political significance and relative cohesion inheres in the tension between how different subjectivities articulate and animate its collective politics. By tracing the main protests and events of its incipient years, I explicate *ribu*'s organizing principles and structuring logics in the formation of this new collective subjectivity. *Ribu*'s organizing principles fostered autonomous action, multidirectional organizing, and a centrifugal dynamic that produced multiple fronts of protest. *Ribu*'s interactions with the New Left, the mass media, and the state constitute several of its diverse sites of intervention and conflict. By delineating *ribu*'s representative events, protests, and campaigns, this chapter demonstrates how the political significance of social movements inheres in the formation of a collective subjectivity that engages in historic critical conflicts and symbolic interventions to forge a new horizon of possibilities.[2]

In the second half of the chapter, I explain how *ribu*'s representative campaigns surrounding abortion and unmarried mothers further illuminate how *ribu*'s core concepts were imprinted by its anticapitalist politics and several of its key activists: Yonezu Tomoko, Mori Setsuko, Tanaka Mitsu, Saeki Yōko, Miki Sōko, and Iwatsuki Sumie. The movement initiated a legacy of activism for reproductive freedom and feminist anti-imperialist organizing and led to the organic development of a women-centered relationality and lesbian love.[3] This chapter underscores the relationship between the collective and the subjective by exploring how the relationships between key activists was pivotal in directing and shaping *ūman ribu*'s distinctive radical feminist politics.

Key Concepts and Core Groups

On April 26, 1970, at a political rally organized by students from Tama Fine Arts University in Tokyo, four women, wearing black helmets with SEX painted in white, hijacked the event by jumping on the stage to announce the formation of their group.[4] Thought Group SEX (Shisō Shūdan Esuīekusu) was one of the earliest *ribu* campus-based groups that formed at Tama Fine Arts University in April 1970. Two of its founding members, Mori Setsuko and Yonezu Tomoko, would continue to be key figures in the movement over the next decade. The conspicuous naming of this group emphatically expresses a determinative concept of *ribu,* namely, the "liberation of sex" *(sei kaihō).* This group sought to politicize a new theorization of sex and to center its relevance. Its practice of disrupting and intervening in an existing political forum was characteristic of many *ribu* groups that adopted the existing style of confrontational direct-action politics. In this manner, many *ribu* groups sought to politicize the exclusion of gender politics from existing student movements, and at the same time, they began to form their own women-only autonomous groups.

Mori Setsuko recounts that it was her visceral and cognitive dissonance within the male-dominated student movement that catalyzed her to form the new women-only group. Despite that she was given "preferential treatment" by male activists and was being treated and trained like the other men (versus being treated like the other women students who were assigned to more domestic duties), she said that the gap between her experience and the treatment of the other women made her acutely conscious of the problem of sex discrimination. Specifically (and akin to Miyaoka's experience, described in chapter 2), Mori states it was during her training on how to use the *gebabō* (bamboo poles, wooden staves, and metal pipes—the symbolic weapons of the student movement and New Left) that she decided to quit following and imitating the men's revolutionary tactics.[5] Rather than learning how to fight the riot police with the *gebabō*, she believed there must be other immediate actions and alternative practices that were integral to achieving liberation. This realization, combined with her keen awareness of the sex discrimination surrounding her, catalyzed Mori to organize Thought Group SEX.

Yonezu Tomoko was another pivotal activist who formed Thought Group SEX, and her presence at *ribu*'s organizing centers would significantly alter and complexify the movement's politics. During her childhood, Yonezu became disabled as a result of spinal cord paralysis and required the use of a brace to walk due to the arrested development of her right leg. The *ribu* women's capacity to comprehend and connect "disability" to the liberation of sex expanded *ribu*'s articulation of body politics. From the beginning of the movement, Yonezu's presence sharpened *ribu*'s critique of capitalist productivity and significantly shaped *ribu*'s stance on abortion and the state's eugenics policies. *Ribu*'s expansive understanding of the liberation of sex involved a critique of the capitalist "logic of productivity" as the measure of the value of life and rearticulated "abject bodies," whether they were disabled persons *(shintai shōgaisha)*, the elderly, criminalized women, sex workers, or comfort women, drawing lines of potential solidarity between those excluded from the state's category of "good productive citizens."[6]

Mori's and Yonezu's formative experiences as part of the student movement and their rejection of the male-centered methods of fighting against the system incited them to create their own space to redefine a new kind of struggle for liberation. After graduating from Tama Fine Arts University in 1971, they began their own communal living collective as an extension of their *ribu* politics. In 1972, they became key activists at the Ribu Shinjuku Center, which remained a formative organizing center of the movement until 1977. The formative role of the Shinjuku Center in the movement is elaborated later in this chapter and in chapter 4.

The Liberation of Sex and Eros

In June 1970, at a rally against the U.S.–Japan Mutual Cooperation and Security Treaty (Anpo) held at Yoyogi Park in Tokyo, a new political group distributed a mimeographed one-page pamphlet called "The Declaration of the Liberation of Eros." At this massive rally, which drew seventy thousand participants, this new group announced itself as the Committee to Prepare for Women's Liberation.[7]

"The Declaration of the Liberation of Eros" was one of the first widely distributed *ribu* manifestos that called for the liberation of sex. It was authored by Tanaka Mitsu, who performed a unique role in the movement as a leading theorist and activist.[8] This manifesto offered a clear critique of both the existing women's liberation movements and Marxist-oriented politics that failed to take into account how gender relations and the family system were fundamental to the operation of the capitalist authoritarian state. This manifesto emphasized sex-based discrimination as "the oldest form of class conflict rooted deeply in the core of human consciousness," criticizing the assumption that such forms of discrimination "will disappear after the overthrow of Japanese imperialism."[9] It ended its appeal by emphasizing its call "from *onna* to *onna*." Its centering of the liberation of sex and eros and its appeal to *onna* would constitute *ribu*'s central tenets.

Ribu's central and symbiotic concepts were the liberation of *onna* and the liberation of sex. For Miki Sōko, the liberation of sex and *onna* were interlinked: "*Onna* has been confined by sex and bound by law. Precisely because *onna* has been considered a 'sexual being' *ribu* called for the liberation of sex."[10] *Eros* would also become a key word in the movement, signifying a shift from a politics based on justice or theoretical correctness to a movement that prioritized relationality and desire, particularly the liberation of *onna*'s desire.

"The Declaration of the Liberation of Eros" echoed the political consciousness articulated in the position papers authored a month earlier by Yonezu and Mori from Thought Group SEX. In her position statement for Thought Group SEX, written in May 1970, Mori writes, "In order to create from our sex *(sei)*, we need to be conscious of our class as *onna*," emphasizing that *onna* constituted another political class that had been suppressed and submerged.[11] *Onna* was the subject who would turn to her sex as a form of power and means of liberation. Mori declares the need to smash the dominant pattern of gender relations where the "woman is too passive toward men" and instead declares that "*onna* must acquire her own violence."[12] This latter comment foreshadows the complex stance *ribu* would take toward expressions of counterhegemonic violence and the violence expressed by *kogoroshi no onna* (women who kill their children).

In her position paper, Yonezu unequivocally declares the need to "smash free sex."[13] From the outset of the movement, *ribu*'s notion of the liberation of sex was not the same as sexual liberation, if the latter were taken to imply the liberalization of sex relations between men and women. To the contrary, the contemporary trend of "free sex" was a problematic practice that *ribu* women would continue to deplore in their manifestos, and they would emphasize instead an alternative relationality between *onna* and between men and women.[14] The new relationality between *onna* would unfold toward women-to-women love and lesbian relations, and the emphasis placed on *relationality* would become another important concept for *ribu*. Because *ūman ribu* called for a new kind of relationality between *onna* and encouraged eros between women, lesbian love was arguably the movement's organic and logical outcome. Several of *ribu*'s core activists, such as Iwatsuki Sumie and Wakabayashi Naeko, would become leading figures of women-centered cultural production and lesbian activism. Although there was space for lesbian representation within *ribu*, in contrast to other lesbian-feminist movements, lesbianism was never privileged, theorized, or affirmed as the most radical alternative to a compulsory heterosexist order.[15] There remained a tension in the movement due to its heterosexual dominance, and this tension is further addressed in chapter 4.

Onna and Anti-Imperialism

The *ūman ribu* movement emerged from the turbulent political context of the late 1960s as an extension and rearticulation of the anti-imperialism of the New Left. On October 21, 1970, the *ribu* movement staged its first public protest on International Antiwar Day. Among the tens of thousands of other protestors at the International Anti–Vietnam War rally, a women-only demo squad pushed their way through the streets of Ginza in Tokyo shouting "liberate *onna!*" Reportedly, about two hundred women joined together with their arms linked in scrum formation. They shouted together and pushed back against the male police officers who were shoving and pushing against them.

女だけの激しいデモに機動隊もややとまどった形 (10月21日，東京・銀座で)

Ribu demonstration at antiwar protest on October 21, 1970. Photograph from *Shūkan Asahi* (November 13, 1970), page 18. Original caption states: "Even the riot police were not sure how to handle this intense women's-only demonstration."

The movement gained significant public visibility because the mass media focused attention on this new women-only demo squad. Until this first major public protest, the movement had existed as a "submerged network"—to use Alberto Melucci's term—forming small, autonomous *ribu* cell groups in different urban centers across the country.[16] This first protest captures many of *ribu*'s formative dynamics, particularly its collective critical intervention within the existing terrain of leftist politics. The performative iteration of the street demonstration displayed the multivalent and multidirectional gestures of resistance that *ribu* embodied, as the women joined themselves together not only during the demonstration but through their many collective forms of protest. Its enunciative power was produced through mimicry of the existing symbolic codes of the street protest, with the women dressed in protest attire, some helmeted and others brandishing the *gebabō* as symbolic weapons against the enemy. As seen in the photo, some *ribu* women used the *gebabō* at this demonstration, signaling the crossover with the direct-action tactics used by student movement and New Left activists. Their chants and slogans brought together the politics of liberation in the context of the U.S. imperialist war in Vietnam, deliberately linking the liberation of *onna* to the international and anti-imperial.

Ribu's key concepts were put forth at the inception of the movement. The centrality of *onna* as a political actor is evident in one of the first manifestos published in 1971 by the Committee to Prepare for Women's Liberation. Its slogans read:

1. Let's protest our internalized *onna*-consciousness
2. Let's liberate *onna* from all her oppressions
3. Let's smash all discrimination between men and women
4. Let's achieve true liberation and autonomy
5. Let *onna* herself organize other *onna*
6. Smash Anpo[17]

The centrality of *onna*, along with the emphasis for *onna* to organize other *onna*, is notable. The call to "smash" Anpo links *ribu* to existing New Left politics, which was directed against Japanese–U.S. imperialism that was manifest in this military security treaty (discussed in chapter 2). The juxtaposition between *onna*, the relationship between men and women, and Anpo were parts of an interlocking system that *ribu* dissected and critiqued, connecting the liberation of *onna* to the state and international politics.

The demand for *onna*'s liberation in the context of an antiwar rally constituted a critical extension of the existing understanding of international politics and how women's liberation and livelihood were thoroughly implicated in this larger violent process. The apparent chasm between international conflicts and localized "personal politics" of women's liberation was reconceived through the creation of a new political ontology.[18] By forging a collective subjectivity as a meaningful way to engage in conflict with the state, *ribu* became a transformative means of self-rearticulation through the creation of the movement as a new form of political ontology. This *onna*-centered movement emphasized the relationality of the domestic and the international, and its localized forms of activism were based on a critique of the totality of interlocking imperialist systems. Because the Japanese government's active support of the United States had material effects as a direct actor on the global stage of international warfare, *ribu*'s antistate protests intervened in and sought to articulate the political relationality between gender and the formation of imperialist projects.

Ribu's anti-imperialist politics, which were inherited from its roots in the New Left, were most strident in its incipient phase. One of the first published manifestos by the Committee to Prepare for Women's Liberation, dated August 20, 1970, states:

> With the emergence of the system of private property and the patriarchal family system, which takes as its fundamental condition the subordination of women to men, it was a historical necessity that sex differentiation became discrimination. We must gain full clarity about the origins of this historical necessity. The reason we must do so is that the ideology and the social formation that is producing the analogous effects of this discrimination against women *(josei)* is that which supports imperialism which is based on aggression.[19]

What is notable here is that the historical reasons for discrimination against women are linked with imperialism and aggression. In this passage, with the emphasis on the relationship between discrimination and aggression and sex, we can see the influence of Iijima Aiko's group (discussed in chapter 1). As Tanaka Mitsu's famous manifesto, "Liberation from the Toilet," declared, the ideological gender structure that divided Japanese women into toilets and idealized wives and mothers was responsible for the production and violation of the comfort women.[20] In making such connections from the beginning of the movement, *ribu*'s analysis of Japanese women was structurally linked with the conditions of how colonized Asian women were exploited and treated. In this manner, *ribu*'s radical feminist discourse was infused with an anti-imperialist gender critique.

In "Imperialism and Gender," feminist scholar Senda Yuki argues that *ribu* emerged with a conscious effort not only to address Japan's imperialist history but, more notably, to face *onna*'s positionality and responsibility in relation to the emergence of Japan's neo-imperialist alliance with the

United States in the postwar.[21] These anti-imperialist feminist politics would articulate through *ribu*'s discourse, particularly in its critiques of the comfort women system and its protests against Kisaeng tourism (sex tourism in South Korea), which is addressed later in the chapter.

What is significant about *ribu*'s discourse is the double identity of *onna* as both victim and accomplice. One of the committee's earliest manifestos describes *onna* as "the greatest victim/greatest accomplice" *(kyōhansha)*.[22] The dual conception of *onna* as both victim and accomplice to domination was intimately linked to *ribu*'s anticapitalist and anti-imperialist politics. Insofar as women were complicit in the structural violence of capitalist and imperialist forms of (re)production, they were both oppressors and victims of the system. This duality or (non)contradictory doubleness constituted the core of *onna*'s subjectivity. This conception of *onna* was a radical departure from women's peace movements, citizens' movement discourse, and liberal feminist discourse that did not address women's complicity in structural violence. This understanding of structural violence provides a feminist conception of violence that takes into account nonvisible forms of systemic and structural violence as constitutive of women's ontology.[23]

Organizing Principles and Major Events

During the initial stages of the movement, core groups such as the Thought Group SEX and the Committee to Prepare for Women's Liberation were formative catalyzing forces involved in organizing many of *ribu*'s main events during the early 1970s. Leading up to the preparation for the antiwar rally on October 21, 1970, the Committee to Prepare for Women's Liberation also began to use the name Group of Fighting Women *(Gurūpu Tatakau Onna)*.[24] The members of these two groups overlapped, and the Group of Fighting Women would continue to be a pioneering core group that was at the center of organizing most of *ribu*'s main events. These major events were the antiwar demonstration on October 21, 1970, the November 14, 1970, meeting, the *ribu* summer camps *(gasshuku)*, and the 1972 Ribu Conference.

The first major *ribu* gathering on November 14, 1970, displays some of the characteristics of the movement. It covered a vast expanse of political issues, indicative of the multifaceted activism of a movement that nonetheless possessed a coherent constellation of concepts and organizing principles. The gathering was held in Shibuya in the Setagaya-ku district of Tokyo. Like *ribu*'s first street protest in October, this first major gathering was organized by two *ribu* cells: the Committee to Prepare for Women's Liberation and the Group of Fighting Women. Approximately two hundred women participated in what was planned as a six-hour forum.[25] Men were shut out of the meeting, a characteristic of the women-only organizing style that *ribu* women predominantly chose. The creation of women's autonomous spaces under women's collective leadership would be another feature of *ribu*'s organizing.

The free-flowing style of the discussion replicated the Zenkyōtō style of "endless debates" *(eien no tōso),* lasting over seven hours. The forum was moderated by the well-known writer Higuchi Keiko, who stated that the purpose of the meeting was "to theorize the new women's liberation movement."[26] Higuchi opened the discussion by noting the different generations of women in attendance. While the *ribu* movement was primarily a movement of young Japanese women in their twenties, this meeting was attended by women in their forties and fifties as well as several women in their sixties. There were students, housewives, academics, journalists, writers, teachers, and veteran leftist women activists, who were all interested and invested in participating in this new movement.

The rich discussion demonstrated how well developed and diverse the views about the liberation of *onna* were at the beginning of the movement. Many of the diverse themes that emerged throughout the discussion would continue to characterize *ribu*'s discourse over the next decade. Among the topics discussed were women's complicity in systems of oppression, especially during wartime; the central importance placed on a revolution of *onna*'s consciousness; a call to reassess the labor of mothering; the relative importance of women's economic independence; and a call to think seriously about masculinity. From the floor, other speakers raised the issues of women's struggles in the workplace, the politics of participation in sex work, the politics of abortion and the pill, and a call for male comrades. Although *ribu* was an *onna*-centered space, it considered the totality of *onna* as connected to Japan's history of imperialism, the economy, the mutual constructedness of masculinity and femininity, and the state's control of women's bodies as linked to foreign policy and immigration.[27]

This meeting was sponsored by the progressive publisher Aki Shobō, which published a transcription of the meeting four months later, in March 1971, titled *Protesting Sex Discrimination: The Contentions of Ūman Ribu.* This volume was *ribu*'s first book publication.[28] In addition to the transcription, the book contained one section devoted to Japanese *ribu* manifestos and essays and an overview of the history and contemporary condition of the women's liberation movement in the United States.[29] For some *ribu* women, the women's liberation movement in the United States became an important site of identification, difference, and critique. Some *ribu* groups, such as Wolf (Urufu no Kai), engaged in English-to-Japanese feminist translation projects as their main activity. Other *ribu* women (such as Iwatsuki and Tanaka) emphasized their own Japanese heritage or solidarity with other Asian women (such as Miki and Mori). As the movement unfolded, differences with the women's lib movement in the United States manifested most saliently in *ribu*'s stance on abortion and birth control, its emphasis on imperialism, and its position on the criminalization of women. These issues would become the driving force of *ribu*'s most sustained campaigns during the first half of the 1970s.

In its earliest stages, *ribu* activists did not prioritize building ties with non-Japanese foreigners living in Japan or other ethnic minority women such as *Zainichi* (resident Koreans), Okinawans, and Ainu, and in this sense *ribu* remained ethnically homogenous, if not exclusive. In this sense, *ribu* replicated the racial, ethnic exclusivity common to dominant white, middle-class feminism in the United States. This limitation can be understood, in part, as a reaction to what many *ribu* women saw as the hypocrisy of the New Left in their claims to solidarity with *Zainichi* (resident Koreans) and Okinawans. Part of the New Left's anti-imperialist politics was to be in solidarity with *Zainichi* and Okinawans, but many *ribu* women felt that this often reflected a leftist compartmentalization of politics without recognizing that discrimination against women was also a serious political problem linked to imperialism and colonialism.

Some *ribu* women did make solidarity with other Asian third world women a political priority. Women such as Iijima, Matsui Yayori, and later other *ribu* activists, such as Kuno Ayako, were important feminist activists who were primarily committed to this anti-imperialist Asian women's organizing. Yet in contrast with how most *ribu* women identified themselves as *ribu*, Iijima and Matsui were involved with the movement but did not primarily identify as *ribu*.[30] This desired solidarity with other Asian women outside of Japan was certainly a characteristic of *ribu* and, like the internationalism of first-world feminist politics, could be criticized for its relative neglect of domestic and local minority women's issues.[31] In contrast to the political condition of Okinawan or *Zainichi* women, for example, the relative power and mobility of Japanese women in Japanese society as the ethnic majority was not often seriously addressed because, ultimately, the radical feminist focus on Japanese women's discrimination was primarily based on their relative domination by Japanese men and how discrimination reproduced the national-patriarchal family system.[32] In contrast with the massive numbers of Japanese women in mainstream women's organizations, *ribu* constituted a radical feminist minority among Japanese women's movements and a political minority within

Japanese politics, which nonetheless iterated a far-reaching critique of the gendered problems of the Japanese state and the Japanese left.

Ribu Summer Camps

The *ribu* summer camp *(ribu gasshuku)* from August 21 to August 24, 1971, marked a watershed in *ribu*'s history for the growth of the movement and networking. After the antiwar demonstration on October 21, 1970, Group of Fighting Women and Thought Group SEX met regularly to form a women's liberation discussion group, which led to the planning of the *ribu* camp. The first *ribu* camp was held in Shinshū, Nagoya, at a ski lodge in the mountains at a location called Shinnohei. Two hundred fifty-seven women gathered from across Japan. They came from as far as Hokkaidō in the north and Kyūshū in the south.

In contrast to the November 14, 1970, meeting at which the participants were mainly women from the Tokyo area, this gathering gave women a sense of how *ribu* consciousness was widely shared across the country, as women from Nagoya, Fukuoka, Tokyo, Hokkaidō, and Kyūshū were able to meet for the first time and share their experiences. The women who attended were from their teens to their forties, students, housewives, career women, teachers, journalists, government employees, part-time workers, and married and single mothers, some of whom came with their children.

While Group of Fighting Women and Thought Group SEX were the main cells that organized the *ribu* camp, there was an open-ended format, and this was communicated to all those who planned to participate.

> Until now, even if you've only thought of yourself as just an "ordinary sister," let's question everything: the class struggle, sex, family relations, Marx, Freud, beauty, common sense, education, labor . . . and what it means to be an *onna*. Although we'll plan 60%, the participants will create the remaining 40%.[33]

This broad range of subjects was indicative of the free-style discussion that took place over the course of the three-night, four-day retreat. The main activity on the first day involved a self-introduction teach-in during which all the women gathered and shared their concerns with the rest of the group. Thereafter, each woman could choose what kind of discussion group she wanted to participate in, while others freely did whatever they liked. The open-ended format was a stark contrast to the rigid hierarchical structure and discipline of the New Left.

Ribu summer camp *(gashhuku)* in Shinshū, Nagoya, August 1971. Photograph by Fukushima Kikujiro.

The second *ribu* summer camp was held in Hokkaidō (the northernmost prefecture) from August 17 to August 21, 1972, and was organized by the *ribu* cell called Metropolitan.[34] The call again emphasized a spirit of self-initiative: "Come and bring with you whatever you want to do. *Ribu* Camp is what you create; you make 90% of it, we've planned 10%."[35] This emphasis and affirmation of subjective desire and autonomy was characteristic of the neo–New Left's affirmation of spontaneity, subjective desire, and autonomous action that was a response to the subculture of the New Left, which had strongly emphasized adherence to a sect's correct theory of revolution and self-criticism. In contrast to what many *ribu* women found to be political posturing and a coercive and suffocating environment, the politics of *ribu* emphasized experiencing an embodied liberation that could and would only begin by facing the contradictory, imperfect self.

> It is from within ourselves that we will birth an abundant future.
> To recognize ourselves, let us *onna* be each other's mirror.
> To see each other without haziness or deception.
> The first step to re-claim and transform ourselves requires us to begin by
> reflecting on our bodies, to reflect from our miserable impotent selves
> and for this reason we are going to have a *ribu* camp.[36]

This kind of explicitly gendered language that recognized a "miserable impotent self" as a starting point signaled a sober self-assessment as well as a hope in self-transformation in relationship with other *onna*. Such self-transformation through relationships with other *onna* characterized *ribu*'s emphasis on both self-determination and the move from the self to the collective. The *ribu* camp, like many previous *ribu* meetings, signaled the conceptual importance of creating *onna*-centered spaces where women would determine for themselves their own agenda. Although there were many existing women's organizations, as noted in chapter 1, such groups were typically hierarchically structured with formal leaders or presidents and were often associated with, or subordinated to, a male-dominated organization or political party. Thus, in terms of its organizing structure, *ribu* broke from this previous formal structure to emphasize the importance of self-determination that began with questioning, confronting, knowing, and transforming the self in a collective space with other *onna*.

The *ribu* camp became the starting point where many *ribu* women connected with each other to begin new projects that would last throughout the decade and beyond. After the *ribu* camp, new *ribu* cells organized across the country. From 1972 to 1973, there was a blossoming of *ribu* cells. According to Miki Sōko, the *ribu* camp was "an opportunity to encounter yourself, to encounter other *onna* and encounter new philosophies."[37] Miki and Saeki Yōko, who continued to be key *ribu* activists and archivists of the movement, initially met each other on the bus en route to the first *ribu* summer camp.[38] Together they began the newsletter *Onna kara onna-tachi e* (From onna to her onna-sisters) and were the editors of *Onna Erosu, ribu*'s first journal, published from 1973 to 1983 by an existing publishing house.

Its first publication was a special issue titled *Unsettling the Marriage System*.[39] This inaugural edition included a report on the "New Wave of American Lib" alongside a reprint of Hiratsuka Raichō's famous inaugural manifesto of the *Seitō Journal*, "In the Beginning Woman Was the Sun."[40] Such essays symbolize how these *ribu* activists and intellectuals clearly saw their movement as linked with both the emergence of women's liberation internationally, with a focus on the United States, and as part of a longer legacy of Japanese women's liberation. Saeki has stated that *ribu*'s conceptualization of eros has remained undertheorized, yet at the same time, the open-ended, polysemic, and somewhat amorphous meaning of eros appropriately signals *ribu*'s turn away from theory-laden politics to an emphasis on the desire emanating from and between *onna*.[41]

Activist-intellectuals like Saeki and Miki have played vital roles in ensuring the legibility of the movement over time. Together with Mizoguchi Ayeko, Miki and Saeki spent over a decade compiling the documents of the history of the movement, which has ensured the legibility of *ribu*'s historical contribution to Japanese and transnational feminist history.[42] The impressive three-volume collection of documents from the movement, edited by Sōko, Saeki, and Mizoguchi, contain the documents of fifty different *ribu* cells, indicating the growth of the movement during this early period (1972–73). Many other *ribu* publications were initiated from the *ribu* camp, such as *Onna's Mutiny (Onna no hangyaku)*, started by Kuno Ayako in Nagoya. This publication has lasted for forty years, and Kuno continues as it editor. The labor of activist-intellectuals like Kuno and archivists like Miki and Saeki, over the span of four decades, is often overshadowed by the iconic figures of *ribu*, such as Tanaka, who are continually spotlighted by the media and women's studies. The political labor of archiving and representing the movement, with all its diversity and limits, contradictions and achievements, is one of the ways the movement continues today. The tensions and conflicts over the representation of the movement is one of the dimensions of *ribu*'s history taken up in chapter 4.

As was the case with many other social movements, the creation of *ribu*'s own alternative media, known as *mini-komi* (mini-communications), was a vital and organic part of its activism. *Mini-komi* became a means for women to forge relationships with each other as they re-created and represented themselves and communicated with each other. This continuous production of *mini-komi* was, in part, also a response to the coverage *ribu* received through the various circuits of the mass media.

Ribu and the Media: The Politics of (In)Visibility

The *ribu* summer camp was covered by newspapers such as the *Mainichi Shinbun* (August 8, 1971) and *Asahi Shinbun* (August 25, 1971). *Ribu* organizers only allowed female journalists to attend and report on the *ribu* camp at a time when there were few women journalists working for major media companies.[43] Much of the coverage of the camp in weekly magazines was written to amuse the readers about this unusual gathering of women. Weekly magazines such as *Shūkan Post* (September 10, 1971), *Shūkan Shinko* (September 11, 1971), and *Shūkan Bunshū* (September 6, 1971) offered negative and mocking coverage. For example, the headline in *Shūkan Bunshū* declared, "The *Ribu* Camp Became a Gathering for Sex Confessions." Its subtitle read, "Challenging the Middle Class in the Nude," pointing out that among the "strange" activities that the women engaged in was a lot of talk about sex and dancing outdoors in the nude. This article also described Japan's *ūman ribu* as an "import" of the women's lib movement from the United States, which became a common misinterpretation used to delegitimize *ribu*'s local and organic formation.

The weekly magazine *Shūkan Shinko* printed a full-page picture of Yonezu, who had attended the *ribu* camp wearing a T-shirt with the graffitied message, "Look at Me!" As a disabled woman, Yonezu's message "Look at me!" was a challenge to the erasure of disabled persons from public view as subjects who were not seen as acceptable.

At public demonstrations, Yonezu would purposely wear this T-shirt, underscoring her challenge to the public's gaze. Her demand clearly engaged with the politics of visibility and the way visual recognition of physical disability disrupts dominant economies of how women's bodies are looked at, sexualized, and commodified.[44] As photos of Yonezu circulated widely through such media coverage and other photographic journalism, she became one of the more visible activists of the movement. A September 11, 1971, edition of *Shūkan Shinko* printed a nude photograph of only the upper half of Yonezu's body, cutting out from public view her full body and her leg brace, which would have been an anomalous sight to see a young disabled woman

Yonezu Tomoko at a demonstration in Tokyo, June 1972. Photograph by Fukushima Kikujiro.

unclothed. The caption next to the photograph read, "We wonder what kind of auntie she will become?" This kind of decontextualized and distorted reporting was typical of the male-dominated mass media.

Inoue Teruko and Ehara Yumiko have written about how the mass media ridiculed and mocked *ribu*.[45] Ehara's chapter "The Politics of Teasing" in *Contemporary Japanese Thought* (2005) has been highly influential in creating the image that *ribu* was "victimized" by this teasing and was unable to respond to this mockery.[46] In her characterization, Ehara reinscribes a binary structure of the powerful media and *ribu* as its powerless victim that was harmed and devastated by such ridicule. While there is validity to this interpretation, Saito Masami's more recent scholarship on *ribu* and the media has criticized the limits of Ehara's reading and instead emphasizes how successfully *ribu* activists were able to strategically negotiate and use media attention. Saito provides an extensive survey of *ribu* media coverage in its early years, from 1970 to 1972, and underscores the extent to which some media venues, particularly newspapers, played a productive role in spreading the movement's message and, at times, provided accurate and favorable coverage.[47]

A closer analysis of *ribu*'s practices and *mini-komi* also amply demonstrate how *ribu* activists strategically and deliberately engaged with the media. *Ribu* activists were able to negotiate with mainstream magazines such as *Shūkan Asahi* and *Asahi Journal* for accurate and significant coverage about the *ribu* movement with articles written by *ribu* intellectuals.[48] Moreover, Ehara's characterization that *ribu* was simply a victim of such mockery disregards the extent to which *ribu* frequently deployed mockery and humor as a primary strategy within its own discourse, eclipsing the interactive circuitry of ridicule and mockery. Although the infrastructure of media production and relative distribution coverage was asymmetrical in terms of its resources and output, throughout their *mini-komi* productions, *ribu* made fun of and sarcastically denounced the mass media, politicians, and leftist men. For example, the Ribu Shinjuku Center published a zine called *Weekly Check on the Mass Media (Shūkan masu-komi chekku)*, which was a parodic critique of the sexist treatment of women across various genres of the mass media.[49] The authors of this zine called themselves the Group of Women Who Fight the Sexism of the Mass Media. The front page featured the "Worst 5 Sexist Commercials" and announced its protest of the weekly magazine *Shūkan Gendai*, which printed a pornographic spread of a young woman, clothed and unclothed, called "The New Real Me." The following illustration demonstrates how the *ribu* women parodied the objectification of women in pornographic magazines by mimicking the same format but using a man's body and pasting on the face of an older man.

The Group of Women Who Fight the Sexism of the Mass Media parodies how a men's magazine displays women's bodies. From the pamphlet *Weekly Check on the Mass Media (Shūkan masu-komi chekku),* distributed by the Ribu Shinjuku Center, October 15, 1975.

This form of parody provides one example of how *ribu* engaged in its own use of mockery and disdain, creating an alternative value system that produced its own codes of humor and pleasure that were shared among its readers. By ridiculing the exposure of a Japanese man's naked body, *ribu* demonstrated its bold political style, crossing lines of acceptable expression that other women's political groups refused to engage. By taking on elements of the mass media, *ribu* engaged in a struggle over the politics of mass culture, demonstrating its expansive agenda that moved beyond personal politics and sought to intervene against the hegemonic common sense that commodified and reduced women's sexuality to entertainment.

Ribu Conference: May 1972

In January 1972, about thirty women began to organize the Ribu Conference.[50] Group of Fighting Women was again at the center of the organizing. The conference was held in Tokyo from May 5 to May 7, 1972.[51] Approximately two thousand people attended the conference. About four hundred women came from the provinces, from as far away as Kagoshima and Hokkaidō; a hundred twenty men and ten American women also participated.[52]

Several events were planned for the conference, such as the Onna and Child's Festival on April 30, which was held at the Yamate Church in the Shibuya district of Tokyo.[53] This event began with a lecture on Kanno Sugako (1881–1911), the anarchist who was executed by the state for plotting to assassinate the emperor. The selection of Kanno Sugako as the featured topic expresses *ribu*'s complex stance toward women and political violence and its anti-imperialist stance. Furthermore, it underscores *ribu*'s consciousness of a Japanese legacy of women revolutionaries. This lecture was followed by a plenary discussion session that included Kageyama Hiroko, Higuchi Keiko, Arima Makiko, Iijima Aiko, Tanaka Mitsu, and Ōzawa Ryōko.[54] The topics addressed during the plenary discussion on the evening of April 30, 1972, represent some of the key issues of *ribu*'s politics at this juncture:

1. Rethinking *ribu* through the United Red Army incident[55]—What is the difference between *ribu* and the New Left?
2. "Men as the Enemy"—How should we *onna* reclaim ourselves?
3. Deepening our realization of the relationship between *onna* and children as our comrades—Confronting the suspicion and hostility between *onna*.
4. How do we want to live? A movement should be a way of living.[56]

The first topic clearly shows *ribu*'s proximity with and distinction from the New Left, specifically marking a confrontation with the political violence of the United Red Army. The second topic declares a new realization and stance toward men, signifying *ribu*'s radical feminist impulse to redefine men as the enemy. This new politicized antagonism toward men should be seen as how *ribu* distinguished itself from existing women's politics and as a reason it made a break from the left (as detailed in chapter 2). However, this principled antagonism should also be read in light of the fact that on May 7, the general plenary session was titled "For men and other friends who consider *ribu* their own issue." The third topic underscores *ribu*'s aim to embody a different logic of relationality, especially with other *onna* and with children, in a paradigm that departed from a male-centered and heterosexist family structure. This was also connected to *ribu*'s communes for women and their children as a positive alternative to the modern family system. The fourth topic indicated how *ribu* emphasized living the movement rather than designating certain activities or topics as political. What distinguished *ribu* from existing forms of issue-driven political activism was how *ribu* women sought to embody and manifest the movement as a *living philosophy*. Thus, rather than only engaging in symbolic actions against the state, the *ribu* women sought to live the totality of their politics, which encompassed the entire spectrum of battling the state's reactionary policies and laws to one's most intimate relationships. Living one's politics was experienced as more challenging and understood as enacting revolution in one's day-to-day existence rather than envisioning revolution as some future goal. This remains one of the most remarkable achievements of the movement, as *ribu* activists continue to live their philosophy in the present-continuous.

Several notable goals and plans were articulated from the Ribu Conference, such as the expansion of the movement against the revisions to the Eugenic Protection Law, an initiative to start "middle-age *ribu*," and a call to organize more child-care centers, communes, and women's clinics.[57] The most significant proposal that was concretized was the call to establish a *ribu* center that would create a constitutive center for the movement.

Constitutive Centers and Campaigns

As discussed in chapter 2, many of *ribu*'s organizing principles were a continuation from the Zenkyōtō and Beheiren movements of the late 1960s, which emphasized antihierarchical structures and valued autonomy and direct action. While these were fundamental organizing principles that *ribu* activists espoused, during the early years of the movement, there were core activists who shaped the movement significantly. Activists such as Yonezu, Mori, Tanaka, Sayama Sachi, and Iwatsuki became key members of *ribu*'s constitutive centers. *Ribu*'s constitutive centers became major centrifugal sites of *ribu*'s activism and discourse production. What made *ribu*'s constitutive centers distinct from a hierarchical organization was that there was no officially recognized authority or headquarters leading the movement. Among those activists who became part of *ribu*'s constitutive centers, a variety of factors differentiated who became most visible and influential. Like other grassroots movements, membership was based on an economy of volunteer participation; however, a person's organizing skills, initiative, commitment, persuasiveness, and charisma differentiated the roles the activists performed. As chapter 4 elaborates, Tanaka's leading role in the movement constituted one of the productive contradictions of *ribu*'s history and the politics of representation. In what follows, I delineate the symbiotic relationships between *ribu*'s key activists, its constitutive centers, and its most representative campaigns.

After the first nationwide Ribu Conference (Ribu Taikai) in May 1972, five *ribu* cells, the Group of Fighting Women, Thought Group SEX, Tokyo Komu-unu, Alliance of Fighting Women *(Tatakau Onna Dōmei)*, and Scarlet Letter (Himonji), worked together to establish and organize the Ribu Shinjuku Center.[58] These groups wanted a space where they could join forces and meet with *ribu* women from other parts of the country and the world.[59] The women who founded the space purposely named it the Ribu Shinjuku Center instead of the Tokyo Center because they wanted to avoid being recognized as the central headquarters of the movement, especially given its location in a central hub of the capital. Despite *ribu*'s attempt to not formally hierarchize its movement or to establish a headquarters, for many reasons the Ribu Shinjuku Center arguably became the constitutive center of the movement. It opened on September 30, 1972. The Shinjuku Center became the constitutive center because several existing cells collaborated in its establishment and its location in Tokyo made it accessible to the media, giving it further visibility. Moreover, the degree to which key activists there shaped the movement was linked to its constant production of *ribu* discourse through its press, which made it distinct from many other *ribu* centers in Osaka, Kyoto, and Hokkaidō.

The Ribu Shinjuku Center was a commune and an organizing center that was open twenty-four hours a day. It was one of the busiest pulsation points of *ribu*'s activities and often functioned as the communication center for nationwide events. It was a dissemination point and publishing house for *ribu*'s largest newspaper *(Ribu nyūsu: konomichi hitosuji)* and a prolific number of other *ribu* publications.[60] The Shinjuku Center organized regular teach-ins on a vast array of topics, such as women who kill their children (*kogoroshi no onna*), the United Red Army incident, abortion and birth control, and men's *ribu*.[61] It operated as a shelter for runaway teenage girls and battered women, and from 1974 to 1977, it provided free legal aid services for women.[62] The sheer amount of activity and the influence of its activists, such as Tanaka and Yonezu, also distinguished it from other *ribu* centers.

Seven women, including Mori, Yonezu, Tanaka, Sayama, and Wakabayashi Naeko,[63] and four cats started living at this two-bedroom apartment (2LDK). About twenty other women commuted from their homes as members of the commune in the autumn of 1972.[64] The division of labor, in principle, was voluntary.[65] There was no one person who decided who would do what. Each woman was supposed to do what she wanted. For example, Mori took charge of running the press. Cooking, doing dishes, or cleaning the toilet was no woman's designated duty. The deliberate avoidance of systematizing domestic duties was seen as a way to negate the modern prescription that a woman's femininity was to be proven through her domestic labors and that anarchistic principles were considered antithetical to the capitalist logic of productivity. The Shinjuku Center became (in)famous for the extent to which it attempted to subvert the dominant ideologies of private property and feminine domesticity. For several years, they practiced the negation of private property by sharing their belongings: women shared their clothing, their underwear, and even their toothbrushes. It was a radical experiment in communal living. These oppositional practices and anarchistic principles contributed to the chaotic quality of the internal life of the commune and made for tough and dirty living conditions.[66] A member of the Shinjuku Center, Wakabayashi Naeko, recalls sleeping at the center and being awakened by a cockroach crawling into her mouth. Wakabayashi states, "In those days, I did not think anything of it, I just took it out and went back to sleep."[67]

The Shinjuku Center became a key organizing site for *ribu*'s major and representative campaigns that it waged from the early 1970s. Five of *ribu*'s most representative campaigns were the protests against the revisions to the Eugenic Protection Law; *ribu*'s support of the "unmarried mother," called K-san; the "Mona Lisa spray incident"; the protests against Kisaeng tourism (sex tourism) in South Korea; and the campaign to support the women of the United Red Army. The United Red Army campaign is addressed in chapter 5. Of these campaigns, the protests against the revisions to the Eugenic Protection Law and the campaign to support K-san aptly exemplify the core concept of the liberation of sex. The protests against Kisaeng tourism represent how the liberation of sex combined with *ribu*'s anti-imperialism. These campaigns were nationwide, expanding the scope of *ribu*'s political organizing, and the establishment of constitutive centers like the Ribu Shinjuku Center was a major step in further enabling these networking capacities.

Eugenic Protection Law Campaign

Ūman ribu's sustained protests against the revisions to the Eugenic Protection Law became the most visible campaign of the movement and initiated a feminist legacy of activism that continues today. *Ribu* activists were fundamentally critical of the government's attempts to control women's bodies as reproductive machinery for nationalist economic growth and clearly saw the proposed revisions in the early 1970s as a recurrence of the government's efforts to utilize women's bodies as it did during wartime to promote capitalist and imperialist expansion.

The history of the state's policies of population control contextualizes *ribu*'s critical stance toward government reproductive control. During the Meiji era (1868–1912), known as a period of intensive modernization, the government sought to regulate the reproductive process, initially by passing laws to control the activities of midwives (in 1869 and 1874) and then by criminalizing abortion in 1880.[68] In addition to the criminalization of abortion, from 1940 to 1941, the government established the Eugenic Protection Law, which legislated contraceptive surgery to prevent the birth of "defective" or "handicapped" children. Alongside these sterilization policies, the law prohibited contraception for "healthy" citizens in order to promote national population growth. *Ribu*'s politics around abortion were forged through its postimperialist critique of how, during wartime, the government encouraged women to produce children in order to build a strong nation and empire.[69]

During the Occupation period, the government made revisions in 1949 to the Eugenic Protection Law, permitting abortions based on "economic reasons" that might harm the mother's health.[70] Although abortion was still deemed a criminal act, this loophole was used liberally for women to legally access abortion with their doctor's consent. After this revision, the number of official abortions from the mid-1950s to 1960 was approximately one million annually, although researchers estimate the actual number of abortions were in fact two to four times higher than the reported rates.[71]

During the 1950s, a right-wing nationalist religious group called Seichō no Ie set out to revise the Eugenic Protection Law in order to ban abortions.[72] Seichō no Ie became increasingly involved in backing politicians of the ruling government party, the Liberal Democratic Party (LDP). Subsequently, during the 1960s, the Ministry of Health and Welfare began to move toward restricting abortions. In 1967, the Minister of Health and Welfare referred to Japan as an "abortion paradise," declaring his interest in doing away with this "dishonor." Government, business, and conservative religious forces aligned behind the impetus to restrict abortions. From 1970 to 1973, on four separate occasions, the LDP proposed revisions to the Eugenic Protection Law in the Diet.[73] One of the proposed revisions would remove the "economic reason" clause and replace it with the "mother's mental health." *Ribu* and other critics saw the revision as signifying an ideological shift that would place blame for abortion on the individual woman instead of improving the societal conditions for giving birth.

Although a woman's right to abortion is often assumed to be a given across feminisms, *ribu*'s politics around abortion did not emphasize "women's rights" to abortion but rather emphasized reproductive freedom from state control.[74] Unlike earlier feminist discourses in Japan and elsewhere, *ribu* did not emphasize that "women's rights" to abortion be granted and protected by the state.[75] This very appeal to state proctorship and protection (that Wendy Brown has cogently emphasized as a pitfall of certain forms of second wave feminist politics in the United States) was antithetical to *ribu*'s fundamental position against state control of women's reproductive freedom.[76]

Ribu's approaches to abortion, birth control, and reproductive freedom demonstrate how *ribu* differed from other radical feminist politics around these issues. *Ribu* activists did not argue that woman's procreative abilities or capacities led to her discrimination or were the source of her discrimination (in contrast to argument by radical feminist Shulamith Firestone in *The Dialectic of Sex*).[77] This also represents *ribu* women's skeptical view of science and Western pharmaceuticals as linked with capitalism and state control (echoing Tokoro Mitsuko's critique of science, discussed in chapter 2). Moreover, the majority of *ribu* groups did not advocate or support the use of the pill. One prominent group, called Chūpiren, which organized in the early 1970s specifically to advocate for the release of the pill, represented a more liberal feminist approach based on individual women's rights and did not reflect the overall political approach of *ribu*.[78] Many *ribu* women were critical of this group's politics and suspicious of their motivations for advocating the pill.[79] *Ribu*'s critique of the pill exemplifies its critical stance toward science and state control of the body and portends how many *ribu* activists would turn toward Eastern medicine.

Ribu's discourses and protests around abortion demonstrate how its anti-capitalist and anti-imperialist politics infused and expanded its feminist articulations of body politics. Rather than politicizing sexism through an analysis that focused on the inequality of rights or power between the sexes, *ribu*'s understanding of sexism was informed by an anticapitalist critique. In its first manifestos on the subject in 1970, *ribu* activists spoke of the revisions as clearly stemming from the "demand of capital."[80] *Ribu*'s critical reception of an almost century-long Marxist legacy in Japan understood capitalism as a dehumanizing system in which women were required to be "accomplices that made men into slaves of capital."[81] Additionally, *ribu*'s critique was directed at how theory and political economy were privileged across Marxist politics over a more thorough critique of common sense and the importance of the ideologies that regulate daily living. In this sense, *ribu* was more invested in a Gramscian notion of hegemony and sought a way to live a politics embedded within a matrix of contradictions.

What is striking about *ribu*'s critique is the extent to which abortion was seen as interconnected to the entirety of the sociopolitical-economic system. In its early manifestos, the Committee to Prepare for Women's Liberation linked the relationship of the control of the womb to the control of national borders.[82] A manifesto titled "The Direction of Our Eros: Immigration Law and Abortion Prohibition Law" (written in August 1970) thoroughly critiques the relationship between laws that restrict the immigration of foreign laborers and laws that restrict abortion. This manifesto declared that the prohibition of abortion is not only "the oppression of sex" but also a "reformation of imperialism."[83] Although conditions such as an anticipated labor shortage were cited as reasons to restrict abortion, the government passed legislation at the same time that would restrict immigration. Therefore, *ribu* critiqued state control of abortion in tandem with the government's exclusivist immigration policies, particularly because these policies excluded immigration from its former colonies.

Ribu not only wished to promote a woman's right over her own individual body but also sought to create a society that would value human relations according to a logic that was not reducible to profit. Its slogan around the issue became "Toward a society where women want to give birth." As evinced by *ribu*'s stance on women who kill their children (elaborated in chapter 1), *ribu* sought to deindividualize the burden of mothering and rearticulate the responsibility of child rearing as a societal and collective duty. *Ribu* affirmed women's power to give birth but sought to liberate birthing from its ideological moorings in the modern family system, which was seen as the state-sanctioned means to reproduce the male-headed nuclear household as the basic unit of capitalist socioeconomic reproduction. *Ribu*'s concept of the liberation of sex translated into *ribu*'s practice of mother–child communes and the refusal of many *ribu* women to enter the modern family system symbolized in the family registration system *(koseki seido)*.

When the revised law was presented before the Diet in 1972, *ribu* groups organized independently, with groups in Sapporo, Hokkaidō, Kyoto, Osaka, and Fukuoka holding their own antirevision demonstrations and meetings.[84] When the revision of the bill was proposed in the Diet the following year, on March 14, 1973, the Ribu Shinjuku Center made an appeal to organize together. In response to its appeal, twenty-nine *ribu* and other women's groups joined to form the Committee to Prevent the Revision of the Eugenic Protection Law (Yūsei Hogo Hō Kaiaku Shoshi Jikkō Iinkai). The establishment of the Shinjuku Center was a major step in enabling this networking capacity. *Ribu* women organized a demonstration and sit-in at the Ministry of Health and Welfare from May 12 to May 15, 1973. They demanded a meeting with ministry officials and denounced them for failing to consider women's perspectives on the issue. Eventually, *ribu* women were physically carried out of the building by ministry officials and police, images of which made the front pages of major newspapers and television news.

Ribu's discourse around abortion was shaped significantly by the presence of Yonezu and Tanaka at the Shinjuku Center. The influence of these two figures provides an example of how particular subjects can shape the collective politics of a movement. As a physically challenged feminist activist, Yonezu's pioneering work during the incipient phase of *ribu* and her active presence at the Ribu Shinjuku Center facilitated the expansion of *ribu*'s politics around abortion as it shifted from an assumption of abortion as a woman's right to a view that critiqued the state control of reproduction and ableism. Tanaka's unique feminist perspective on abortion and child killing was discussed in chapter 1. Tanaka has acknowledged how her close relationship with Yonezu, as co-organizers and cohabitants at the center, challenged and expanded her views on abortion and infanticide. Insofar as Tanaka was arguably the most influential and prolific theorist of the movement, the relationship between Tanaka and Yonezu altered the direction of *ribu*'s politics around abortion.

Yonezu acted as bridge builder to work in solidarity with disabled citizens' groups. The Ribu Shinjuku Center organized in conjunction with Aoshiba no Kai, an advocacy group for people with cerebral palsy. Disabled citizens' groups protested against the revisions, which would include a "fetal conditions clause" that would further strengthen the eugenic aspect of the existing law. Aoshiba no Kai was the most active disabled citizens' group to protest the revisions.[85] In October 1972, Ribu Shinjuku Center printed a pamphlet authored by Tanaka Mitsu called "Is Abortion a Vested Right?" In this text Tanaka cites a pamphlet from Aoshiba no Kai and links the morality of child killing and abortion to the case of a parent who killed his "handicapped child." Tanaka echoes the critique of Aoshiba no Kai that also denounces a "society that values humans depending on their labor capacity."[86]

> In this world, where the strong devour the weak, its order is established through the logic of productivity . . . those like the elderly, children, the sick, the "handicapped." . . . This logic measures the dignity of a person's life on the basis of whether or not a person is useful to a corporation and this logic permeates our consciousness and life daily.[87]

Two weeks after the Ribu Shinjuku Center initiated the formation of the Committee to Prevent the Revision of the Eugenic Protection Law, it organized a meeting with Aoshiba no Kai on March 29, 1973, which three hundred people attended. Aoshiba no Kai argued that the state should create societal conditions where disabled people "could lead happy, productive lives" rather than promote discrimination against the disabled and, in effect, cut off their lives before they are born.[88] The striking similarity between Aoshiba and *ribu*'s approach to abortion signifies the degree of cross-fertilization between these movements. Yonezu's presence at the center of the movement and the movement's collaboration and dialogue with Aoshiba no Kai distinctively shaped its feminist stance toward abortion, critiquing the discrimination based on a capitalist logic of productivity.

The direct protest actions by Aoshiba no Kai appeared effective because the fetal conditions clause was removed from the proposal to revise the bill in 1974. The degree to which the activism by *ribu,* disabled citizens' groups, and other women's and family planning groups influenced the parliamentary process is open to question, because the strongest lobby groups were medical interests and doctors who had close ties with the government. Researchers such as Tiana Norgren, who have closely studied reproductive politics and policy in Japan, have noted that the reactionary revisions themselves proved to be effective catalysts to ignite and strengthen both feminist and disabled citizens' movements. In July 1974, when the revisions bill failed to pass a vote in the Upper House of Councilors, several groups, including Nichibo (the organization representing the doctors authorized to perform abortions), disability groups, and women's groups all considered this a political victory.[89]

Campaign to Support K-san—An Unmarried Mother

In the midst of the struggle against the revisions to the Eugenic Protection Law, another emblematic *ribu* protest ignited when the media covered a story in February 1973 about a mother who was fighting to win custody of her child. This campaign became known as the Keiko or K-san case. K was an unmarried mother *(mikon no haha)* and teacher who lived and worked in Osaka. On March 16, 1970, nine days after she gave birth, she went to speak with N, the biological father, because they were no longer together. Without her knowledge or consent, the father took the child, who was sleeping in another room. He then brought the infant to his new partner, S, and claimed that the baby belonged to them. In an attempt to get her newborn infant back, K appealed to the family courts, which began a battle that would ensue for the next four years.

In February 1973, the mass media reported that the court ruled against K's right to raise her child. The judge's ruling declared, "The birth parent is not qualified to raise the child," and no kidnapping charge was made against N for taking the child from K. This news immediately catalyzed a support movement for K by *ribu* women. A few months after a support network was organized, a few *ribu* members in Osaka planned and executed a direct action that successfully returned K's child to her on May 5, 1973. The mass media immediately framed K as a "bad mother" and "criminal." The May 7, 1973, edition of the *Asahi Shinbun,* for example, stated, "This emotional attempt to retrieve [her child] by her own means is deplorable. . . . If she had maternal love, she would have given up the child and sacrificed herself."[90] *Ribu* women protested the conformity of the mass media to police authority in their coverage of the incident and supported K's struggle across both legal and extralegal fronts.[91] *Ribu* women protested the ruling, critiquing the language the judge used in passing judgment on her as an "unwed" mother who chose to have an "'illegitimate child' . . . knowing that her child would have to face such unhappy circumstances."[92] From the fall of 1973 to the winter of 1974, K continued to appeal within the legal system to win back the custody of her child. On February 26, 1974, the supreme court ruled against the previous judgment and ordered the parties into mediation. From April to July, the parties negotiated, and on July 4, 1974, they came to the agreement that K would raise the child, but she would have to pay N and S compensation.[93]

Ribu understood how this case had implications beyond K and was a symbolic judgment against all working and unwed mothers. Alongside the state's capitalist rationale of the Eugenic Protection Law, the K-san case provided a vivid dramatization of the state's will to thoroughly control women's reproduction and regulate motherhood. Because the family registration system functioned as a state apparatus to restrict women's freedom to give birth, by legally rendering unmarried women's children "illegitimate," *ribu*'s protests were set against the deep imbrication of the modern family system and the state.

According to Miki Sōko, *ribu* demonstrated an anti-individualist economy of identification that moved beyond the self to understand that "I am Keiko."[94] The declaration "I am Keiko" signifies a deeper and broader understanding of a collective subjectivity. The conception of a collective identity of *onna* would imply that if such persecution and discrimination can happen to one *onna*, then it could happen to any other *onna*. This anti-individualist economy, as we see again in chapter 5 in *ribu*'s response to the United Red Army, was a core element of *ribu*'s collective subjectivity. The K-san case demonstrated that *ribu*'s politics were not based on the existing identity of women but constituted an explicit articulation of a political identification with women who defy the system, whether these women were criminalized mothers like K or other abject figures like *kogoroshi no onna*, comfort women, or sex workers. This political identification with abject subjects constituted *ribu*'s collective subjectivity and political ontology that moved beyond "personal politics" or meeting one's individual needs and rights. By understanding the relationality between subjectivity and collectivity, and how these were interconstituted, *ribu* focused simultaneously on a revolution of the self and on societal transformation. By grasping how one's subjectivity was forged through collectivity, *ribu* acted as a collective-subject performing symbolic social interventions against the fragmenting effects of individualism that fuels capitalism and liberalism. There was thus both a centripetal and centrifugal dynamic to *ribu*'s political praxis, creating a generative tension between the need to transform the self by transforming how the self engaged with the other and rest of society.[95]

Kisaeng Tourism

Ribu's praxis of the liberation of sex was directed against the regulatory and ideological power of the state's family system to control reproduction and motherhood. Its notion of the liberation of sex went beyond the confines of the nation-state and the family system to critique how the emergent neo-imperial formation also implicated the politics of sex. The movement's protests against Kisaeng tourism represented the intersection of the liberation of sex and *ribu*'s anti-imperialist feminist politics. Kisaeng tourism involved organized tours in South Korea that included sexual services provided by young South Korean women at what were called Kisaeng clubs. According to *ribu*'s perspective, this form of tourism represented the reformation of

Japanese economic imperialism in Asia and was a system that exploited the sex of other third world Asian women.

In December 1973, as part of a longer campaign of anti-Japanese protests, Korean women college students from the elite Eiwa College demonstrated against the Japanese men arriving at the Kimpo Airport in Seoul. The demonstration was televised in Japan, and in direct response, several Japanese anti-imperialist women's groups organized a demonstration at Haneda Airport in Tokyo on December 25, 1974.[96] Several women of the Ribu Shinjuku Center, including Mori, took part in this protest. Mori decided that she would graffiti the message "Against Kisaeng Tourism" on the large windows of Haneda Airport. Although she knew she would be arrested for this symbolic protest, being open to such forms of criminalization was integral to *ribu*'s antistate politics and its close identification with and support of criminalized women.[97] Mori's day-to-day labor as an activist who ran the presses at the Ribu Shinjuku Center performed a crucial role in disseminating *ribu*'s discourses across Japan and beyond. In this moment, she became a medium to send a message of solidarity with Korean women who had protested against the Japanese exploitation of Korean women's sexuality.

The demonstration in December marked the beginning of a nationwide movement to stop Kisaeng tours. On March 9, 1974, a gathering of three hundred women on International Women's Day focused on the imperative to oppose Kisaeng tourism. From Kyūshū to Hiroshima, from Kanazawa to Okayama, tour companies became the target of protest actions, and demonstrations were staged at several airports around the country. In response to these nationwide protests, JATA (Japanese Association of Travel Agencies) changed its policy regarding Kisaeng tours to prohibit their advertising and promotion.

Ribu's involvement in the anti–Kisaeng tourism effort represented one way in which some *ribu* women consciously engaged in solidarity-building actions with other Asian women, whom they recognized as former colonized subjects of the Japanese empire who were now subjected to emergent neo-economic-imperialist formations. During an interview in February 2003, Mori stated that in spite of the consequences of her having been marked with a criminal record for her graffiti protest against Kisaeng tourism, she had no regret for doing what she did. "There was no choice as I saw it, I had to do it. That is what I felt."[98] Like many other *ribu* women, Mori's affective response to her self-critical recognition of her location moved her to this feminist anti-imperialist practice. As part of an extralegal protest that was not just transnational but anti-imperial, these *ribu* women embraced this form of criminality as a response to their position of privilege and power as middle-class Japanese women.[99]

What's in a Name?

Ūman ribu's anti-imperialist transnationalism constituted its centrifugal direction, which was simultaneous with its centripetal drive toward the creation of local community networks and spaces. Much of *ribu*'s activism focused on creating *onna*-centered spaces and cultural productions. A key activist in this regard has been Iwatsuki Sumie (also known as Asatori Sumie), a lesbian activist who has been a vital force in organizing many forms of *onna*-centered cultural production. In the late 1960s, Iwatsuki was also involved in leftist politics, including sectarian student activism and protests around Sanrizuka.[100] Through her involvement, she also had direct encounters with the use of political violence, so much so that at times she had to fight for her life against other sect members. Given the kind of antistate battles in which her comrades engaged, she questioned whether the current form of political protest would be sustainable in the long run. Before becoming part of the *ribu* movement, Iwatsuki had already begun to forge new roads. Iwatsuki's predictions were correct. Having survived physical attacks by other sect members, Iwatsuki successfully removed herself from the destructive violence of the left and became one of *ribu*'s key cultural producers. In 1969, for example, she started working in construction and became determined to build her own home. With little resources, she audited architecture classes and worked on a construction site. When she started building her house, other construction workers would donate supplies and volunteer to assist her because they were so amused that a woman was trying to build a home on her own.

When Iwatsuki first became involved in the *ribu* movement, she was not informed by the women's lib movement in the United States, nor did she study it. Iwatsuki emphasizes that she did what she felt she had to do for herself and the women around her. She states,

> I didn't feel the need to use the term *ūman ribu* because there already existed the concept of *onna*, and we emphasized *onna* in the plural— *onna-tachi*. There have been so many *onna* flowing like a river with their own history, legacy and spirit, and although this history has been ignored by men, it is for *onna* themselves to recognize this.[101]

Iwatsuki states that she prefers not to use the term *ribu* but deliberately emphasizes *onna-tachi* to underscore the legacy of Japanese women activists and to accentuate the importance of the relationship between *onna*. "I prefer the word *onna-tachi*, but if a fine *(sutekina)* woman asks me, 'Are you *ūman ribu?*' I'll say yes. Like being a lesbian, I don't think that there is a need to say it to everyone."[102]

In 1970, Iwatsuki was central in establishing a women's café called Three Points in the Ginza district of Tokyo. This café was designed as an *onna*-centered space where women could come and exchange information. Three Points became the first "open space" for *onna* in Tokyo.[103] Iwatsuki spent much of her time there sharing with and counseling women on how to deal with the problems they faced. *Ribu mini-komi* and pamphlets were available at the café, and *ribu* women would gather at Three Points for meetings and to exchange information.

Witch Concerts

Three Points became another kind of *ribu* center. One of the core members of Three Points decided to become an "unmarried mother."[104] Thus, when news of the K-san case arose in the media, the women at Three Points immediately began organizing meetings to demonstrate their outrage. Three Points became the center of organizing for Japan's first Witch Concert. Planning for the Witch Concert began in 1973, and Iwatsuki worked as its central organizer. Initially, it was conceived as a means to raise funds for K, but by the time the event took place on July 27, 1974, the K-san case was resolved. The Witch Concert was to feature exclusively women, ranging from jazz and rock bands to folk singers. The announcement for the event expresses how *ribu* continued to center and privilege *onna* during its early years:

> Until now, we have known too little of the pleasure of *onna* encountering each other. Moreover, we have seen women through the eyes of men, but now we are starting a new perspective. Before each *onna* is crushed one by one, let's try to discover *onna*. Without formal titles or proper names, let's invest in encountering other *onna* as our allies. This is the purpose of our concert. We call it the "Witch Concert." Witch is the word that is imputed to women who try to choose, with a clear vision, a way of living that is acceptable to us. Therefore, witches are all the more so attractive. Let's fill up the hall with witches. Let's share and send out the bonds that are created there to all *onna* throughout Japan.[105]

The Witch Concert was designed and produced by *onna* for *onna*. With three thousand people in attendance, the Witch Concert was the largest *ribu* gathering to date. The Witch Concert, more than any *ribu* event until that point, was the manifestation of how *ribu* developed in terms of understanding the importance of pleasure *for* and *with onna* and thus was very much an expression of *ribu*'s notion of eros. The concert signified how the creation of new cultural practices that celebrated *onna* were simultaneous with the creation of a new sensibility, new values, and new forms of *onna*-centered pleasure.

There were some men who were interested in being involved in the event. Therefore, the concert organizers decided that their role would be to babysit the children. The men interested in participating underwent six months of child-care training at Three Points. *Ribu* thus went beyond critiquing a sexist division of labor and engaged in new cultural practices that would liberate both men and women from their prescribed roles. Some of these men went on to work as preschool teachers after the concert. Thus, even though *ribu* emphasized an *onna*-centered political activism, it did not exclude men who were willing to transform themselves and practice a new form of relationality with *onna* and children. As the following photo depicts, the purposeful inclusion of men and children in their new forms of radical relationality was also part of *ribu*'s politics and legacy that understood the importance of liberating men from sexism, misogyny, and the national-patriarchal family system.

Three Points was closed in 1975 (because the building's owner did not continue the lease), and the following year Iwatsuki opened Hōkiboshi, which was located in the Shinjuku district of Tokyo. Hōkiboshi was a restaurant and space for women where alternative media was available and sold. Hōkiboshi became the organizing center for two more Witch Concerts that were held on September 10, 1976, and May 22, 1977.[106]

In 1977, Iwatsuki changed her name to Asatori Sumie. Asatori's renaming of herself represents the conscious self-transformation that takes place through a new matrix of relationality. Even within her own family, she stopped calling her family members by "mom" *(okaasan)* or "older sister" *(oneesan)* but insisted on calling them by their own names, which was a countercultural practice within the intimate familial space. The will to transform these mundane, normalized practices was indicative of the depth of her consciousness about the links between language, power, family ideology, and the social, subjective, and collective force of normativity.

Akin to Asatori, all of the core activists discussed in this chapter—Mori, Yonezu, Tanaka, Wakabayashi, Miki, and Saeki—have refused to live within the marriage–family system for the past forty years as the lived expression of their politics. Wakabayashi went on to become a pioneering activist of Regumi Studio, one of the first lesbian resource organizations in Japan.[107] Although lesbian activism was not her focus, Yonezu lived long term with a woman partner, whom she describes as a woman she fell in love with. Yonezu

Men carrying babies participate in a *ribu* demonstration. The banner reads: "Fix the World! Abolish This Paternal Rights Society."

went on to become a central feminist organizer for reproductive freedom and for decades has labored as a key archivist of the movement along with Miki and Saeki. Tanaka and Saeki had children outside of the family system and raised them in Japan despite the many forms of discrimination they faced as unmarried mothers of children classified by the state as "illegitimate" (*hi-chakushutsushi*). *Ribu*'s praxis of mother–child communes and giving birth outside of the family system emblematized how *ribu* women live the liberation of sex on a daily basis by going against the heteronormative male-headed family.[108]

Mona Lisa Spray Protest

Ribu maintained a core set of concepts, such as the liberation of sex, but also saw the entirety of the sociocultural politicoeconomic system as ideologically interconnected. This overarching political analysis fostered expansive and multidirectional fronts of activism and intervention. *Ribu*'s investment and solidarity in protesting discrimination against the disabled was again evinced in what became known as the Mona Lisa Spray Incident. The Mona Lisa was displayed at the Tokyo National Museum in Ueno Park in April 1974. The museum announced that because it anticipated the exhibit to be crowded, it would deny access to those who might need assistance, which implied the elderly, the disabled, and those with infants. When the activists at the Ribu Shinjuku Center heard about this policy, they determined to protest in solidarity with other disabled groups, such as Aoshiba no Kai. In the course of discussing how to protest the exhibit, Yonezu decided that she would graffiti the glass case of the exhibit to symbolize their protest.[109] On April 20, 1974, the opening day of the exhibit, the Ribu Shinjuku Center and *ribu* activists from the *ribu* commune called Tokyo Komu-unu staged a demonstration. On this same day, Yonezu went into the exhibit and spray painted the glass encasement of the Mona Lisa with red spray paint. She was arrested at the museum, detained for a month, and a court battle ensued for the next year. In June 1975, she was convicted of a misdemeanor and made to pay a fine of three thousand yen.[110]

Their main purpose was to protest discrimination against the disabled; a 1974 pamphlet states: "Insofar as the Mona Lisa Exhibition is symbolic of the outrageous discrimination against handicapped people in society, we will struggle against it."[111] The decision to engage in this form of protest can be seen as both the expansiveness of *ribu*'s politics and an overextension of its limited resources and energy. By 1975, after simultaneously waging campaigns on multiple fronts and sustaining support for the women of the United

Red Army (discussed in chapter 5), the women at the Shinjuku Center certainly felt the strain and pressure of constantly fighting against the system.

The women at the Shinjuku Center also lived with frequent ridicule from the mass media and criticism from both conservatives and other leftist sects. As the *ribu* movement cast itself outward in its protests, its centrifugal movements were suppressed by the juridical and policing power of the state. *Ribu* women were arrested, detained, jailed, and indicted for their various protest activities. Because of *ribu*'s affiliation with and support for the women members of the United Red Army, the *ribu* women of the Shinjuku Center were kept under state surveillance, and *ribu* organizing centers in Tokyo were raided by the police.[112] Battling the state through court cases and being followed around Tokyo by plainclothes police officers added to the pressures of life at the Shinjuku Center.

The Shinjuku Center did not receive any state funding or have any sponsors, and thus raising money to run the commune was a constant pressure. It took 300,000 yen per month to run the Shinjuku Center.[113] The women who lived there took turns (in approximately three-month shifts) between working outside and working full time in the center. The women took various day jobs, such as waitressing, working at ramen (noodle) shops, nude modeling, and hostessing in the sex-entertainment industry to make money to run the Shinjuku Center.

In addition to the daily stress of living in these conditions, with at least six or seven other women cramped in a small two-bedroom apartment, the nonstop schedule of the Shinjuku Center made life tense and harsh. Looking back on their life at the center, Namahara Reiko complains that she was always sleepy.[114] Although there was no such thing as a typical day, because the schedule was constantly changing, Namahara describes what one day at the collective might look like. "After waking up from sharing a single futon with another woman, the day might begin with going out before breakfast to hand out pamphlets, then coming home and fixing a meal, then going to work for the day, then returning to the Center to organize a meeting, then doing laundry, and then writing and printing the handouts for the next meeting, before finally going to sleep."[115] Different women moved in and out of the Shinjuku Center, visitors came at any time, and there were constant changes in the schedule and uncertainties about its future.

In 1974, the women began to discuss the possibility of reducing the activities of the Shinjuku Center to allow the women to work more on their interpersonal relations. The constant pressure, fatigue, and repeated disappointments in each other had strained their relationships so much that some *ribu* women described their relations as "warped."[116] Starting in 1975, many key *ribu* activists, such as Tanaka, Wakabayashi (along with Takeda Miyuki), and Asatori (aka Iwatsuki), left Japan to live abroad for a period. In 1975, Tanaka and Wakabayashi went to the United States and then to Mexico City to participate in the United Nations Conference for the International Year of the Woman.[117]

After being immersed in the activism of the movement and experiencing her own disappointments, in 1978, Asatori left Japan and traveled around the United States to visit different lesbian-feminist friends and communes. She then went to Europe. Through her travels from 1978 to 1980, Asatori discovered what she interpreted to be a transcultural commonality, that is, women living by loving other women.

> I discovered that the women around the world who were doing women's
> activism were women who loved other women. They are like me, lesbians.
> And even though you don't have to necessarily have a woman-lover [to be
> a lesbian], I think that this love for other women was the key and it made
> me so happy.[118]

After returning to Japan, in 1982, Asatori started a women's band *(onna kurabu bando)* that produced its first recording a few years later. She went on to build a women's recording studio and martial arts dōjo as part of a women's communal housing project in Ichikawa City in the Chiba Prefecture.

Asatori also became involved in the second major protest against the revisions to the Eugenic Protection Law. In 1982, the government again attempted to remove the "economic necessity" clause as a legal means to obtain an abortion. This movement catalyzed the formation of Shoshiren, a nationwide coalition that continues today as a political legacy of *ribu.*[119] As did *ribu,* Shoshiren has continued to work with disability groups to fight against the eugenics rationale of Japan's legislation that hierarchizes human life through laws that prohibit the birth of "inferior descendents." Shoshiren emphasizes the "body of *onna*" as its point of departure and aims to abolish the eugenics rationale.[120] Yonezu has continued as a leading activist in the struggle for reproductive freedom over the last forty years and remains a central figure in this organization that continues to rearticulate *ribu*'s slogan, "*Onna*/I will decide to give birth or not give birth." More than forty years later, this slogan continues to emphasize the politics of birthing, not a discourse of rights. This is one vital example of how the *ribu* movement continues to shape feminist politics into the twenty-first century.

Asatori became a member of Shoshiren, where she works with Yonezu and other women continuing the legacy of *ribu.* She is also involved in Regumi Studio, the lesbian collective started by Wakabayashi Naeko. While activists like Tanaka, Wakabayashi, and Asatori were abroad, Yonezu and Mori started their own small publishing company in 1977, called Aida Kōbō. During the early 1980s, Aida Kōbō, Shoshiren, and Regumi Studio all worked out of the same building in Tokyo.[121] The close working relationship between the *ribu* women who formed these new political collectives and the organic and fluid movement of the women between these groups exemplifies the multifaceted approaches and fronts of activism in which *ribu* women continue to engage today.[122] In contrast with so many activists of the 1960s and 1970s who defected or became cynical reactionaries, most *ribu* women continue to live their politics. Key activists like Miki, Saeki, Wakabayashi, and Yonezu still gather at annual *ribu* retreats that are held in different parts of the country. What is striking about these ongoing *ribu* gatherings is how each *ribu* woman has her own subjective way of living her *ribu* and values the cohesiveness, openness, and critical support of the ongoing collectivity of *ribu*. At these retreats, younger generations of feminists often join veteran *ribu* activists, rearticulating and discussing the legacy as well as passing on the spirit of *ribu*.[123]

Many outside observers have stated that the *ribu* movement ended in 1975. Feminist scholars like Ehara Yumiko have reiterated the view that the movement "died" in 1975.[124] Such interpretations fail to provide an account of how the political ontology of *ribu* extends beyond the rubric of a social movement defined by the public visibility of its activists and campaigns. Rather than declare its premature death, by tracing the continued activities of *ribu* activists, we can recognize the multiple temporal ontologies of *ribu* that are rearticulated across different horizons: lesbian activism, feminist music and martial arts, women's communes, and ongoing reproductive freedom movements. *Ribu* remains a political identity and a living philosophy that thrives through the lives of hundreds, if not thousands, of women who continue to embody the legacy of *ribu* into the present continuous.

CHAPTER FOUR

Ribu and Tanaka Mitsu

The Icon, the Center, and Its Contradictions

The Medium and Its Excess

In the summer of 1970, Tanaka Mitsu appeared at leftist political gatherings, agitating and handing out her handwritten manifestos that called for the "liberation of eros" and the "liberation of sex." In August 1970, for example, she went to the Asian Women against Discrimination conference at Hosei University in Tokyo. This meeting was attended by about two thousand politically active women from across Japan. Other *ribu* women remember her, raising her voice, wearing a white mini skirt, and handing out her manifesto, "Liberation from the Toilet."[1] This six-page pamphlet became the most well-known manifesto of the movement. At the dawn of *ribu*, Tanaka wrote the manifestos that became its symbolic texts, such as "The Liberation of Eros" and "Liberation from the Toilet."[2] Tanaka was a member of the Committee to Prepare for Women's Liberation and also formed another cell called the Group of Fighting Women.[3] From the beginning of the movement, although she organized as a part of the groups noted above, her handwritten manifestos often ended by stating that the author and "the person to contact is Tanaka Mitsu."[4]

Tanaka began her *ribu* in Tokyo just as other women throughout Japan began forming their own *ribu* cell groups. From 1970 until 1975, she was involved in organizing most of *ribu*'s major activities and through her involvement became its most visible iconoclast.[5] During this five-year period, she played a formative if not pivotal role in the movement. She performed many functions within the movement: she was an agitator, activist and organizer, spokeswoman, philosopher, writer, and leader. At the genesis of the movement, she forwarded a comprehensive and cogent argument of why women's liberation had to be the liberation of sex, and in this sense, she was a vanguard theorist of the movement.

Despite the fact that the *ribu* movement formally recognized no one leader or representative *(daihyō)*, very few women of *ribu* would dispute that Tanaka had a highly influential role in the movement. Akiyama Yōko writes that from 1970 to 1975, Tanaka was "the eye of *ribu*'s typhoon."[6] This metaphoric description of Tanaka's role in the movement is suggestive of her paradoxical position at the center of a movement that purported to have no one center, or leader. In *Notes on a Personal History of Ribu* (1993), feminist scholar Akiyama writes, "Even if the person called Tanaka Mitsu did not exist, there would have been a *ribu* movement in Japan. But then again, without her, I don't think that it would have been *that ribu*" (emphasis mine).[7] Akiyama here makes two important points: first, that the rise of the *ribu* movement cannot, and should not, ever be reduced or solely attributed to Tanaka Mitsu; second, that Tanaka was nonetheless a remarkably influential figure who definitively shaped the movement.[8] In this vein, sociologist Ichiyo Muto, an outsider to the movement, has stated, "Though Lib was a collective movement from which no personality should be singled out as the 'mastermind,' Japanese Lib thinking cannot be properly evaluated apart from Tanaka's originality, power of language and personality."[9] Muto's statement points to an inherent tension and contradiction between understanding *ribu* as a collective movement, with its antihierarchical principles, and the distinctive and substantive role that Tanaka embodied.

In addition to Tanaka's role in the movement from 1970 to 1975, over the past forty years, Tanaka has arguably become the icon of *ribu*. For example, in a 2001 interview, when questioned about Tanaka's relation to the movement, Akiyama stated, "In history, sometimes a charismatic leader is born that symbolizes an era. I think that Tanaka carried out that role."[10] Inoue Teruko, a prominent women's studies scholar and *ribu* participant also stated, "She is the person who symbolizes Japan's *ribu*. After all, it was her individual personality that shaped Japan's *ribu*. . . . Sometimes an era chooses one, and that one was Tanaka Mitsu."[11] Through such retrospective commentary from Japanese feminist scholars, Tanaka has become for many the *one* who symbolizes the movement, the proper name that is associated with *ribu*. This metonymic structure of representation is problematic for many reasons.

Given the antihierarchical principles of *ribu,* other *ribu* women have been critical of, if not offended by, the role Tanaka has been given by the mass media and women's studies scholars as "the representative of *ribu*."[12] Mizoguchi Ayeko has stated that it was contrary to the principles of *ribu* to focus on a single member as "its star" as women's studies in Japan and the mass media have done.[13] According to Saeki Yōko, one of the editors of the *ribu* journal *Onna Erosu* (published 1972–83), "*Ribu* is a movement of nameless women who remain nameless and struggle to create their own lives. . . . To become famous or the leader of a group would be a problem and contradiction."[14] From this viewpoint, fixing Tanaka as the one proper name and leader contradicts *ribu*'s own antihierarchical and antielitist principles. The making of Tanaka into the movement's representative or icon, in other words, has arguably been contrary to what many consider to be *ribu*'s antihierarchical philosophy and thus an "anti*ribu*" effect.

Like the process of canonization, the process of iconization is replete with divergent effects. An icon at once marks a historical moment or era and serves as a symbolic replacement of a more complex and dynamic set of meanings and conditions. An icon often masks an antagonistic, unpresented, and unrepresentable history and thus makes for a preferred substitute for the more laborious process of critical engagement that challenges accepted forms of knowledge about the past and present.

In producing a narrative of *ribu*'s history, I aim to move beyond the recognition of Tanaka as an icon and resist the hazards of hagiography that often conceal the excesses and contradictions of political leaders and public figures. My goals are to critically understand Tanaka's formative presence as an activist and organizer, assess her contributions as a feminist theorist, and elucidate the process and effects of her iconization. If chapter 3 provided a macroassessment of the movement's history and main interventions and successes, this chapter engages in an analysis of the micropolitics of the movement, exploring the difficult internal and interpersonal dynamics of this movement with a focus on the group dynamics involving Tanaka. Tanaka's role in *ribu* was pivotal and consequential, though not without problems, excesses, and limitations. By revisiting several conflicting and critical responses to Tanaka's role in the movement, I examine how Tanaka's position in the movement was contestatory and indicative of the challenges of *ribu*'s organizing principles. Tanaka's role in the movement, in many respects, was indicative of the strengths and limitations of *ribu*'s formation; therefore, a close analysis of the tensions and conflicts within the movement provides insight into the pitfalls and problems of certain organizing styles and ideals that often fail to effectively deal with power differences. What did the other *ribu* women think and feel about her? What does this tell us about the challenges of the collective dynamics of radical social movements and their difficulties dealing with internal power dynamics? Such an analysis of *ribu* affords lessons for the future, especially because many of its problems remain common among other grassroots, progressive, feminist, and leftist movements. In the course of this discussion, I elaborate how these contradictions, tensions, and excesses in the formation of the movement are also integral to Tanaka's philosophy of liberation, marking both the uniqueness of Tanaka's theories and their potential pitfalls and blind spots. This focus on Tanaka and the groups she was involved with, however, should not be taken to be representative of the entire *ribu* movement. On the contrary, Tanaka's character and unique role arguably had a distinct effect on those who worked most closely with her. This critical focus on Tanaka's relation to the movement plays into the danger of metonymic ellipsis but hopefully sheds light on how we might better understand and theorize the potential violence of—and between— feminist subjects.

In this chapter, I also trace and critique the historical process through which Tanaka became *ribu*'s icon. Although Tanaka did not continue to be centrally involved in the collective activities of the *ribu* women after 1975, she continues to perform the role of the icon of *ribu*. I conclude this chapter with an analysis of Tanaka's own participation in her iconography and ask: Who benefits from this iconization, and what discursive work do specific icons like Tanaka perform? What are the seductions and dangers that come with the discursive power of an icon?

The Visibility of the Messenger

Tanaka has described herself as *ribu*'s messenger—its *yobikake nin*—implying that she announced the message of *ribu* and appealed to and moved people with her words.[15] From the early days of the movement, Tanaka purposely engaged with various kinds of media, placing herself in the public eye. She exposed herself time and again in magazines, in newspapers, and at political rallies, announcing a new women's movement called *ūman ribu*.[16] Tanaka's appearances in the mass media and her prominent role in many of *ribu*'s major nationwide events made it seem to some that she was a spokeswoman for *ribu* and thus its representative.

By the fall of 1970, Tanaka became the face and the proper name associated with the Group of Fighting Women. On October 25, 1970, the *Asahi Shinbun,* one of Japan's widest circulating daily newspapers, published a close-up of Tanaka with an article that features her as a member of the Group of Fighting Women.[17] This image of her face captures the defiant stance that would characterize *ribu*, and Tanaka Mitsu's name is used to introduce many of *ribu*'s key concepts.

This photograph of Tanaka captures an intent, if not glaring, insolent gaze, looking away from the camera as if she sees something beyond that moment in time. The journalist who wrote the article commented that he thought Tanaka could be a *miko,* that is, a medium or shaman. In my view, Tanaka

Photograph of Tanaka Mitsu printed as a representative of the Group of Fighting Women in *Asahi Shinbun* on October 25, 1970, Tokyo morning edition, page 23.

was a medium for *ribu,* its *miko,* and its excess. She played the role of the charismatic authority figure.[18] Tanaka laid a cornerstone of the movement; however, the cornerstone was not laid through the strength of one woman but through the coming together and combined power of those hundreds of other women who came to identify with and as *ribu*. It was a mutual and dialectic process involving tension, struggle, desire, conflict, and contradiction.

Through this dialectic process, Tanaka's thoughts, words, and actions combined, collided, and synthesized with the energies and labor of many other women and became a mediating force of the movement.

Ribu's Charismatic Leader

Throughout the *ribu* movement, as well as in her later writings, Tanaka has maintained a contradictory style of self-identification that is at once emblematic of *ribu*'s antielitism and yet also sets her apart from other women.[19] In contrast with the majority of *ribu* women who were college educated, Tanaka's last level of formal education was public high school. After she graduated from Toshima Metropolitan High School in Tokyo, she went to work for about a year as a copywriter at an advertising company. After quitting her job because of a complicated affair with a male coworker, she worked some odd jobs and helped at her parents' restaurant until she began her *ribu*. Tanaka's family environment did not provide her with a leftist political education. Tanaka's parents were not part of a professional intellectual class. They were, as Tanaka insists, common *(futsū)* working people who ran a fish shop and later started a small restaurant. Tanaka deliberately emphasizes her class background as a means to critique what she regards to be the classism and elitist tendencies of many feminists in Japan and, by contrast, identifies herself as an intellectual who is "closer to the people."[20]

Although Tanaka has at times referred to herself as "closer to the people," taking a kind of antielitist stance, she also actively participated in her own iconization, which constitutes another significant tension in how Tanaka represents herself. In her writings, Tanaka has theorized many aspects of her past into a kind of personal legacy, contributing to her own iconography. For example, during the early 1980s, she gave a talk titled "The Time When I Was That Era."[21] Such a statement reveals Tanaka's recognition of her historical significance and her willingness to participate in her own reconstruction as the symbol of *ribu*.

In her second book, Tanaka republished her manifesto, "Liberation from the Toilet (rev.)." She introduces her manifesto saying,

> Humans are strange. Not having ever read a single book on women's liberation, suddenly one day, in one sitting, I wrote this thing called "Liberation from the Toilet." . . . Until then I was basically just chillin', helping out at my parents' restaurant, sweeping, wiping . . . you could say that I live listening to "voices from the heavens" so I don't worry too much about what I am doing. When I handed out this pamphlet, I could feel that I had grasped the spirit of the times.[22]

It is evident from this passage that Tanaka does not represent herself as a political activist prior to writing this pamphlet. What is notable here is that she refers to the "voices from the heavens." Commentators both within and outside the movement have characterized Tanaka as the charismatic figure of *ribu* at its outset (referring to her as the *"karizuma-teki sonzai"* and *"karizuma-sei"*). Tanaka's own forms of self-representation shore up Max Weber's classic definition of the charismatic leader as someone extraordinary and "otherworldly." To recall Weber's definition, the charismatic leader is "set apart . . . treated as endowed with supernatural, superhuman, or at least specifically exceptional powers or qualities" that are supposedly of "divine origin" or "exemplary."[23] Tanaka's own selection of otherworldly references shore up her charismatic identity and are also suggestive of the spiritualism that becomes more pronounced in her later writings. This explanation is also indicative of her diminished reliance on the language of the New Left and her minimal acknowledgment of her political work with others. Here she does not mention the leftist circles and the *ribu* women that were vital to her intellectual formation.[24] Such pronouncements invite critical attention by implying that she operates on a different dimension than others, and her role as a medium, *miko*, or shaman aligns with that of the charismatic authority figure.

During her midtwenties, Tanaka lived in the Hongo district of Tokyo, a stone's throw from the University of Tokyo. There she witnessed the symbolic victories of the student movement—when the students of Zenkyōtō took over the university—and its ensuing breakdown. During this time, she became involved in the anti–Vietnam War movement. She was a founder of a group called Sending Love to the Injured Orphans of the Vietnam War, which she started, she said, because she could identify with these injured orphans due to her childhood experience of sexual abuse.[25] She also became involved in the immigration law struggle *(Nyūkan tōsō)*. Through her involvement in various leftist circles, Tanaka became familiar with the political culture of the New Left. Tanaka educated herself through her interactions with other leftist intellectuals and activists such as Iijima Aiko, who started the group Asian Women against Discrimination as Aggression.[26] She familiarized herself with the leftist literature of the day, such as Karl Marx, Friedrich Engels, Jean Paul Sartre, and Wilhelm Reich. Tanaka's reading of Reich's *The Sexual Revolution* was pivotal in recasting her understanding of class exploitation and oppression. *The Sexual Revolution* is the one book that Tanaka explicitly advocated reading.[27]

Tanaka rarely mentions her intellectual sources, and when she does, it is often in the form of a joke. In one of her early manifestos, she writes, "Having read Marx, Engels and de Beauvoir, I now am left with a big wrinkle in my left brain."[28] To joke about and sarcastically mock the existing hierarchies within leftist intellectual culture was another characteristic of Tanaka's dexterous rhetorical style. Tanaka cites Marx, Lenin, Sartre, Reich, and Angela Davis. These names point to the four intellectual traditions that inform her theory of liberation: Marxism, existentialism, psychoanalysis, and black liberation thought.[29] Like many other radical feminist thinkers, Tanaka's relation to black liberation thought, Marxism, and the New Left provided the conceptual grounding that gave birth to *ribu*. Through a creative synthesis of these traditions, Tanaka forged her theory of the liberation of sex.

Tanaka and Her Original Écriture Féminine

Tanaka's speeches and writings were shocking, bold, and moving; they heralded a different kind of discourse. Akiyama states that Tanaka's was a new form of writing distinct from the agitation writings of the New Left at the time and from the extant theories of women's liberation. The "scream from the womb" and the "truth spoken from the vagina" were examples of the powerful and unsettling way Tanaka expressed the body in language, in ways that had rarely before been expressed as part of leftist political culture. Her rhetorical flare and poetic creativity made her a powerful figure in the movement. Fujieda Mioko has said that Tanaka's works are near impossible to translate, her meaning difficult to grasp. Other women in the movement refer to her writing and speaking style as difficult at times to comprehend. Her writing often has a chaotic quality; her sentences are sometimes ungrammatical, flowing in multiple directions, involving an almost schizophrenic variety of tones. In Japanese, it can be said to constitute a new form of *onna kotoba* (woman's language/langue de femme), or what in other Euro-American contexts has become known as écriture féminine.[30]

In her nuanced essay "Feminism and Tanaka Mitsu: The Body, Eros and Écriture Féminine," Kanai Yoshiko points to the connection between écriture féminine and Tanaka.[31] Écriture féminine—a form of writing through and of the body—is commonly thought to be French in origin, beginning in the mid-1970s with Hélène Cixous's seminal essays "The Laugh of the Medusa" and "Sorties" from *La Jeune Née* (1975) (translated as *The Newly Born Woman* [1986]).[32] However, Tanaka and other *ribu* women could be said to be its forerunners, albeit in a different context.

Tanaka and the other women of *ribu* spoke the forbidden. Tanaka's writings heralded a political voice from places hitherto unheard, declaring that her voice spoke from "the dark place of the womb" and brought forth messages about the "blood of children who were killed by their mothers."[33] Tanaka thus functioned as a medium (or shamanlike figure), ventriloquizing messages from those who could not speak. By speaking of woman's sex, her vagina, her sexual desires, her longings, and the fluidity of her erotic sensuality from the subjective perspective of *onna*, this pouring forth was a watershed. This writing of the feminine, her body, her sex, as the repressed and oppressed aimed to speak of the other, expressing the *eros* of the feminine. Although these forbidden zones had previously been explored in literature (notably by writers such as Morizaki Kazue, among others), Tanaka's discourse placed these terms at the front of a new political movement.[34]

In her first book, *To Women with Spirit: A Disorderly Theory of Ūman Ribu (Inochi no onna-tachi e: torimidashi ūman ribu ron),* for example, she begins the chapter "The New Left and *Ribu*" by infusing her bodily response and the onset of the flow of her menstrual blood into her political discourse.[35] When she writes about hearing the news of the political violence in the United Red Army (URA), she says that the combined effects of the "psychological shock and her menstrual cramps" knocked her down so she could not write.[36] She dared to compare the masculinism of dominant capitalist society to that of the culture of the New Left, stating, "Whether it is the logic of the productivity of revolution, or the corporate logic of productivity—they equally abhor woman's menstruation."[37] Tanaka's ability to speak in relation to existing political discourses enabled *ribu* to derive its politicality and relevance. Suddenly, a voice who referred to herself as *onna* began sarcastically questioning and exposing the shortcomings of Marxism. In a voice full of insolence and irreverent laughter, she mocked the notion that women would be liberated after a socialist revolution. She frequently referred to the "impotence" of the men of the left, explicitly referencing the gendered and sexualized economies that were not deemed a significant part of the left's political dynamic. In "Liberation from the Toilet," she refers to the dominant system that renders women's sexual function into "toilets" for men whose sexuality is also reduced to "excrement."[38] Her irreverence extended as well to the activists of the former women's liberation movements, whom she describes as "scrawny, unattractive ugly ducklings."[39] She critiques these former women activists, saying, "The kind of hysterical unattractiveness of the women's liberation movements since the Meiji period [1868–1912] was due to the fact that, in order for women to be liberated as women, it was historically necessary for women to go through the process of becoming men."[40] In line with Weber's notion of charismatic authority, Tanaka "repudiates the past" women's liberation movement.[41] It was the penetrating tone and content of this *onna*'s speech that reveals an intimate but critical relation to Marxism, the New Left, and the existing women's movements, positioning *ribu* as a critical extension of these political genealogies.

The Demon Child of the New Left

Tanaka refers to herself as a descendant of the New Left. She calls *ribu* the demon child *(onigo)* of the New Left. It was in the midst of the violent internecine battles of the New Left that Tanaka conceived of her political philosophy. Along with many other women who experienced firsthand the blatant masculinism of the New Left, Tanaka recalls attending New Left meetings where she could "smell the hypocrisy" of the men who posed as revolutionaries by putting up the facade *(tatemae)* of their impressive-sounding revolutionary theories.

> Women have been suppressed while bearing the unspoken forms of violence by [leftist] men, taking on the vast portion of the burden of the banal work that remains unseen like the mountain beneath its snow covered surface . . . raising money for those men who are supposedly revolutionaries, doing house work, raising children, and doing laundry and so on . . . it has been the men's struggle and their theory that has formed the outer coating of this snow covered mountain, the visible part, exhibited on the stage for all to see. . . . When the men were waxing eloquent about international proletarianism . . . the women sensed deceit in the air; they could smell the lie of the men's posturing.[42]

Tanaka called the New Left her *han-men kyōshi*—her teacher of what not to do. In the preceding passage, Tanaka criticizes what she saw as the male centered *(dansei-chūshin)* modality of the New Left that not only was evident in the sexist division of labor but permeated the very understanding of revolution itself.[43] Tanaka wrote, "The 'politics' of today's New Left is such that only its words and theories advance, which are cut off from the practice of daily living."[44]

Alongside many other *ribu* women, Tanaka explicated and argued how the family *(ie)* system was a microcosm of the nationalist-imperialist system.[45] This critique constituted a fundamental element of *ribu*'s politics and encapsulated *ribu*'s critique of the imbrication of gender and Japanese imperialism. Despite the general anti-imperialism of the Japanese left, the majority of men and many women failed to reject or even have a critique the family system. In her critique of the New Left, Tanaka points to its failure to have a theory of the sexes.

> Even in movements that are aiming towards human liberation, by not
> having a theory of struggle that includes the relation between the sexes,
> the struggle becomes thoroughly masculinist and male-centered *(dansei-chūshin shugi)*.[46]

In Tanaka's eyes, the New Left had become caught up in the dominant logic
of production and too exclusively preoccupied with opposition to state power.
Tanaka rejected the notion that revolutionary politics could and should be
confined to symbolic opposition to state power as the preeminent strategy
to bring about the revolution. According to Tanaka, the New Left failed to
account for the way revolution was being defined from a man's viewpoint. In
this connection, Tanaka insisted that the "liberation of *onna*" could not and
should not be subsumed under what men had defined as "human liberation."

> Even though women themselves somehow sensed that the emancipation of
> human beings sounded vain and without substance . . . they did not pay
> attention to the fissure or cleavage that existed between "the fact of being
> *onna*" (woman) and "revolution."[47]

It was because of this fissure or cleavage Tanaka sensed, and the dissonance it
produced for her, that she found it necessary to insist on a new understanding
of revolution. It was between the interstices of this fissure that Tanaka began
to speak of a new kind of liberation that brought together the terms "revolution" and *"onna"* and "liberation" and "sex."

Tanaka's Theory of the Liberation of Sex

Tanaka was prolific during the 1970s, and she has produced a corpus of writings that remains as a record of her philosophy of liberation. Her writings
have been an organic part of her political practice and constitute the thread
that weaves together her involvement in the movement, her iconization, and
her contribution as a feminist philosopher. For Tanaka, sex was a key concept
not only for women's liberation but for human liberation. Wilhelm Reich's
The Sexual Revolution figured significantly in Tanaka's conception of sex
and sexuality in relation to politics.[48] Tanaka's earliest manifestos contained
what became the key terms of the *ribu* movement: sex, *onna*, eros, and relationality. Among Tanaka's hundreds of pages of pamphlets and essays, three
of her manifestos written between June and October 1970 clearly map out
her argument for the liberation of sex: "The Declaration of the Liberation
of Eros" (June 1970),[49] "Liberation from the Toilet" (original, August 1970;

revised, October 1970),[50] and "Why Sexual Liberation? Raising the Problem of Women's Liberation" (September 1970).[51]

Tanaka's understanding of the liberation of sex entailed a complex and expansive theoretical schematic. Like many other radical feminists, Tanaka used the Marxist notion of class oppression and exploitation as a heuristic device to analyze sex. By theorizing sex as class, she adapted a Marxist notion and made a critical shift by stating that a primary axis of oppression from *onna*'s perspective was none other than sex itself.[52] In a deliberately jestful manner, Tanaka began one of her earliest manifestos, "Why Sexual Liberation?," by mimicking Marx's famous opening passage from the Communist Manifesto, "For women, the history of the oppressor and the oppressed has been none other than a history of misery inflicted on women's sex."[53] Tanaka thus made a critical revision to Marxism not only by arguing for a materialist analysis of sex as class but also by making a fundamental move from a politics based on class exploitation to theorizing sex as the fundamental determinant of power relations. Insofar as sex became a corrective to the existing dominance of class as the primary category of analysis, *ūman ribu* did not attend to race and ethnicity as a determinant of power, which was also indicative of an absence of a racial analysis in the intellectual culture of the Japanese left.

Tanaka's notion of sex *(sei)* was not simply equivalent to an English definition of sex, referring to the sexual difference between females and males, sexuality, or sex acts. She theorized sex in a more specific and expansive sense. For Tanaka, sex was multivalent. Sex was not only a socially constructed category that functioned as a class, but it was also at the core of a repressed ontology that constituted a contradictory and potentially liberating force (following Reich's theory). Tanaka asserted that women's sex was the target of oppression and also held within it a key to emancipation as a potentially liberating and violent force. Tanaka (re)conceived the abject condition of women's sex as "hiding within it essentially anarchistic tendencies" and therefore saw women's position in the social matrix as potentially radical.[54] By summoning women to reassess their sex as something that could essentially be subversive to the social order, Tanaka was suggesting that sex was an inherent power that they could use as a revolutionary force.[55] Because of women's role in reproducing the system, they could either maintain or radically transform it.[56]

Although sex and sexed relations appear to be the core or the nucleus of her argument, Tanaka argued that sex is only a part of the "Totality" *(zentaisei)*. The Totality, for Tanaka, referred to the system, that is, the modern capitalist-imperialist state and authoritarianism. Tanaka's critique located the roots of oppression not in a static notion of sex but in the dynamic and contradictory relationality of the Totality of the system. Sex was one part of the dynamic relationality of the Totality. Tanaka's theory of liberation was concerned with the tension between the part and the Totality and how women's liberation figured in this tension.[57] In the following quote, we can see how Tanaka conceives and situates her notion of the liberation of women in the tension *between* the part and the Totality.

> Based on the fact that we will achieve the liberation of *onna* as a proletarian liberation, as we head toward world revolution we must deepen our struggle against authority. As for the struggle against authority, which is a Totality due to its inherent globality *(sekai-sei)* and universality, our relations with men make up part of that Totality. Even though it is a part of the Totality, it is thrown aside as a part, and rather than only measuring subjective formation against the struggle against authority=Totality, women have to form their own subjectivity in the midst of the tensions of the relation between the part and the Totality. In the midst of the tense relations of our struggle against authority, without continually questioning what it means to be an *onna* and the way that we individually relate to man, child, and the family, and the contradictions inherent to these relations, we will not be able to grasp the means by which to universalize what it means to be human.[58]

Tanaka's attention to the philosophical question of what it meant to be an *onna* remains in tension with the struggle against the Totality. Tanaka was concerned with the gendered constitution of the subject in the system, and her philosophy of the liberation of sex was a means to point out the relationality of sex within the Totality of the system.

As a version of radical feminism, *ribu* sought a total revolution of cultural values that would enable a different kind of relationality, which it saw as the goal of human liberation. In the original version of the "Liberation from the Toilet," Tanaka writes, "What is important for women (and for men as well) is not to seek power as such, but to live as an *onna,* which means to live as a human. The struggle for power is no more than a means to that end."[59] By clearly differentiating between struggle for power as a temporary process and the eventual goal, which was for human liberation, this distinction significantly altered and shaped the form of *ribu*'s struggles. Rather than thinking of women's rights as separate and against the rights of others, Tanaka conceived of *ribu* in relation to other struggles against domination. Tanaka emphasized that women's liberation must be part of a universal and global struggle against authority, for if it failed to become a part of this universal struggle, then it would become nothing more than a struggle for a particular group of "women's rights in contest against the rights of other oppressed peoples." Such a narrow struggle was then in danger of becoming nothing more than what she saw as the American women's liberation movement, which she called a "nationalistic form of women's rights."[60] This is what she saw as the problem of liberal feminism. Tanaka's *ribu,* like other forms of radical feminism, can be understood as a critique of liberal feminism. In her original version of "Liberation from the Toilet," Tanaka made a jab toward what she understood as the U.S.-based women's liberation movement. Although Tanaka was not aware of the multitude of feminist positions that comprised American women's lib, she describes it as a copycat version of Japan's first wave, given its central concern with women's "equal rights."[61] Rather than looking to what she referred to as the U.S. women's lib movement for direction, Tanaka rebukes it for being shortsighted, arguing that altering relations with men offers only a partial answer to more far-reaching problems. Although *ribu* struggled against sex discrimination, unlike liberal feminism, equality with men was not the aim of the movement. Tanaka argued that insofar as *ribu* was a part of a universal and global struggle against authority, its goal was not to increase Japanese women's power and authority over others but to transform the ideologies that structure social relations.

Tanaka's theory of liberation refrained from determining in advance an agenda for *ribu* or what the revolution should look like. She insisted that "women's theory" *(onna no ronri)* itself required a protracted period of time before it would arrive at any clear-cut conclusions.

> In contrast to men's arrogance about the rationale of their theory, with its immediate efficacy, and the simplicity of planned results that can be calculated in one's head, women's theory is such that it requires an unhurried process before it can produce its results.[62]

Rather than deciding for women what they should prioritize or how they should live, Tanaka's theory of liberation circles back to the self, emphasizing the creation of one's own practice of liberation and the open-endedness of what women may become in the future. While this open-endedness was a response to the rigidity of leftist orthodoxies, it would entail its own difficulties and problems in the context of sustaining a collective movement.

Internal Differences and Criticisms

Throughout *ribu*'s history, there were conflicts and disputes about what emphasis and direction the movement should take and who and what qualifies as *ribu*. Differences existed among the women in terms of their involvement and their ability to communicate their views and their desire to change society. And there were, of course, expectations, desires, disappointments, and power struggles among the women of the movement. The most significant power struggles within *ribu* were over the focus and direction of the movement, and Tanaka's involvement in many of these struggles consequently shaped *ribu*'s historical trajectory. As a speaker, Tanaka's determination to express her own views combined with her rhetorical abilities, which enabled her to dominate debates; she commanded the attention of some and drew criticism from others. Because there was no formal hierarchy, and *ribu* events and meetings were often open-ended, the women with the most persuasive arguments and strongest personalities often dominated debates.

From the early days of *ribu*, many women were drawn to and moved by Tanaka. Depending on their expectations, desires, and projections, women responded differently to her. Some were enamored by her. Takeda Miyuki, another highly visible woman in the movement, states, "We adored her, we were all enamored with her."[63] But for others who lived with her, she was a source of pain and trauma by whom they felt dominated.[64] As a highly visible and vocal figure, Tanaka also became an object of criticism. Tanaka's leadership style, manner of expression, powerful personality, and political priorities were criticized by other *ribu* women.

There are several published records of women complaining about what they experienced as Tanaka's domineering manner and overbearing presence. When women from across Japan gathered in Nagano for the *ribu* summer camp *(gasshuku)* in August 1971, some criticized Tanaka in their reports about the event. Many perceived Tanaka to be the leader of the Group of Fighting Women. For example, in a report from a group called Ribu Fukuoka (from the southwestern part of Japan), a member singles out Tanaka, describing her as the "de facto leader of the Group of Fighting Women," who wouldn't stop talking at the *ribu* camp. The same report describes Tanaka as the "representative" of the organizers of the *ribu* camp and criticizes her for not responding to more concrete issues and going on endlessly about abstract existentialist questions.[65] Although many women were moved and inspired by what she had to say, some women felt strongly that Tanaka's discourse was too obtuse and abstract.[66] There were similar complaints about Tanaka at the May 1972 Ribu Conference (Ribu Taikai) in Tokyo. In a *ribu* newsletter, *Onna's Mutiny* (*Onna no hangyaku*, August 26, 1972), a woman who attended the Ribu Conference criticizes Tanaka:

> As usual, she was using her difficult expressions and speaking so fast that
> I couldn't even take notes. If I had asked all those who understood what

she was saying to raise their hands, I wonder if even a third of the audience would have raised their hands.[67]

Tanaka's dominance was thus resisted and criticized by other women in the movement, but it was never fundamentally displaced or completely negated. Some *ribu* women were critical of Tanaka's role but not hostile enough to organize against her or attempt to delegitimize her leadership.

Although autonomy was valued, *ribu* activists debated about who and what constituted the legitimate or authentic *ribu*. Tanaka publicly debated others, like Enoki Misako, the leader of Chūpiren, making clear distinctions about what she believed should constitute the politics of *ribu* and how groups such as Chūpiren did not, in her opinion, qualify as *ribu*.[68] Such debates to define what constituted *ribu*'s core political issues bore the traces of the exclusionary effects resulting from defining a radical position and stance. Forming one's ideology or principles of membership can be a necessarily exclusionary process; however, the priority to attract more potential participants was in dynamic tension with the process of defining the "correct" political analysis. The political subculture of *ribu* groups would therefore differ depending on what priorities and personalities were central.[69]

As the movement unfolded from 1970 onward, it was Tanaka's version of *ribu* that became hegemonic.[70] Insofar as Tanaka's political vision provided a theoretical schematic for the movement, the criticisms of Tanaka's political vision were relevant to the movement. These criticisms of *ribu* had to do with Tanaka's and *ribu*'s emphasis on sex and her insistence that each woman's liberation ultimately had to be a *personal struggle* against the system and her own contradictory self. Tanaka emphasized that liberation must begin with the immediate state of one's own contradiction:

> As for our struggle as women, it does not begin with being a "perfect revolutionary woman," who in fact exists nowhere, but it begins with the me here, with all the contradictions, and the contradictions that defy reason, that is the here-existing *onna (koko ni iru onna)*.[71]

What characterized Tanaka's theory of liberation was the nonexclusion of contradiction; contradiction was not only the inevitable and necessary point of departure but the perpetual condition of the struggle for liberation.

After witnessing firsthand the self-destructive masculinization of the New Left, Tanaka believed that women had no choice but to take their liberation into their own hands. At the beginning of the movement, Tanaka turned her own six-mat apartment in the Hongo district into one of the first spaces in Tokyo for women in the movement to gather, organize, and live.[72] Tanaka and a handful of women from the Group of Fighting Women, such as Asakawa

Mariko and Machino Michiko, began an urban commune in January 1971 called the Medaka Collective (Piranha Collective). Having run away from home at the age of nineteen, Sayama Sachi joined the Group of Fighting Women collective in May 1971.[73] The collective was said to be a space for the "daily creation of a revolutionary subject . . . to see to what extent each person could practically experience the benefits of communistic social relations."[74] Many of these women went on to live and work at the Ribu Shinjuku Center.[75]

One of the tensions within the movement was between its heterodominance and its *onna*-centered principles. Although Tanaka wrote and spoke of eros between women, one of the major limitations in Tanaka's theory of the liberation of sex was her investment in a heterosexual logic.[76] As a woman who identified explicitly as heterosexual, Tanaka was concerned with transforming sexual relations with men. In her famous manifesto "Liberation from the Toilet," Tanaka foregrounds heterosexual desire as natural, referring to the "totally natural desire" of a fifteen-year-old boy to want to "fulfill himself in body and soul" with a fifteen-year-old girl.[77] Her manifestos argued for the naturalness of heterosexual love and desire, which had been repressed by the current system.[78] She did not espouse lesbianism as a radical alternative to the force of compulsory heterosexuality, which for some radical feminists was the logical outcome of a woman-centered existence.[79] In the absence of a principled lesbian-positive practice or a discourse that theorized the potential radicality of lesbian love, a heterodominance prevailed in the movement.[80] Moreover, the periodic homophobia expressed within *ribu* spaces—which lacked an adequate degree of intervention and critique— caused some lesbian-identified women to withdraw from the movement.[81]

If these were some of the negative contradictions of the movement, they must be understood in tension with how several of the forerunners of lesbian activism (Wakabayashi Naeko and Asatori Sumie) were also part of the *ribu* movement even though they did not identify as lesbians when they first began organizing as *ribu* activists in the early 1970s. Yonezu Tomoko stated that another characteristic of the movement was that "many *ribu* women could immediately understand same-sex love *(dosei ai)* and went beyond making gestures toward the inclusion of lesbian women by becoming lesbians themselves."[82]

Lesbian voices and perspectives on women's liberation began to emerge in *ribu* publications in the early 1970s. For example, the inaugural edition of Gurūpu Kan's (グループ姦) bulletin, published in 1973, includes what approximates a lesbian manifesto.[83] The author, Fuyumi, argues from the perspective of "a woman who loves women," protesting how "same-sex love" is considered a sickness or perversion *(hentai)*. She calls for women to unite and fight the legal restrictions on abortion for how they obstruct love between women. The earliest editions of *Onna Erosu,* volumes 2 and 3, published Amano Michimi's translations of the sections about lesbian sexuality from *Our Bodies, Ourselves* and Matsumoto Michiko's photographs of lesbian couples in New York City.[84] Many seeds of lesbian activism were thus planted during the *ribu* movement and would eventually become a distinct lesbian movement.

Conflict at the Commune

Tanaka's presence was a significant factor that brought attention to the Ribu Shinjuku Center and had distinct ramifications for the power dynamics of the women who worked and lived there. The women of the Shinjuku Center sought to create a collective that was nonhierarchical; however, it was undeniable that the women did not have equal strengths, skills, or experiences. At age twenty-nine, Tanaka was the eldest of those living at this collective. Most of the other women were in their late teens to their early twenties. Tanaka also had more work experience than most of the other women. Before the Shinjuku Center opened, she already had established a network with select media reporters and had published articles in a variety of magazines, such as *Shisō no kagaku, Gendai no me,* and *Josei Jishin.* Earlier that year, she had published her book *To Women with Spirit,* which was read by most *ribu* women and has since been called the classic book of the movement.[85] It was advertised and sold at the May 1972 Ribu Conference. Given her appearances in the mass media and that she was one of the few published writers of the movement, she had already gained a name for herself at the outset of the movement. Thus, even before the Shinjuku Center was established in September 1972, Tanaka was not in an equal position vis-à-vis the other women.

When the Shinjuku Center opened, Tanaka already could state her position clearly. She published an article in the inaugural issue of *Ribu News* called "To Theorize the Ribu Center."[86] The Ribu Shinjuku Center was, for Tanaka, intended to be an experimental place to forge a new kind of relationality between women that would be predicated on the attempted negation of the logic of productivity, private property, and hierarchical organization. Yet insofar as these ideologies had already been instilled into the bodies and consciousness of these women, Tanaka never believed they would achieve their total eradication, nor was their total eradication the aim of *ribu*—the point was to struggle to articulate and bring into being different ontological principles. Before the Shinjuku Center opened, Tanaka writes,

No matter what you say, there is no way that the collective will ever be a
utopia. There is no reason why it could ever be . . . it's an experiment.
The collective is not simply a space where we share our material belongings, its a name for what we call the relationality *(kankeisei)* that we *onna*
comrades create on a daily basis between us.[87]

This statement points to how Tanaka sees the commune as a new kind of
relationality between *onna,* knowing from the outset that utopia was not
going to be found in these experimental conditions. Although forging a new
relationality between *onna* was fundamental to the practice of *ribu,* from the
outset Tanaka did not believe this new relationality would ever be outside
power, conflict, and misrecognitions. She writes,

The Ribu Center is not a place where *onna* comrades get together to sit
around smiling at each other, rather, our Ribu Center is, to the very end,
a place where the self of each *onna* draws out her life *(inochi)* from herself,
as the life force and life force of each *onna* encounter each other. . . . Of
course, as long as this world is our world, there is no way to exist outside
the relations of power and authority *(kenryoku)*.[88]

The Ribu Center was to be a place where *onna* would struggle together toward creating a different kind of relationality that was at odds with dominant
society. Tanaka spoke of living in the collective with other *onna* as a way to
see the self and to see how *onna* is reflected in the lives of the other; she spoke
of the other as a mirror of *onna* and oneself. The encounter *(deai)* with the
other *onna* would inevitably involve conflict and confrontation *(taiketsu),*
and for Tanaka, this ability to confront herself through the other was integral
to the practice of *ribu.* However, precisely because the women were not confronting each other outside a grid of already established power differences,
the consequences of these conflicts and confrontations affected the women
differently. The commune could not be a blank tabula rasa because it was a
communal site for the overflow, residue, and traumas of all the women coming together and colliding even as they tried to live and work, think and love
differently.

Hierarchy at the Ribu Shinjuku Center

According to Wakabayashi Naeko, a veteran *ribu* activist (who would later
become a lesbian activist), Tanaka became the main spokeswoman for the
Shinjuku Center.[89] Even though there was no formally recognized representative, Tanaka acted most often in this capacity.[90] Although Tanaka was
under various kinds of pressure, as a highly performative character, she was

not averse to being on stage or to being the focus of attention.[91] Her eloquent, witty, and sharp verbal abilities made her effective. Moreover, no other woman within the movement or at the Shinjuku Center effectively challenged Tanaka's role. Although Tanaka initially started working as a hostess (in the sex-entertainment industry) for several months, she quit after a short time and earned money by working as a writer.[92] According to Machino Michiko, monetarily speaking, Tanaka contributed to the center by working as a writer, and the rest of the women did more "physical labor" *(nikutai rōdo)*.[93]

Although the division of labor at the Shinjuku Center was done on a volunteer basis, other women's labor—whether cooking and cleaning or working the printing presses like Mori Setsuko—did not gain as much social recognition as Tanaka's work as a writer and speaker.[94] The combination of her visibility, authority, and influence was exceptional. The women did, however, resist seeing Tanaka's work as a writer as more important than their own and struggled against the way outsiders evaluated their division of labor. For example, Mori states,

> I felt that there was not anything so great about writing, that was her responsibility, it was her job *(buntan)* to do that work . . . we should have just recognized our different abilities and our different personalities.[95]

As discussed in chapter 3, Mori was a pioneering activist in Thought Group SEX. During the first decade of *ribu,* her role running the presses was pivotal in ensuring the legibility of *ribu,* and her design work greatly enhanced the aesthetic appeal of *ribu* publications. However, her role and labor in the movement was certainly not as visible as Tanaka's or Yonezu Tomoko's.[96] Yet, insofar as Mori's labor was also crucial for *ribu*'s legibility, she acted as a vital medium of the movement in the same way that the labor of Miki, Saeki, Mizoguchi, Kuno Ayako, and countless others have made *ribu* legible through history by their less visible labors.

In spite of how the women at the center struggled against the dominant ideologies that they had internalized, given that the women were constantly being reminded of how outsiders assessed the collective in hierarchical terms, it was difficult not to reproduce and experience a hierarchized sense of who was running the center and whose labor was being recognized and valued. Yonezu rightly states, "There was a kind of reproduction taking place that was beyond us, no matter even if we thought differently about it."[97]

Rather than working toward a different notion of hierarchy or difference, the antihierarchical stance itself proved to be a conceptual knot, a double bind that produced expectations among the women that would never be fulfilled. The expectations that the relations between the *onna* comrades could be nonhierarchical amid their intense living conditions set the women up for greater disappointments, anger, hurt, and resentment. The attempt to live according to an antihierarchical oppositional consciousness produced various points of collision at the center. In the midst of their struggles and conflicts with each other, their attempt to re-create nonhierarchized relations proved to be a Sisyphean task.

Although the women sensed the contradictions among themselves, and they began to try to remedy them by discussing the need to reduce the center's activities in 1974 to work on their interpersonal relations, by 1975, many women were exhausted.[98] During this politically volatile period, and given all the pressures the women faced on a daily basis, those working at the Shinjuku Center were unable to prioritize working out the problematic dynamics between them. Instead, the emphasis was directed toward political organizing, protesting the government's reactionary initiatives, and battling the system simultaneously on multiple fronts. Because of their overextended commitments and the manifold pressures of daily living, their limited energies were not directed toward developing alternative models of leadership or more acceptable hierarchies for the movement. Thus, rather than establishing a new means of achieving collective leadership and collective decision making, the women were not prepared to confront Tanaka's authority and were left to extemporaneously resist, deny, and conceal the emergent hierarchy.[99] After Tanaka's departure from the center, the women were able to begin talking about and analyzing why the power relations had become so unbalanced and unhealthy.[100]

The reemergence of hierarchy and power differences within leftist organizations is common, and yet what often is lacking (and remains underexplored) are effective practices to address and work through interpersonal friction and conflict, especially as it intertwines and meshes with political differences. A concerted effort to collectively decide what principles and values should determine courses of action, how resources should be allocated, and what terms should apply to responsibility and decision making is typically a time-consuming and difficult process that at times fails. Such nonguaranteed conditions are part of the experimental, unprescribed, and arduous process of creating an alternative and sustainable subculture.

Unfulfilled Ideals

Even though equality was never one of *ribu*'s key concepts, nor was it necessarily one of *ribu*'s fundamental organizing tenets,[101] this political ideal came back to haunt the activists who lived and worked at the Shinjuku Center. In the center's antihierarchical model of organization, equality was presumed to be an unspoken ideal and outcome, but it was not guaranteed. Equality among women at the Shinjuku Center became an unfulfilled and elusive ideal. This dynamic and expectation is apparent in Mori's critique of Tanaka: "I could not have an equal relationship with [Tanaka] Mitsu-san, it felt to me that she was not invested in creating one."[102] Mori's statement indicates that her problem with Tanaka extended beyond their division of labor or external recognition. Mori felt that Tanaka was not committed to creating equal relations with the other women.[103] Although creating equality among the women was not the stated goal of the collective, the desire for equality inevitably reemerged as an impossible ideal; equality became a residual value that mediated these relationships, the absent thing for which the women yearned. In spite of her ability to speak eloquently of the collisions and conflicts among *onna* comrades as an inevitable part of a process of establishing a new subjectivity, Tanaka's unequal power vis-à-vis the other women was not addressed sufficiently. Instead, Tanaka also seemingly succumbed to the seduction of the ideal of equality among the women, expecting and longing for the other women to be her equal. Yonezu states, "Tanaka was constantly disappointed in us, because she wanted us to live up to her expectations, she wanted us to be her equal." But, for Yonezu, "Tanaka was an overwhelmingly powerful person, and even though I kept thinking that I wanted to become equal with Tanaka, no matter how much I tried to extend and exert myself, I felt that I could not reach her level."[104] Tanaka's own reflections indicate a similar mistaken expectation of herself and the other women, stating that she too overemphasized equality. One of the ways she expressed this desire was to want all the women to write as an expression of their political practice. Due to this unrecognized and underarticulated idealization of equality, and the value placed on the practice of writing, Tanaka encouraged other women to write, saying that "they could do this kind of work as well."[105] Some women, like Wakabayashi Naeko, perceived this as an encouragement, but other women took it to mean they should become like Tanaka.[106] In this instance, equality became synonymous with sameness, and difference became a marker of unequal power.

Although there were many university-educated women who had produced their own alternative media publications before joining the Shinjuku Center and were polished and competent writers, Tanaka took it upon herself to edit other women's writing. Even though she was not the designated leader as such, in her capacities as writer and editor, Tanaka exerted her views, and her editorial interventions were clearly an example of her power to shape the discourse of the movement.[107] By editing other women's writing, she became an unnamed cowriter on behalf of other women, and this was clearly a way that Tanaka's own political vision could be inserted and overlaid through the writing of other women.[108] Her labor as an editor was one more means by which Tanaka's views gained hegemony within the movement, and thus the relative coherence of *ribu*'s discourse can in part be seen as an effect of Tanaka's relative power within the movement.

Tanaka took upon herself a sense of responsibility for how the movement was represented and perceived. She felt responsible for what others wrote, especially when other women were writing on behalf of the Group of Fighting Women or the Ribu Shinjuku Center. While it was understandable that Tanaka was concerned with the reputation of *ribu*, other women have commented on Tanaka's role at the center, saying, "She tried too hard, and she outdid herself" *(ganbari sugita)*. As ironic as it may seem, it was precisely Tanaka's all-consuming conviction about the "correctness" of her position and her destructive and reconstructive power and drive that propelled the movement forward in its incipient years. Were she a less powerful or determinative personality, the movement would not have been so deeply imprinted by Tanaka's views.[109] Consequently, her passion and militancy were directed not only toward those perceived "enemies of *ribu*" but also, at times, toward other *ribu* women.

Tanaka's Vexed Position as Leader

The women at the Shinjuku Center were unable to address adequately their power dynamics, and Tanaka was also ambivalent about her leadership function. Consequently, Tanaka was uneasy, frustrated, and inconsistent in how she dealt with her position of power. On the one hand, she states that she resisted and struggled against acting as the leader because she felt there should be no one leader of the movement. To have a leader was a contradiction of Tanaka's philosophy of liberation. Nevertheless, her own actions signaled her shifting desire to be recognized as the representative of *ribu* and, at other times, to be free of that responsibility and accountability to other *ribu* women. Her central involvement in organizing and defining the movement from its outset, her writing practice and its impact, and her actions at the Shinjuku Center combined to make her into a de facto leader without bearing an official title in the movement.

Without a doubt, many women looked to Tanaka for leadership, but at times Tanaka sought to share decision making and tried to push responsibility onto the other women. Tanaka's resistance and periodic refusal to take leadership also angered and disappointed women. Some *ribu* women mention stories of Tanaka leaving in the middle of a rally because of her frustration that so many women were relying on her to make the decisions. At these moments, leaving the rallies was Tanaka's way of refusing to be the leader and refusing the responsibility to make the decisions, but other women could not understand her abrupt and seemingly irresponsible actions. Many *ribu* women have attested that much of Tanaka's exhaustion and her eventual withdrawal from the center stems, in part, from sensing that some women relied on her to be the leader when Tanaka knew that she should not fulfill this role. As Tanaka has said, she felt that at times she was playing the role of "the man." This was a striking contradiction in light of the struggle to create an *onna*-centered collective and movement. At times, Tanaka became angry and yelled at the other women, but not all of the women could yell back or desired to engage in such confrontational forms of communication. In her book, Tanaka writes about how she even hit Sayama Sachi, a member of the Medaka (Piranha) Collective, for mistakenly leaving the gas burner running unattended.[110] Tanaka includes this incident to represent the "disorder and chaos" of their struggles and conflicts and the *imperfect* conditions of their collective. However, it was Tanaka, not Sachi, who was able to publish her perspective of this incident as part of a narrative that has become canonized as the monumental text of the movement. The power of Tanaka's message cuts many ways. To include this incident testifies to the mistakes made within the collective, which were at once mundane and dangerous (leaving on the gas burner) and in some cases personally harmful, as this incident was to Sachi both in the moment and for her body-memory in the aftermath, further accentuating the power difference between her and Tanaka. This anecdote functions as a multivalent form of transgression by revealing to the public the wrongs done in times of pressure and also provides an opportunity to further examine such dynamics. This form of accounting reveals that Tanaka is able to speak of her own contradictions on her terms and provide lessons about the forms of violence that erupt between feminist activists.

By 1974, the pressures of operating the center were taking its toll on the women and their interpersonal relationships. They began to talk of changing the structure of the center, and about this time, Tanaka also began discussing leaving the center and Japan. In 1975, Tanaka, along with Takeda Miyuki and Wakabayashi Naeko, left Tokyo to travel to the United States. Once in the United States, they decided to go to Mexico to attend the United Nations' Conference for the International Year of the Woman in Mexico City.[111] As the women at the Ribu Shinjuku Center discussed Tanaka's imminent departure, Tanaka gave directives about how she thought the center should be run. Even though some members of the center thought it was not right that Tanaka was giving orders if she was leaving, they could not, at that time, speak back to her authority. The women who remained at the center felt Tanaka's departure had left them with a heavy burden to bear, given its breadth of activities and the financial responsibilities accrued in opening and running the center. After Tanaka left, they changed how they ran the center, limiting its hours of operation so it was no longer open twenty-four hours a day.

Even after her departure, Tanaka continued to express her opinions on how she thought the center should be run by writing letters from Mexico, where she resided until 1979.[112] The women who remained at the center were hardly pleased with Tanaka's attempt to direct its activities even though she was not there to perform the labor. Such clashes occurred, however, because they were never able to work out what Tanaka's authority at the center ought to be.[113] Because of the exceptional circumstances of the Shinjuku Center, the women were unable to work through how the new hierarchy represented a set of values that resembled what was common to the subculture of the New Left.[114] This inability to deal openly with power relations is also common in other liberal, progressive feminist organizations. What was lacking was a political discourse and the analytical tools to deal with these power differences and reemergent hierarchies. Because there was no established route by which *onna* was supposed to achieve her liberation, this experimental practice of communal living would reveal how a woman's desire and struggle for liberation could often clash with and hurt the other.[115] It also revealed the need for a continual debate about the relationship between the collective struggle and the subjective *onna* and how the liberation of an individual *onna* would inevitably come into conflict and might supersede the priority to work toward collective liberation. Even decades later, Tanaka would often avert critique and accountability for her actions toward other *ribu* women, using her adept skills of argumentation and publicly stating that she simply was not "the type of person" who should form groups or could deal with "collective" living.[116] Also lacking was a form or practice of accountability and a commitment for further communication when *ribu* women felt harmed or hurt by their interpersonal interactions. This inability to move beyond hurt, defensiveness, and judgment is not unique to *ribu* movement dynamics but an endemic problem of interpersonal communication and relations.

As stated in chapter 3, *ribu*'s dynamic was founded on a fundamental contradiction involving the creation of a collective subjectivity that would affirm and value self-determination and autonomy while seeking to transform the self and the self's relationship with the other. The fundamental tension between the liberation of the self and the liberation of the collective could not be resolved but rather constituted the very conditions of possibility for liberation that was essentially defined as perpetual struggle in and from a site saturated with contradiction. Given how contradiction and anarchist principles were at the heart of Tanaka's theory of the liberation of sex, it is not surprising that they manifested in her style of organizing and her relations with others.[117] The recognition of constitutive contradiction as a perpetual condition of the human subject is a valuable insight, but if it is not coupled with some form of accountability for harm done to others, constitutive contradictions threaten to become the limit or end point that defines the trajectory of the struggle.

Tanaka's Iconography

As noted in previous chapters, the imperative to emphasize *ūman ribu*'s localized Japanese New Left origins makes Tanaka an apt symbol of *ribu* precisely because she resisted looking to the women's liberation movement in the United States as a model and rather voiced her critiques of its shortfalls in her earliest manifestos. When we seek to know what was different about *ūman ribu* compared with other forms of feminism, Tanaka's *ribu*-era writings on the issues of abortion, child killing, and women and violence render her strain of radical feminist thought compelling and distinct.

Tanaka's departure from Japan in 1975 and her relative distance from *ribu* women's collective movements after her return also makes her a convenient representative for scholars and commentators who wish to emphasize *ribu*'s discontinuity and relegate *ribu* to the past as a bygone social movement. In the *Women's Studies Dictionary,* published by the prestigious Iwanami Shoten press, feminist sociologist Ehara Yumiko writes that 1975 is usually recognized as the "end" or "death" *(shūen)* of *ribu*.[118] Ehara's description is paradigmatic of most secondary commentary that describes *ribu* as a past social movement that was succeeded by more established, institutionalized, and academic forms of feminism. What is troubling is how these narratives enact a premature symbolic death of *ribu* based on Tanaka's departure. For example, Ehara states that the Shinjuku Center closed in 1975 when in fact it remained open until 1977.[119] Ehara writings, along with the prolific writings of Ueno Chizuko, have contributed to the production of a master narrative of Japanese second wave feminism whereby the rise of *ribu* in 1970 is followed by its demise in 1975 and the succession of more established forms of feminism.[120]

Other widely circulating narratives, such as the documentary film about the *ribu* movement, *Ripples of Change: Japanese Women's Search for Self* (1993), reinscribe this master narrative of Japanese women's studies, conflating Tanaka's departure with the movement's demise. Nanako Kurihara, a Japanese filmmaker, produced and directed this fifty-seven-minute documentary. She began making the film in the late 1980s, while she was residing in New York, where she met a woman named Fumiko who was involved in *ūman ribu*. Because of her close friendship with Fumiko, Kurihara wanted to learn more about the *ribu* movement. Kurihara casts herself in the film as the protagonist in search for answers about the *ribu* movement. This documentary, which has circulated in the United States since the early 1990s, serves as a visually rich introduction to the history of the movement. The film focuses on five *ribu* activists: Funamoto Emi, Iwatsuki (also known as Asatori) Sumie, Fumiko's sister Setsuko, Murakami Tomoko, and Tanaka Mitsu. In the narrative voice-over, Kurihara states that she went looking for Tanaka in the late 1980s but was "disappointed to find she [Tanaka] seemed to have given up her activism." One of Kurihara's comments provides an example of the extent to which Tanaka's role as the leader of *ribu* is overevaluated: "It seemed to me that if she continued to lead it *[ūman ribu]*, things might be better for Japanese women today." More acutely than other secondary commentary on *ribu*, *Ripples of Change* charges Tanaka with an excessive degree of responsibility for *ribu*'s success and failures. Kurihara's framing and casting of Tanaka as *ribu*'s leader who left the movement provokes a defensive response from Tanaka in a scene where Kurihara directly questions Tanaka about why she left the movement. In response, Tanaka rejects Kurihara's suggestion, which implies that she should have remained a movement activist, saying, "What are you talking about? Basically *ribu*'s founding principle is for the 'I' *(watashi)* to be liberated."[121] This statement by Tanaka in the late 1980s is indicative of how Tanaka's rearticulations of *ribu* emphasize the priority of the "I" to be liberated. In this moment, in the late 1980s, Tanaka's discourse is notably more aligned, if not convergent, with a liberal feminist goal of individual liberation. Although the overarching premises of Tanaka's liberation discourse during the 1970s was embedded within a critique of the interconnected aspects of an oppressive system and was largely antagonistic to liberal notions of the individual, her discourse about *ribu* and her relationship to movement organizing underwent several shifts after her return to Japan.[122]

During her time in Mexico, Tanaka had a baby boy with an indigenous Mexican man who was her lover. She returned to Japan with her son in 1979 and raised him as an unmarried mother, consistent with *ribu*'s political stance on women's freedom to have children outside the Japanese marriage system. In this sense, upon her return, Tanaka continued to live the politics of *ribu*. After her return to Japan, Tanaka studied Eastern medicine and trained to become an acupuncturist. This choice of acupuncture also points to her political, intellectual, and spiritual shift from centering sex to focusing on the body. In reading her published works over a forty-year span from the 1970s to the present, Tanaka shifts from an emphasis on the primacy of the liberation of sex to the need to care for and heal the body. After the 1980s, her work and writing takes on a more spiritualist value system wherein she advocates different methods of healing oneself, such as visualization techniques. Some *ribu* women recognize this as an extension of her liberation politics. It is notable that many other *ribu* activists also became practitioners of Eastern medicine and focused on the body as different kinds of healers.

In a public lecture in 2000, Tanaka Mitsu stated that she began her *ribu* in Hongo, in the same district that Hiratsuka Raichō had lived and in the same area that the ashes of Itō Noe were stored.[123] In making these references, Tanaka approximates herself with the most famous figures of *Seitō* (Blue Stockings), which is generally recognized as the first wave of radical feminism in Japan (1910–20).[124] She has also stated that Hiratsuka Raichō was a *te-ate* practitioner, that is, someone who could heal through laying one's hands on the body of a sick person. In doing so, Tanaka situates herself in this longer legacy of Japanese radical feminists, healers, and revolutionaries who lived against the grain of society's parameters for acceptable women. In these ways, Tanaka does not shy away from claiming for herself a place among this legacy of Japan's most significant historical feminist figures. For forty years now, Tanaka has lived her own style of liberation and is confident that she carried out her role in history.

In her published dialogue with Ueno Chizuko (1986), the most prominent feminist scholar in Japan today, Tanaka names 1975 as the beginning of *ribu*'s "defeat."[125] Although Tanaka should not bear responsibility to have continued to lead the movement after 1975, she nonetheless participates in reproducing the narrative that *ribu* ended in 1975, and she willingly continues to perform the role of its icon to the present. Narratives that conflate Tanaka's departure in 1975 and *ribu*'s demise are problematic in that they place an excessive amount of responsibility for the movement's success and demise on Tanaka. In so doing, such narratives reproduce the discursive power of the icon and the idealism and mysticism that surrounds charismatic authority, implying that the power of the movement rested with and emanated from her actions as its leader. The seductive quality of such a narrative to create a heroine, larger than life, is an all-too-common yet persistent form of storytelling. The charismatic appeal and significatory power of the icon relies on this aura of the extraordinary, if not transcendent, qualities of this individual. Secondary commentary about Tanaka also contributes to a hagiographic tendency to idealize her leadership rather than account for the diversity and conflict involved in how other *ribu* activists experienced her will to power.[126]

Tanaka's own forms of self-representation have reproduced and guarded her status as a living icon.[127] However, investing such power in an icon comes becomes dangerous when that person no longer represents the political principles of the movement.

Rather than concur with the overevaluation of Tanaka that renders her solely responsible for the demise of *ribu*, I caution that this explanation deflects attention away from a historical understanding of the formation of a new hegemonic political bloc that can be broadly characterized as a liberal feminist coalition. In response to the UN International Year of the Woman in 1975, a new women's coalition was organized comprising fifty-two existing women's organizations, many of which were continuations of prewar and wartime groups. This coalition was called the Liaison Group for the Implementation of the Resolution from the International Women's Year Conference of Japan (Kokusai Fujin-ren Renraku-kai) and worked closely with the government. In 1975, the government established the Headquarters for the Planning and Promotion of Policies Relating to Women, which was to implement decisions that were made at the International Women's Year Conference. The government also became involved in promoting women's studies and soon after built the National Women's Education Center in Saitama-ken, where the first large international women's studies conference was convened. This liberal feminist political bloc was reformist and sought to work with the government and within the existing logic of the system. The organization of these forces coincides with what many have called the shift to the era of feminism. Ehara periodizes the shift from the "era of liberation" to that of the "development of feminism and women's studies," describing the shift in the following terms:

> The changes of the 1970s and 1980s are reflected in shifts from the [*ribu*] movement to institutions such as the legislature and universities, which themselves underwent change in the process. In response to these shifts, public officials and university scholars began to speak out and take an active role in the feminist movement.[128]

Insofar as Tanaka's departure from Japan also coincides with such developmental narratives of second wave feminism, Tanaka's iconic status as a metonym for the movement serves the needs of women's studies and other dominant forms of history that limit the politics of the 1970s as a period of exceptional radicalism. On the other hand, Tanaka's own turn away from her radical politics of the 1970s reinforces the developmental narratives that presume that radicalism is necessarily equivalent with immaturity and an underdeveloped political analysis.[129] Although the movements of that era were not without their problems, critical analysis of them offers lessons that remain relevant today and that we can take into the future.

In contrast to the iconization of Tanaka through women's studies and the mass media, the fifteen-hundred-page monumental collection of original *ribu* documents, *The Documents of the History of Women's Lib in Japan,* compiled by Saeki Yōko, Miki Sōko, and Mizoguchi Ayeko, assert a significantly different time line and trajectory. Their time line begins in 1969 and ends in 1982, situating *ribu*'s origins in closer relationship with existing women's leftist movements, such as the Asian Women Association (Ajia Fujin Kaigi), and includes the emergence of lesbian groups within its history. This collection successfully demonstrates the nationwide breadth of the movement and does not attribute to Tanaka a special place in the series. Consistent with the politics of *ribu,* there is no single voice or star that is privileged above others. Their goal in producing this series was to demonstrate the depth and breadth of the collective labor and struggle that was the power of the movement that continues to sustain and inspire the lives of *ribu* women today.

Conclusion

The historic figure Tanaka Mitsu would not exist as such without the hundreds of other women who came to identify as *ribu,* who struggled and collided with the state's imposed system of gender norms, policies, and ideologies regulating women's bodies and reproductive capacities. The name Tanaka Mitsu, in fact, was the new movement name she took on at the beginning of her activism that would signify her identity and persona in relation to *ūman ribu.* The proper name Tanaka Mitsu marked the creation of a new political subject, but its referent also embodied the identity and excesses of the person who deployed that name in relation with *ūman ribu.* The woman who used the name Tanaka Mitsu was a medium for *ribu* and also its excess. The invocation of the name Tanaka Mitsu derives political significance and cultural capital from the history of the movement without necessarily recognizing the significance of the heterogeneity of that collectivity, which has often been disregarded in relation to the unifying discourse and gaze that is directed by and toward the power of the icon.

Tanaka has continued to speak publicly and to write about *ribu* without denying or relinquishing her privileged position as the representative of *ribu.* In 1983, Tanaka published her second book, *No Matter Where I Go, I Am a Riber: Tanaka Mitsu's Collection of Expressions.*[130] The title expresses how Tanaka's rearticulations of *ribu* have become more personalized and how she continues to live *her ribu* wherever she goes. Tanaka has repeatedly insisted that she lived *her ribu*, and that *her ribu* cannot be someone else's. This personal yet open-ended notion of liberation that valued and affirmed notions of eros and contradiction did not prioritize expansion as a social movement. Rather, Tanaka emphasized the formation of one's subjectivity as an *onna*, as a philosophy of committed struggle and opposition from the contradictory position of the here-existing *onna*. Tanaka continually says that it is not the past but the present that matters; she has at times refused to talk about the past as the past, insisting that "the act of talking about the past is really a reflection of one's present."[131] Tanaka's reluctance to talk about the past with other women of the movement can also be read as a reluctance to work through what happened at the Shinjuku Center and how her politics today may differ from her politics of the 1970s.[132]

At a symposium in Tokyo in September 2009, there was a moment of open tension and conflict between Tanaka and a veteran *ribu* activist, Wakabayashi Naeko, who publicly articulated her "deep disappointment" in Tanaka when they recently tried to work together to organize a *ribu* retrospective event. In response to Wakabayashi's critical comment, Tanaka emphasized that she was "not only an oppressor, but also a victim" *(higaisha)*, inferring that she was also hurt through her complex, tense, and conflictual relationships with other women. The condition of her iconic status, all its contradictions notwithstanding, undoubtedly includes Tanaka's own sense of hurt, woundedness, guilt, and exhaustion from which she sought healing and respite through her departure from the movement. Her claims to victimhood, however, also serve to deflect criticism of her own shortcomings and responsibility for how her militancy and attacks were, at times, directed against other *ribu* women when they got in the way of her practice of liberation. Consequently, her manner of leading the movement effectively alienated a significant number of *ribu* women, and Tanaka's asserted authority, by 1975, was already in question among many of those women who worked closely with her.[133] Over the years, she continues to assert her authority over the history of *ribu*, acting as a kind of gatekeeper of the movement. At times, Tanaka has denied other *ribu* activists' claims to collaborative work, guarding her authorship with vigilance.[134] Thus, one of the notable contradictions of *ribu*'s history remains in how its iconic figure often sought and achieved her liberation in the process of disregarding and harming other *ribu* women.

Ultimately, the historical process that made Tanaka an icon of *ribu* was not orchestrated from a single source; rather, a complex set of factors converged to produce this discursive and historical effect. It was the fusion of Tanaka's multifaceted roles within the movement—as a pioneering messenger and medium, as a key organizer and visible spokeswoman—that combined with the repeated recognition of her from those outside the movement. Tanaka's iconization has been a result of numerous forces, intentions, and desires that extend beyond and outside the *ribu* movement, involving the mass media, photographers, publishers, and women's studies *(joseigaku)* scholars. In addition, her representations of herself have also contributed to her iconization. She has certainly benefited from her relative fame and reputation through the continual invitations and opportunities to speak, teach, and publish. In spite of the efforts of other *ribu* women to resist this process, dominant forms of narrativity and historiography and studies such as my own tend to single out a subject as particularly compelling and worthy of critical attention.

My treatment of Tanaka and her significant role in the *ribu* movement attempted to go beyond an iconic understanding of her place in history and to assess her philosophy, actions, and contributions in order to raise larger questions about the common problems among collectivities that struggle to create alternative forms of relationship. Beyond recognizing Tanaka as an icon, or as an appropriate symbol of *ribu,* it is important to recognize the original, vital, and pivotal role Tanaka played in the movement at its dawn as its charismatic figure and the productive and limited effects of such a model of leadership. Her role shaped the movement's direction and flow and infused *ribu* with a creative and defiant ferocity without claiming to be without contradiction and imperfection, but rather embracing them as the conditions of struggle. Because of linguistic constraints, neither Tanaka nor the hundreds of lesser-known *ribu* women have been accorded significant attention outside of Japan. And yet *ribu*'s goals were not solely aimed at gaining external recognition: they also aimed at transforming the conditions of possibility of the terms of recognition and relationality. This history, with all its complexities, not only is often wrongly assessed or belittled but remains largely unknown. This study of Tanaka's role in the movement will hopefully encourage others to fill in the gaps and provide their own interpretations and analysis of what transpired.

Rather than simply exposing the internal conflicts of the center to air the "dirty laundry" as a spectacle for voyeuristic consumption, it is my intention to encourage feminist and other liberation movements to further theorize the contradictions within and among the proponents of radical, revolutionary, and transformative politics. Reflecting on the radicalism of the late 1960s and the 1970s affords us the benefit of hindsight to confront, embrace, and analyze the shortcomings, necessary imperfections, and mistakes of past social movements and leadership models in order to devise and craft constructive and productive ways to work through the precarious process of relationship and movement building. Rather than only mourn and criticize the problems of charismatic authority and the master narratives that have failed to examine the problems of violence among and within feminist subjects, it is necessary for cultures of resistance to continually confront, theorize, and develop new practices that recognize the inevitability of conflicts and clashes that are simultaneously political and interpersonal. There is a need to continually assess the necessity, desirability, and viability of coalitional politics not only by asking the same questions in a new context—at whose cost and to what ends?—but also by attending to the violations and the violence that transpire in our struggles for collective liberation.

III

BETWEEN FEMINISM AND VIOLENCE

Ribu's Response to the United Red Army

Feminist Ethics and the Politics of Violence

Political violence remains as an aporetic condition.[1] It is an ineluctable problematic bound to politics, ethics, sovereignty, and power. The definition of political violence is debated and unsettled, involving a spectrum of violence for political ends that can include state-sponsored violence and terrorism; military and policing actions; incarceration and torture; and insurgent, counterhegemonic uses of violence and terrorism.[2] As a radical feminist movement that formed amid the turbulence of the early 1970s, *ūman ribu*'s approach to political violence was both compelling and complex. This chapter examines *ribu*'s relationship to the United Red Army (Rengo Sekigun; hereafter URA), a group considered by many to have been Japan's most violent domestic underground revolutionary sect.[3] The following discussion of the URA demonstrates that the interpretability and contestability of any action or event is what renders its violence political, justifiable, and/or abhorrent. The events surrounding the URA in 1972 became a turning point for Japanese leftist radicalism because of the way political violence was deployed in the name of revolutionary purposes. The URA's use of violence in the name of the revolution has been regarded as a disturbing and tragic event that marked the downfall of the Japanese New Left. To this day, the causes, residues, and scars of this self-destructive phenomenon have haunted many of those involved in the political movements of that era.

Ribu's critical feminist approach to violence was evident in how it related to the URA. While rejecting the URA's use of violence as fundamentally misguided, many *ribu* women collectively engaged in various supportive actions toward the women of the URA. *Ribu*'s support of the women of the URA provides a critical reframing of how the state and the mass media constructed the female leader of the URA as a "violent threat" to national security. Through this analysis of *ūman ribu*'s approach to the political uses and abuses of violence, I argue that their praxis of critical solidarity and radical inclusivity offers a creative way to work through the causes and effects of different forms of violence and expresses an alternative feminist ethics of violence. In the second half of the chapter, I discuss Tanaka Mitsu's complex approach to different manifestations of violence as one element of her philosophy of liberation. I demonstrate how her philosophy of liberation involves the principles of *torimidashi* (contradiction and disorder), contingency, violence, relationality *(kankeisei),* and eros, which are all integral to her existentialist approach to liberation. I conclude with Tanaka's approach to the URA's female leader, Nagata Hiroko, as a powerful and symbolic distillation of *ribu*'s crucial intervention at this pivotal moment in Japan's political history.

The United Red Army

Ūman ribu emerged at a time when political violence was rampant across the political spectrum from the far left to the far right. University campuses were rife with battles between right-wing student groups, leftist sects, and student activists. As the Japanese government continued its support of the United States' war in Vietnam, thousands of Japanese took to the streets to battle against the riot police to express their solidarity with the Vietnamese. As the state increased its police powers and continued its repression of protests by arresting thousands of activists, some far-left groups also increased the intensity of their tactics against the state. The URA emerged amidst this escalation of violent resistance.

The URA became the most infamous sect of the Japanese New Left. It formed through a merger of two far-left sects on July 15, 1971. The merger involved one wing of the Japanese Red Army (JRA) and the Revolutionary Left Faction, an offshoot of the Marxist Leninist Faction (ML Ha).[4] The leader of the JRA at the time of the merger was Mori Tsuneo (1944–73), and the leader of the Revolutionary Left Faction was a woman, Nagata Hiroko (1944–2011). Nagata became second-in-command of the URA, after Mori.[5] One of the reasons Mori merged with the Revolutionary Left Faction was that his JRA division was unable to acquire any arms or weapons. Under Mori's leadership, the political aim of the URA was to escalate conflict with the Japanese government.

The JRA, which should be distinguished from the URA, was known as the most militant revolutionary group in Japan. Its other cells had engaged in several successful missions, including a series of robberies and attacks against politicians and police officials and the hijacking of an airplane to

North Korea in 1970. In 1971, some of its members left Japan and aligned themselves with the PFLP (Popular Front for the Liberation of Palestine). Led by Shigenobu Fusako, the JRA division based in the Middle East continued its activities for the next few decades. After November 1971, nine of the ten most wanted "criminals" in Japan were members of the two sects that comprised the URA. This was indicative of the state's efforts to prioritize the targeting of leftist insurgents.

In the winter of 1971, the URA retreated to mountain training camps in the Japanese Alps in Gunma-ken to undergo revolutionary training. The URA intended to prepare for armed struggle against the state and to liberate one of its leaders who had been incarcerated. During this revolutionary training period, under the directives of Mori and Nagata, the group engaged in a violent and lethal internal purge. This purge began as a process of *sōkatsu* (which took the form of collective and individual self-criticism) but quickly escalated into a form of testing and measuring each member's revolutionary commitment. During various training activities, Mori and Nagata accused members of not possessing or demonstrating sufficient revolutionary consciousness. For example, when two of the members (Katō Yoshitaka and Kojima Kazuko) were found to be engaging in romantic relations, this was interpreted as evidence of a lack of revolutionary commitment. Within this logic of organizational discipline, having a romantic relationship was deemed counterrevolutionary. During the course of this internal purge, Mori and Nagata ordered other members to punish those they deemed as lacking in their revolutionary commitment. These forms of punishment involved beatings and torture and exposure to the elements without food and shelter.[6] In the course of this purge, the sect tortured and killed twelve of its members, most of whom were in their early twenties. Between January 1 and early February 1972, the leaders of the URA ordered the torture or execution of:

Ozaki Michio (21, male)
Shindō Ryuzaburo (21, male)
Namekata Masatoki (22, male)
Kojima Kazuko (22, female)
Toyama Mieko (25, female)
Katō Yoshitaka (22, male)
Teraoka Koichi (24, male)
Yamazaki Jun (21, male)
Ōtsuka Setsuko (23, female)
Kaneko Michiyo (23, female and eight months pregnant)
Yamada Takeshi (27, male)
Yamamoto Junichi (28, male)

Torturing and killing one's own comrades, who were suddenly designated as lacking in revolutionary commitment, became a means of both proving one's own revolutionary commitment and ensuring one's own survival. Two others had previously been killed in August 1971, when they had tried to leave the Revolutionary Left Faction: Hayaki Yasuko (21, female) was killed in Inbanuma, and Mukaiyama Shigenori (21, male) was murdered in an apartment in Kodaira.

In early February 1972, Mori and Nagata left the camp in the Gunma mountains to go to Tokyo. After they left, members of the URA began to escape, fearing they would be the next one singled out to be killed. By mid-February the police began closing in on the URA. On February 19, the police arrested Mori and Nagata.

The last five remaining members of the URA were on the run, armed with rifles and explosives. They were hiding out in a mountain lodge in the Japanese Alps and had taken the wife of the owner of the lodge as a hostage. Between February 19 and 28, these five remaining members of URA held off over fifteen hundred riot police at the lodge, called Asama Sansō, near Karuizawa. This armed standoff and hostage-taking incident became an unprecedented television spectacle. Television news coverage of the incident began on February 19, and hundreds of media staff were on site to work the story. The continuous live televised news coverage lasted for ten hours and forty minutes and constituted an unprecedented broadcasting event in Japan's media history that has never been surpassed in terms of its duration and ratings. At the climax of the police operation, when the "radicals were arrested and the hostage rescued," with almost 90 percent viewer ratings, according to NHK (Nippon Hōsō Kyōkai), "almost the entire country was watching the same thing on TV."[7]

The orchestration of this prolonged televised broadcast recast the URA's form of small-scale insurgency into unprecedented national spectacle, producing the hypervisibility of the actions of a handful of militant New Leftists. In the month following this standoff, as the police interrogated the incarcerated members of the URA about the whereabouts of the remaining sect members, the details of the internal purge were gradually divulged. The police immediately released these details to the mass media, which promptly disseminated stories about the killings across the nation. Revelations about the URA's murders and the exhumation of corpses made the front pages of major newspapers and top stories of television news during the first half of March 1972.

The collaboration between the police and the mass media rendered the killing of these twelve Japanese as an exceptionally heinous spectacle of violence. In the wake of the Asama Sansō incident, the reportage about the URA

The grave of two victims of the United Red Army lynching incident. *Asahi Shinbun*, March 10, 1972.

tied the image of armed resistance to the murder of one's comrades. This misuse of counterviolence served to delegitimize militant leftist struggles, as these young leftist revolutionaries were portrayed as ruthless extremists. The URA incidents thus became an ideal opportunity to hegemonize the state's monopoly on political violence. In Patricia Steinhoff's words, "As the gory details emerged, the entire nation recoiled in shock, and the New Left was shattered."[8]

The unprecedented hypervisibility of this (ab)use of revolutionary violence, as an effective discursive tactic, eclipsed the incommensurate magnitude of mass militarized massacre being perpetrated against the Vietnamese. This incident deeply disturbed the Left and New Left. Immediately following the revelation, established leftist organizations such as Zengakuren (All-Japan Students Association) publicly stated their unequivocal condemnation of these violent actions. The chairman of Zengakuren, the largest communist (anti–Japanese Communist Party) student organization, stated to the news media on March 15, 1972, that the URA and other militant groups, such as Kakumaru (Revolutionary Marxist) and Chūkaku (Middle Core), were "undermining democratic forces in Japan."[9] In the spring of 1972, the JRA members based in the Middle East condemned the activities of the URA and officially declared their disassociation from them. As a consequence of the mass media's coverage of the lynching incidents, Nagata became arguably the most notorious and reviled woman of her era, if not throughout postwar Japanese history.

Ribu's Critical Reframing

In March 1972, just as the news of the lynchings was breaking, *ribu* women from different regions of Japan confronted how the media was framing the story. Even though the news was horrific, and all the more sensational because of the role of a woman in leadership, many *ribu* activists responded in the moment to the mass media as part of a complex and multifaceted approach to the URA. Rather than condemn or single out the URA, *ūman ribu*'s response was based on a broader analysis of the interconnectedness and gendered regulation of the political system. Through their alternative media, *ribu* activists created a counterdiscourse critically reframing the complex convergence represented by the URA and Nagata Hiroko.

For example, the inaugural issue of one of the long-standing *ribu* newsletters, *From Woman to Women (Onna kara onna-tachi e)* addressed the URA and its media coverage as an issue related to all women. This *ribu* newsletter was edited by Miki Sōko and Saeki Yōko and was published from 1972 to 1982. Writing in a regular column under the pen name "witch," or *majo,* Miki Sōko critiques the coverage of the URA. She analyzes the March 11 and 12, 1972, editions of the *Asahi Shinbun* and argues that this kind of coverage by sexist male reporters "disseminates discrimination throughout the nation" and thereby "oppresses women."[10] The morning edition on March 12, for example, ran headlines such as "The Onna Called Nagata Hiroko" and "Cruelty That Even the Men Feared," along with commentary such as "You can hardly say Nagata was a beauty."[11] Miki also critiqued the publication of a roundtable composed exclusively of men, who comment on the high number of women in the URA and how they were stronger [than the men in the group].[12] One of the commentators repeatedly remarks on how the URA members were very "feminine" *(joseiteki)* and how what transpired was due to "extreme emotions" within the group.[13] Another commentator suggests that perhaps it was not Mori, but Nagata, who was at the center of the events. Another states, "Women's participation in the movements is not only a problem for the URA, but a new problem today."[14] Because of this kind of coverage, *ribu* activists took to task the skewed and sexist editorials that suggested such violence was to be blamed on women's involvement and the feminine characteristics of the group. By responding to the gendered representations of the URA, *ribu* activists offered a critique of the gendered economies deployed to render aberrant particular expressions of violence, especially when they were framed as emanating from a "feminine source."

Nagata as Female Terror

Ribu activists addressed how Nagata was displayed as a spectacle and an object of loathing for the entire nation.[15] They thoroughly objected to how the media declared that Nagata was "inhuman," "a murdering devil," and a "witch."[16] In the newspaper and magazine photos selected to represent the story, Nagata was often portrayed with her face down, tied up with a rope around her waist like an animal as she is being escorted by the police.[17]

Even though Mori was captured at the same time, similar pictures of the male leader, being tied with a rope and escorted by the police, rarely appear alongside Nagata's. Compared with the more neutral facial photos of Mori, the photos of Nagata tied up with a downcast face indicate how the media chose to portray her in such a way that her very image was meant to be seen as an object of shame. Indeed, one of the first lines of the story about her confession published by *Asahi Shinbun* on March 14, 1972, begins, "Even her

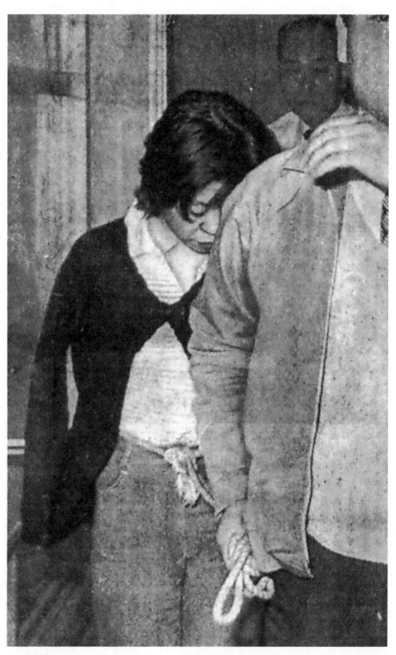

Nagata Hiroko. Photograph from *Asahi Shinbun*, March 14, 1972.

Mori Tsuneo. Photograph from *Asahi Shinbun*, May 11, 1972.

own comrades called her an 'old hag' *(onibabā)* behind her back."[18] This kind of news reporting unabashedly emphasized Nagata's sexual difference, as a female leader, mediating how she would be viewed by multiple publics.

Patricia Steinhoff, who has conducted extensive research on the history of the URA, also underscores the disparity in how the two URA leaders were treated: "Both the court and the public have treated Mori as a political leader whose plans went astray, they have treated Nagata as a menacing crazy-woman motivated by spite and jealousy."[19] Steinhoff further notes that the judge had a "misogynous opinion" of Nagata, describing her as possessing an "emotional and aggressive personality, she is suspicious and jealous, and to these are added the female characteristics of obstinacy, spitefulness, and cruel sadism."[20] That such a gendered discourse was used to condemn Nagata highlights the degree to which her actions were being interpreted through a debased view of her sex. The *ribu* women clearly understood that treating and blaming Nagata as the source of the problem was a means to attack women more generally. These examples of the sexist discourse used to condemn Nagata contextualize the significance of *ribu*'s intervention.

The *ribu* movement was forming in the midst of the breakdown of the New Left. The planning for the first major *ribu* conference was ongoing just as the March news of URA incidents was revealed. In the newsletters leading up to the May 1972 Ribu Conference, many women took up the thematic of the URA right alongside issues such as unmarried mothers, abortion, women who kill their children *(kogoroshi no onna)*, contraception, and child raising. They considered the problem of women engaging in different forms of violence as connected with other political problems.

> It is important to consider the various problems of daily life, seeing the problems of sexual discrimination, the problem of how to organize the movement and what form the struggle against authority should take, and the pain that Nagata Hiroko experiences as an *onna* alongside each other.[21]

Rather than seeing Nagata as an aberration, *ribu* understood her as caught within a matrix of interconnected political issues, a symptom of how state violence and leftist political violence, sexual discrimination, and movement organizing had collided in a self-destructive cycle. Alongside a much needed critique of the sexist and misogynist discourse of the mass media, *ūman ribu* forwarded a timely and trenchant critique of the URA tragedy as a catastrophic outcome of the masculinism of the New Left and the state.[22] As discussed throughout chapter 2, the *ribu* women questioned and critiqued the

masculinist culture of the New Left and how revolutionary action was conflated with one's willingness to engage in violent action against symbols of
the state (such as politicians and police).[23] *Ribu* women drew the connections
and parallels between the masculinist values of the power structure, the New
Left, and the mass media.[24] A *ribu* activist named Kazu states that both the
New Left and the state are engaged in a power struggle "based on the same
set of values which is a fight between men to seize power and authority."[25]
Therefore, any woman who tries to continue working within this thoroughly
masculinist structure would eventually be found to be "counterrevolutionary."

Along with their criticism of the New Left, *ribu* women recognized their
relative proximity and relationality with them, as their progenitors. In this
connection, another *ribu* pamphlet states:

> There is no way that it should be said that *ribu* has no relationship to the
> New Left. Surely, the first thing that can be said that it [the New Left] was
> the parent that spawned and gave birth to *ribu,* and the fact that it has
> manifested such an aspect and broke down, with other parts in shock and
> struggling to survive, is a serious situation for *ribu* as well.[26]

Thus, rather than conceiving of themselves as somehow outside of or un-
tainted by its politics, along with its strident critique of the New Left, *ribu*
activists recognized their own political genealogy and formation in relation
to the New Left.

In addition to their critique of the media's sexist representations of
Nagata and the masculinist culture of the New Left, *ribu* activists had to
respond to the many ways the mass media linked the URA with *ūman ribu*.
Nagata's leading role provided a facile means to sensationalize the event, and
her role as a female leader became a convenient way to connect and conflate
ūman ribu with the URA. Miki Sōko also points out that the evening edition
of the *Asahi Shinbun* (March 11, 1972) reported that one of the members of
the JRA was also a member of the Group of Fighting Women, *ribu*'s most
well-known group.[27] Although this information was not accurate, in this way,
the mass media linked the URA and *ūman ribu* in multiple ways.[28] Linking
ribu to the URA was a way to prevent some women from joining the movement, by casting *ūman ribu* as a "dangerous" affiliate of the URA. The *ribu*
women recognized that this was an attempt to cast a shadow over *ūman ribu*
and malign the image of women's participation in revolutionary politics.
The conflation of *ūman ribu*'s politics with the URA suggested that horrible
things happened when women become too strong and too powerful, deflect-
ing a broader critique of the masculinism of the New Left and the state.

Critical Solidarity

Even as they maintained their critique of the masculinism of the New Left and URA's militaristic tactics, many *ribu* activists supported the women of the URA, understanding the significance of this juncture and what was at stake. Based on their critical analysis of the URA, as symptomatic of the masculinism of the New Left and the state, and their supportive actions for the women involved, I describe this distinctive relationality as a feminist praxis of critical solidarity and radical inclusivity. The key words used in *ribu*'s discourse and alternative media to describe their relation to the women of the URA were *shien,* meaning support or backup, and *kyūen,* generally referring to rescue and relief work, in contrast to the term for solidarity *(rentai).*[29]Although the *ribu* women were critical of the philosophy and practices of the URA, they still engaged in a wide range of supportive political action for the women of the URA that not only constituted rescue and relief work but, I would argue, went beyond merely rescuing those in critical condition as the condemned and rendered socially dead through their criminalization. Through their political actions, they produced a new form of relationality with these criminalized subjects.

Ribu's collective actions to support the women of the URA can be theorized as a radical feminist practice of solidarity based on how *ribu* activists sought to identify *as onna* with the *other onna* of the URA. *Ribu* activists readily understood that Nagata's treatment and condemnation was inseparable from her identity as an *onna,*[30] which was in turn linked to the generality of *onna.*[31] Reflecting on their actions toward the URA, in the mid-1990s, Mori Setsuko stated, "We wanted to point out that these women [of the URA] were being criminalized for being *onna. . . .* We were not supporting the philosophy of URA. We were supporting the *onna* that was already being condemned as *onna.*"[32] Nagata was being condemned not simply because of her actions but because she was an *onna* who had stepped far beyond the acceptable boundaries for women to act. In the context of the 1970s, based on her position of power over men in a paramilitary organization, Nagata embodied a subversion, if not what some might consider a perversion, of gender roles. Even in the context of revolutionary praxis, she was a gender-nonconforming anomaly.

Even as they completely rejected the use of violence against one's own comrades, *ribu* activists stridently objected to the ways in which the state and the male-dominated media attempted to dehumanize the members of the URA and cast Nagata as some kind of female monster or witch. In her explanation as to why they organized in support of the URA, activist Namahara

Reiko ("Nora") emphasizes, "These people were not considered human."[33] *Ribu* activists were concerned with how other middle-class Japanese women were abjected and dehumanized through this process of criminalization. The fact that Nagata engaged in this form of political violence was an opportunity to amplify the criminalization of violent women as particularly heinous, rendering her status as a woman at once both questionable and yet the basis of her condemnation. Rather than disavowing or disassociating from her, Nagata was treated as an *onna* who had committed a fatal and tragic series of mistakes and as an important opportunity to question the conditions that could compel *any woman* to act as Nagata did.[34]

Ribu activists were motivated by a radical feminist logic that sought to affirm their own sex and revolutionize their immediate surroundings; they identified with other Japanese women who could be interpreted as rebel women committing mutiny against the dominant system. In doing so, they articulated a bold new approach to violence expressed by women. Akin to how the *ribu* women declared solidarity *(rentai)* with women who killed their children—while they in no way advocated killing children—*ribu* women understood the larger political discursive structure that had to be rejected and intervened upon. As seen through *ribu*'s solidarity with women who killed their children (discussed in chapter 1), *ribu* refused the complete repression and disavowal of women's inherent capacity for violence, which then necessitated their pathologization, rendering violent women aberrant. By supporting the women of the URA and declaring solidarity with mothers who killed their children, *ribu* activists engaged in a form of feminist support and solidarity that was nevertheless critical of the context and effects of interpersonal and structural violence. Even though *ribu* activists did not agree with these women's actions, they chose to support these women on the basis of their broader feminist concerns regarding the conditions that led these women to express their violent potential. *Ribu*'s form of feminist identification included active support of violent women and violent mothers who were criminalized and condemned by dominant society. Insofar as violence was thoroughly regulated through gendered economies, *ribu* women interpreted the expression of violence by women as necessarily political.

This praxis of critical support and solidarity is based on a broader analysis of the interconnectedness of the political system that illuminated the connections between the gendering of state power and authority, as maintained through violent domination, and how this gendering infected the culture of the Japanese New Left. *Ribu* took issue with this ideological gendering of domination that made violent physical domination of bodies a normalized form of expression for men in power but rendered it aberrant for women. They sought to expose how both the men who govern the nation and certain members of the New Left were upholding the same form of armed, lethal military power as the chosen and most valued tactic. *Ribu* intellectuals Saeki, Miki, and Mizoguchi summarize the URA as a militant group that emphasized that "it is the *gun* that creates the party" and sought to "battle to the death with guns."[35] Such a reductive and destructive approach to revolutionary change was antithetical to *ribu*'s all-encompassing approach to social transformation and desire to prioritize human relationality. Their use of the terms *shien* (support) and *kyūen* (rescue and relief), instead of *rentai,* mark this political distinction in their approach to revolution as a representational strategy that signified a constitutive distinction.[36]

Radical Inclusivity

Ribu's feminist approach self-reflexively embraced the problem of the URA as its own. In so doing, *ribu* engaged in a challenging form of critical solidarity, a praxis I call radical inclusivity. In March 1972, Mori Setsuko, a core *ribu* activist, stated, "I think that the essence exposed by the URA is actually within each one of us, and within me."[37] In making such a statement, Mori approaches the violence expressed by URA and the complicity of the other URA women in that violence as a means to examine the self and locate the other within the self, enacting a self-reflexive form of radical inclusivity that enables solidarity and a complex political identification with these other women. Rather than disidentify or disassociate from the women of the URA, this was seen as an important opportunity to question the conditions that had compelled them to act as they did. Similarly, veteran *ribu* activist Yonezu Tomoko states why she went to the URA hearings:

> We wanted them to have a proper trial, because if it was rushed, there would be no chance for the causes of what happened to be made clear. When I went to the public hearings, I thought about . . . what was the difference between me and those women standing there as defendants, not only just Nagata Hiroko, but also some younger women who did not have much of a leadership role in the group. . . . Fortunately, I was in a university where the New Left guys were more flexible . . . so we were able to make a women's-only group. But what would have happened if I were in a university where there were only people who were more like Nagata and her people? My reality was that I did not go in that direction, but there was a possibility that I could have walked down that path. . . . I could sense how awful it was for those defendants standing there, and wondered

how they would be able to go on with their lives, and so I could not allow myself to avert my eyes from them.[38]

In this case, Yonezu's gaze is not one that objectifies but that seeks ways to connect with these women. Both Mori's and Yonezu's explanations highlight how *ribu*'s discourse and actions sought to interrogate and emphasize the potential commonality, as well as differences, they had with the women of the URA. They recognized that they too could have become entangled in such misguided violence had they not been fortunate enough to start a life-affirming movement like *ribu* that valued relationality with other *onna*. They therefore related to the women of the URA not as abjected others but sought to understand and imagine what they experienced, and they reflected deeply about the root causes of such violence. *Ribu*'s approach to violence was thus highly self-reflexive (and self-critical), for they did not simply reject and disavow the potentiality of such violence within themselves. Critical solidarity involves a praxis of political identification based on a philosophy of existence that emphasizes the contingency of one's life and destiny and the realization of one's potential commonality with the other, including the potential expression of violence.

Ribu did not have the luxury to philosophize about the URA from a safe distance. Because of the tactics deployed by the mass media, the battle over the representation of the URA became the terrain of *ribu*'s own struggle. Not only was *ribu* falsely connected by the media to the URA, but a few *ribu* women had various kinds of connections with the URA. As addressed later, Nagata Hiroko had solicited Tanaka to work with them prior to the lynching incidents.[39] *Ribu*'s response to the URA was thus infused with multiple agendas and dangers.

In the wake of the May 1972 Ribu Conference, women from five *ribu* groups together established the Ribu Shinjuku Center in September 1972.[40] Alongside their activism on a myriad of interrelated issues, *ribu* women continued their support for the women of the URA. One woman, who is described in the *Ribu News* as a member of the Group of Fighting Women, had a previous connection with members of the URA.[41] Her movement name was Kunihisa Kazuko. She was arrested on July 18, 1972, under the suspicion of aiding and concealing Nagata Hiroko and Sakaguchi Hiroshi. Sakaguchi was another leader of the URA, who was married to Nagata and involved in the lynching incidents. Rather than trying to disassociate from or disown Kunihisa, the *ribu* women organized to support her case.[42] Even though Kunihisa was accused of concealing Nagata and Sakaguchi in April 1971, more than half a year before the internal purge, the media coverage of her arrest deliberately overlapped the story with the lynching incidents. In this manner, the media linked *ūman ribu* with the URA, casting *ribu* in the shadows of the URA. The *ribu* women recognized that such reportage was an attempt to use the violence of URA as an opportunity to destroy their own movement by "blurring the distinction between the existing struggles and *ribu*."[43]

The inaugural edition of the *Ribu News,* published in September 1972 from the Shinjuku Center, ran a full-page article by Kunihisa called "The Gap between the Popular Image and Reality." Kunihisa describes her experience—as a mother of two—of being arrested on July 18, while her child was at home with her.[44] The article discusses in detail how she was detained, interrogated, and indicted by the police and her emotional state throughout this process until she was released on bail on August 16, 1972. The largest-circulating newspaper of the *ribu* movement (with a circulation of several thousand copies) thus publicized *ribu*'s support of and relationship with Kunihisa and, in doing so, reframed and shed light on her (contingent) relationship with the leaders of the URA. Kunihisa's voice and perspective, articulated through the *Ribu News,* enabled the reader to connect with her experience as an "ordinary woman and mother." Kunihisa speaks of her struggle between her conflicting desires to keep her political integrity on the one hand (by not giving the police any information) and her worries about her children, on the other hand, due to her near month-long detainment.[45] The space enabled by the *Ribu News* forged vital connections and a means of relating to a criminalized *onna,* in this case, Kunihisa, and understanding how Kunihisa was related to Nagata and Sakaguchi. Generating Kunihisa's discourse enabled a recognition of how the fate of one woman and her criminalization is connected to others.

Alongside Kunihisa's own account, Yonezu writes an article titled "From the Side That Supports Kunihisa-san"[46] in which she emphasizes a kind of relationality that was core to the politics of *ribu*. This relationship recognizes subjective agency but also emphasizes the degree to which coincidental factors beyond one's control also determine the course of one's life.[47] Yonezu concludes her article by saying, "We want to move forward by treating these women's achievements and past mistakes as the accumulated resources of *onna*'s struggle."[48] In this manner, rather than repressing *onna*'s errors and mistakes, Yonezu includes them and critically embraces them as lessons for the future of the struggle. Critical solidarity thus involves a praxis of political identification that recognizes the inevitable imperfections and mistakes involved in any struggle.

On January 20, 1973, the Shinjuku Center organized a teach-in called On the Support of Nagata Hiroko.[49] This meeting became the starting point of a support group for the women of the URA composed of many of the women of the Shinjuku Center and other non-*ribu* movement activists. The full name of this group was How Much of the Essence of the Thing Can We Hone In on by Supporting the Women Defendants of the United Red Army. The long, circuitous name of the group reflected the group's inquisitive and deliberately measured stance toward their support activities, and it demonstrates how critical solidarity emphasizes that the "essence of the problem" extends beyond the individuals involved in an act of violence. Rather than individualizing acts of violence, this approach analyzed violence as exceeding the individual and not being reducible to group dynamics of the militant New Left. The group's titling also signals a radical Marxist approach—questioning the question—aligning this feminist politic with that of the New Left it also criticized.

This group began to print a newsletter called *Ashura* in February 1973, with the contact address of the Ribu Shinjuku Center. Naming the newsletter *Ashura* invoked the image of a well-known Buddhist guardian deity (deva) with three faces and six hands, serving as a reminder of how one body can possesses many faces.[50] One of its first newsletters printed Nagata's own appeal that she wrote while in detention on February 13, 1973.[51] In this appeal, Nagata writes in bold language, expressing a determined fighting stance.[52] Nagata states that she knows the trial of the URA and the special policies the court is trying to institute to rush the process is part of a larger "counter-revolutionary campaign" to target "extremist groups."[53] In her appeal, she explains why she and other URA defendants are protesting the proceedings of the court, through a hunger strike, because of how the authorities are trying to hasten the duration of the trial. Nagata writes:

> From within this trial which is all about an ideological struggle *(shisō tōso)*, I will endeavor to continue thinking about the death of my fifteen comrades. I want to move forward in my life struggle from within this context. I think that our struggle is one part of the class struggle.[54]

Printing Nagata's own appeal from a newsletter emanating from the Ribu Shinjuku Center linked the voice of the most maligned woman of the era with one of the main centers of the women's liberation movement. This collective thus provided support for a woman who was fighting without hesitation or apology against the authorities even though her tactics may have been fatally wrongheaded. The cogency and analytic urgency of Nagata's appeal contrasts sharply with the media representations of her as a menacing crazy woman given to fits of hysteria.

Ashura calls for a rally with the declaration: "We Will Not Allow Them to Use the United Red Army Trial to Promote Fascism," forwarding a bold and unflinching critique of the state. But in contrast to this strident style of political writing, what characterizes many of *Ashura*'s articles is the non-jargonistic, down-to-earth style of its prose:

> We started our actions, moving forward with baby steps. We take our time to figure out what we can do. . . . What is necessary to do at this time? . . . We attended the public hearings and visited them at the Tokyo Detention Center. . . . Others came after school and after work, and stayed to help make pamphlets, rubbing their sleepy eyes.[55]

Articles such as "Why We Bring Our Children to the United Red Army Hearings" argued against the assumption that *ribu* women were endangering their children by bringing them to the hearings and questioned how such a trial can be more dangerous than living in a society where children have been known to die from food contaminated by toxins.[56] These articles thus forwarded a logic that went against the dominant narratives that sought to set apart and render hypervisible the URA as though they were a group of loathsome criminals. They expressed how "ordinary," rather than radical or extreme, supporting the women of the Red Army should be. In an article titled "Why We Are Supporting the Women Defendants,"[57] the author expresses her sense that "next, they are going to come after me." Refusing to single out Nagata or the URA as dangerous extremists, *ribu*'s counterdiscourse consistently directs its critical lens on a system that continues to "threaten our existence," underscoring a political subjectivity and ontology based on a collective form of existence.[58]

Ashura also served to document the various support activities this group engaged in, which included corresponding with the defendants, responding to relevant inquiries from other parts of the country, and collecting donations to support their legal defense.[59] In addition to visiting them at the detention center and attending the hearings, the *ribu* women and other supporters went to bear witness to all the irregularities of the proceedings and to keep a record of them.[60] Even though the hearings were formally public, the authorities tried to control who could enter and created special kinds of restrictions that were not part of the normal procedures. For example, the court required all those who came as spectators to the hearings to undergo a body search.[61] In these ways, the creation of such special procedures to deal with the URA hearings signaled the way the state would continue to increase its forms of control and policing, using the URA as an example of why the state must take extreme and invasive measures to rid society of such left-wing threats to national security.

The choice and commitment by *ribu* activists to continue an affiliation with this underground revolutionary sect—which was condemned by so many—points to how their principles of collectivity went against what would typically be considered more pragmatic tactics. A more pragmatic feminist approach may have involved publicly condemning the actions of the women of the URA as masculinist and distancing and isolating them as violent extremists. Their affiliation with the URA rendered the *ribu* women the objects of police surveillance and *ribu* centers the target of police raids.[62] By going to the hearings and visiting them at the detention centers, the *ribu* women moved their bodies into physical proximity with the women of the URA. In doing so, they risked being identified as part of the URA networks and placed their lives in the line of a state-orchestrated criminalizing gaze.[63] Rather than staying within the comforts of the middle-class mainstream, their relatively privileged position as middle-class Japanese women enabled this kind of political action whereby they could choose to make themselves vulnerable to the state.

Through a combination of coincidence and subjective will, the women of *ribu* found themselves in the crossfire of a decisive struggle in Japanese political history. *Ribu*'s decision to support the women of the URA was a difficult, if not precarious, action for the movement, but all the more profound given the political climate at the time. This willingness to embrace those who were criminalized and not considered human was *ribu*'s most dangerous encounter.

Tanaka Mitsu and Her Philosophy

As she watched the New Left face its demise, Tanaka Mitsu forced herself to continue writing during the spring of 1972. Over the course of about forty days and nights, Tanaka struggled to complete her book *To Women with Spirit: A Disorderly Theory of Women's Liberation (Inochi no onna-tachi e: torimidashi ūman ribu ron)*.[64] Described as the monumental text of the *ribu* movement, *To Women with Spirit* remains the most widely read book of the *ribu* era.[65] Tanaka's philosophy of liberation is woven into this highly personalized text alongside her critique of the New Left, the URA, and Nagata Hiroko.[66]

Tanaka articulated a philosophy of liberation that departed from a particular understanding of *onna*'s subjectivity and ontology. Tanaka's notions of *torimidashi*, contingency, violence, relationality *(kankeisei)*, and eros are all important principles in understanding *onna*'s ontology as a desiring subject. Tanaka philosophy of liberation and *onna* involved a complex approach to different manifestations of violence constituting a distinct feminist epistemology and ontology. Through this analysis of Tanaka's critical approach to different forms of violence, I argue that it serves as a point of departure to reconceive the relationship between violence and feminist subjects.

Tanaka's earliest manifestos spoke of a political subject who was not singular in her desires but existed in the tension of her conflicted and contradictory desires. Tanaka referred to this subject as the here-existing *onna (koko ni iru onna)* in contrast to the nonexistent fantasy woman *(doko ni mo inai onna)*. This here-existing *onna* sensed her miserable and wretched condition and could no longer bear to continue to live according to a heterosexist system that defined her as either a nurturing sacrificial wife and mother or a toilet for male sexual desire.[67] She was a split subject: split between living a lie and sensing that lie, knowing she lived a performance and not knowing herself as a living woman, knowing there must be something other than what she was living but not knowing how to become that not-yet-living woman. She was caught between sensing her oppression and knowing she participated in the system that (re)produced her oppression, between learning to survive in the system and finding pleasure in her unfulfilled, unfree condition. This subject did not and could not know herself, because she had never been free to be herself. Regarding "the here-existing *onna,*" who existed in her state of contradiction and chaos, Tanaka writes,

> Within each person, there are different intentions that contradict each
> other, and because they shift back and forth, you have this essential
> derangement and disorder. Therefore, from the outset it is impossible to
> express one's real intent with words. That momentary constantly shifting
> real intention *(honne)* can only at moments be expressed as *torimidashi*—
> chaos, derangement and disorder.[68]

This condition of perpetual contradiction that Tanaka describes as *torimidashi* was the essence of what it meant to live as a human. Tanaka sensed that the orderly and abstract theories about human liberation failed to encompass what it meant to live as an *onna* in this condition of derangement. It was this existential inquiry, a conscious turning toward the painful and contradictory condition of one's existence, that produced Tanaka's conception of liberation as a chaotic and disorderly process. This sense of disorder is expressed in the subtitle of her book. Contradiction and derangement were at the core of a subject's ontological condition. Tanaka's conception of subjective and collective action for *ribu* was captured in her oft repeated phrase *"torimidashi tsu tsu,"* which referred to this continual state of disorder and derangement.

For Tanaka, the way the Left privileged its theories of liberation over practice and lived experience was symptomatic of a masculinist modality that would rather exclude, repress, or deny the importance of this condition of perpetual contradiction or the significance of the visceral differences of woman's sex. One of the reasons for Tanaka's desire and will to assert this principle as the core of subjectivity derives from her assertion about the anarchistic tendencies of woman's sex. For Tanaka, this core essence of women's sex as anarchistic was a potential counterhegemonic force against the orderly forces of modern capitalism and a masculinist and male-centered civil society.[69]

To begin to know and recover herself, the here-existing *onna* had to confront herself and the misery of her life condition. In doing so, she would realize that her subjective condition did not originate or emanate solely from within herself but also formed from the outside by the system that constituted her as a social being. Tanaka held that the here-existing *onna* must turn away from the forces that negate her and look elsewhere for her definition of who she is and who she will become. She needed to learn how to affirm and live as the here-existing *onna*.[70] She must affirm herself not as a perfect revolutionary subject but rather, in her totality, as an imperfect, contradictory subject, for there was no other place of departure other than the here-existing *onna*. Therefore, Tanaka's concept of the revolutionary subject was precisely that of the imperfect subject who was necessarily constituted by contradictory and even conflicting desires.

Tanaka's theory of liberation called for an episteme of the self, an episteme that recognized and confronted one's own state of contradiction and relationship with violence. Tanaka's theorization of violence provides a striking contrast with common feminist conceptions of violence as inherently masculine or as a manifestation of male dominance.[71] One's own contradictoriness, excess, and otherness were linked to the conception of relationality and how one encounters the other. Tanaka rejected the dominant definitions of the "individual" based on binary models that separated and hierarchized the mind/body, theory/experience, rationality/sexuality. Part of Tanaka's project was to displace this paradigm of the individual by theorizing through and centering the body-of-contradiction of the here-existing *onna*. For Tanaka, a capitalist society that alienates, divides, and splits subjects into categories of the "individual," the productive and nonproductive, and cuts off relationality *(kankeisei)* according to the logic of capitalist productivity, was cruel and inherently violent. Thus, Tanaka did not emphasize individual acts of violence but rather the violence of the system.

Tanaka speaks of various kinds of violence that differ in each context. In *To Women with Spirit,* in one passage, Tanaka writes about her desire for violence as a desire to be able to *express her own violence,* because she felt that as a woman she was not able to adequately express the violence that she knew resided within her. Tanaka's articulation of her desire to express her own violence suggests that she does not idealize nonviolence, but rather, depending on the context, she sees and recognizes the efficacy of expressions of violence, particularly in the case of self-defense. "One thing that I don't quite have that I want is violence *(bōryokusei)*. Perhaps my very existence is violent but within me what is lacking is its concrete expression that one can understand such as the raised fist."[72] Tanaka makes this statement as she recalls how her father would beat her and her mother. Growing up, Tanaka lived in fear of her father's violence until the day she fought back. Tanaka's experience of using counterviolence against her father's violence protected and validated her existence. Her own use of counterviolence was, in this case, a form of self-defense used to stop the perpetuation of domestic interpersonal violence against her and her mother.[73] Insofar as she describes it as an effective means to break that cycle of domestic violence, she represents this form of counterviolence as seemingly having a desirable or positive effect. Therefore, the use of such counterviolence must be interpreted or attributed value according to its context. Nowhere does Tanaka advocate that such particular uses of violence are generalizable as an ultimate principle for political action.

In another passage in *To Women with Spirit,* Tanaka writes about her excitement as she watches her first *uchigeba* (intra-/intersectarian violent conflict) between the men of two left sects, Kakumaru (Revolutionary Marxist) and the JRA. Even though the young men from the JRA were well outnumbered, they won. At that time, Tanaka was with a Kakumaru man, watching from a distance.[74] When the fight was over, she recalls feeling repulsed by what she realized was her disdain of her companion's lack of virility. Her reflections about her own desires and the lure of violence mirror her fantasies about masculinity and how that fantasy constitutes her own sense of femininity and heterosexual desire.[75] Through her inclusion of these anecdotes, Tanaka implicates herself and attempts an articulation of her location as a woman in the desire for violence and how it is linked to her fantasies about masculinity and power. Thus, even though she critiques these men, she places herself in intimate proximity and relation with those whom she criticizes. Tanaka's analysis of the contradictoriness and fantasy-driven dynamic of her desire speaks to a fundamental inconsistency of desire as a force that is always potentially dangerous.

Philosopher Ukai Satoshi states, "The fundamental task of the current era is how to evaluate the differences among violences."[76] This task would involve an elaboration of what Randall Williams describes as "a defense of the ethicality of using violence as a strategic method—and when, where and under what conditions such strategic actions might be deemed both necessary and morally justifiable."⁷⁷ In this connection, I would add that when a subject is always already constituted within, by, and through a matrix of historical, structural, and systemic violence, this underarticulated historicity of violence can serve as the ontological basis and epistemic point of departure for a feminist ethics of violence. Therefore, in certain contexts, such as the ones described earlier, violence can be interpreted as exerting a particular set of effects and can be precariously open to different kinds of interpretations. In one instance, it is deployed and narrativized as self-defense, and in another, it serves to shore up dominant fantasies of masculinity. Tanaka's self-reflexive and critical discourse offers a means to consider the productivity of a feminist ethics of violence that examines the subject's historicity, positionality, and desires as constituted by differentiated relations of violence and power.

Tanaka went beyond what was typical among leftist discourses at the time by elaborating a gendered analysis of the violence of the right and the left and the violence within and between women themselves. In her earliest manifestos, Tanaka pointed to the contiguity of Japanese women's structural relationship to heinous forms of violence against other colonized Asian women, speaking of the relationship of the "chastity of the wives of the military nation" in direct relation to "the dirtied pussies of the comfort women."⁷⁸ Even if there is no direct physical manifestation of violence by an individual Japanese woman against the comfort women, we should recognize historical and structural violence that produces their positionalities in a structure of correlation. In her writings, Tanaka makes it clear that Japanese women (notably the middle class) are also oppressors in the system, playing a distinct role in reproducing men as slave workers under capitalism. According to Tanaka, women were not only participants who reproduced a violent social structure: beyond being subjects that reproduced violent social effects, a potential for violence was inherent to the specificity of a woman's body and being, to the particularity of her sex.

As noted in chapter 1, for Tanaka, the womb was not only the symbolic and material site of the creation of new life, it was also the origin of violence. Tanaka conceptualized the womb as the place that carried the grudge (怨) of women's history, containing forces that were generative and violent. By positing a woman's womb as a source of potential violence, Tanaka suggests the female body is no longer seen as only a victim of external violence but bears the potential to become a force of destruction and death. Thus, women are not separate from violence; rather, a potential for violence is located within women. By theorizing the female body as a site and source of violence, Tanaka's ontology leads to profoundly different conclusions than feminist discourses that almost exclusively posit women as the victims of male violence.

Tanaka saw the capacity and desire for violence and revenge in the bodies of all women, and she spoke of the capacity for violence as inherent to women's sex, as part of her will to power and her will to survive. Therefore, women who killed were not depraved or aberrant but were expressing a force both within them and beyond them. Rather than trying to speak to why women killed, Tanaka asks, What is it that keeps us from becoming murderers?

> Isn't having to exist in this society itself already agony enough? How
> can we go on living without engaging in such dishonorable tactics such
> as attacking men, attacking women, attacking children, and attacking
> ourselves?[79]

"I am not going to attack, I do not want to attack when the other/enemy is off guard" is the title of one of the sections of Tanaka's book on the disorderly theory of women's liberation. This contemplation of whether to attack the other expresses the force and singularity of Tanaka's philosophy of liberation. Tanaka's capacity to tarry with violence, and the desires for and against committing violence, and the contradiction and contingency between these desires are distinctive features of her feminist philosophy of liberation and also relate to this radical inclusivity of contradiction and chaos within the subject. Tanaka's conceptualization of violence contours her texts not only as eruptions or obstacles on the way to liberation but also as the interminable reality of human subjectivity and power struggle and therefore not only unavoidable but integral to the movement of liberation.

Tanaka says that what prevents people from taking out their revenge against others is that they have become numb to their pain and numb to the real violence of society; they deceive themselves into thinking they are all right, that they are living "in the light."[80] The majority of people refuse to confront the fundamental violence of society and also refuse to confront themselves, for doing so would bring them face to face with their own relationship to violence. A confrontation with the self requires an understanding of who one is in society and how one is supposed to live.

The meaningful potentiality of Tanaka's oeuvre to liberation inheres in becoming a subject that is open to this kind of self-identification, which becomes a way to identify with the other. Tanaka's theorization involved a radical pursuit of the other within the self, which became a way to forge a radical relationship to the other beyond the self. It is through this inward turn that a subject confronts one's own violence and realizes that one could have become a child killer or a "Nagata Hiroko." It is this same inward turn that leads to new possibilities of conceiving and embodying liberation. Because no one was beyond or outside the violence of the system, it was crucial to grasp one's own relationship to violence and one's position in a violent system.[81] Tanaka was thus open to identify with and theorize a relationship to various expressions of violence. She therefore did not see violence as an aberration, or essentially evil, nor was it something that could be totally repressed or expunged from society. Although she recognized that violence was part of the struggle for liberation, Tanaka also refused to idealize or advocate violence as the ideal way to achieve liberation. Although violence was part of the ineluctable condition of existence and struggle, Tanaka recognized the multiple and relational consequences of violence. Tanaka's grasp of the subject's relationship to violence was why violence was not idealized or reified but understood as integral to the perpetual condition of struggle and therefore something to be understood and judged according to its context, its relational causes and effects. As a radical feminist movement, an integral aspect of *ribu*'s liberation praxis was predicated on struggling toward an identification and relationality with the existential possibility that one could have become that other, whether that other be a child-killing *onna* or an even more notorious woman such as Nagata Hiroko.

Tanaka and Nagata

Tanaka states that she began her *ribu* because she was disgusted with the kind of revolution espoused by the New Left. In her words, *ribu* was the "demon child" *(onigo)* of the New Left—a painful birth that was well past its due date. In her dealings with the New Left, Tanaka writes about her observations of the JRA. Having been asked to allow members of the JRA to stay at her apartment (as was common practice among leftist activists at the time), she had the chance to observe the JRA up close. She writes, "Their lines sounded great, but they did not give a damn about me even though I was proposing to organize. What the hell kind of revolutionaries are they?!! . . . It was from this kind of anger that I began my ribu."[82]

Immediately following the first *ribu* camp *(gasshuku)*, held in August 1971, Tanaka received a call from Nagata Hiroko.[83] Because their sect was already under surveillance by the police, Nagata's group was looking for other groups to assist them. Nagata invited Tanaka to their mountain base to stay overnight to observe their "extralegal activities" (非合法活動).[84] Tanaka states that although she had no interest in covert activities, at this point, she agreed to meet with them. Although she had never met Nagata before, Tanaka states she was "curious" about this woman who symbolized a "woman revolutionary."[85] According to Nagata's account, from the time they met, Tanaka expressed her criticisms of the JRA. Nagata writes in her memoirs that it was clear that "Tanaka's group would not support any kind of armed struggle that did not have the support of the masses."[86] Tanaka states she could not even consider merging with them because she could already see that this group did not grasp the difference between reality and their dream of "simultaneous world revolution."[87]

Having met Nagata and other members of the JRA, Tanaka was shocked by news of the lynchings.[88] She had met many of the members face to face when she visited the mountain camp.[89] Tanaka's trauma from these events would haunt her for years.[90] Decades later, Tanaka recounts the unforgettable laughter and smile of Kaneko Michiyo, who was eight months pregnant.[91] She began writing *To Women with Spirit* in the wake of these revelations and would reiterate her explanations for years to come. In *To Women with Spirit*, she begins her chapter about *ribu* and the New Left as if she sees the body of twenty-three-year-old pregnant Kaneko, who was killed by Nagata and Mori in the purge.

> The tragically brutalized corpse of an eight month pregnant woman emerged from the other side of the fluorescent light. It was frightening. Whether it is the corporate logic of productivity or the logic of the productivity of revolution—they equally abhor woman's menstruation. It is not the United Red Army that scares me. To live on in this society is for me what is frightening.[92]

This quote captures the radical inclusivity of Tanaka's style of discourse, encompassing a critical analysis of the relationality of unnecessary death, capitalism, revolution, menstruation, misogyny, and fear. In an article published in 2009, thirty-seven years after the incidents, Tanaka explains, "I loathed Nagata. But even as I was shaking from disgust and fear, as I watched Nagata being lynched by the media, I asked myself, can I just let this go on?"[93] Tanaka describes how, because Nagata was being treated like a devil and a witch by the media, and because the rest of the nation had fallen silent from fear, despite her shock and horror, she could not remain silent.[94] Of the incident, Tanaka wrote,

> The bizarre incident that happened in the middle of the mountains was one of the effects of the lies of this society that insists that a woman must exert herself "twice that of a man" in order to rise in the ranks in this male-dominated society.[95]

According to Tanaka, Nagata was a woman who, like other career women, had to outdo men in order to prove her worth. But this base competition with men, whether it be in mainstream society or in the New Left, forced women to become like men and to compete within masculinist economies. Within the New Left, the women of *ribu* had already criticized how the very meaning of revolution had been defined by men, and Nagata was caught in this competition of proving herself within the economy of revolutionary violence. Tanaka writes, "Nagata martyred herself to the justice of man's revolution, although it might be said that she was crueler than the other men, she had to exert twice the power."[96] Nagata was caught up in performing a role defined by a masculinist subculture and in becoming the ideal revolutionary who outdid the men in her ranks. But even though Nagata may have been exceptional in her accomplishments by outdoing men, Tanaka argues that the desire that drove Nagata was symptomatic of women (and men) who seek recognition within male-centered economies. In Nagata's case, this economy was based on proving and measuring one's commitment through "revolutionary violence," which became a self-destructive quotient.

Immediately after the incidents in 1972, in *To Women with Spirit*, Tanaka wrote, "All those women who wag their tails to please men are Nagata Hirokos."[97] This desire to flatter men by demonstrating one's self-sacrificing devotion was not, however, a quality that was singular to Nagata: "Insofar as women exert themselves outdoing men in order to 'subjectively' carry out the men's theories of revolution, they are all Nagata Hirokos."[98] In forwarding this argument, Tanaka sought to lay bare the contagiousness of a male-identified logic that motivates many women to act as they do to compete for the (revolutionary) male gaze. Tanaka writes that Nagata's determination to prove her own revolutionary intent was what compelled her to the point of denying and disidentifying with her own sex. Nagata had become what Tanaka theorized as the nonexisting woman (*doko ni mo inai onna*), a woman who proved herself by denying the nature of her sex and the contradictions of her sex to become a woman who does not exist.[99]

Tanaka as Nagata

In Nagata's *Sixteen Graves,* her memoirs written from prison, she reflects on her past.[100] Nagata writes that she came from a background in which she was never able to openly deal with her sex, and it became, more than anything, a shameful thing for her. Moreover, Nagata had been unable to deal adequately with the sexual violence she experienced in her sect at the hands of its male leader, Kawashima Tsuyoshi. In August 1969, Nagata was working late at

Kawashima's home when his wife was away. That night, Kawashima raped Nagata.[101] In response to her rape, Nagata writes, "I ignored my character *(jinkaku)* as a woman. . . . . I could not at that time possess any demands or realize myself as a woman."[102] Nagata's discourse contrasts starkly with *ribu*'s approach to the indivisibility of *onna*'s identity, her sexuality, and her liberation.

According to Patricia Steinhoff, Nagata's sect took the position that "women's liberation required women to be revolutionaries first and women second."[103] But it was precisely this kind of separation or bifurcation that Tanaka and the *ribu* women rejected in terms of the essential indivisibility of being an *onna* and what it meant to be a revolutionary. They felt it was a grave mistake to base one's politics on the notion that one's identity as a woman should or could be repressed so that one could be a "pure revolutionary"—*a doko ni mo inai onna*—a nonexisting *onna*. Tanaka sensed that Nagata failed to recognize how she was connected to the other women in her sect and refused to recognize her own contradictions, which could have prevented her from killing her comrades.

Tanaka writes that Nagata could probably sense that she had the here-existing *onna (koko ni iru onna)* within herself and was torn between the "nonexisting woman" and the "here-existing *onna*."[104] Tanaka argues that if Nagata had been able to confront her own sex, and the meaning of that sex, she would have realized the contradictoriness and excessive condition of the subject. Instead, in order to prove her pure revolutionary intent, she did not allow for the here-existing *onna* to exist within herself or outside herself. Rather than recognize the here-existing *onna,* Nagata killed the women who reminded her of the here-existing *onna*.[105] When the other men and women of the sect displayed their sexual desires, or when other women acted too feminine, Nagata determined that these actions were counterrevolutionary. Tanaka writes that Nagata felt she had to kill the woman who was eight months pregnant who had "too much of an attachment to her accessories."[106] In so doing, Tanaka writes that Nagata was the one who killed and the one who was killed.[107]

In the *Ribu News,* Tanaka writes, "I desire to meet those members of the United Red Army, those who are dead and those who are alive."[108] By speaking of her desires to meet both the living and dead members of the URA, Tanaka's discourse was both poetic and spiritual, gesturing toward desires that could not be categorized as purely political or rational. Thus, her desires to meet the dead members of the URA, as well as her vision of Kaneko's corpse heavy with an unborn child, are suggestive of how some have commented that she seemed like a *miko* (shaman) or medium for the movement.[109] Her affective response to those killed in the URA's lynchings was thus not simply about empathy for those wrongly killed. It emanated from her own precarious relationality with those who killed in the name of a misconceived revolutionary ideal.

Even though Tanaka critiques Nagata as the embodiment of a woman symptomatic of the masculinist and self-destructive economies of the left, Tanaka also expressed her *will* to protect Nagata and support her. In spite of her own sense of revulsion—in her own condition of *torimidashi*—Tanaka cast her being toward Nagata, grasping the gravity of this historical moment.

Tanaka states, looking back on her actions at this time, "In a sense, in order to protect her whole body, I used my entire being to shield her."[110] On June 1, 1972, in *Nihon Dokusho Shinbun,* she wrote, "First we must be clear about who the self is. I am Nagata Hiroko" *(Atashi wa Nagata Hiroko desu).*[111] Given the context in which Nagata was displayed, as a national object of shame and abjection, Tanaka intervened by declaring that she was Nagata Hiroko. It goes without saying that Tanaka did not attempt to make sense of Nagata within a commonsensical schema of identity. In this statement, Tanaka opened up a different possibility of political identification and relationality. Tanaka's statement forwards a philosophical assertion that reconfigures the relationship of the self to the other. This statement involved the articulation of an imaginative possibility, of a consciousness that moved beyond the borders of what is said to constitute the self and the "I." Tanaka's use of the I in her statement "I am Nagata Hiroko" brings together her I and Nagata Hiroko and at once recasts the meaning of Nagata Hiroko and the I through a new episteme. When she speaks of the "Nagata Hiroko who is named Tanaka Mitsu,"[112] Tanaka's understanding of Nagata Hiroko is not as an individual or singular subject; rather, she grasps her as a convergence and culmination of animate and violent historical forces that Tanaka was open to identifying with and a part of. The mass media's misogynist representation of Nagata had rendered her inhuman, but Tanaka's reclamation of Nagata entailed a double movement that simultaneously deindividuated and humanized her. For Tanaka, Nagata was more than human, but she was not just an individual. Tanaka rather understood Nagata as the embodiment of a set of thematics and ontological principles, a woman who embodied the crises and contradiction of sacrificing *onna*'s sex for the revolution.

In the years following the incident, Tanaka continued to generate a discourse that inspired affection and eros between *onna*. In 1973, for example, Tanaka wrote a pamphlet titled "Your Short Cut Suits You, Nagata!"[113] This affectionate expression and compliment of Nagata's appearance, which had been continually trashed by the mass media, was Tanaka's way of reaching out with warmth toward a woman who was reviled by so many. In light of what happened, Tanaka carefully expresses her potential admiration for Nagata.

> If she hadn't been arrested as the ringleader in the lynching incident, she would have continued to be someone who I looked up to. The encounter is always an accident, contingent, and sometimes it is irony that is the primary factor that mediates the encounter. I have no doubt whatsoever that she is a "kind woman," I have this image that we overlap in ways, as ordinary women *(atarimae no onna)*.[114]

In this passage from the *Ribu News,* Tanaka again publicly declared her potential admiration for Nagata as a woman who was both ordinary and a product of her times. Rather than basing her support on a "rational" political choice, Tanaka's relationship with Nagata and the URA was based on a series of chance encounters, a constellation of affinities and (un)fortunate crossroads.

Throughout *To Women with Spirit,* Tanaka refers to the facticity of contingency as the foundational condition of being in the world. She elaborates a concrete example of this "chance," which she attributes to the contingent factor *(tama tama)* of the diseases each of them had contracted as young women. Tanaka, who had contracted syphilis in her early twenties, says that her disease, precisely because it was a sexual disease, did not allow her to deny her sex. "Without a doubt, the kind of sickness that I had made me conscious of a woman's sex."[115] By contrast, Nagata's illness, Graves disease, allowed her to deny her sex. Thus, when one attempted to relate to or identify with the other, it was important to understand that one's differences were often related to such contingent conditions.[116] When a subject realized that her position in the world was ultimately contingent, this understanding could potentially work to mitigate the tendencies toward fundamentalism, fascism, nationalism, and absolute notions of what constitutes good and evil. Such contingent conditions, which permeate and extend beyond the subject, largely determine one's life and death. On February 5, 2011, Nagata died of brain cancer in a Tokyo prison. She had been living on death row for almost thirty years.[117]

Conclusion

Tanaka was critical of any reductive prescription about revolution that necessitates violent action. Instead, she reconceived of revolution through a notion of relationality as figured in conditions of perpetual struggle and tension. She recognized that violence, contingency, contradiction, and relationality are all conditions of being in the world; therefore, she rejected any idealization of violence because of its interconnected, potentially irreversible, uncontrollable effects. Her ontological principles of contradiction and derangement *(torimidashi)*, violence and contingency, relationality and eros, are all to be held in tension such that one should not be idealized over the other, and she did not advocate that nonviolence must be the basis of political struggle.

Tanaka's analysis of the historical significance of Nagata and her capacity to articulate her relationship with her exemplified *ribu*'s creation of a different logic of relationality. Rather than turning against the other of the self, Tanaka could see the other *within* the self. She was a messenger of the force of *ribu*, which moved, articulated, and enacted a different logic of liberation and relationality that emanated from a place permeated with eros and violence. Tanaka's discourse about Nagata expresses *ribu*'s praxis of radical inclusivity and critical solidarity as the symbolic condensation of *ribu*'s alternative relationality.

Tanaka's analysis of Nagata constituted a complex modality of political and ethical identification that is philosophical and affective, political and spiritual. Within this form of identification lies the potential for a kind of liberatory relationality, which can form the basis of a different kind of feminist ethics of violence. These epistemological and ontological principles defy the ideology of individualism, liberalism, and by extension, liberal feminism. This relationality was deeply political insofar as it gestured toward the potentiality of more liberatory human relations. It required a different economy of identification that was not to be understood within the existing terms of identity and individuality.

In this dark hour of Japanese history that marked the demise of the New Left, through their collective actions and words, *ribu* women reflected the light in the shadows and created a space to support the lives of those who were condemned. Most immediately, *ribu* activists had to respond to a grotesque spectacle that would summon a nation to render militant leftist groups as the chosen objects to fear and to loathe, to be complicit with the state's will to criminalize and punish insurgent subjects. *Ribu*'s praxis of critical solidarity inhered in the tension between the collective and subjective, feminism and the New Left, in the attempt to build a collective approach to how individualized subjects become the agents and targets of different forms of violence within hegemonic gendered economies of power. *Ribu*'s relationality with these criminalized and insurgent women enabled *ribu* women to confront and work through the contingencies conditioning the potential effects of various forms of hegemonic and counterhegemonic violence. *Ribu*'s alternative modes of epistemology and ontology could constitute the basis for a feminist ethics of violence that refuses to idealize either nonviolence or revolutionary violence. By recognizing the subject's constitution in a system of historical and structural violence, such a feminist ethics would recognize that the eruption of counterviolence becomes recognizable only through its break with the normalized (and often nonvisible) conditions of state violence. Thus, violence itself is not a break or exception but rather largely unrecognized due to the banality of its most pervasive forms. Insofar as the URA came to symbolize an extremist group that posed a mortal threat to an "innocent nation," *ribu*'s approach to political violence and its praxis of critical solidarity remains trenchantly relevant today in a world where the discourses of terror and terrorism have all but foreclosed on the possibility of a sober and critical engagement with the vexed and vexing questions of political violence.

Lessons from the Legacy

Ūman ribu's legacy remains vital to understanding the subsequent trajectories and contentions across feminist formations in Japan and offers lessons for the future of social movements beyond the Japanese context. While many books could be written about the complex conditions of post-1970s feminism in Japan and how the women involved in *ribu* continue to shape this horizon, in what follows, I touch on a few significant fissures, transformations, and lessons from *ribu*'s legacy as points of reflection for the future.

The relationship between *ūman ribu* and feminism *(feminizumu)* in Japan has been a complicated one that begs to be understood not simply as a smooth transitional development but as a heterogeneous terrain that has involved political antagonisms and transformations. As noted in the Introduction, *ūman ribu* and feminism are not used interchangeably within the Japanese context. Whereas *ribu* has been associated with the movement era of the late 1960s and early 1970s, the usage of the transliterated term *feminizumu* to mean feminism began in the late 1970s and early 1980s.[1] Although there is a constituency of women who identify as both *ribu* and feminist, during my fieldwork from 1999 to 2002, I found it noteworthy that many *ribu* women refused to call themselves feminists and were resistant to the term. During this same period, I encountered even more Japanese feminists who would not identify as *ribu* because of its meaning and associations in Japan.[2] The political differences that demarcated this rift can be traced to *ribu*'s antiestablishment origins in the wake of the radicalism of the late 1960s and early 1970s in contrast to the institutionalized characteristics of academic feminism, which has arguably become the most visibly dominant form of feminism since the 1990s.

The semantic distinction between *ribu* and *feminizumu* is embedded within a specific political history. Inoue Teruko has stated that the term *feminizumu*

has academic and foreign associations compared to older terms such as
fujin kaihō undō (women's liberation movements) and *josei kaihō* (women's
liberation).[3]

> The way that feminism is used in Japan has a distinct nuance, a sense of
> it being academic or neutral. . . . It sounds like an imported or borrowed
> word . . . feminism refers to something distant from oneself, referring to
> European or American thought or movements.[4]

One of the turning points in the usage of *feminizumu*/feminism began with the
publication of a bilingual Japanese and English magazine called *Feminisuto*,
which began in 1977 and continued through the 1980s. This magazine was
launched by a group of academic and professional women in collaboration
with a few (white) American and European feminists. These feminists funded
their magazine by selling advertising space to corporations such as Shiseido
and Seibu Department Store, taking a different posture toward corporate
capital. Many *ribu* women noted the significance of this new alliance with
major corporations, because they had made it a deliberate practice to engage in self-publishing to maintain autonomy of their form, content, and
distribution.[5] According to Saeki Yōko, when the founders of *Feminisuto* first
launched their magazine in 1977, they called a press conference at which they
announced a "new era had begun" that was going to spread feminism in
Japan in more effective ways than *ribu*.[6] This move to mainstream or popularize feminism through women's commercial magazines is a post*ribu* phenomenon that I have examined elsewhere.[7] Many of the brief histories of
postwar women's movements printed in *Feminisuto*'s English editions make
little or no mention of the *ūman ribu* movement, disregarding the significance
of *ribu*'s interventions during the 1970s. Many *ribu* women interpreted these
moves as an attempt to negate their movement and render it obsolete. The
subsequent emergence of feminism after the genesis of *ribu* thus involved
what some women experienced as a history of betrayal that has remained as
an affective structure. This history of betrayal remains in excess of the history of *ribu* that has been canonized through the establishment of women's
studies.

Women's Studies and *Ribu*

The establishment of women's studies *(joseigaku)* in Japan became another
site of contestation.[8] In the late 1970s, many women invested in academic
research organized to establish women's studies in Japan. The formation of
women's studies was a response to *ūman ribu,* the development of women's

studies in the United States and Europe, and the UN Decade for Women.[9] From its emergence, there has been debate and critical exchange about the purpose of women's studies, the process of its establishment and hierarchical structure, its methodology and pedagogy, and its hegemonic position within the current feminist movement.[10]

Many of the founders of women's studies distanced themselves from the *ribu* movement.[11] Because these academics sought to establish women's studies in Japan as a respectable and bona fide scholarly practice, the radicalism of the *ribu* movement and its hysterical image that had been created by the mass media as a group of disruptive young women were regarded as incongruent with and unsuitable for its academic goals.[12] Instead of seeking to forge links with the existing women's movements in Japan, many founders sought to legitimate their project by referring to women's studies in the United States as the model to follow.

In 1978, in *ribu*'s most widely circulating journal *Onna Erosu,* Miki Sōko published a prescient and discerning critique of women's studies just as it was emerging in Japan. In the eleventh edition, Miki wrote an article called "What Is Women's Studies without *Ribu*'s Spirit?" In this short but often cited essay, Miki criticizes the two newly formed women's studies associations, the Women's Studies Association of Japan *(Nihon joseigaku kai)* and the International Society for Women's Studies *(Kokusai joseigaku kai).*[13] Miki criticizes these two associations for trying to distance themselves from *ūman ribu* and for purporting to have no ideological stance except an academic and objective perspective.[14] Key founders of women's studies, such as Iwao Sumiko, were interested in collecting data about the life cycle of women's lives, asserting that a women's lifestyle was her "individual free choice," without questioning the ideological aspects of the dominant sex-role division of labor.[15] Miki noted the imitative and assimilationist tendencies of these proponents of women's studies who claimed to want to be objective about the conditions of women's lives without recognizing that the production of knowledge was always political. Miki advocated for a women's studies that emanated from the oppositional consciousness of the *ribu* movement and would challenge and critique existing power structures between men and women across all social institutions. For Miki, women's studies should not be a vehicle of assimilation but a field of transformative knowledge production based on *ribu*'s alternative ways of knowing and analyzing women's conditions.[16] This rift posited between political activism and professional assimilation has been a common issue in the establishment of ethnic, women's, feminist, gender, and queer studies in the academy beyond the context of Japan.

In contrast to some of the founders of women's studies who purposely distanced themselves from *ūman ribu,* there are women who identify with both *ribu* and *feminizumu,* such as Inoue Teruko, Akiyama Yōko, Tanaka Kazuko, and others, who were involved in the *ribu* movement and went on to invest themselves in the project of women's studies. Inoue Teruko has been a pivotal figure in this regard, as a person involved in the early stages of *ribu* who went on to become a prolific and highly influential participant in women's studies in Japan. Inoue writes that she first heard about women's studies at the 1971 *ribu* summer camp in Nagano, when the journalist and feminist activist Matsui Yayori reported on the conditions of the women's liberation movement in the United States.[17] At the time, Inoue was already on an academic track as a doctoral student at the University of Tokyo. Upon hearing about women's studies, she felt her future vision for her research was crystallized. In 1975, Inoue was one of the first scholars to establish and teach a women's studies class at Wako University.

Inoue has carried out an important role in terms of bridging and theorizing the relationship between *ribu* and women's studies. Inoue is cited as one of the key proponents of women's studies, who defines it as being "the study of women, by women for women."[18] For Inoue, women's studies is the "academic version of *ribu*" and the "academic version of feminism" more broadly.[19] Inoue invested in the project of establishing women's studies within the university as part of a transformative feminist agenda that is, for her, connected with her experience of *ribu.*

The institutionalization of women's studies over the last thirty years has thus had diverse political effects and produced a range of feminist positions. Works such as *Japanese Women: New Feminist Perspectives on the Past, Present and Future* (1996), *Voices from the Japanese Women's Movement* (1996), and *Broken Silence: Voices of Japanese Feminism* (1997) represent a diverse range of feminist perspectives, demonstrating a robust and rich range of feminist debates from ecofeminism to housewife feminism and feminist critiques of Japanese pornography and the sex industry. A substantive body of feminist, women's, and gender studies literature is now available in Japanese, and although these subjects remain marginal in the Japanese academy, gender and women's studies courses have been institutionalized from the undergraduate to graduate level. By the mid-1990s, approximately 25 percent of Japanese colleges and universities offered some form of women's studies courses.[20] By the 1990s, women's studies had gained enough recognition that prestigious academic publishing houses such as Iwanami Shoten and journals such as *Gendai Shisō* began to produce book series, anthologies, and specialized encyclopedic dictionaries devoted to the subject of *feminizumu.*

A bloc of prolific feminist scholars, which has included Inoue Teruko,

Ehara Yumiko, Ueno Chizuko, and Kano Mikyo, incorporated and produced a history of *ribu* that connects academic feminism to this movement era. By linking the history of women studies directly to the *ribu* movement, this narrative has, to some extent, worked to bridge the divide by recognizing and acknowledging *ūman ribu* as the beginning of what has been dominantly periodized as the genesis of second wave feminism in Japan. The adoption of the term "second wave feminism" in Japan from the U.S. and European context is also indicative of the ways in which the establishment of women's studies has largely adopted Eurocentric paradigms of feminist knowledge production. Moreover, as I discussed (in the Introduction and chapter 4), this periodization also effectively narrated the end of *ribu* in 1975, discursively producing its premature obsolescence through feminist scholarship.[21] Furthermore, the way Japanese women's studies has repeatedly spotlighted Tanaka Mitsu as *ribu*'s icon has been frequently criticized by *ribu* activists and other feminists.[22] This selective adoption and canonization of *ribu* has had the polyvalent effect of rendering it a *past* social movement, which in turn has deemphasized the ways in which many *ribu* activists remain involved and committed to various localized and transnational political struggles beyond the academy. The master narrative that the movement era ended in the 1970s has many negative effects, when in fact movements have taken on new forms, sizes, spaces, and interfaces.

Feminism and the State

The establishment of women's studies has occurred alongside the increasing corporatization of the university and adoption of a state feminism. This converged with the reformation of a new liberal feminist bloc of fifty-two women's groups that have worked with the government to implement various reforms since the beginning of the UN Decade for Women in 1975.[23] State feminism has managed to promote and regulate a liberal feminist discourse that endorses equality between the sexes. The enactment of the Equal Employment Opportunity Law in 1986 was emblematic of an emphasis on equality for women's participation in the labor market based on the individual's "abilities and willingness."[24] During the 1980s and 1990s, which saw the rise of state feminism, the government continued to maintain its discriminatory practices against immigrant labor from third world nations. The government at the same time denied state compensation to those women who attempted to sue the Japanese government for their forced labor and systematic rape as military sex slaves in Japan's military comfort station system. The rise of liberal state feminism thus demands a continual critique of how certain forms of feminism can benefit select groups and individuals, as evidence of "progress," and at the same time deny political rights and self-determination to others. In this regard, Matsui Yayori summarily stated, "I am suspicious about the American model of empowerment, which means the right to grasp for power just as men do."[25]

A case that illustrates some salient fissures across feminist formations was the Women's International War Crimes Tribunal for the Trial of Japanese Military Sexual Slavery held in December 2000. One of the leading forces organizing this tribunal was the Violence Against Women in War–Network Japan (VAWW-Net).[26] VAWW-Net was established by Matsui Yayori, and the forum in many ways symbolized the culmination of her decades of anti-imperialist feminist work that focused on Japan's responsibility toward other Asians. Rather than join efforts led by VAWW-Net to indict the Japanese government for war crimes in this international forum, leading feminists like Ueno Chizuko and Tanaka Mitsu sought to establish nongovernmental citizens' funds to compensate and aid former comfort women and to forward their own extensive critiques of the sexual politics of this imperialist system.[27] This fund-raising was part of their alternative feminist response, which also entailed their critique of the government's establishment of the Asian Women's Fund, which asked for donations from Japanese citizens to compensate the so-called comfort women. While many forms of reparation, education, and transformation must be pursued, a focus on monetary compensation from Japanese citizens can function to detract from and obscure state accountability. These differences between Japanese feminists can also be traced to how the *ribu* movement and Ueno's brand of feminism were more explicitly prosex than Matsui's politics, which were largely critical of prostitution/sex work. Matsui's stance on prostitution/sex work was informed by her anti-imperialist concern with its impact on Asian women and has also been attributed to her Christian background. In turn, Matsui criticized how *ribu*'s focus on sexuality became too self-referential.[28] Such differences signify how Japanese feminists prioritize and negotiate the importance of anticolonial and anti-imperialist politics given the afterlife of Japanese colonialism that continues to the present.

The strategic production of liberal feminist discourse as part of state feminism has been simultaneous with the production of feminist discourses that are compatible with neoliberalism. The emergence of nongovernmental organizations that take on feminist projects and work in cooperation with the state is another area to be reevaluated in terms of how feminists negotiate reformist relationships with the state.[29] The production of feminist celebrities and their hypervisibility during the rise of neoliberalism also warns of how the empowerment of individual feminists often operates as a politics of representation that substitutes for a more substantive politics of redistribution of power and resources.[30]

Ribu's Rearticulations

Since the 1990s, there has been a significant number of *ribu* retrospective publications and collections. The leftist press Inpakuto Shuppan-kai has published four collections: *Twenty Years of Ribu* (1992), *From Zenkyōtō to Ribu* (1996), *The Revolution Called Ribu* (2003), and most recently, in 2008, the *Collection of Documents of the Ribu Shinjuku Center,* a massive three-volume collection of *ribu* manifestos, newspapers, bulletins, and pamphlets.[31] These publications signal an ongoing interest in and rearticulation of *ribu*'s politics well beyond its initial context of emergence. These retrospective collections indicate a renewed interest in the 1960s and 1970s, inviting activists to reflect on and reiterate the meaning of their participation in political movements.

Rather than producing such knowledge as historical relics to be consumed as commodities within a neoliberal market, such work becomes particularly meaningful and relevant when we can discuss how such movements relate to the current horizon of politics. It is important to understand the purpose of (re)articulation (following Stuart Hall) as a strategy to reiterate and re-animate political antagonisms that exceed narratives of inclusion and recognition. Thus, eschewing a nostalgia for a bygone era, it remains imperative to rigorously examine the interventions, practices, limits, and mistakes of these formations and how they should inform and transform the present in the current context of militarized neoliberal globalization.

In 2004, feminist filmmakers Yamagami Chieko and Seyama Noriko produced a *ribu* retrospective documentary, *30 Years of Sisterhood*. This project was initially planned as a means for *ribu* women to document their own stories and was meant to contrast with other filmic representations, such as *Ripples of Change* and Hara Kazuo's *Extreme Private Eros,* that are seen by *ribu* women as produced by outsiders to the movement.[32] This compilation of video interviews, filmed in 2003 and 2004, captures many conversations during the annual *ribu* retreat.[33] The synopsis line on the DVD cover states: "This is the herstory of women who have taken action against a sexist society and tried to live life as freely as they could." *Ribu* activists discuss why and when they joined *ribu* and what they gained from the movement. The interviews are edited in such a way to create a coherent "herstory" of sisterhood and produces a representation of *ribu* that is readily recognizable as a mirror image of radical feminism in the United States. This kind of narrative of sisterhood is informative and valuable, cohesive and inspiring, but in my view, it simplifies the complex multi-issue, anti-imperialist feminist politics of the movement into a single-axis, antisexist feminist politics. Some of the most significant and striking aspects of *ribu*'s activism, such as the women's experimental work in the sex industry, their solidarity with women who killed their children, and their position on abortion that was informed by an anticapitalist stance on disability, are not mentioned. Moreover, *ribu*'s complex affiliations with the New Left and its radical critique and support of the United Red Army fall outside of this narrative of Japanese feminist sisterhood. While this sisterhood has sustained me and this project, a narrow notion of feminism emerges that highlights individual freedom over the messy, difficult work of collective struggle.[34] This reiteration constructs the movement's legacy primarily by having women speak of their liberation in terms of achieving their own forms of self-expression. Tanaka Mitsu, for example, speaks of the importance of being "one's own cheerleader" and states that "*ribu* was a platform for *her* to become no one other than *herself* (emphasis mine)."[35] Feminist discourse that reduces systemic critique to the aim of individual liberation has become commonplace and is highly compatible with neoliberalism.

In February 2006, a tour of *30 Years of Sisterhood* was organized across universities and college campuses in the United States. Joining the codirectors, Yamagami and Seyama, were three ribu activists: Doi Yumi, a veteran member of the Group of Fighting Women and the Ribu Shinjuku Center who lives in San Francisco; Miki Sōko, veteran *ribu* activist and scholar who is now a retired professor and an active organizer of feminist film festivals in Asia; and Akiyama Yōko, a feminist scholar of Chinese literature involved with women's studies in Japan. These veteran *ribu* activists were joined by Urara Satoko, a younger-generation lesbian-identified filmmaker, and Tomomi Yamaguchi, a U.S.-based Japanese feminist scholar and the lead organizer of the tour. This tour of *30 Years of Sisterhood* marks a significant moment in the narration of *ribu*'s legacy and how its transnational networks have often been routed and directed toward the United States as a metropole and site of recognition, solidarity, and difference. The tour also constituted a merging of veteran *ribu* activists, women's studies scholars, and a younger generation of Japanese feminists to disseminate the knowledge of *ribu* beyond Japan across multiple temporalities. This U.S. tour of *30 Years of Sisterhood* is one example of how some of the domestically situated rifts between *ribu* and feminism from the late 1970s and 1980s are no longer salient when *ribu* and feminist activists dialogue and travel across transnational feminist networks.[36]

After the screening of *30 Years of Sisterhood* across college campuses, feminist bookstores, and LGBT community centers in 2006, viewers of the documentary raised questions about how *ribu* relates to ongoing feminist contentions such as the gap between political activism and women's studies, the relationship between *ribu* and lesbian movements, and *ūman ribu*'s relationship with other "minority" women in Japan. These gaps and fissures remain as part of the legacy of *ribu* and as areas for further interrogation and elaboration.

Conclusion

I began this book by suggesting the need for a new feminist analytics and ethics of violence that takes into account the historical and systemic forms of violence constitutive of our ontologies and epistemologies of liberation. My intent to problematize the various forms and effects of violence among women, feminists, and other leftist activists suggests the imperative to reckon with the harms that transpire in the very pursuit of liberatory politics. From *ūman ribu* (and other movements) we can learn of the dangers that accompany the reification of a revolutionary subject or icon and how equality remains an illusive ideal that can unsettle leftist hierarchies. Progressives, leftists, and radicals are often caught up in their own forms of contradiction and competition for recognition and resources. If we recognize that interpersonal harm is more than likely, if not inevitably, going to manifest across the complex conditions and relationalities of the Left, then it is necessary to collectively create productive and constructive practices to deal with these contradictions and conflicts rather than conceal, internalize, or displace responsibility and accountability. This kind of work is integral to this feminist analysis and ethics of violence.

The cumulative effects of differential power and harm may be—like an internal hemorrhaging wound—what diffuses our collective force, preventing more powerful movements, imaginative alliances, and unforeseen insurrections. By heeding the screams from the shadows, we might learn from the experiences of those who have given their lives and those whose lives were lost in the imperfect, fractured, and unfinished struggle for liberation.

ACKNOWLEDGMENTS

This book was made possible through the support of multiple communities of activists, teachers, mentors, colleagues, friends, comrades, and loved ones. I have lived with this project for a long time, and its deepest roots exceed my own life and genealogy. My journey through the archives and fieldwork to the completion of this book took many detours and processes of protracted renegotiation and resolution. As a 1.5-generation privileged Japanese immigrant, born in Denenchōfu, Tokyo, but raised in a white working-class Canadian neighborhood in Surrey, British Columbia, my experience of the uneven assemblages of racism, sexism, and classism informed my motives for pursuing a graduate degree in the humanities. I went to graduate school at Cornell University, thanks to Tom Lamarre's mentorship when I was an undergraduate at McGill University.

Cornell proved to be a stimulating and fertile terrain. After a full-time immersion in those texts and theorists across the overlapping fields of continental philosophy, feminist theory, and Japanese philosophy, my relative dissonance with how feminist high theory meant almost exclusively Eurocentric feminist criticism impelled me down new paths of inquiry. I wondered about those lesser or unknown feminist revolutionaries and radicals who could challenge the boundaries of feminist theory and explode orientalist myths of the other. I first heard of Tanaka Mitsu from former members of the Japanese New Left who were visiting scholars at Cornell. After I located some of Tanaka's writings as a graduate student in the late 1990s, her Japanese words of poetic rage became my entry point into the history of the movement.

I am fortunate to have been the beneficiary of a constellation of scholars at Cornell who all taught me important lessons. The patience and support of my committee members as I made plenty of detours, including martial arts as a feminist praxis, was deeply appreciated. Naoki Sakai, my advisor, modeled the importance of taking a stance based on the political stakes of knowledge production; his imprint has been formative, and I am indebted to his support and principled generosity. I am grateful for Brett de Bary's sensitive and meticulous approach to handling people and texts, for Victor Koschmann's breadth of knowledge and consistency, and to Shelley Wong for introducing me to Asian American and ethnic studies. Gary Okihiro's commitment to mentoring graduate students and his reflections on the greater purpose of the struggle from within the academy remain with me. My friendship with Susie Lee (Pak) and Jean Kim, as well as my other compadres during my graduate school years, sustained me in the early phases of this work; Jolisa Gracewood, Tamara Loos, Sara Friedman, Katsu Endo, Ilse Ackerman, Paula and Joshua Young, and Rich Calichman were notable in this regard.

The first fourteen months of my fieldwork, from October 1999 to December 2000, was generously supported by a Japan Foundation Dissertation Research Grant. My original plans to study at Ochanomizu Women's University were not feasible due to Tachi Kaoru's leave of absence, so I ended up at the University of Tokyo, where Ueno Chizuko was generous enough to serve as my official advisor. It was an eye-opening experience to be a participant–observer in her famous seminars. Seeing how feminism can be transfigured and co-articulated in the most unexpected and innovative ways is one of Ueno's trademarks and has enabled her unparalleled contribution to postwar Japanese feminist history and publishing. I was able to extend my field research for two more years, from March 2001 to March 2003, as a recipient of a Monbusho Research Scholarship. I appreciated the opportunity to conduct such extensive research over this three-year period from 1999 to 2003, when I was able to interact with and get to know many *ribu* activists and Japanese feminist scholars. Because of my affiliation with Ueno Chizuko and the University of Tokyo, it was sometimes difficult to negotiate the preexisting tensions and conflicts between some *ribu* activists and Ueno and the signifying power of the imperial university.

During my fieldwork, I spent a significant amount of time with Tanaka Mitsu. I studied Eastern medicine *(tōyōigaku)* with her for six months as a student in her classes at the Asahi Cultural Center in Shibuya, and I worked as a volunteer for the Okinawan music concerts she organized in Tokyo. Tanaka knew that she was a focal point of my dissertation research; she was highly receptive to this and generously shared with me unpublished documents and writings. By the end of my fieldwork, and over the course of ten years, I had conducted a long series of recorded interviews and had numerous meetings and conversations with her over meals, at her apartment, and in different cafés across Tokyo. Spending so much time with Tanaka and reading her body of work from the 1970s to 2010 had a profound impact on how I understand her role in the movement in all its rich complexity and contradictions.

I am deeply indebted to the kindness, warmth, and generosity of the women of the movement and other leftist women activists I met along the way who shared their stories and writings and their candid opinions about their experiences as activist–intellectuals. From 2000 to 2002, I participated in several *ribu* annual retreats, including two *onsen gasshuku* (hot springs retreats), feminist film festivals, and reunion gatherings. At these events, I had extended conversations with many *ribu* women, such as Funamoto Emi, Azumi Yōko, Wakabayashi Naeko, Kitamura Mitsuko, Asakawa Mariko, Kuno Ayako, Wada Aiko, Shimemura Fuyuko, Masai Reiko, Terazaki Akiko, Miki Ayako, Nakajima Satomi, Fuji Mitsuko, and Yamagami Chieko; all were helpful in shaping my appreciation of *ribu*'s dynamic history. I conducted recorded interviews with the following *ribu*-identified women: Yonezu Tomoko, Endō Misaki, Mori Setsuko, Sayama Sachi, Akiyama Yōko, Inoue Teruko, Iwatsuki/Asatori Sumie, Miki Sōko, and Saeki Yōko, as well as leftist organizers such as Hama Retsuko and Abe Shigeko. It was a special privilege to interview Iijima Aiko in March 2001 before she passed in 2005. I especially thank Hama Retsuko for arranging this opportunity. Meeting and conversing with the late Matsui Yayori, before she passed in 2002, was a dialogue that I wish I could have extended. Younger-generation, queer-identified women who organized with *ribu* women, such as Inaba Mizuki, and others such as Yuki Hirano, also helped shape my understanding of *ribu*, Japanese feminism, and queer politics.

In September 2002, I participated in a study retreat on *Documents of the History of Ūman Ribu in Japan* (Shiryō Nihon ūman ribu shi, 1969–82). I am especially grateful to Saeki Yōko and Miki Sōko, two of the editors of this monumental three-volume collection of the movement's original documents, with whom I had the opportunity to travel. My extended conversations and correspondence with them over the course of many years were influential in forming my understanding of the movement's history.

I prolonged publishing this work for many reasons. One was my sense of obligation to the women of the movement, as I feared that any work that represents them will inevitably be incomplete, fall short of the mark, and not do adequate justice to their labor, sacrifice, and kindness. Another difficulty involved my need to reconfigure my focus on Tanaka Mitsu in the dissertation and work through the tensions of her relative power in the movement vis-à-vis other *ribu* activists. Mizoguchi Ayeko, the third editor of *Documents of the History of Ūman Ribu in Japan,* and Yamaguchi Tomomi were among the first Japanese feminist scholars who alerted me to the problematic power status of Tanaka. It took a long time to resolve how to distill into words that complex set of relations and historical processes. Having contemplated the stakes of producing this book and directing it to an English readership, I came to realize that it remains important to fully comprehend the symbolic value and pragmatic function of leaders and icons. It is just as imperative to resist idealizing them and to be ethical and meticulous in our critical assessment of the fissures and conflicts within movements through our production of alternative histories.

Watanabe Fumie, a *ribu* activist from Hiroshima, was a vital supporter of my project and read most of the manuscript. She helped translate two of my chapters into Japanese so that *ribu* women could read them. Her kindness, knowledge, and advice were a lifeline in difficult times. Miki Sōko was consulted in this process, and I especially thank Yonezu Tomoko, Wakabayashi Naeko, and Sagama Sachi for reading these chapters and offering comments and factual corrections.

Feminist publisher and activist Hashimoto Iku, of Ochanomizu Shobō, provided great support, a wealth of knowledge, and advice throughout many years of this project. Saitō Masami, a former "housewife activist" and Japanese feminist scholar of the media and *ribu*, has been a wonderful and well-informed interlocutor over the years. Kobayashi Sachiko and Hara Kazuo were very generous in allowing me to interview them about their relationship with the *ribu* movement and their filmmaking practice. I appreciated the opportunity to meet and converse with Nanako Kurihara, the director and producer of *Ripples of Change,* in New York City.

Many others aided in my multilayered knowledge of Japan's leftist history. Nagahara Yutaka taught me how the violence of that New Left history did not end in the 1970s. Another former New Left activist and scholar, Iwasaki Minoru, has been a wonderful teacher, friend, and colleague. Time and again he informed me of the meaning of key terms and concepts of the 1970s and offered his reflections on that period. His brilliance, self-effacing humor, and revolutionary spirit has endeared him to many. I also appreciated learning from the historian Narita Ryūichi, who enlightened me about complex relationships across postwar leftist history.

I gained much from many conversations with the feminist scholar Yuki Senda about the contemporary state of Japanese feminism and the major feminist debates during the 1990s. In September 2009, Yuki Senda, Akiyama Yōko, and Muto Ichiyo gave me comments on three of my chapters at a forum at the Tokyo University of Foreign Studies facilitated by Iwasaki Minoru.

When I first moved to Riverside, California, conversations with Piya

Chatterjee and Jared Sexton, who offered critiques of the movement, were helpful. During my postdoctoral years at Stanford from 2005 to 2006, Michele Mason and Kiyoteru Tsutsui were ideal fellow postdocs. I especially thank Wesley Sasaki-Uemura for reading and commenting on chapter 2 and for his advice on related sources. I thank Erica Edwards for comments on chapter 4 and her help in thinking through the seductive perils of charisma and charismatic leaders. Stephen Wu, Ricardo Bracho, and Randall Williams read chapter 5 on the United Red Army and offered much encouragement. Randall Williams's work and our ongoing conversations have been sustaining, inspiring, and illuminating. I thank him for help with the final title of the book. The opportunity to present chapter 5 at Harvard University in 2011 at the workshop Radical Feminism in Japan, organized by Tomiko Yoda, was greatly appreciated. The workshop's participants (Anne Allison, Brett de Bary, Rebecca Jennison, and Adrienne Hurley) provided a stimulating space. Adrienne has been a long-time comrade in Japan studies and an incredible and life-sustaining friend. Conversations with James Welker, another scholar of *ribu* and the lesbian movement in Japan, have been most helpful in figuring out interesting ironies of the movement. Mark Pendleton, Daisy Kim, and Gavin Walker have been wonderful interlocutors in recent years.

My colleagues in my home department of Media and Cultural Studies (MCS) at University of California–Riverside—Lan Duong, Wendy Su, Derrick Burrill, Ruhi Khan, Ken Rogers, and chair Toby Miller—provided a collegial working environment. I especially thank my next-door MCS hallmates Keith Harris and Freya Schiwy, whose modes of inhabiting the university have been a sustaining force. Andy Smith's work has been paradigm-shifting in recalibrating my feminist politics. Our amazing MCS departmental staff, Brandy Quarles-Clark and Mike Atienza, keep our spirits and students going in tough times. Colleagues and friends like Traise Yamamoto, Jennifer Doyle, Vorris Nunley, Devra Weber, Farah Godrej, Jeff Sacks, Mariam Lam, Brinda Sarathy, Karthick Ramakrishnan, Amar Raheja, Cecily and Jonathan Walton, Sarita See, David Lloyd, Ofelia Cuevas, Dean Saranillio, and Sharon Heijin Lee provide a wonderful community in Riverside and beyond. I thank our supportive Dean Steve Cullenberg. The late Emory Elliot was a stalwart supporter, and Laura Lozon has made UCR a livable place. A Regent's Faculty Fellowship in 2009–10 and the support of the UCR Academic Senate facilitated the final phases of this project. Thanks to David Martinez, who copyedited an early draft of the manuscript and produced the index. I also thank Masahito Kawahata, who assisted me in 2008, and Akinobu Okajima, my research assistant in 2009.

During this journey, I diverged and coedited the anthology *Militarized*

Currents: Toward a Decolonized Future in Asia and the Pacific with Keith Camacho. This five-year project expanded my horizons, and Keith helped navigate new terrains. I also am grateful for those who inspired and shared in the process of making *Visions of Abolition: From Critical Resistance to a New Way of Life,* our film project that coincided with the last few years of finishing the book. In this regard, Melissa Burch, Susan Burton, Jolie Chea, Treva Ellison, Kiana Green, David Stein, Anthony Rodriguez, Tasneem Siddiqui, and Craig Gilmore were important. My coproducers, Cameron Granadino and Gina Gonzalez, have become great friends and comrades and allowed me to talk through many ideas during our countless hours together in the editing lab.

Japanese women's historian Kathleen Uno and feminist scholar Anne Russo were my external reviewers and gave me excellent feedback on the first draft of my book; their suggestions significantly strengthened it. Lisa Yoneyama and Lisa Lowe provided wonderful examples of scholarship for me. The global political–intellectual breadth and magnanimity of Cynthia Enloe has been inspiring. Rita Wong, Angela Davis, Ruthie Gilmore, and Beth Ritchie model the kind of feminist scholar–activist life work to which I aspire.

Bearing, birthing, breastfeeding, and raising Taer and Saya have given me a radically new perspective on life. Their changing beings every day bring a new appreciation for mysteries of DNA as a construct in tension with social-ization. Raising these two kids and living with Dylan Rodríguez for the past ten years have taught me many lessons in the importance of rethinking family configurations and creating "extended family networks." Dylan's loyalty and devotion have sustained me in some of the toughest moments of this project. His consistent criticism of "Eurocentric feminist tendencies" and first-world Japanese privilege have been most helpful in seeing the limitations of *ribu*'s politics. Through this relationality, I learned much about how to embrace the work of intellectual insurgency and the effects of taking unpopular political positions in the university as a vital site of politics. In our family, we include Viet Mike Ngo, one of Taer's godfathers, who has also sustained me and loved our family as he struggled from inside California's prisons to freedom.

I thank the fabulous women in my UCR writing group who read parts of the manuscript: Tamara Ho, for her generosity of spirit; Michelle Raheja, for being such a sophisticated stealth thinker; and the virtuosity of Amalia Cabezas, for encouraging me to boldly call out the repressive tendencies among feminists and in feminist theory. And last but certainly not least is the multifaceted brilliance of Jodi Kim: I could not have completed this book without the consistent, loving support of my dear friend, colleague, and soul sister. She was always there for me, giving smart advice, reading multiple drafts, and providing a patient listening ear to help me work through the vortex of difficulties and obstacles and fruitful detours on the long road to completing this project.

My siblings, Rie, Ken, Hana, and Tetsuro, have, from their diverse careers and vantage points, always been encouraging, and they reinforced my determination to carry through while keeping perspective and reminding me to laugh. My parents have always modeled for me divine values: holding together knowledge with kindness, that learned generosity and graceful humility is a form of dignity, and that you can never give too much to the universe. Both Yoshiko's and Akira's bilingual expertise as writers and journalists helped me navigate the difficulties of nuance and polysemy as well as the nontranslatable in the work of translating from Japanese to English.

Finally, the fantastic people at the University of Minnesota Press. Erin Warholm, Anne Wrenn, Carol Lallier, Nancy Sauro, Rachel Moeller, and Daniel Ochsner made the process of working with this press ever pleasant and smooth as possible. I especially thank Richard Morrison for his consistent support, humor, and editorial acuity.

There have likely been many others I may not have named here who helped this project; I take responsibility for its shortcomings, and my gratitude does not end here. This book is devoted to all the lives of those committed, however imperfectly, to the shared work of our ongoing struggles.

NOTES

Translation and Romanization

Japanese names and authors of Japanese texts are cited with the surname followed by given name. Conversely, Japanese authors of English publications follow standard convention. If an English translation of a book title, film, political party, or group has already been in circulation, I use the existing title. Unless attributed, all translations are my own. I use the modified Hepburn system for the romanization of Japanese, with macrons to indicate long vowels.

Preface

1. Ann Russo, "The Feminist Majority Foundation's Campaign to Stop Gender Apartheid: The Intersections of Feminism and Imperialism in the United States." *International Feminist Journal of Politics* 8, no. 4 (2006): 557–80. The Feminist Majority Foundation has been one of the more visible U.S.-based feminist organizations that endorsed American intervention in Afghanistan by linking "anti-American terrorism" with that of the "oppression of Afghan women." On September 18, 2001, President Eleanor Smeal wrote, "The link between the liberation of Afghan women and girls from the terrorist Taliban militia and preservation of democracy and freedom in America and worldwide has never been clearer." Chicago Women's Liberation Union, Herstory Project, http://www.cwluherstory.com. See also Catharine A. MacKinnon, "State of Emergency," in *Aftershock: September 11, 2001, Global Feminist Perspectives,* ed. Susan Hawthorne and Bronwyn Winter (Vancouver: Raincoast Books, 2003), 467–73. For a critique of how Western liberal feminist discourse colludes with imperialism, see Nima Naghibi, *Rethinking Global Sisterhood: Western Feminism and Iran* (Minneapolis: University of Minnesota Press, 2007).

2. In a 1996 interview with Lesley Stahl on CBS's *60 Minutes,* Stahl stated, "We have heard that half a million children have died [as a result of sanctions]. I mean,

that's more children than died in Hiroshima. And, you know, is the price worth it?" Albright replied: "I think this is a very hard choice, but the price—we think the price is worth it." "Madeleine Albright—60 Minutes," accessed September 2008, http://www .youtube.com/watch?v=FbIX1CP9qr4.

3. My work responds to Chandra Mohanty's call for "an explicit analysis" of the "potentially imperialist complicities of U.S. feminism," in "US Empire and the Project of Women's Studies: Stories of Citizenship, Complicity and Dissent," *Gender, Place and Culture* 13, no. 1 (2006): 7–20. In her characterization of hegemonic feminism, Becky Thompson writes that it is "white-led, marginalizes the activism and world views of women of color, focuses mainly on the United States, and treats sexism as the ultimate oppression. Hegemonic feminism deemphasizes or ignores a class and race analysis, generally sees equality with men as the goal of feminism, and has an individual rights-based, rather than a justice-based vision for social change." (337). Becky Thompson, "Multiracial Feminism: Recasting the Chronology of Second Wave Feminism," *Feminist Studies* 28, no. 2 (2002): 336–60; see also, Valerie Amos and Pratibha Parmar, "Challenging Imperial Feminism," *Feminist Review,* no. 17 (Autumn 1984): 3–19.

4. Barbara Ehrenreich, "Feminism's Assumptions Upended," first published in *Los Angeles Times,* May 16, 2004.

5. Jacinda Read, *The New Avengers: Feminism, Femininity and the Rape–Revenge Cycle* (New York: St. Martin's Press, 2000).

6. Some conservative critics, pundits, and journalists blamed feminism, with statements that implied that such scenes of women's involvement in Abu Ghraib were the "cultural outgrowth of a feminist culture which encourages female barbarians" See George Neumayr, "Thelma and Louise in Iraq," *American Spectator,* May 5, 2004, p. 220. Online essays, such as Angela Fiori's 2004 "The Feminist Road to Abu Ghraib" (http://www.lewrockwell.com/orig/fiori4.html), blame the scandal itself on the presumably (liberal) feminist inclusion of women into the military.

7. I am not arguing that there has been a complete reticence or lack of feminist responses to U.S. imperial violence since the onset of the war on terror. Preexisting organizations such as Women in Black and newer organizations such as Code Pink, as well as others, have made significant contributions to feminist and women-centered organizing against war and occupation. The cited collections are examples of such responses. I am troubled rather by the seeming inability of U.S. feminists to make a more *effective intervention* in U.S. politics given our current state of organizations, movements, tactics, and positions within the U.S. academy. See Elizabeth A. Castelli, "Reverberations: On Violence," *Scholar and Feminist Online* 2, no. 2 (2004), http:// bcrw.barnard.edu/publications/reverberations-on-violence/; and anthologies such as *Feminism and War,* ed. Robin Riley, Chandra Mohanty, and Minnie Bruce Pratt (London: Zed Press, 2008).

8. Thompson, "Multiracial Feminism"; Andrea Smith, "Without Bureaucracy, Beyond Inclusion: Re-centering Feminism," *Left Turn,* June 1, 2006, accessed November 2008, http://www.leftturn.org/without-bureaucracy-beyond-inclusion-re-centering-feminism.

9. A major federal law that NOW (National Organization of Women) promoted for over a decade was the Violence Against Women Act of 1994 (VAWA); see Pat Reuss, "The Violence Against Women Act: Celebrating 10 Years of Prevention," accessed October 19, 2009, http://www.now.org/nnt/fall-2004/vawa.html. This body of legislation was reauthorized in 2005. Passed as Title IV of the Violent Crime Control and Law Enforcement Act of 1994, this feminist victory was part of the passage of the largest crime bill to date in U.S. history, producing 100,000 more police officers and $9.7 billion in more funding for prisons. Violent Crime Control and Law Enforcement Act of 1994. U.S. Department of Justice Fact Sheet, accessed October 19, 2009, http://www.ncjrs.gov/txtfiles/billfs.txt.

10. Angela Y. Davis, *Are Prisons Obsolete?* (New York: Open Media, 2003); Dylan Rodriguez, "(Non)Scenes of Captivity: The Common Sense of Punishment and Death," *Radical History Review* 96 (Fall 2006): 9–32; Human Rights Watch, *Targeting Blacks: Drug Law Enforcement and Race in the United States,* accessed March 5, 2011, http://www.hrw.org/en/reports/2008/05/04/targeting-blacks.

11. Feminist-abolitionist scholars, such as Angela Davis, Andrea Smith, Beth Richie, Julia Sudbury, and Andrea Ritchie, have criticized how mainstream feminist reliance on and support of the state's criminal justice system has been ineffective and has resulted in the increased rates of women's incarceration. See Andrea Ritchie, "Law Enforcement Violence against Women of Color" (138–56) and "Gender Violence and the Prison Industrial Complex" (223–26) in *The Color of Violence: The Incite! Anthology,* eds. INCITE Women of Color Against Violence (Boston: South End Press, 2006); Jael Silliman and Anannya Bhattacharjee, eds., *Policing the National Body: Sex, Race, Gender and Criminalization* (Boston: South End Press, 2002).

12. UNIFEM Annual Report, 2009–2011, accessed April 12, 2011, http://www.unifem.org/materials/item_detail.pho?ProductID=176; Martha Chen, Joann Vanek, Francie Lund, and James Heintz, eds., *Progress of the World's Women 2005: Women, Work and Poverty,* accessed April 12, 2011, http://www.unifem.org/materials/item_detail.php?ProductID=48. According to a 2011 report by the Global Fund for Women, "women and children comprise 80 percent of the world's 50 million who are displaced persons by war and conflict." "Militarism Facts," accessed March 2011, http://www.globalfundforwomen.org/component/content/article/156-general/1826-militarism-facts. See also the PeaceWomen Project for sources on the impact of women in conflict zones. PeaceWomen Web site, accessed March 2011, http://www.peacewomen.org.

13. See, in particular, Angela Davis's classic essay, "Rape, Racism and the Myth of the Black Rapist," in *Women, Race and Class* (New York: Vintage, 1983), 172–201.

Introduction

1. Edward Said, *Orientalism* (New York: Vintage Books, 1979); Lisa Lowe, *Critical Terrains: French and British Orientalisms* (Ithaca, N.Y.: Cornell University Press,

1991); Stefan Tanaka, *Japan's Orient: Rendering Pasts into History* (Berkeley: University of California Press, 1993).

2. Compared with other postwar women's organizations, the size of the movement was relatively small. Numbering less than an estimated three thousand women, this movement was numerically marginal compared with other women's leftist organizations that numbered in the tens of thousands to mainstream women's organizations such as Chifuren that had well over six million members in the 1950s. Wake A. Fujioka, trans. and ed., *Women's Movements in Postwar Japan: Selected Articles from Shiryō: Sengo Nijyu-Nen Shi* (Honolulu: East-West Center, 1968). *Ribu*'s largest publications, such as *Onna Erosu*, sold between two thousand and three thousand copies per issue through the 1970s, indicative of the approximate size of the movement. The last issue of *Onna Erosu*, no. 17, was published in 1982. Interview with the Saeki Yōko, one of the editors of *Onna Erosu*, Tokyo, November 28, 2002.

3. This new organizing style is elaborated in chapter 2. Leaders like Tanaka Mitsu emerged, and their relative power within the movement and iconic status remain as contradictions of the movement's history. I address this issue in chapter 4 and the Epilogue.

4. Orie Endo, "Aspects of Sexism in Language," in *Japanese Women: New Feminist Perspectives on Past, Present and Future,* ed. Kumiko Fujimura-Fanselow and Atsuko Kameda (New York: Feminist Press at the City University of New York, 1995), 30. Endo writes that to say that one has become an *onna* usually refers to the "female subject's first experience of menstruation or sexual intercourse" (30).

5. Email interview with Sayama Sachi, August 20, 2010.

6. Inderpal Grewal and Caren Kaplan, eds., "Introduction," *Scattered Hegemonies: Postmodernity and Transnational Feminist Practices* (Minneapolis: University of Minnesota Press, 1994), 17. My introduction seeks to underscore that transnational feminism is not necessarily anti-imperialist. Furthermore, transnational feminist practices and first-world anti-imperialist feminist practices must also be interrogated for the ways they reproduce hegemonic power-knowledge formations and relations.

7. Masao Miyoshi and H. D. Harutoonian, eds., *Learning Places: The Afterlife of Area Studies* (Durham, N.C.: Duke University Press, 2002).

8. Saul-ling Wong, "Denationalization Reconsidered: Asian American Cultural Criticism at a Theoretical Crossroads," in *Amerasia Journal* 21, no. 1–2 (1995): 1–27.

9. See Tani Barlow, "Theorizing Woman: *Funū, Guojia, Jiating* (Chinese Women, Chinese State, Chinese Family)," *Genders* 10 (Spring 1991): 132–60. Reprinted in Grewal and Kaplan, *Scattered Hegemonies,* 1994.

10. The phrase "translational trouble" emerged from our conversations during the Genealogies of Radical Feminism in Japan Workshop organized by Tomiko Yoda at the Reischauer Institute, Harvard University, January 29, 2011.

11. Matsui Yayori (1934–2003) was one of the most prominent advocates of this form of Pan-Asian feminist solidarity. Matsui identified herself as part of the libera-

tion movement, and although her feminist political views did not become hegemonic within the movement, the organization she established, Asia-Japan Women's Resource Center, exemplified this sustained attention to and solidarity with Asian women. She also established the Violence Against Women in War–Network Japan (VAWW–NET Japan), which involved Pan-Asian organizing to criticize the system of militarized sexual slavery, known as the comfort women, during the Asia–Pacific Wars. Many *ribu* activists continued their solidarity with Asian women for decades. Charlotte Bunch, ed., *Voices from the Japanese Women's Movement* (London: M.E. Sharpe, 1996), 38–52. See chapter 1, note 62, and chapter 3, note 30.

12. Further details of the antagonism between *ribu* and *feminizumu* are elaborated in the Epilogue. For a history of radical feminism in the United States, see Alice Echols, *Daring to Be Bad: Radical Feminism in America, 1967–1975* (Minneapolis: University of Minnesota Press, 1989); Flora Davis, *Moving the Mountain: The Women's Movement in America since 1960* (Chicago: University of Illinois Press, 1999); Sara Evans, *Personal Politics: The Roots of Women's Liberation in the Civil Rights Movement and the New Left* (New York: Vintage, 1980); Judith Hole and Ellen Levine, *Rebirth of Feminism* (New York: Quadrangle Books, 1971). For a critical counterhistory of radical feminism, see *This Bridge Called My Back: Writings by Radical Women of Color,* ed. Cherríe Moraga and Gloria Anzaldua (Watertown, Mass.: Persephone Press, 1981); Thompson, "Multiracial Feminism."

13. Inoue Teruko, *Joseigaku to sono shūhen* (Tokyo: Keisō Shobō, 1980); *Joseigaku e no shōtai: kawaru, kawaranai onna no isshō* (Tokyo: Yūhikaku, 1992); interview with Inoue Teruko, Tokyo, February 24, 2001.

14. Machiko Matsui, "Evolution of the Feminist Movement in Japan," *National Women's Studies Association Journal* 2, no. 3 (1990): 435–49; Ichiyo Muto, "The Birth of the Women's Liberation Movement in the 1970s," in *The Other Japan: Conflict, Compromise and Resistance since 1945,* ed. Joe Moore (London: M.E. Sharpe, 1997), 147–71.

15. Imelda Whelehan, *Modern Feminist Thought: From the Second Wave to Post Feminism* (Edinburgh: Edinburgh University Press, 1995).

16. Ibid., 65. In Whelehan's work, she refers specifically to the U.S. New Left, but her description is pertinent here insofar as many *ribu* activists also reacted to the male dominance of the Japanese New Left.

17. Ibid.

18. Miki Sōko, Saeki Yōko, and Mizoguchi Ayeko, eds., *Shiryō Nihon ūman ribu shi* [The Documents of the History of Women's Lib in Japan], 3 vols. (Kyoto: Shōkadō, 1994), 2:176–79.

19. Nishimura Mitsuko, *Onna-tachi no korekutibu: nanajyū nendai ūman ribu o saidoku suru* [The Women's Collective: Rereading 1970s Women's Lib] (Tokyo: Shakai Hyōronsha, 2006).

20. For example, from January 1970, the news media covered the U.S. women's

liberation movement, disseminating information about the movement across Japan. In particular, the *Asahi Shinbun,* a major national daily, ran a story covering the U.S. women's liberation movement almost every month from January to August 1970. The national women's strike in August 1970, for example, was covered in (at least) three major national newspapers, the *Mainichi Shinbun, Yomiuri Shinbun,* and *Asahi Shinbun.*

21. Tanaka Mitsu's early writings, for example, criticized what she perceived to be an overemphasis on "women's rights," which she understood to be central to the U.S. feminist movement. Cf. chapter 4, notes 60 and 61. Early issues of the *ribu* journal *Onna Erosu* also contained articles on the women's liberation movement in the United States, comparing and contrasting it with the *ribu* movement in Japan. See, for example, Yoshihiro Kiyoko, "Amerika no ribu no atarashii nami," in *Onna Erosu,* no. 1, *tokushū: kekkon seido o yurugasu* (1973).

22. Sharon L. Sievers, *Flowers in Salt: The Beginnings of Feminist Consciousness in Modern Japan* (Stanford, Calif.: Stanford University Press, 1983); Vera Mackie, *Feminism in Modern Japan* (Oxford: Oxford University Press, 2003). See also Hiroko Tomida, *Hiratsuka Raicho and Early Japanese Feminism* (Boston: Brill, 2004); Akiko Tokuza, *The Rise of the Feminist Movement in Japan* (Tokyo: Keio University Press, 1999).

23. Chandra Talpade Mohanty, *Feminisms without Borders: Decolonizing Theory, Practicing Solidarity* (Durham, N.C.: Duke University Press, 2003). See, in particular, "Under Western Eyes: Feminist Scholarship and Colonial Discourses," and "Cartographies of Struggle: Third World Women and the Politics of Feminism."

24. Chizuko Ueno, "Are the Japanese Feminine? Some Problems of Japanese Feminism in its Cultural Context," in *Broken Silence: Voices of Japanese Feminism,* ed. Sandra Buckley (Berkeley: University of California Press, 1996), 297–302. Ayako Kano, "Toward a Critique of Transhistorical Femininity," in *Gendering Modern Japanese History,* ed. Barbara Molony and Kathleen S. Uno (Cambridge, Mass.: Harvard University Asia Center, 2005). Both Kano and Ueno have described how orientalism and the reactionary discourse of reverse-orientalism have had an antifeminist effect in the Japanese context. Kano and Ueno describe reverse-orientalism respectively as an "internalization of the orientalist paradigm" (Kano 522) where an "Orientalist perspective is taken up to define a positive national identity" (Ueno 295). The result of this double-orientalist configuration operates to feminize Japan such that Japan has always already been feminine and therefore does not need feminism, which is presumed to be somehow alien to an already feminized Japan (Kano 543). In this dubious schema, Japan is indigenously feminine, but feminism is somehow posited as foreign, alien, and nonindigenous; therefore, Japanese feminism is rendered an import and imitation of Western women.

25. Richard F. Calichman, *Takeuchi Yoshimi: Displacing the West* (Ithaca, N.Y.: Cornell University East Asia Program, 2004).

26. Nomura Kōya, *Muishiki no shokuminchi shugi: Nihonjin no Beigun kichi to Okinawajin* (Tokyo: Ochanomizu Shobō, 2005).

27. *Ribu* activists were critical of Japan's neo-imperial relations with Korea and Okinawa and engaged in direct actions and campaigns to protest this resurgence and reformation of neocolonialism.

28. Naoki Sakai, *Translation and Subjectivity: On "Japan" and Cultural Nationalism* (Minneapolis: University of Minnesota Press, 1997).

29. I derive the concept of U.S.-based third world liberation movements from Cynthia Young, *Soul Power: Culture, Radicalism, and the Making of a Third World U.S. Left* (Durham, N.C.: Duke University Press, 2006). See Wesley Iwao Ueunten, "Rising Up from a Sea of Discontent: The 1970 Koza Uprising in U.S.-Occupied Okinawa," in *Militarized Currents: Toward A Decolonized Future in Asia and the Pacific,* ed. Setsu Shigematsu and Keith L. Camacho (Minneapolis: University of Minnesota Press, 2010), 91–124; William Tucker, "Yellow Panthers: Black Internationalism, Interracial Organizing and Intercommunal Solidarity" (thesis, Brown University, 2004).

30. I address these political problems in more depth in "Militarized Occupations and the Spectacle of Asian/Japanese-Black Feminist Transgression: Subversive Appropriation and Post-liberation Blues," a forthcoming article. See chapter 4, note 29.

31. Many *ribu* women continue their various forms of *ribu* activism today. Ongoing activism is discussed in chapter 3 and the Epilogue.

32. Akiyama Yōko, *Ribu shi shi nōto* (Tokyo: Inpakuto Shuppankai, 1993), 194–95.

33. Masami Saito, "Feminizumu riron ni yoru hihan-teki disukōsu bunseki (FCDA) no tenkai—ūman ribu undō no media gensetsu o jirei toshite" (PhD diss., Ochanomizu Joshi Daigaku, 2001).

34. See Acknowledgments for more details of my interviews and time spent with the women of *ribu*.

35. James Welker, "Transfiguring the Female: Women and Girls Engaging the Transnational in Late Twentieth-Century Japan" (PhD diss., University of Illinois at Urbana–Champaign, 2010). Welker traces some of the roots of the lesbian movement to the *ribu* movement and emphasizes *ribu*'s transnational connections. Setsu Shigematsu, "Feminism and Media in the Late Twentieth Century: Reading the Limits of a Politics of Transgression," in Molony and Uno, *Gendering Modern Japanese History,* 555–89. Tomiko Yoda's paper, "Radical Feminism and Media Culture in Early 1970s Japan," tracks the dissemination of radical feminist discourses into women's commercial magazines (paper presented at the Genealogies of Radical Feminism in Japan Workshop, Reischauer Institute, Harvard University, Cambridge, Mass., January 29, 2011).

36. Many Japanese feminist scholars have reproduced this dominant periodization that *ūman ribu* was the beginning of second wave feminism in Japan. See the Preface of Inoue Teruko, Ueno Chizuko, Ehara Yumiko, and Amano Masako, eds., *Nihon no Feminizumu,* vol. 1, *Ribu to Feminizumu* (Tokyo: Iwanami Shoten, 1994), i.

37. Fujieda Mioko, "Onna no sengoshi—ūman ribu," *Asahi Jānaru* (February 1985): 78.

38. According to Jo Freeman, in *The Politics of Women's Liberation* (New York: David McKay Co., 1975), radical feminism in the United States took off in the 1970s (148). See Smith, "Without Bureaucracy, Beyond Inclusion."

39. *Ripples of Change: Japanese Women's Search for Self,* directed and produced by Kurihara Nanako (New York, Women Make Movies [distributor], 1993).

1. Origins of the Other/*Onna*

1. Here I deliberately use the phrase "Japanese women's movements," although I recognize that it has the discursive effect of potentially homogenizing a diverse array of women's movements. I do so because many Japanese women's movements consciously identified themselves as "Japanese women" and purposefully contributed to the formation, (re)production, and homogenization of a constellation of identities for Japanese women such as housewife, citizen, mother *(shufu, shimin, haha)* without problematizing their nationalist, essentialist, and homogenizing function. I contrast *ūman ribu* to such nationalist Japanese women's movements. Cf. notes 42, 43.

2. The title of one of *ribu*'s longest-lasting newsletters, *Onna's Mutiny (Onna no hangyaku),* captures the essential sentiment of defiance that characterized the political style of these radical feminists. Its inaugural issue was published in January 1971 and, to my knowledge, continues to the present. The last copy I received from Kuno Ayako, its founding editor, was in 2009.

3. Lisa Yoneyama, "Liberation under Siege: U.S. Military Occupation and Japanese Women's Enfranchisement," *American Quarterly* 57, no. 4 (2005): 885–910; Lisa Yoneyama, "Feminizing National Memory," *Hiroshima Traces: Time Space and the Dialectics of Memory* (Berkeley: University of California Press, 1999).

4. Noriko Mizuno, "Family and Family Law in Japan," in *Gender and the Law in Japan,* ed. Miyoko Tsujimura and Emi Yano (Sendai: Tohoku University Press, 2007), 147–56. Mizuno writes, "The 20th century became the first century in Japanese history to enforce family law through civil codes, and to this day Japanese families have been under control of this code. . . . The Meiji Civil Code was originally created under diplomatic pressure; the then world powers refused to relinquish extra-territorial rights unless a Euro-American civil code was established in Japan. . . . The Civil Code was created to center family law on a patriarchal *ie* as the foundation of the family within the register" (147–51).

5. Lois J. Naftulin, "Women's Status under Japanese Law," *Feminist International* 2 (1980): 13; Susan Pharr, "The Politics of Women's Rights," in *Democratizing Japan: The Allied Occupation,* ed. Sakamoto Yoshikazu and Robert E. Ward (Honolulu: University of Hawaii Press, 1987).

6. Kiyoko Kinjo, "Legal Challenges to the Status Quo," in *Japanese Women: New*

Feminist Perspectives on the Past, Present and Future, ed. Kumiko Fujimura-Fanselow and Atsuko Kameda (New York: Feminist Press, 1996).

7. This law prohibited women from participating in political meetings or becoming members of political parties. Tokuza, *The Rise of the Feminist Movement in Japan,* 156–57. Vera Mackie, *Creating Socialist Women in Japan: Gender, Labor and Activism, 1900–1937* (Cambridge: Cambridge University Press, 1997).

8. Yoneyama, "Liberation under Siege," 887.

9. Wakita Haruko, Narita Ryūichi, Anne Walthall, and Hitomi Tonomura, "Past Developments and Future Issues in the Study of Women's History in Japan: A Bibliographical Essay," in *Women and Class in Japanese History,* ed. Hitomi Tonomura, Anne Walthall, and Wakita Haruko (Ann Arbor: Center for Japanese Studies University of Michigan, 1999). These historians write, "The position of women fell when governmental and corporate organizations grew large, replacing the many functions of the *ie* and relegating it to the task of reproducing daily necessities only. This eventually created the modern situation in which child rearing was considered the heavenly ordained job of women" (306). In this vein, they argue, "Japan's tremendous industrialization and capitalist growth in the 1970s and 1980s, however, preserved gender inequality and forced people to realize that modern, even more than pre-modern, society enforced on all people—including the commoners—the principle of patriarchal authority based on the sexual division of labor in which men were equated with the sphere of outside work and women with domestic labor" (305).

10. Ibid. In summarizing Murakami's findings, Wakita, Narita, Walthall, and Tonomura write, "It was the Meiji family system, built upon patriarchy, that invited gender inequality even for commoners whose earlier freedom in daily life had depended on the legacy of community principles" (302). These historians also emphasized the importance of class distinctions, stating, "Because the position of women and the development of patriarchal institutions are class specific, research [on women's history] had to address class differences in each historical period" (303).

11. Naoki Sakai, "Modernity and Its Critique: The Problem of Universalism and Particularism," in *Translation and Subjectivity* (Minneapolis: University of Minnesota Press, 1997), 153–76.

12. Sharon Sievers, "Women in the Popular-Rights Movement," in *Flowers in Salt,* 26–53; Vera Mackie, "Kishia Toshiko and the Torch of Freedom," in *Feminism in Modern Japan.* Ueno Chizuko, however, cautions against using the particular term *feminist* to describe women's movements prior to the actual use of the term in Japan, which began in the late 1970s. Interview with Ueno, November 27, 2002.

13. Formed during the first decades of the twentieth century, the *Seitō* (Blue Stockings) movement led by Hiratsuka Raichō has been widely considered Japan's first radical feminist movement. *Seitō* heralded the "New Woman" *(atarashii onna)* who defied the conventions of proper femininity as circumscribed by the patriarchal *ie* system. Tomida's *Hiratsuka Raicho and Early Japanese Feminism;* Jan Bardsley, *The Bluestockings of Japan: New Woman Essays and Fiction from Seitō, 1911–16* (Ann

Arbor, Mich.: Center for Japanese Studies, 2007); Noriko Lippitt, "Seitō and the Literary Roots of Japanese Feminism," *International Journal of Women's Studies* 2, no. 2 (1975): 163–88; Pauline C. Reich and Atsuko Fukuda, "Japan's Literary Feminists: The Seitō Group," *Signs* 2, no. 1 (1976): 280–91; Mikiso Hane, *Reflections on the Way to the Gallows: Rebel Women in Prewar Japan* (Berkeley: University of California Press, 1988), and Hélèn Bowen Raddeker, *Treacherous Women of Imperial Japan: Patriarchal Fictions, Patricidal Fantasies* (London: Routlege, 1997) are works that have explored and documented the legacy of Japan's leftist women intellectuals and Japanese anarchist women martyrs Kanno Sugako (1881–1911) and Kaneko Fumiko (1905–26).

14. For *ribu* citations of Hiratsuka Raichō, see Miki, Saeki, and Mizoguchi, *Shiryō Nihon ūman ribu shi,* 1:152, 1:389, 1:400, 2:275, 2:283, 3:326. For citations of Takamure Itsue, see ibid., 1:48, 1:50, 1:86, 1:87, 1:158, 1:297, 2:93, 2:98, 2:272, 2:303, 2:233, 2:332, 3:79, 3:207–9, 3:234, 3:236.

15. Toshitani Nobuyoshi, "The Reform of Japanese Family Law and Changes in the Family System," trans. Amy Searight, *U.S.-Japan Women's Journal: English Supplement,* no. 6 (1994): 66–82.

16. Postwar reforms legally allowed for either the husband's or wife's name to be chosen as the family name; however, approximately 98 percent of families continued to choose the husband's name. See Kinjo, 358–59. The *koseki* impacts the lives of virtually all Japanese because it is required to obtain government benefits such as education, income assistance, and a passport. The *koseki* system thereby functions to regulate and track the movement of Japanese citizens both domestically and outside of Japan. Taimie L. Bryant, "For the Sake of the Country, for the Sake of the Family: The Oppressive Impact of Family Registration on Women and Minorities in Japan," *UCLA Law Review* 39 (October 1991): 109–68.

17. Kathleen Uno writes, "*Ryōsai kenbo* defined women's contribution to the good of the nation to be their labor as 'good wives' and 'wise mothers' in the private world of the home." Kathleen Uno, "Death of 'Good Wife, Wise Mother'?," in *Postwar Japan as History,* ed. Andrew Gordon (Berkeley: University of California Press, 1993), 279; Kathleen Uno, *Passages to Modernity: Motherhood, Childhood, and Social Reform in Early Twentieth Century Japan* (Honolulu: University of Hawaii Press, 1999), 44–45, 48–50, 105, 108, 122, 145–46, 147. Andrew Gordon, "Managing the Japanese Household: New Life Movement in Postwar Japan," in Molony and Uno, *Gendering Modern Japanese History,* 423–60.

18. Uno, "Death of 'Good Wife, Wise Mother'?," 295.

19. Vera Mackie, "Feminist Critiques of Modern Japanese Politics," in *Mapping the Women's Movement,* ed. Mónica Threlfall (London: Verso, 1996), 260; Vera Mackie, "Feminist Politics in Japan," *New Left Review* 167 (1985): 53–76.

20. Chizuko Ueno, "The Enigma of Japanese Women's Movements," unpublished essay. Ueno writes that "while feminism is a women's movement, women's movements are not necessarily feminist movements" (5). Feminist sociologist Senda Yuki also cautions against assuming that "women's agency" automatically renders social action

"feminist" or politically legitimate. In her article, "What Is 'Japanese Feminism'?," Senda calls for a critical examination of the social effects of actions to determine whether they are feminist or even detrimental to feminist causes. Senda Yuki, "'Nihon no feminizumu' to wa nanika?" *Daikōbō* 39 (2001): 182–98. For an extensive discussion of defining feminist organizations in Japan, see Diana Khor, "Organizing for Change: Women's Grassroots Activism in Japan," *Feminist Studies* 25, no. 3 (1999): 633–61. In this article, Khor draws on Patricia Yancey Martin's criteria to define feminist organizations. These criteria offer a broad definition of feminist organizations: "an organization is feminist if it meets any one of the following criteria: (a) has feminist ideology; (b) has feminist guiding values; (c) has feminist goals; (d) produced feminist outcomes; (e) was founded during the women's movement as part of the women's movement." Khor's approach is highly indeterminate, to the extent that she seeks to "define feminism in a way that does not align it with any particular orientations or strategies." Such an open-ended approach to defining feminism can render its politics so relative that the term loses its political meaning. For a critical redefinition of feminism, see Cheryl Johnson-Odim's essay, "Common Themes, Different Contexts: Third World Women and Feminism," in *Third World Women and the Politics of Feminism,* ed. Chandra Talpade Mohanty, Ann Russo, and Lourdes Torres (Bloomington: Indiana University Press, 1991).

21. My definition of radical feminism draws largely on the work of Whelehan, *Modern Feminist Thought.* See discussion and definition of radical feminism in Introduction.

22. The Zen-Nihon Fujin Renmei [All-Japan Women's Federation], for example, was affiliated with the ruling party and one of the most conservative women's organizations.

23. This group later changed its name to the Nihon Fujin Yukensha Dōmei (Japan League of Women Voters) after women were granted the right to vote in the first election in 1946.

24. The club was established to attain and safeguard peace. However, after the Occupation adopted a clearly anticommunist agenda, this club managed to maintain a leftist agenda by distancing itself from government institutions. The Women's Democratic Club tended to see Japanese women as victims of the war and stated that its goal was to prevent women from being "blindly led into war again." The initial founders included Katō Shizue, Akamatsu Tsuneko, Sata Ineko, Matsuoka Yōko, Miyamoto Yuriko, and others. Wake A. Fujioka, trans. and ed., *Women's Movements in Postwar Japan: Selected Articles from Shiryō: sengo nijū-nen shi* (Honolulu: East-West Center, 1968), 20. Its newspaper is *Fujin Minshū Shinbun.*

25. Inoue, *Joseigaku to sono shūhen,* 178–79.

26. The historical and political context of the U.S.–Japan Mutual Cooperation and Security Treaty, known in Japanese as "Anpo" (an abbreviated reference to the Anzen Hoshō of the Nippon-koku to Amerika-gasshūkoku to no Aida no Sōgo Kyōryoku oyobi Anzen Hoshō Jōyaku) is discussed in chapter 2.

27. Saito Masami, "Haisen chokugo no shinbu ni miru 'josei sanken,'" *Joseigaku* 6 (1998): 94–115.

28. The bourgeois leadership also shifted their efforts to promote the "full utilization of women's abilities in the work place" and to promote a "peaceful" and "democratic" society. Inoue, *Joseigaku to sono shūhen,* 179.

29. Mizoguchi Ayeko, "Josho: fujin undo kara josei undo e," in Miki, Saeki, and Mizoguchi, *Shiryō Nihon ūman ribu shi,* 1:19. Although Mizoguchi is not listed or named as author, the other editors, Saeki Yōko and Miki Sōko, confirmed her authorship of this entry.

30. Kazuko Tanaka, "The New Feminist Movement in Japan, 1970–1990," *Japanese Women: Feminist Perspectives on the Past, Present and Future,* 343.

31. Kiyoko, "Legal Challenges to the Status Quo," 354.

32. Kazuko, "The New Feminist Movement in Japan," 344. "Work, Education, and the Family," in *Japanese Women: New Feminist Perspectives on the Past, Present and Future,* ed. Fujimura-Fanselow and Kameda, 295–308.

33. Legal scholar Kiyoko Kinjo writes, "Discrimination against women in the workplace has been a source of huge profit to companies; indeed, it has been a main source of economic power for Japan." "Legal Challenges to the Status Quo," 418.

34. Sandra Buckley's 1994 essay, "A Short History of the Feminist Movement in Japan," is a notable example of this production of continuity in the history of feminism. Buckley places the *ribu* movement within a framework that she calls "the development of Japanese feminism over the postwar period." In constructing her developmental narrative, Buckley does not make any meaningful distinction between women's groups and feminist groups. Consequently, mainstream women's consumer organizations, such as Shufuren and massive nationwide organizations like Chifuren, are said to constitute one of the "structures [that] came to characterize postwar Japanese feminism from the 1960s." In *Women of Japan and Korea: Continuity and Change,* ed. Joyce Gelb and Marian Lief Palley (Philadelphia: Temple University Press, 1994), 150–88.

35. Kathleen Uno describes early postwar women's movements (1945–60) as being based on women's identities as wives and mothers, which emphasized their roles as "guardians of the household and nurturers of life" who "banded together under desperate conditions to try to achieve minimal subsistence." "Death of 'Good Wife, Wise Mother'?," 317. Kathleen Uno writes, "Women in the early postwar period justified their public activities in terms of motherhood" (308).

36. Shufuren is an abbreviation of Shufu Rengokai. Its first group began in Tokyo with the aim of ridding undesirables *(furyō)* from their neighborhood. Fujioka, *Women's Movements in Postwar Japan,* 24–31. Shufuren's slogan was, "If we set out to work positively, we'll be sure to succeed and see hope in our lives as housewives and members of the Japan Housewives Association. The object is to link government directly with our life" (217). According to Akiko Tokuza, its monthly newspaper circulation was approximately 100,000 in 1987.

37. Inoue Teruko, Chizuko Ueno, Yumiko Ehara, Mari Ōsawa, and Mikiyo Kano,

eds., *Iwanami joseigaku jiten* [Iwanami dictionary of women's studies] (Tokyo: Iwanami Shoten, 2002), 193–94. This class of women emerged in the Taisho period (1912–26) as part of the formation of a modern capitalist economy with a class-specific and gendered division of labor, referring to women who were married to white-collar workers and were responsible for the domestic work. Ochiai Emiko, *The Japanese Family System in Transition: A Sociological Analysis of Family Change in Postwar Japan* (Tokyo: LTCB International Library Foundation, 1997).

38. Narita Ryūichi, "Shufuren," in Inoue et al., *Iwanami joseigaku jiten*, 350.

39. Tokuza, *The Rise of the Feminist Movement in Japan*. The founder of Shufuren, Oku Mumeo, was a prominent leader in prewar and wartime women's movements and was an elected member of the Diet in the postwar. Oku Mumeo, who donned a white apron to "catch the eye of the media," describes her intention as a Diet member: "I was determined with work, with an image of a rice scoop always in my mind" (216–17). The rice paddle was Shufuren's symbol.

40. *Asahi Shinbun*, October 25, 1970, 23. In this article, Tanaka also declares that the *ribu*'s "enemies" *(teki)* are women like the actress Yoshinaga Sayuri and the writers such as Kamisaki Fuyuko and Sono Ayako.

41. *Asahi Shinbun*, October 6, 1970, 24.

42. Chifuren is an abbreviation for Zenkoku Chiiki Fujin Dantai Rengō Kyōgikai (National Federation of Regional Women's Organizations). Fujioka, *Women's Movements in Postwar Japan*, 67–68. In 1951, Tanaka Sumiko, head of the Women's Section of the Women's and Minors' Bureau of the Ministry of Labor, reported that there were over six million members of regional women's organizations, indicative of the massive base of women's organizations (4).

43. Ibid., 33. Chifuren's stated goals were "to establish in ourselves a sound world view; to strive toward our moral development; to safeguard our families; to educate women; to open our eyes and become informed about economic and social matters; to formulate sound opinions free of political and ideological bias; to live by a sense of mission that we are Japanese; and to protect a true democracy" (55).

44. For example, the first issue of *Onna Erosu* sold twenty thousand copies in 1973, but its average circulation per issue through the 1970s was between two thousand and three thousand copies. Interview with Saeki Yōko, one of the editors of *Onna Erosu*, November 28, 2002. The number of copies of *Ribu News (Ribu nyūsu konomichi hitosuji)* was estimated at around three thousand during the time of its printing from 1972 to 1976. Correspondence with Yonezu Tomoko, September 15, 2010. See details in *Ribu nyūsu konomichi hitosuju: Ribu Shinjuku Sentā shiryō shūsei*, ed. Ribu Shinjuku Sentā Shiryō Shūsei Hozon Kai (Tokyo: Inpakuto Shuppankai, 2008), vi.

45. Imelda Whelehan, "Radical Feminism: Redefining Politics," in *Modern Feminist Thought*, 70–73; Echols, *Daring to Be Bad*.

46. Aki Shobō Henshū Bu, ed., *Sei sabetsu e no kokuhatsu: ūman ribu wa shuchō suru* (Tokyo: Aki Shobō, 1971), 107.

202

NOTES TO CHAPTER 1

47. Ibid., 18.

48. Ibid., 11.

49. She met Ōta Ryū (whose legal birth name is Tōichi Kurihara) and began a relationship with him when she was fifteen years old.

50. Because Iijima's group had been organizing outside of the established party lines and supported autonomous leftist and antiwar struggles, in July 1970, the Japan Socialist Party (and its affiliate women's organization) purged Iijima and formally prohibited any of its members to organize with her group, the Committee of Asian Women (Ajia Fujin Kaigi). Iijima was cut off from the old Left for expressing too much support for the New Left, which was the rebel offspring that detested the authoritarianism of the established political parties. This was the end of Iijima's long-term affiliation with the established left. Iijima, "Naze Shinryaku=Sabetsu to Tatakau Ajia Fujin Kaigi," in Miki, Saeki, and Mizoguchi, Shiryō Nihon ūman ribu shi, 1:186.

51. She divorced Ōta in 1964 after being married for twelve years. Iijima Aiko, "Shinryaku=sabetsu" no kanata e: aru feminisuto no hansei (Tokyo: Inpakuto Shuppankai, 2006), 363–65.

52. This monumental three-volume collection, which spans from 1969 to 1982, was compiled by several ribu intellectuals and represents a conscious attempt by women of the movement to write their own history. Saeki Yōko, Miki Sōko, and Mizoguchi Ayeko are the editors. By the time they reached the third volume, Sōko and Saeki were the primary editors of the project. This collection is an implicit critique of established women's studies periodizations about the movement, which consistently state that the movement ended or died in 1975 or 1977. See, for example, Ehara Yumiko's entry on ribu in Inoue et al., Iwanami joseigaku jiten, 39–40. This narrative is also reproduced in Ueno Chizuko and Tanaka Mitsu's published dialogues, Mitsu to Chizuko no kontonton karari: Tanaka Mitsu Ueno Chizuko taidan (Tokyo: Mokuseisha, 1987); Tanaka Mitsu, "Tanaka Mitsu intabyū: mirai wo tsukanda onna-tachi," in Iwasaki Minoru and Takashi Tsujii, eds., Sengo Nihon sutadīzu, Vol. 2, 60–70 nendai (Tokyo: Kinokuniya Shoten, 2009), 270–334.

53. Iijima discusses how the JCP-affiliated women's organization Shin Nihon Fujin no Kai had come to dominate the politics of the Mother's Convention by the late 1960s. She harshly criticized the organization for disconnecting the meaning of the security treaty from the structure of imperialism, reducing it to simply the issue of the "Treaty."

54. This is an abbreviated summary of the objectives of the Mother's Convention. For a longer description, see Uno, "Death of 'Good Wife, Wise Mother'?"; Kamichika Ichiko and Tanaka Kazuko, Josei no shisō shi (Tokyo: Aki Shobō, 1974).

55. Iijima Aiko, in Miki, Saeki, and Mizoguchi, Shiryō Nihon ūman ribu shi, 1:27. Iijima writes, "Formerly, the system used to define women as the 'mothers of Yasukuni.'" From its origins in 1868, the Yasukuni Shrine has been dedicated to the spirits of those who have died in Japan's wars and has been closely connected to the impe-

rial family. Those who died in battle are worshiped as the *kami* (deities) of Yasukuni Shrine. During the war, mothers who sacrificed their sons to the great imperial cause were idealized as the "mothers of Yasukuni." See Kano Mikiyo, *Josei to Tennosei* (Tokyo: Shisō no Kagaku, 1979).

56. Iijima also spoke to the efforts of the mothers to protect their revolutionary children from harm and therefore try to dissuade them or support them after they were arrested or beaten down. In other words, she points to the role of mothers' participation in the political process. Miki, Saeki, and Mizoguchi, *Shiryō Nihon ūman ribu shi*, 1:24–25.

57. Ibid., 1:23., 1:399, 2:29, 2:67, 2:231, 2:239, 3:152, 3:288.

58. Iijima Aiko, "Naze 'Shinryaku=Sabetsu to Tatakau Ajia Fujin Kaigi,' datta no ka," *Zenkyōtō kara ribu e: jyūgo shi nōto sengo hen* [From *Zenkyōtō* to Ribu], ed. Onna-tachi no Ima o Tou Kai (Tokyo: Inpakuto Shuppankai, 1996), 188.

59. Iijima Aiko, "Dono you ni tatakau koto ga hitsuyou to sareteiruka," in Miki, Saeki, and Mizoguchi, *Shiryō Nihon ūman ribu shi*, 1:23.

60. First published in Aki Shobō Henshū Bu, *Sei sabetsu e no kokuhatsu*, 131. This manifesto was from the group the Committee to Prepare for Women's Liberation (Josei Kaihō Undō Junbi Kai), dated August 20, 1970.

61. The full name of the group is Shinryaku=Sabetsu to Tatakau Ajia Fujin Kaigi. For an abbreviated history of the group, see Setsu Shigematsu, "Shinryaku=Sabetsu to Tatakau Ajia Fujin Kaigi," in Inoue et al., *Iwanami joseigaku jiten*, 263–64; for a fuller history, see Iijima Aiko, *"Shinryaku=Sabetsu" no kanata e: aru feminisuto no hansei* (Tokyo: Inpakuto Shuppankai, 2006).

62. This Pan-Asian solidarity became a foundational political principle for feminist activists like the late Matsui Yayori, who established the Asian Women's Resource Center (the basis of what developed into today's Asia-Japan Women's Resource Center) and VAWW-NET (Violence Against Women in War–Network Japan). See http://www1.jca.apc.org/vaww-net-japan/english/ (accessed August 2010). Matsui identified herself as a member of the women's liberation movement, although many *ribu* activists thought that her politics differed substantially from what they defined as the core of *ribu*'s liberation of sex; Matsui would later criticize how privileging the "liberation of sex" could be reduced to little more than a self-centered form of liberation for Japanese women. Cf. chapter 3, note 30, and Epilogue, note 28.

63. The Shibokusa women are rural farming women who for decades have resisted the appropriation of their lands by the U.S. and Japanese military at the north foot of Mount Fuji. Matsuoka Yōko, "Shibokusa Haha no Kai," Tokushū: kyōdōtai no gensō e no hangyaku, *Gendai no me* (May 1971) 216–21; Kaji Etsuko, "Peasant Guerrillas on Vietnam Second Front: A Report on the 25-Year Struggle for Land of Kitafuji," *AMPO*, no. 13–14 (May–July 1972); Leonie Caldecott, "At the Foot of the Mountain: The Shibokusa Women of Kita Fuji," in *Keeping the Peace: A Women's Peace Handbook*, ed. Lynne Jones (London: Women's Press, 1983). Sanrizuka refers to the

protest that began in the latter half of the 1960s when farmers refused to give up their land in response to the government's plan to build Narita Airport. New Left sects, nonaffiliated students, and other leftists joined in solidarity with the farmers, and this organized struggle, which lasted for over a decade, became a symbol of the struggle of the people against the state. For a rich and detailed account of the history of this struggle, see David Apter and Nagayo Sawa, *Against the State: Politics and Social Protest in Japan* (Cambridge: Harvard University Press, 1984); "The Sanrizuka Farmers' Struggle," *AMPO*, no. 3–4 (1970): 20; "Sanrizuka Fight Continues," *AMPO*, no. 5 (1970). Miki, Saeki, and Mizoguchi, *Shiryō Nihon ūman ribu shi,* 1:24–28.

64. Matsuoka Yōko, "70 Taikai kichō hōkoku: '8 gatsu 22 nichi' Shinryaku=Sabetsu to Tatakau Ajia Fujin Kaigi " in Miki, Saeki, and Mizoguchi, *Shiryō Nihon ūman ribu shi,* 1:43.

65. This identity politics for *ribu* was based on the politicized understanding of the term *onna* as its key word and the core concept of the liberation of sex *(sei no kaiho)*. The liberation of sex is more fully elaborated in chapter 3.

66. Such comparisons were also made within *ribu*'s discourse referencing, for example, how blacks in America were protesting against the discrimination they faced.

67. Iijima writes, "What I feel is that this world and theory itself is male *(otoko),* and therefore we need *onna*'s theory *(onna no ronri).*" Iijima Aiko, "Onna ni totte sabetsu towa nanika," in Miki, Saeki, and Mizoguchi, *Shiryō Nihon ūman ribu shi,* 1:47, 1:52.

68. Ibid., 1:47. Iijima criticized how Marxist theory assumed that women were socially degraded because they were forced to perform the mundane and nonproductive work of domestic labor. Iijima argued that even if more women were organized as part of the labor movement, this would not lead to women's liberation. Iijima argued that increasing women's participation in the labor force would only further assimilate women into the capitalist structure by simply expanding the lowest paid strata of the labor force. Iijima wanted to emphasize that regardless of the intention of women laborers, "they were serving the interests of capital" (49).

69. Ibid., 49.

70. Iijima theorized that by splitting and opposing the concepts of sex and birthing, birthing was cut off from "living" and that living and sex were simultaneously split from each other, compartmentalizing these concepts.

71. Interview with Iijima Aiko, Tokyo, March 11, 2002.

72. According to Iijima, her position was distinct from Tanaka's position on three major points. First, given her long background in the established left, she ultimately could not let go of the centrality of labor as being a fundamental organizing concept and allow it to be replaced with the emphasis on sex that Tanaka proposed. Second, she felt that Tanaka's practice of liberation ultimately emphasized "self-liberation" more than it emphasized social transformation. Third, Iijima stated that even though she wrote about the meaning of the liberation of *onna,* ultimately, she felt she could not identify herself as an *onna.* Interview with Iijima Aiko, March 11, 2002.

73. Inoue, *Joseigaku to sono shūhen*, 176–93.

74. The *Kojien Japanese Dictionary* (Tokyo: Iwanami Shoten, 2000) defines *shufu* as the "wife of the master of a household." Ehara Yumiko writes that the term *fujin* refers to an adult woman and a woman who is married, noting that much of the post-1970 criticism of *fujin* had to do with the meaning of the Chinese character that comprised *fujin,* which entailed the radical for "broom," implying that a *fujin* was a woman who used a broom inside a house (Inoue et al., *Iwanami joseigaku jiten,* 412). See Ochiai, *The Japanese Family System in Transition;* Ueno Chizuko, "The Genesis of the Urban Housewife," *Japan Quarterly* 34 (1987): 130–42.

75. Endo, "Aspects of Sexism in Language," 30. Cf. Introduction, note 4. Kano Masanao, *Fujin, Josei, Onna: Josei shi no toi* (Tokyo: Iwanami Shinsho, 1989), 12.

76. Email interview with Sayama Sachi, August 20, 2010.

77. Verta Taylor and Nancy E. Whittier, "Collective Identity in Social Movement Theories: Lesbian Feminist Mobilization," in *Frontiers in Social Movement Theory,* ed. Aldon D. Morris and Carol Mueller (New Haven: Yale University Press, 1992), 104–29.

78. Ochiai Emiko notes that the activists of the *ūman ribu* movement did not seem to make an analytical distinction between what they criticized as the *ie seido* and the contemporary male-centered nuclear family system. Ochiai, *The Japanese Family System in Transition,* 101.

79. Although I wish to emphasize the symbolic distinction and shift from *josei* to *onna,* some *ribu* groups that were established later still used the term *josei.* For example, Watanabe Fumie writes that she used the term *josei* to name the second *ribu* group she started at Hiroshima University in 1974 (女性解放研究会). Email interview with Watanabe Fumie, August 18, 2010. Although there were many exceptions, *ribu* discourse centers *onna* as a key word and political subject of its discourse.

80. In some of the early *ribu* literature, the term *josei* was used. However, very quickly, with the theorization of the term *onna* by *ribu* intellectuals, *onna* was overwhelmingly referred to as the signifier of *ribu*'s political subject. Tanaka Mitsu emphasizes the choice of *onna* in "'Matsu onna' kara dappi," *Asahi Shinbun,* October 25, 1970, 23.

81. There are two versions of the pamphlet "Liberation from the Toilet" ("Benjo kara no kaiho"): the six-page original (August 1970) and the seven-page revised version, "Benjo kara no kaiho" (kaisei ban) ["Liberation from the Toilet" (rev.)] (October 1970). Both manifestos are cited throughout the work. I cite the original version, which is reprinted in Miki, Saeki, and Mizoguchi, *Shiryō Nihon ūman ribu shi,* 1:201–8, hereafter "Liberation from the Toilet." The original is also reprinted in Inoue et al., *Nihon no feminism=feminism in Japan,* vol. 1 (Tokyo: Iwanami Shoten, 1990), 39–56. The revised version is reprinted in Tanaka's *Inochi no onna-tachi e: torimidashi ūman ribu ron* [To Women with Spirit: Toward a Disorderly Theory of Women's Liberation] (Tokyo: Pandora: 2001), 333–47, and *Doko ni iyou to riburian: Tanaka Mitsu hyōgenshū* (Tokyo: Shakai Hyōron Sha, 1983), 265–80. I cite the version in *Doko ni*

iyou to riburian (1983) hereafter cited as Tanaka Mitsu, "Liberation from the Toilet" (rev.), 277. Three versions are reprinted in *Ribu Shinjuku Sentā shiryō shūsei: bira hen,* eds. Ribu Shinjuku Sentā Shiryō Hozon Kai (Tokyo: Inpakuto Shuppankai, 2008), 20–25; 27–33; 40–46. The first version is attributed to Tanaka Mitsu (20–25), the same pamphlet is also attributed to Josei Kaiho Renraku Kaigi (27–33); and the third revised version is attributed to Gurūpu Tatakau Onna, hereafter Group of Fighting Women. I use the translation Group of Fighting Women here instead of Group of Fighting *Onna* because this translation has been widely used in extant works.

82. Kathleen Uno and Ueno Chizuko have both argued that the role and concept of "mother" *(haha)* and "motherhood" *(bosei)* define the bases and recurring thematics of postwar women's movements. In "The Making of a History of Feminism in Japan" (*Asian Journal of Women's Studies* 2 [1996]: 170–91), Ueno writes, "Japanese feminism has been characterized by maternalism from the beginning" (180). Ueno, "Umu sei, umanai sei: haha ni naru obseshion," *Onna to iu kairaku* (Tokyo: Keisō Shobō, 1986); Uno, "Death of 'Good Wife, Wise Mother'?," 293–322.

83. Miki, Saeki, and Mizoguchi, *Shiryō Nihon ūman ribu shi,* 1:152, 1:192, 1:195, 1:200, 1:205, 1:208, 1:372, 2:34, 2:42, 2:64–65, 2:73, 2:143, 2:144, 2:270, 2:311. Shimazu Yoshiko, "Unmarried Mothers and Their Children in Japan," *U.S.–Japan Women's Journal* 6 (1994). "In looking at history we see that the family registry system that was created over the thirty-year period from early Meiji through the establishment in 1898 of the Meiji Civil Code is the culmination of a system that was formulated to further paternal lineage" (109).

84. *Ribu* activist Watanabe Fumie writes that in the beginning of the movement women started using "male language" (男言葉), which is considered rough or rude. Email interview, August 19, 2010.

85. Nishimura, *Onna-tachi no kyōdōtai,* 45–46.

86. Images of Tokyo Komu-unu appear in Hara Kazuo's film *Kokushi-teki erosu: Koi-uta 1974,* which has international circulation through film screenings and DVD sales.

87. Takeda Miyuki, "'Tokyo Komuunu' kaitai—sono sōkatsu," in Miki, Saeki, and Mizoguchi, *Shiryō Nihon ūman ribu shi,* 2:36.

88. Kristin Luker, "Women and the Right to Abortion," in *Abortion and the Politics of Motherhood* (Berkeley: University of California Press, 1984).

89. Some of the consequences of rejecting the marriage–family system for the children of *ribu* women and men are depicted in the documentary film *Ripples of Change: Japanese Women's Search for Self,* dir. Nanako Kurihara (New York: Women Make Movies, 1993).

90. Group Tatakau Onna, "Haha e no rabu letā: kogoroshi no onna e rentai suru ware ware ribu no sono 'rentai' to iu kotoba no imi wa nani ka," in Miki, Saeki, and Mizoguchi, *Shiryō Nihon ūman ribu shi,* 1:240–46.

91. *Ribu Shinjuku Sentā shiryō shūsei: bira hen,* 197.

92. The government responded to this crisis by allocating 110 million yen in 1972 to childcare for babies ages one to three. Tanaka Mitsu, *Inochi no onna-tachi e—torimidashi ūman ribu ron* (Tokyo: Kawade Shobō, 1992), 170. I cite the Kawade Shobō edition of *Inochi* unless otherwise stated.

93. *Ondoro ondoro* (Tokyo: Group of Fighting Women [Gurūpu Tatakau Onna]), May 8, 1971). These figures are confirmed by Tama Yasuko's study *Boseiai to iu seido: kogoroshi to chūzetsu no poritikusu* (Tokyo: Keiso Shobō, 2001; repr. 2008), 71–104.

94. Tama, *Boseiai to iu seido,* 73.

95. Ibid., 72. The number of stories that reported mothers killing their children was double the number that reported fathers killing their children. The number of reports of such incidents peaked in 1973, with newspapers such as *Mainichi Shinbun* and *Asahi Shinbun* reporting 169 and 221 incidents respectively, doubling and tripling the numbers of stories published a decade earlier (in 1963).

96. Ibid., 44–62.

97. Interview with Yonezu Tomoko, July 12, 2009. Yonezu emphasized to me during an interview that it was not Tanaka Mitsu who led or ordered this solidarity movement, but the sense of identification with *kogoroshi no onna* was shared among many *ribu* activists who engaged this issue. The number of different authors of the writings and data collected on *kogoroshi no onna* in *Ribu Shinjuku Sentā shiryō shūsei: bira hen* and *Ribu Shinjuku Sentā shiryō shūsei: panfuretto hen,* ed. Ribu Shinjuku Sentā Shiryō Hozon Kai (Tokyo: Inpakuto Shuppankai, 2008), attest to how many activists were involved in this organizing work at the Ribu Shinjuku Center.

98. The following citations refer to *kogoroshi no onna* in the historical documents of the movement compiled in Miki, Saeki, and Mizoguchi, *Shiryō Nihon ūman ribu shi,* 1:164, 1:165, 1:176, 1:184, 1:186, 1:228, 1:240–46, 1:251, 1:323, 1:354; 2:15, 2:17, 2:24–25, 2:30, 2:37, 2:61, 2:68–69, 2:114, 2:150, 2:178, 2:200, 2:232, 2:246–47, 2:315, 2:326, 2:363–64, 2:365, 2:379, 2:381. The large number of citations are indicative of the significance of *kogoroshi no onna* in the consciousness, writings, and activism of *ribu* women.

99. Interview with Yonezu Tomoko, July 12, 2009.

100. Minpō Kaisei o Susumeru Gurūpu, ed., *Minpō kaisei soko ga shiritai: sentaku bessei to kodomo no byōdou* (Kyōto: Kamogawa Shuppan, 1996). Until 2001, the *Minpō kaisei nettowāku* was still lobbying for changes regarding the discriminatory inheritance laws that discriminate on the basis of nonmarital children *(chakushutsu denai ko)* (unpublished *Minpō kaisei nettowāku* booklet from March 2001). Shimazu, "Unmarried Mothers and Their Children in Japan." Shimazu writes, "In Japan it is the mother who ends up bearing all of the child-rearing responsibilities for those children who live away from the paternal home or who do not contribute to the continuance of the paternal bloodline" (84). Shimazu notes, "The family register . . . conveys an image of what is considered appropriate in relationships between people" (85).

This unfavorable treatment of the nonmarital child, which continues to the present, began in modern Japan.

101. I owe the translation of the first part of this title (To Women with Spirit) to James Welker. He used this title in his paper at the annual meeting of the Asian Studies Association in Philadelphia, March 27, 2009.

102. Tanaka's views concerning violence are further elaborated in chapter 5.

103. Tanaka, *Inochi no onna-tachi e*, 196.

104. Ibid., 201.

105. Ibid., 171.

106. Ibid., 189.

107. Ikeda Sachiko, Akiyama Yōko, and Inoue Teruko, "Zadankai: todai tōsō kara ribu, soshite, joseigaku, feminizumu," *Zenkyōtō kara ribu e*, 52. Akiyama Yōko discusses how Tanaka Mitsu readily connected the issue of abortion to its imperial history, which regulated women's bodies through the Eugenic Protection Law.

108. During the Meiji era (1868–1912), known as a period of intensive "modernization," the government sought to regulate the reproductive process. In 1880, abortion was made a crime and remains so under current criminal law. In addition to the criminalization of abortion, from 1940 to 1941, the government established the Eugenic Protection Law that legislated contraceptive surgery to prevent the birth of "defective" or "handicapped" children.

109. Article 14 of the Eugenic Protection Law allows women access to abortion under certain conditions. See Ōhashi Yukako, "My Body Belongs to Me: Women Fight against a Retrogressive Revision of the Eugenic Protection Law," *AMPO* 18, nos. 2–3 (1986): 94–99. Ōhashi writes, "According to the law, abortion is a punishable crime, and a woman must bear the baby once she gets pregnant" (95). "With the aborticide law intact on the one hand, the Eugenic Protection Law was enacted in 1948. . . . Women literally became the 'child-bearing corps,' and child-bearing was considered a 'national mission'" (95). Under the Eugenic Protection Law, abortion was still considered a criminal act, although the clause permitting "economic reasons" provided a legal loophole for women in the postwar period to use abortion as a means of birth control. See, Tiana Norgren, *Abortion before Birth Control: The Politics of Reproduction in Postwar Japan* (Princeton, N.J.: Princeton University Press, 2001).

110. Miki, Saeki, and Mizoguchi, *Shiryō Nihon ūman ribu shi*, 2:61.

111. Ibid., 2:63.

112. Ibid., 1:178. Morioka Masahiro published several works that interpret Tanaka and *ribu*'s politics on abortion as converging with prolife views of abortion as murder. This conclusion that abortion is murder should be fully assessed within the discursive, historical, and political contexts of each of these movements. Tanaka did not begin her argument with the intention of an alliance with prolife movements. To the contrary, the movement Seicho no Ie, which emphasized the essential morality of giving birth, was one of the groups that catalyzed the restrictions of abortion that *ribu* activ-

ists fought against. For more information about Seicho no Ie, see Norgren, *Abortion before Birth Control,* and the notes to my discussion on abortion in chapter 3. Morioka Masahiro, *Seimeigaku ni nani ga dekiruka* (Tokyo: Keisō Shobō, 2001); Morioka Masahiro, "*Ūman Ribu* to Seimei Rinri," in *Onna to otoko no jikyū: Nihon josei shi saikō,* ed. Yamashita Etsuko (Tokyo: Fujiwara Shoten, 1996).

113. Tanaka Mitsu, "Aete teiki suru-chūzetsu wa kitoku no kenrika?" in Miki, Saeki, and Mizoguchi, *Shiryō Nihon ūman ribu shi,* 2:63.

114. I interpret this as constituting a protofeminist abolitionist politics. See note 118.

115. Tanaka Mitsu, "Aete teiki suru-chūzetsu wa kitoku no kenrika?" in Miki, Saeki, and Mizoguchi, *Shiryō Nihon ūman ribu shi,* 2:63.

116. Tanaka, *Inochi no onna-tachi e,* 61. Tanaka, "Onna ni totte kogoroshi to wa nannika," Doko, 83–100.

117. Tanaka Mitsu, "Aete teiki suru-chūzetsu wa kitoku no kenrika?" in Miki, Saeki, and Mizoguchi, *Shiryō Nihon ūman ribu shi,* 2:63.

118. For further reading on sources that inform my notion of feminist-abolition, see Angela Davis, *Abolition Democracy: Beyond Prisons, Torture and Empire* (New York: Seven Stories Press, 2005), and *Abolition Now: Ten Years of Strategy and Struggle against the Prison Industrial Complex,* ed. CR10 Publications Collective (Oakland, Calif.: AK Press, 2008). For a filmic representation of my notion of a feminist-abolitionist politics see *Visions of Abolition: From Critical Resistance to a New Way of Life,* directed by Setsu Shigematsu (2011), 87 min., http://www.visionsofabolition.org.

119. My discussion of *ribu*'s response to the women of Rengo Sekigun (United Red Army) in chapter 5 further elaborates my concept of a feminist ethics of violence.

120. To say that lethal violence is an act of feminist resistance is a stance that must be further examined, especially for its danger of being co-opted by the state for national-imperialist purposes, as it was in Japan's past imperialist legacy.

121. English language pamphlet of the Ribu Shinjuku Center, April 1, 1975. Reprinted in *Ribu Shinjuku Sentā shiryō shūsei: panfuretto hen,* 276.

2. Lineages of the Left

1. For histories of the New Left, see Takazawa Kōji, Takagi Masayuki, and Kurata Kazunari, *Shinsayoku nijyūnen shi: hanran no kiseki* (Tokyo: Shinsensha, 1995); Kurata Kazunari, *Shinsayoku undo zenshi* [The Complete History of the New Left Movement] (Tokyo: Ryūdō Shuppan, 1978); Oguma Eiji, *1968,* 2 vols. (Tokyo: Shinyōsha, 2009).

2. The massive struggle regarding the 1960 renewal of the security treaty is referred to as 1960 Anpo. Cf. chapter 1, note 26.

3. Wesley Sasaki-Uemura, *Organizing the Spontaneous: Citizen Protest in Postwar Japan* (Honolulu: Hawaii University Press, 2001); George Packard, *Protest in Tokyo:*

The Security Treaty Crises of 1960 (Princeton, N.J.: Princeton University Press, 1966); Robert Scalapino and Junnosuke Masumi, "The Crises of May-June, 1960," in *Parties and Politics in Contemporary Japan* (Berkeley: University of California Press, 1967), 125–53.

4. Matsushita Keiichi, "Citizen Participation in Historical Perspective," in *Authority and the Individual in Japan: Citizen Protest in Historical Perspective,* ed. J. Victor Koschmann (Tokyo: University of Tokyo Press, 1978), 171–88; Takabatake Michitoshi, "Citizen's Movements: Organizing the Spontaneous," in Koschmann, *Authority and the Individual,* 189–99.

5. Ellis S. Krauss, *Japanese Radicals Revisited: Student Protest in Postwar Japan* (Berkeley: University of California Press, 1974); Usami Shō, "Zengakuren," *Japan Quarterly* 15, no. 2 (1968): 233–44; Kazuko Tsurumi, "The Student Movement," in *Social Change and the Individual: Japan before and after Defeat in World War II* (Princeton, N.J.: University Press, 1970), 307–69.

6. Ellis Krauss, *Japanese Radicals Revisited,* 4; Muto Ichiyo and Inoue Reiko, "Beyond the New Left (Part 1): In Search of a Radical Base in Japan," *AMPO* 17, no. 3 (1985): 20–35.

7. Packard, *Protest in Tokyo;* Sasaki-Uemura, *Organizing the Spontaneous.*

8. Sasaki-Uemura, *Organizing the Spontaneous,* 44, 48, 52, 162–63; Muto and Inoue, "Beyond the New Left (Part 1)," 27; Krauss, *Japanese Radicals Revisited,* 1.

9. In *Organizing the Spontaneous,* Sasaki-Uemura writes that on June 19 when an estimated 330 thousand people demonstrated around the Diet, "those present felt as if they were mourning for both Kanba and democracy" (53) and that "most protesters saw her [Kanba] as a victim of state violence" (162).

10. Kanba Michiko's death marked the violence inherent to the policing of Japanese postwar democracy and the recognized sacrifice of a young elite Japanese woman who believed in the meaning of political protest. Ibid., 44, 48, 52, 162–63.

11. J. Victor Koschmann, "Introduction to the Individual as Citizen: Postwar Japan," in *Authority and the Individual,* 144–53. Koschmann writes, "In short, the opposition parties had become part of the 'system,' and the established movements they controlled were no longer flexible and responsive to minority demands or new issues" (146).

12. For example, in the immediate postwar period, the JCP aimed for a peaceful revolution, epitomized in the slogan "The Lovable Communism Party." However, with the onset of the Cold War and the fate of international communism in the balance, the Japanese left was compelled to respond to the changes in international politics. As a result of the U.S. involvement in the Korean War, the Cominform (Communist Information Bureau) strongly criticized the JCP for its moderate reaction. The Cominform was established in 1947 and was the first official organization of the international communist movement since the disestablishment of the Comintern (the Communist International or the Third International). It was a Soviet-dominated organization that

was dissolved in 1956. Munemutsu Yamada, "The Development of Left-Wing Intellectuality," *Social and Political Ideas in Japan* 2, no. 1 (1964): 59–64. In response, the JCP dramatically switched its position to promoting armed conflict with the state. However, after realizing such tactics would greatly weaken its domestic support, it again switched its position to espouse its support of a gradual two-stage revolution and staunchly committed itself to playing within the rules of parliamentary politics. Muto and Inoue, "Beyond the New Left (Part 1)," 22–23. This program stipulated that Japan had to undergo a national democratic revolution before it could achieve a socialist revolution.

13. Krauss, *Japanese Radicals Revisited,* 4–5; Muto and Inoue, "Beyond the New Left (Part 1)," 25.

14. Sasaki-Uemura, *Organizing the Spontaneous,* 52.

15. The police denied responsibility for her death, stating that she was trampled to death by other student protestors. Ibid., 44.

16. Apter and Nagayo, *Against the State;* Packard, *Protest in Tokyo*. The peak in Zengakuren's membership and activity was in 1949, and then it went into decline from 1950 to 1955. In 1956, it began a renaissance. In 1959, it had about 300,000 members over 140 campuses, gearing up for the 1960 Anpo protest. Muto and Inoue, "Beyond the New Left (Part 1)," 30. Bund had emphasized underground activity, armed struggle, and world revolution. The year 1965 also marked the formation of the Sanpa-Zengakuren, an acrimonious coalition of Bund, Chūkaku, and Kaihō. Regarding itself as a revolution-oriented organization, Sanpa-Zengakuren declared that in order to engage in an anti-imperialist struggle, "we are prepared to suffer repression, denunciation, and isolation."

17. Takazawa Kōji, Takagi Masayuki, and Kurata Kazunari, *Shinsayoku nijyūnen shi: hanran no kiseki* (Tokyo: Shinsensha, 1981), 234.

18. Junrō Fukashiro, "The New Left," *Japan Quarterly* 17, no. 1 (1970): 27–36; Muto and Inoue, "Beyond the New Left (Part 1)," 20. In 1965, the Antiwar Youth Committee known as Hansen (Hansen Seinen Iinkai) organized workers to protest the normalization treaty between Korea and Japan. Hansen comprised the class-based component of the New Left. Muto Ichiyo and Inoue Reiko, "Beyond the New Left (Part 2): In Search of a Radical Base in Japan," *AMPO* 17, no. 4 (1985): 51–59.

19. Muto and Inoue, "Beyond the New Left (Part I)," 31.

20. William Marotti, "Japan 1968: The Performance of Violence and the Theater of Protest," *American Historical Review* 114, no. 1 (2009): 97–135.

21. Muto and Inoue, "Beyond the New Left (Part 2)"; "Student Murdered by Riot Police," *AMPO,* no. 2 (1969): 6.

22. Donald Wheeler, "The Japanese Student Movement: Value Politics, Student Politics and the University of Tokyo Struggle," (PhD diss., Columbia University, 1974). October 21, 1969, saw the massive arrests of 14,748 demonstrators and activists, which cost various factions 150 million yen in bail money and depleted the resources of the

antiwar and New Left movements (258). Beheiren provided the umbrella organization for this demonstration, with 860,000 participants.

23. Patricia Steinhoff writes, "By the late 1960s, a 29,000-man elite police force, the Kidōtai, devoted its time to controlling student riots and gathering intelligence on specific student organizations; plainclothes police conducted round-the-clock surveillance of more than a hundred student activists. . . . Several thousand college students acquired arrest records during the late 1960s and early 1970s, and hundreds have served time for a variety of offenses related to participation in the student movement. . . . Substantial numbers of individuals were losing social rights and privileges because of their participation in such activities." Patricia Steinhoff, "Student Conflict," in *Conflict in Japan,* ed. Ellis S. Krauss, Thomas P. Rohlen, and Patricia G. Steinhoff (Honolulu: University of Hawaii Press, 1984), 175–76; Patricia Steinhoff, "Protest and Democracy," in *Democracy in Japan,* ed. Takeshi Ishida and Ellis Krauss (Pittsburgh, Pa.: University of Pittsburgh Press, 1989).

24. Ehara Yumiko, *Josei kaihō to iu shisō* (Tokyo: Keisō Shobō, 1985), 105. Ehara discusses three conditions that enabled the birth of *ribu* women out of the New Left. First, the New Left offered a critique of the existing political parties; second, it had developed tactics for organizing and executing a political action; third, it provided a politicized consciousness about inequality, discrimination, and social contradiction.

25. Gotō Motoo, "Crises in Japan-U.S. Relations," *Japan Quarterly* 15, no. 4 (1968): 421–29.

26. For a rich and thorough account of the Sanrizuka struggle, see David Apter and Nagayo, *Against the State.*

27. The spokesman of Beheiren was Oda Makoto. Muto and Inoue, "Beyond the New Left (Part 2)," 61.

28. Kurihara Yukio, "Sengo minshūshugi o koeta undō rinen—beheiren," in *Rekishi no dohyō kara* (Tokyo: Renga Shobo, 1989), 280–90; Yoshiyuki Tsurumi, "Beheiren: A New Force on the Left," *AMPO,* no. 1; Muto Ichiyo, "'Beheiren' undō no shisō," *Shisō no kagaku,* no. 5 (January 1967): 11–21.

29. Oda Makoto, "The Ethics of Peace," in Koschmann, *Authority and the Individual,* 154–70; "Interview with Makoto Oda, Beheiren Chairman," *AMPO,* no. 1 (1970); "Intellectuals and the Movement in Japan and the U.S.: Noam Chomsky and Makoto Oda," *AMPO,* no. 5 (1970).

30. By confronting state violence, Beheiren became radicalized. For example, Beheiren's folk guerrilla movement used to gather crowds of up to five thousand that were forcefully dispersed by the riot police. This forced dispersal led to its fragmentation and multiplication to other local areas, which in turn produced a new slogan: *"hiroba,"* which means "open space" and implied the concept of a liberated zone. In spite of its strikingly decentralized and antibureaucratic mode of organization, Beheiren provided the most effective umbrella organization leading up to the 1970 Anpo struggle. For the first time since 1960, under Beheiren's banner, all the major groups of the New

Left, including students, young workers, and various citizen groups, numbering approximately seventy-five thousand people, came together in united action on June 15, 1969, to peacefully protest the war in Vietnam. Fukashiro, "The New Left."

31. Wheeler, "The Japanese Student Movement," 132. Wheeler writes, "Joint Struggle Committees (Zenkyōtō) were formed to coordinate campus-wide struggles at Keio University in 1965 and at Waseda in 1966. Student leaders at other universities also formed Joint Struggle Committees; however, it was the University of Tokyo student leaders whose interpretation became the hegemonic meaning of these Zenkyōtō struggles as a new style of student movement. After the University of Tokyo struggle, the Zenkyōtō style spread to struggles all over the country" (132). The hierarchy of theorists of Zenkyōtō reproduced the existing prestige hierarchy of the imperial university structure.

32. Ibid., 132.

33. Tokoro was born in 1939 and was an undergraduate in the sciences at Ochanomizu Women's University. She went on to study microbiology at Osaka University. She returned to Tokyo after becoming ill in Osaka. At the University of Tokyo, she belonged to the University of Tokyo Newspaper Research Center (Daigaku Shinbun kenkyū jo), which is now the Media Research Center.

34. Tokoro Mitsuko, "Tokoro-san no byōki," in *Waga ai to hangyaku* (Tokyo: Shinmu Shobō, 1969), 138.

35. Guy Yasko, "The Origins of Zenkyōtō Thought: Tokoro Mitsuko's Road to Zenkyōtō," in "The Japanese Student Movement 1968–1970," (PhD diss., Cornell University, 1997), 19. Ōta Kyōko, "Onna-tachi no Zenkyōtō undo," in *Zenkyōtō kara ribu e*, 76. Tokoro is remembered as a pioneering visionary who devoted herself to the cause of the revolution. The University of Tokyo struggle, which took off in 1968, is often considered the beginning of Zenkyōtō. Yasko calls Yamamoto the "chair" of Zenkyōtō because he was in the position to speak for the students of the University of Tokyo's Zenkyōtō movement (76).

36. Yasko, 20.

37. Ibid., 21.

38. Tokoro's "Yokan sareu shoshiki ni yosete" [The Organization to Come] was an award-winning essay that was published in the October 1966 issue of *Shiso no kagaku*. Authored under the pseudonym Tomano Mimie, it won the Nakai Shō. It was republished in Tokoro, *Waga ai to hangyaku*, 149–59.

39. Ibid., 150.

40. Ibid., 145–47.

41. Ibid., 145–48.

42. Ibid., 149.

43. Yasko, "The Japanese Student Movement 1968–1970," 31. Tokoro, "Yokan sareru shoshiki ni yosete," 157–58. Inoue Teruko stated that she belonged to a study group with Tokoro Mitsuko at the University of Tokyo, where they read Simone de Beauvoir and Simone Weil together. Interview with Inoue Teruko, February 24, 2001.

44. "How Does *Onna* Desire to Exist?" originally published as Tokoro Mitsuko [Tomono Mimie, pseud.], "Onna Wa Dou Aritai ka," *Shisō no Kagaku*, no. 2 (1967). Reprinted in Tokoro, *Waga ai to hangyaku*, 168–70.

45. Iijima, "Naze 'Shinryaku=Sabetsu to Tatakau Ajia Fujin Kaigi' data no ka," 189–90. Iijima elaborated Tokoro Mitsuko's reading of Takemure Itsue's pantheistic materialism as calling for a "woman's theory." Additionally, Inoue Teruko refers to how the women of *ribu* discussed the works of Wilhelm Reich, Morisaki Kazuke, and Tokoro Mitsuko, in "Shutaiteki kakumeisha e no ishi hyōgen," Miki, Saeki, and Mizoguchi, *Shiryō Nihon ūman ribu shi,* 1:384–85.

46. According to Iwasaki Minoru, a former member of the New Left and specialist in German philosophy and the politics of the 1960 and 1970s, Tanaka's critique of the analogous problems of the logic of productivity was an apt observation of a broad spectrum of the New Left. Correspondence with Iwasaki Minoru, September 10, 2003.

47. Cf. note 34.

48. Wheeler, "The Japanese Student Movement." Wheeler writes that at the University of Tokyo, nonsect radicals who were dissatisfied with the student politics of "both the JCP Zengakuren and anti-JCP Zengakuren sects, were able to capture the leadership of the campus struggle" (132). David Apter writes, "The movement was characterized by study groups, discussion, soul searching, and an absence of doctrinarism. In 1969 eight anti-JCP sects formed Zenkyōtō. The relatively open organization and the emphasis on diversity made it into a model movement for citizen participation." Apter and Nagayo, *Against the State,* 119–22; "Student Rebellion at Nihon University: Interview with Akehiro Akita," *AMPO,* no. 5 (1970).

49. Iijima, "Naze 'Shinryaku=Sabetsu to Tatakau Ajia Fujin Kaigi' data no ka," 189–90; Ōta, "Onna-tachi no Zenkyōtō undo," 75–77. See also Tomono Mimie [Tokoro Mitsuko], "Onna wa do aritai ka?" *Shisō no kagaku* (February 1967): 44–49. Miki, Saeki, and Mizoguchi, *Shiryō Nihon ūman ribu shi,* 1:50, 1:52, 1:279. Cf. note 38.

50. Komashaku Miki, "Ūman ribu to watashi: sengo shakai ni okeru ribu no imi," *Shisō no kagaku,* no. 6 (1976): 98–112; Muto, "The Birth of the Women's Liberation Movement," 147–49.

51. Muto and Inoue, "Beyond the New Left (Part 2)"; Wheeler, "The Japanese Student Movement," 131–32. "Yokan sareru shoshiko ni yosete" [The Organization to Come], cf. note 38.

52. "The key was to develop an organization, practice and theory that could accommodate a society in which fundamental contradictions could surface on multiple fronts." Yasko, "The Japanese Student Movement 1968–1970," 25.

53. Wheeler, "The Japanese Student Movement," 123.

54. Wheeler writes, "There was considerable frustration and disgust among students with the dogmatic, exclusivist, self-centered sectarianism and factional strife of the early and middle 1960s. It was quite clear that there was no hope for student unity in a sect dominated movement. One sect would have to encompass all the others and there was no possibility of doing this peacefully or by force." Ibid., 188.

55. "*Ūman ribu* zadankai: dakareru onna kara 'otoko o daku onna' e," *Shūkan Asahi,* November 13, 1970, 22.

56. *Ribu*'s break from Zenkyōtō and the New Left is typically attributed to sexism of the student movement culture. Ozawa Yōko, "Ūman ribu no hachijyū nendai," *Gendai no me* 17, no. 1 (1976), 136–43. Ozawa cites a case in which a male student activist referred to a woman as a "public toilet" (136). In some cases, the rape of the women of rival sects became part of the New Left's tactics. See Oguma Eiji, *1968,* for accounts of such incidents of sexual violence.

57. Ōno Tsutomu, "Student Protest in Japan—What It Means to Society," *Journal of Social and Political Ideas in Japan* 5, no. 2–3 (1967); Patricia Steinhoff, "Student Conflict," 174–213.

58. Yasko, "The Japanese Student Movement 1968–1970," 8. Yasko writes, "Most Zenkyōtō activists did not believe that a revolution within university walls could substitute for a more generalized social transformation, but simply insisted that one's own immediate surroundings offered the best opportunities for change" (9).

59. Takada Motomu, "'Nichijo-sei' to 'jiko-hitei,'" in *Zenkyōtō no shisō to sono shūhen* (Tokyo: Shin Nihon Shuppan, 1969).

60. Yamamoto Yoshitaka, *Chisei no hanran* (Tokyo: Zeneisha, 1969), 113.

61. The influence of the philosopher Yoshimoto Taka'aki stressed the "practice of overcoming/living through the contradiction of one's position." Yasko, "The Japanese Student Movement 1968–1970," 88.

62. According to Yasko, a kind of negative mode of self-criticism and self-denial became the privileged view that justified one's point of relationality to other struggles. Yasko states, "Rather than the interests, desires, and needs of the subject leading to multiple struggles, it was the subject's essential criminality" (or complicity) that would connect the campus struggle to other battles. Ibid., 37.

63. "*Ūman ribu* zadankai," 22.

64. Miki, Saeki, and Mizoguchi, *Shiryō Nihon ūman ribu shi,* 1:33.

65. Ibid., 1:39.

66. Miyaoka Maki, "Zengakuren dai 30 kai teiki zenkoku taikai deno sei no sabetsu=haigaishugi to tatakau ketsuihyōmei," in *Onna no shisō,* ed. Saeki Yōko (Tokyo: Sanpō Books, 1972), 43–44. This manifesto, in a slightly altered form, was republished in Inoue et al., *Nihon no feminizumu,* vol. 1. I chose to work from the original 1972 publication of this manifesto instead of the reprinted edition because I am interested in the form of the text as it was disseminated during the early 1970s. The 1994 reprinted edition also does not include the name of any author. The given name of the author, Miyaoka Maki, according to editor Saeki Yōko, was most likely a pen name used to help conceal her identity.

67. As I theorize in chapter 5, *ribu*'s libratory praxis involved creating relationships that previously did not exist. They were based neither on personal experience nor direct contact but on an analysis of one's positionality within the discriminatory social relations of classism, nationalism, and imperialism. In order to oppose these

discriminatory social relations, *ribu* engaged forms of politicized identification in an attempt to forge solidarities with criminalized women and women who killed their children (see chapter 1).

68. Miki, Saeki, and Mizoguchi, *Shiryō Nihon ūman ribu shi,* 1:118, 1:124, 1:127, 1:157, 1:159–62, 1:165–66, 1:280, 1:321, 1:399, 2:29, 2:67, 2:231, 2:239. The performative enactment of these textual critiques, as one articulation of their politics, informed some *ribu* women's efforts to form alliances with Okinawan women's groups.

69. According to a *ribu* pamphlet written in 1970, a government census in 1969 counted 7,362 registered prostitutes in Okinawa. However, the pamphlet suggests there were actually twice as many. Miki, Saeki, and Mizoguchi, *Shiryō Nihon ūman ribu shi,* 1:157–59. At this time, two-thirds of all labor in Okinawa was dependent on the military industry.

70. These oppositional practices involved a diverse range of actions, from transforming one's way of speaking and one's sexual practices to confronting government officials and confronting one's own state of contradiction.

71. Insofar as postwar debates on subjectivity were concerned with the subject's "incomplete" state, *ribu*'s focus and pursuit of the formation *(keisei)* of the subject of *onna* can be understood within a broader trajectory of modernity and its subject. J. Victor Koschmann, "The Politics of Democratic Revolution in Postwar Japan," and "Modernity and Its Subject," in *Revolution and Subjectivity in Postwar Japan* (Chicago: Chicago University Press, 1996).

72. On January 18, 1969, eighty-five hundred riot police stormed the campus and forcefully removed the student protestors. Muto Ichiyo and Inoue Reiko, "Beyond the New Left (Part 2)," 52.

73. Photograph is from Yamamoto Yoshitaka's *Chisei no Hanran.*

74. Mori Setsuko, "Otoko narami onna kara ribu e," *Zenkyōtō kara ribu e,* 164–71.

75. Interview with Mori Setsuko, Tokyo, February 5, 2003.

76. Yasko, "The Japanese Student Movement 1968–1970," 19.

77. The climax of the movement was the National Zenkyōtō massive demonstration held on Antiwar Day, October 21, 1969. Zenkyōtō peaked before 1970 and the reversion of Okinawa. "The National Zenkyōtō stayed together until June 15, 1971" (265). Wheeler, "The Japanese Student Movement," 258.

78. Ibid., 369.

79. Ibid., 368. Zenkyōtō justified this refusal of the category of the citizen as an attempt to "negate the concept of nation."

80. Takeda, "Minshushugi hitei no shisō to ronri," in *Zenkyōtō no shisō to sono shūhen,* 51–55.

81. This was eleven days after *ribu*'s first major gathering in Tokyo on November 14, 1970. Before committing hara-kiri, Mishima reportedly shouted praises to the emperor: "Tenno heika banzai!" (akin to "Three cheers to the divine Emperor!") Henry Scott Stokes, "Hara-kiri," in *The Life and Death of Yukio Mishima* (Tokyo:

Charles E. Tuttle, 1975), 48. Muto Ichiyo, "Mishima and the Transition from Postwar Democracy to Democratic Fascism," *AMPO*, no. 9–10 (1971): 34–50.

82. John Nathan, *Mishima: A Biography* (Tokyo: Charles E. Tuttle, 1974), 247–49. In response to the University of Tokyo Struggle, Mishima states, "Observe and remember . . . when the final moment came, there was not one of them who believed in what he stood for sufficiently to hurl himself out of a window or fall on a sword." Ibid., 248. Guy Yasko, *Mishima Yukio vs. Todai Zenkyōtō: The Cultural Displacement of Politics* (Durham, N.C.: Asian/Pacific Studies Institute, Duke University Press, 1995).

83. Tanaka Mitsu, "Shinsayoku to ribu: harakiri to junshi," in *Inochi no onna-tachi e*. See my translation of this chapter in Setsu Shigematsu, "Tanaka Mitsu and the Women's Liberation Movement in Japan: Towards a Radical Feminist Ontology" (PhD diss., Cornell University, 2003), app. 3, 300.

84. Wheeler, "The Japanese Student Movement," 267.

85. Tanaka Mitsu, "Naze 'Sei no kaihō' ka: josei kaihō e no mondai teiki" (September 1970). Reprinted in Miki, Saeki, and Mizoguchi, *Shiryō Nihon ūman ribu shi*, 1:210–12, and in the latest edition of Tanaka's *Inochi no onna-tachi e* (Tokyo: Pandora, 2010), 307–10. See my translation in Shigematsu, "Tanaka Mitsu and the Women's Liberation Movement in Japan," app. 2, 298.

86. Mishima's criticism had pointed to this failure. See note 82.

87. Tanaka argued that people were alienated by the conditions of a capitalist society, and they therefore desired to flee from the mundane and oppressive conditions of everyday life. The use of violence was in itself extraordinary, and thus to fight against the riot police allowed one to escape one's oppressive sense of isolation and momentarily feel alive and feel fear and exhilaration.

88. Shigematsu, "Tanaka Mitsu and the Women's Liberation Movement in Japan," app. 3, 308.

89. Iwatsuki Sumie (later known as Asatori Sumie), "Karada kara no hassō," *Onna Erosu: Tokushū: Onna no karada wa uchū o hagukumu*, no. 5 (1978): 7–8.

90. Miyaoka Maki, "Tōsō no naka deno mezame: gakusei undō," in Saeki, *Onna no shisō*, 12–46.

91. Ibid., 14.

92. She began reading more of Marx's works after noting his statement in the *Economic and Philosophical Manuscripts* that "the fundamental human relationship is the relationship between men and women" and serves as the "barometer to measure human development."

93. Miyaoka, "Tōsō no naka deno mezame: gakusei undō," 16, 20–23.

94. Ibid., 23.

95. Ibid., 25.

96. Ibid., 16.

97. Ibid., 28.

98. Ibid., 29.

99. Ibid., 37.

100. Ibid., 18.

101. Ibid., 25.

102. Ibid., 37.

103. One example of the erasure of *ribu*'s presence from the history of the New Left is noted by Ichiyo Muto, who states that Kurata Kazunari's *Shinsayoku undō zenshi* fails to mention *ribu*'s debut demonstration at the October 21 International Antiwar Demonstration Day. Muto, "The Birth of the Women's Liberation Movement," 171.

104. Shigematsu, "Tanaka Mitsu and the Women's Liberation Movement in Japan," app. 3, 302.

105. Toyama Mieko (age 25) and Namekata Masatoki (age 22) were tortured and beaten to death as punishment for their inappropriate nonrevolutionary expression of their sexual attraction to each other. *The Japan Times* reported that they had been accused of having sexual intercourse while "on duty" (March 14, 1972). These internal dynamics of the United Red Army were widely reported in newspapers in March 1972. Patricia Steinhoff, "Death by Defeatism and Other Fables: The Psychodynamics of the Rengo Sekigun Purge," in *Japanese Social Organization,* ed. Takie Sugiyama Lebra (Honolulu: University of Hawaii Press, 1992); Steinhoff, *Nihon Rengun ha: sono shakaigakuteki monogatari* (Tokyo: Kawade Shoten, 1991); Steinhoff, "Three Women Who Loved the Left: Radical Women Leaders in the Japanese Red Army Movement," in *Re-imaging Japanese Women,* ed. Anne Imamura (Berkeley: University of California Press, 1996); Ueno Chizuko also writes about Tanaka's critique in "Rengo Sekigun to feminizumu," in *Bungaku o shakaigaku suru* (Tokyo: Asahi Shinbun Sha, 2000), 163–82.

106. Miki, Saeki, and Mizoguchi, *Shiryō Nihon ūman ribu shi,* 1:345.

3. The Liberation of Sex, *Onna,* and Eros

1. The term *onna* (woman) is elaborated in chapter 1.

2. As noted in the Introduction, my purpose here is to offer a critical historiography that best captures *ribu*'s distinct feminist politics, both in the context of the 1970s and from the perspective of transnational feminisms in the twenty-first century.

3. Welker, "Transfiguring the Female." Welker's study examines the relationship between *ribu* and the emergence of lesbian culture and politics. Sachiko Ishino and Naeko Wakabayashi, "Japan: Lesbian Activism," in *Unspoken Rules: Sexual Orientation and Women's Human Rights,* ed. Rachel Rosenbloom (San Francisco: International Gay and Lesbian Rights Commission, 1995), 95–102; Sharon Chalmers, *Emerging Lesbian Voices from Japan* (New York: Routledge, 2002).

4. Miki, Saeki, and Mizoguchi, *Shiryō Nihon ūman ribu shi,* 1:169–87.

5. Mori Setsuko discusses this turning point in the video documentary *30 Years*

of Sisterhood: Women in the 1970s Women's Liberation Movement in Japan, directed by Yamagami Chieko and Seyama Noriko (Tokyo: Herstory Project, 2004). Tanaka Mitsu also criticized this privileging of the *gebabō* by implying that it symbolized the masculinist modality of revolutionary action within the ranks of the New Left. See Part 5, "The New Left and *Ribu*," in Tanaka, *Inochi no onna-tachi e.*

6. I take my notion of abjection from Julia Kristeva. John Fletcher and Andrew Benjamin, eds., *Abjection, Melancholia, and Love: The Work of Julia Kristeva* (New York: Routledge, 1990). See also Hara Kazuo's film *Goodbye CP* (1972) for a critical cinematic exposé regarding the politics of visibility of the disabled body.

7. At the beginning of the movement, this group was also called the Committee to Contact and Prepare for the Women's Liberation Movement (Josei Kaihō Undo Renraku Junbi Kai). This pioneering *ribu* group began with members such as Asakawa Mari, Garido, and Tanaka Mitsu. Garido was a pseudonym. Many *ribu* women created other names when they participated in the *ribu* movement, including Miki Sōko, Saeki Yōko, and Tanaka Mitsu.

8. Tanaka's name appears on this manifesto and other manifestos as the author and person to contact, indicative of the role she would perform as a pioneering theorist and writer of the movement. It is notable that this manifesto explicitly referenced Wilhelm Reich. Reich is the only name cited in the manifesto, and its opening paragraph is taken directly from Reich's book *The Sexual Revolution.* The Japanese translation of *The Sexual Revolution* was published in 1969 by Keisō Shobō and was arguably one of the most influential texts on Tanaka's early thinking. Translated in Japanese as *Revolution of Sex and Culture* (published as *Sei to Bunka no Kakumei*), this 1945 work by the dissident psychoanalyst appears as the first title on the list of recommended books compiled by the Group of Fighting Women. Reich's critique of dominant sexual morality as central to the maintenance of an authoritarian state was pivotal in reshaping Tanaka's focus on the necessity to liberate sex as key to a radical cultural revolution.

9. Miki, Saeki, and Mizoguchi, *Shiryō Nihon ūman ribu shi,* 1:194–95. See my translation in Shigematsu, "Tanaka Mitsu and the Women's Liberation Movement in Japan," app. 2, 298.

10. Miki, Saeki, and Mizoguchi, *Shiryō Nihon ūman ribu shi,* 2:168.

11. Mori Setsuko, "Shisō shūdan SEX: soshiki ron? yosetsu," in ibid., 1:172.

12. Ibid., 1:171.

13. The language of these texts invoked common terms of the New Left, such as the call to "smash" *(funsai)* what was deemed to be the problem. The radical declarations of these two young intellectuals of this pioneering *ribu* cell went on to pose a feminist critique of Marx as one way of critiquing the sexist behavior of male leftists and the false "neutrality" of what was being called "human liberation." Mori's and Yonezu's clear consciousness of sexual difference as a site of political antagonism was initially articulated through a Marxist concept of class oppression. It was a reaction to the existing gender politics of leftist student movements whereby the liberalization

of sexual relations should be critically distinguished from *ribu*'s notion of the liberation of sex.

14. Ibid., 171. By the late 1960s, "sex" had become a politicized term among leftist intellectual discourse. The works of Wilhelm Reich and Herbert Marcuse were read and debated by students and leftist intellectuals. In October 1969, for example, *Shisō no kagaku* published a special issue on the politics of sex, "Sei no shisō o ikani henkaku suruka." [How Will the Ideology of Sex be Transformed?].

15. James Welker describes the tensions between *ribu*-lesbian feminists and other less politicized lesbian groups in his dissertation, "Transfiguring the Female."

16. Alberto Melucci, "A Strange Kind of Newness: What's 'New' in New Social Movements?" in *New Social Movements: From Ideology to Identity,* ed. Enrique Larana, Hank Johnston, and Joseph R Gusfield (Philadelphia: Temple University Press, 1994), 101–30. Autonomous *ribu* cells determined their own agendas, emphasizing direct participation, self-transformation, and the reformation of day-to-day living.

17. Aki Shobō Henshū Bu, *Sei sabetsu e no kokuhatsu,* 130.

18. There is a field of philosophy and continental thought concerned with political ontology. While my understanding of political ontology is informed by thinkers such as Baruch Spinoza, Martin Heidegger, and Emmanuel Levinas, among others, I use this phrase to reconceptualize how social movements can constitute a new kind of political ontology qua collective subjectivity.

19. Aki Shobō Henshū Bu, *Sei sabetsu e no kokuhatsu,* 132.

20. See chapter 1, note 81 for an explanation of this pamphlet.

21. Senda Yuki, "Teikokushugi to jendā: *Shiryō Nihon ūman ribu shi o yomu*" [Imperialism and Gender: Reading the Documents of the history of Women's Lib in Japan], in *Ribu to iu kakumei: kindai no yami o hiraku* [The Revolution Called Ribu: Uncovering the Darkness of Modernity], ed. Kanō Mikiyo (Tokyo: Inpakuto Shuppankai, 2003), 57–69.

22. Aki Shobō Henshū Bu, *Sei sabetsu e no kokuhatsu,* 131. Tanaka did not view women as victims. She rather observed that through their active participation in the family *(ie)* system, women serve as the crucial link binding men into the system. In Tanaka's view, women's reproductive (unpaid) labor served to maintain the capitalist division of labor. Tanaka refers to the idealized full-time housewife *(sengyō shufu)* as a "slave-dealer" who enables her husband to be a productive slave of capitalism. In "Liberation from the Toilet (rev.)," Tanaka writes, "Women execute the task of slave dealers by taking care of the men who are worn down through the survival of the fittest . . . so that they can be sent out again into the market place as labor commodity" (273). A women's unpaid labor has the dual effect of maintaining her own economic dependency and supporting the exploitation of her husband's labor under the capitalist system.

23. This political ontology involves forms of political identification that punctures a linear notion of time to connect with affective immediacy with other historical moments, movements, and subjects.

24. This naming characterized the deliberate centering of the term *onna* and a move away from the more generic term for women, *josei*. Tanaka was a key figure in both of these groups, and her presence in these core groups would shape the movement.

25. Aki Shobō Henshū Bu, *Sei sabetsu e no kokuhatsu*, 3.

26. Ibid., 3.

27. A significant theme that repeatedly emerges throughout the discussion is the need for a women's or *onna*'s theory *(onna no ronri)* to resist the domination of "male theory" as well as the prevalent consciousness of male superiority (23). Although *ribu* has also been mischaracterized by scholars as "allergic to theory," it would be erroneous to assume that *ribu* was antitheoretical or antiphilosophical. *Ribu* did, however, reevaluate how theory and philosophy were privileged above actually living one's politics. Philosophical questions—such as Does *onna* even exist in this system? Can *onna* exist in this system? What does it mean for *onna* to exist?—were examples of some of the first interrogative slogans posed at the International Antiwar Rally on October 21, 1970. Slogans such as, "What is femininity?" (Onnarashisatte nāni?) were published in *Asahi Shinbun*, October 20, 1970, Tokyo edition, 24. What emerges in the course of this open-ended discussion, and throughout *ribu*'s literature, is a critique of the inadequacy of Marxist and Leninist theory. One woman at the meeting forwards a gendered analysis of how the labor market is a dehumanizing system, asserting that the labor market was under the process of masculinization.

28. Aki Shobō Henshū Bu, *Sei sabetsu e no kokuhatsu*.

29. The first and longest section of the book offers a 126-page transcription of the November 14, 1970, discussion. The book enacts the collective process of self-definition. From an early point in the discussion, a speaker makes reference to how Hiratsuka Raichō started a movement against the family system during the Taisho period (1910–29), indicative of how *ribu*'s emergence entailed a consciousness of the heritage of Japanese women's movements alongside a recognition of new women's liberation movements elsewhere. In regard to the feminist movement in the United States, a speaker indicates that she thinks the *ribu* movement in Japan differs slightly from the *ribu* movement in the United States but is not yet sure how to articulate that difference.

30. Matsui was involved in the *ribu* movement. She attended the first *ribu* summer camp, and some of *ribu*'s important main events were held at her parents' church, Yamate Kyōkai in the Shibuya district of Tokyo. Some *ribu* women suggested that Matsui's Christian background informed her feminism, and her politics differed from *ribu*'s on subjects such as sex work. She later grew more critical of what she observed as *ribu*'s overemphasis on sexuality when, in her view, there were more urgent political issues at hand, such as the plight of other third world Asian women. Kuno Ayako, a veteran *ribu* activist in Nagoya, has been committed to working with third world Asian women in Japan, particularly those who come as workers and entertainers. Until 2007, she worked as a counselor at a shelter for foreign women workers. Broadly speaking, the women's movements that were explicitly anti-imperialist focused more

on solidarity with Asian women, whereas liberal feminists emphasized links with Euro-American feminisms.

31. See, for example, Yuriko Iino, "The Politics of 'Disregarding': Addressing *Zainichi* Issues within the Lesbian Community in Japan," *Journal of Lesbian Studies* 10, no. 3/4 (2007): 65–85; Sonia Ryang, "Love and Colonialism in Takamure Itsue's Feminism: A Postcolonial Critique," *Feminist Review* 60, no. 1 (1998): 1–32.

32. This postcolonial and neocolonial distinction between the Japanese mainland and mainlanders *(yamatonchu)* and Okinawa remains a conflictual political issue. Even though Okinawa is officially a prefecture of Japan, it remains a de facto military colony of the United States, and therefore its former colonial status has been criticized as a dual occupation by both the Japanese and the U.S. military. An article in a November 25, 1971, *Asahi Journal* special issue on *ūman ribu* examines why there is not an equivalent women's liberation movement in Okinawa and underscores how Okinawan women's status contrasts with that of mainland Japanese women. The author writes that Okinawan women "have not even secured for themselves the basic conditions of human existence" and thus are in no position yet to be questioning "femininity" (26).

33. Miki, Saeki, and Mizoguchi, *Shiryō Nihon ūman ribu shi*, 1:317.

34. Metropolitan was a *ribu* group based in Hokkaido. This group began organizing on October 21, 1970, after participating in an International Antiwar Day demonstration in Hokkaido. Ibid., 1:147. The third *ribu* summer camp was held in Izu, on Shikine Shima in the Kanto region, between August 23 and August 27. Approximately one hundred women participated.

35. Miki, Saeki, and Mizoguchi, *Shiryō Nihon ūman ribu shi*, 2:18.

36. Ibid., 1:317.

37. Ibid., 1:315.

38. *30 Years of Sisterhood.*

39. *Onna Erosu: tokushū kekkon seido o Yurugasu* [Onna Eros: Special Issue Shaking-up the Marriage System], no. 1 (1973).

40. Bardsley, *The Bluestockings of Japan;* Lippitt, "Seitō and the Literary Roots of Japanese Feminism"; Reich and Fukuda, "Japan's Literary Feminists."

41. Interview with Saeki Yōko, March 8, 2001.

42. Although the editors, Miki, Saeki, and Mizoguchi, state in newspaper interviews that they spent seven to ten years compiling the documents, they tell other *ribu* women that the process actually took fifteen years from start to finish. "*Ribu* no rekishi tsutaetai: kiroku 3 kan kankō e," *Kyoto Shinbun,* March 25, 1992; "Nihon no *ribu* shi sho no shiryō shū: dai ichi maku 10 nen kake shuppan," *Kyoto Shinbun,* January 15, 1993; "Zenkoku kara shiryō atsume: henshū ni 7 nen," *Mainichi Shinbun,* January 29, 1993; "Josei kaihō no yoake: *ribu* o minaosu," *Mainichi Shinbun,* January 23, 1993. This process of compiling the documents was discussed at the first Shiryō Nihon Ūman *Ribu* Shi—Dokushokai [Study Group of the Documents of the History of Women's Lib in Japan], September 14–16, 2002, held in Izu, in which I participated.

43. The articles and coverage in women's magazines, such as "Ūman ribu shinya no hakunetsu daishūkai," *Josei Seven* (September 8, 1971), and Sugiura Rei, "Ūman ribu gasshuku taikenki," *Bishō* (September 11, 1971), were not entirely favorable. For example, the reporter's subtitle in *Bishō* reads, "Although I have been very interested in the *ūman ribu* movement, this was the first time I actually participated. As part of this women-only group that I didn't know, frankly, I was a little frightened." *Bishō*, September 11, 1971.

44. Cf. note 6.

45. Inoue, *Joseigaku to sono shūhen.*

46. Ehara Yumiko, "The Politics of Teasing," trans. Ayako Kano, in *Contemporary Japanese Thought*, ed. Richard Calichman (New York: Columbia University Press, 2005), 43–55. Ehara Yumiko, "Karakai no seijigaku," ["The Politics of Teasing"] in Ehara, *Josei kaihō to iu shisō* [The Ideology of Women's Liberation], 172–94. First published in the journal *Josei no shakai mondai* [Women's Social Problems], no. 4 (1981).

47. Masami, "Feminizumu riron ni yoru hihan-teki disukōsu bunseki (FCDA) no tenkai."

48. *Asahi Journal* published a special issue on *ribu* on November 25, 1971, devoting thirty pages to *ribu* coverage and other women's movements in China.

49. *Ribu Shinjuku Sentā shiryō shūsei: bira hen*, 630.

50. In December 1971, the Group of Fighting Women organized with other groups who had attended the *ribu* camp to reflect on the first year and plan for the next. Out of this series of meetings came two major proposals: to organize a *ribu* conference and to establish a *ribu* center for the purpose of networking.

51. May 5 was a plenary session, and May 6 was devoted to breakout sessions. The topics of the breakout sessions included the following: (1) what it means for *onna* to work, (2) toward a day when *onna* and children can live—thinking about *ribu* for *onna* and children, (3) the path our mothers have lived, the path I desire to live—rethinking the split between mothers and daughters, (4) *onna*'s sex—premarital, extramarital—rethinking the "one-husband-one-wife" system, (5) *ribu* and the United Red Army—*onna*'s possibilities and those new directions, (6) liberation from sacrificial death, and (7) a collective for *onna*'s independence: a problem forwarded by a women-only commune (Miki, Saeki, and Mizoguchi, *Shiryō Nihon ūman ribu shi*, 2:332). May 7 involved a discussion session followed by a demonstration.

52. According to Mizoguchi Ayeko, the Ribu Conference represented a clear step forward for the movement by providing a forum to assess *ribu* as a departure from former models of leftist politics. Miki, Saeki, and Mizoguchi, *Shiryō Nihon ūman ribu shi*, 1:331.

53. Matsui Yayori's parents were both ministers of this church. Unlike in the United States, through Japanese history, Christianity has often been a site of resistance to the state and is much more marginalized. Less than 1 percent of the population identifies as Christian.

54. Arima Makiko, a journalist, went on to become the Japanese representative to the United Nations Commission on the Status of Women and the director of the Asian Women's Fund, which was first established in 1995. The Asian Women's Fund was a joint initiative between the government of Japan and its citizens to provide compensation and atonement for the so-called comfort women system, the military sexual slavery system implemented during Japan's wars of aggression in Asia and the Pacific.

55. The United Red Army (Rengo Sekigun) was an underground revolutionary group that engaged in armed resistance against the state. *Ribu*'s relationship with this group is discussed in detail in chapter 5.

56. Miki, Saeki, and Mizoguchi, *Shiryō Nihon ūman ribu shi,* 1:332.

57. Ibid., 1:331.

58. Ibid., 2:58.

59. Ibid.

60. *Ribu News* published sixteen issues from 1972 to 1976, with its final notice of its closure in 1977. Originals are archived at the Yokohama Women's Forum library and reprinted in the *Ribu nyūsu konomichi hitosuji.* Cf. chapter 1, note 44.

61. Miki, Saeki, and Mizoguchi, *Shiryō Nihon ūman ribu shi,* 2:59–91. In April 1973, Ribu Shinjuku Center began to organize "men's *ribu.*" See ibid., 3:397–421.

62. Ibid., 2:59.

63. Sayama Sachi was another original member of the Shinjuku Center. She identifies as a lesbian and lives in San Francisco, California. She has been involved in Japanese diasporic lesbian activism.

64. The Shinjuku Center officially opened on September 30, 1972.

65. Such antihierarchical organizing styles entail their own difficulties and contradictions that I examine in chapter 4. Chapter 4 addresses the inevitable power differentials and conflicts within movements.

66. This commitment to antihierarchical forms of organizing was an extension of the principles of Beheiren, Zenkyōtō, and the anarchism of the counterculture movement generally. The deliberate choice to refuse to appoint a leader or to validate established structures of authority was also related to this anarchistic political stance. This model of organizing was a direct response to the hierarchical and militaristic tendencies of the New Left sects and the established Left.

67. "Zadankai: ribu sen o taguri yosete miru," in *Zenkyōtō kara ribu e,* 234. This roundtable discussion *(zadankai)* was led by historian Kano Mikiyo and included Endō Misako, Oda Michiko, Takeda Miyuki, Namahara Reiko, Machino Michiko, Mori Setsuko, Yonezu Tomoko, and Wakabayashi Naeko. Shiryō Nihon Ūman *Ribu* Shi—Dokusho Kai, workshop in Izu, September 14–16, 2002.

68. In 1869, the government passed the first law that criminalized the sale of abortive medicines by midwives and then, in 1874, passed a law to regulate and license the practice of midwifery. In 1880, abortion was made a crime and remains so under current criminal law.

69. According to Japan's imperialist ideology, women's wombs were to produce babies for the nation as the "Emperor's children." See Kano, *Josei to tennosei*.

70. In 1952, another revision to the regulations was made that simplified administrative access to abortions. Only a certified doctor's permission was needed to acquire an abortion. During the 1970s, the official number of abortions declined to less than one million annually.

71. Norgren, *Abortion before Birth Control*, 5, 49.

72. Seicho no Ie emerged in the early 1950s and formed a coalition to abolish the Eugenic Protection Law that included Catholic and Shinto organizations.

73. Nagano Yoshiko, "Women Fight for Control: Abortion Struggle in Japan," *AMPO*, no. 17 (1973); reprinted in *Japanese Women Speak Out*, ed. Mioko Fujieda, Pacific-Asia Resources Center, and "White Paper on Sexism–Japan" Task Force (Tokyo: Tokyo International, 1975).

74. For example, in 1967, at the second national convention of the National Organization of Women (NOW), the organization voted on a bill of rights for women that included a clause to repeal penal laws governing abortion: "The right of women to control their reproductive lives by removing from the penal code laws limiting access to contraceptive information and devices and by repealing penal laws governing abortion." Judith Hole and Ellen Levine, "Abortion," in *The Rebirth of Feminism*, 279.

75. Tomida, *Hiratsuka Raicho and Early Japanese Feminism*; Shidzue Ishimoto, *Facing Two Ways: The Story of My Life* (Stanford, Calif.: Stanford University Press, 1984); Sievers, *Flowers in Salt*; Joyce Gelb, "Reproductive Rights Policy in Japan and the United States," in *Gender Policies in Japan and the United States: Comparing Women's Movements, Rights and Politics* (New York: Palgrave Macmillan, 2003); Linda Gordon, *Woman's Body, Woman's Right: A Social History of Birth Control in America* (New York: Penguin Books, 1974); Luker, *Abortion and the Politics of Motherhood*.

76. Wendy Brown, *States of Injury: Power and Freedom in Late Modernity* (Princeton, N.J.: Princeton University Press, 1995). In *Woman's Body, Woman's Right*, Linda Gordon describes the legalization of abortion as a "significant victory," but she also points to how the state has deployed the legalization of abortion as a means of sterilization of "poor women and non-white women" (415). In pointing to this the danger of state control of abortion, Gordon's critique resonates with *ribu*'s stance on abortion as potentially dangerous and its strong suspicion of state control of reproduction.

77. Firestone concludes *The Dialectic of Sex* (1970) with the imperative to free women from "the tyranny of their reproductive biology by every means available." She also calls for "the diffusion of the childbearing and child-rearing role to the society as a whole, men as well as women." Shulamith Firestone, *The Dialectic of Sex: The Case for Feminist Revolution* (New York: Bantam Books, 1970), 206.

78. Chūpiren was an abbreviation for Chūzetsu Kinshi Hō ni Hantai Shi Piru Kaikin o Yōkyū Suru Josei Kaihō Rengō, meaning the Women's Liberation Federation

for Opposing the Abortion Prohibition Law and Lifting the Pill Ban. Enoki Misako was the leader of this group. She attended the May 1972 Ribu Conference, where she tried to organize women to form Chūpiren. Chūpiren members referred to themselves a "neolib" or neo-*ribu*. Miki, Saeki, and Mizoguchi, *Shiryō Nihon ūman ribu shi*, 2:144–52. As documented by Akiyama Yōko, Chūpiren's approach toward the pill differed from that of the majority of the *ribu* movement. See Akiyama Yōko, "Enoki Misako to Chūpiren" in *Ribu shishi nōto: onnatachi no jidai kara* (Tokyo: Inpakuto Shuppankai, 1993), 121–38. Chūpiren's politics emphasized the discourse of women's rights, and it protested husbands who tried to divorce their wives. In so doing, *ribu* women interpreted such protests as maintaining the marriage system. Its tactics also involved seeking maximum coverage from the mass media, and this entailed wearing "pink helmets" at its protests. Hence, Chūpiren also became known as the "pink helmets."

79. Enoki Misako, the leader of Chūpiren, started her involvement with the *ribu* translation group called Wolf Group (Urufu no Kai). Akiyama writes that *ribu* groups experimented with the pill and concluded that because of its negative and unnatural side effects on women's bodies, it was an undesirable method of birth control. Because its distribution was controlled by the government, *ribu* women were reluctant to rely on a birth control that the state could easily regulate. When Enoki initially distributed the pamphlet that called for the release of the pill, Enoki used the name of the Wolf Group (Urufu no Kai), which angered the women of the group because they did not endorse her position. In short, she was not trusted by many *ribu* women, and women within Chūpiren also became critical of her leadership style. Akiyama, "Enoki Misako to Chūpiren," 125–38. Akiyama stated that Enoki seemed to appear out of nowhere and then disappeared from activism. Interview with Akiyama Yōko, Saitama-ken, February 26, 2001.

80. Aki Shobō Henshū Bu, *Sei sabetsu e no kokuhatsu*, 133.

81. John Crump, *The Origins of Socialist Thought in Japan* (London: Croom Helm, 1983); Mackie, *Creating Socialist Women in Japan*.

82. Committee to Prepare for Women's Liberation, "The Direction of Our Eros: Immigration Law and Abortion Prohibition Law," in Aki Shobō Henshū Bu, *Sei sabetsu e no kokuhatsu*, 133.

83. Ibid., 134.

84. Miki, Saeki, and Mizoguchi, *Shiryō Nihon ūman ribu shi*, 2:171–72.

85. Ibid., 2:61, 2:90, 2:128, 2:129, 2:171, 2:173, 2:174, 2:236.

86. Ibid., 2:61.

87. Ibid.

88. *Asahi Shinbun*, May 14, 1973; *AMPO*, 17 (1973).

89. Nichibō is the organization representing the group of obstetricians and gynecologists officially authorized to perform abortions. See Norgren, *Abortion before Birth Control*, for a detailed account of postwar abortion history and policy changes.

90. Miki, Saeki, and Mizoguchi, *Shiryō Nihon ūman ribu shi,* 2:201–2.

91. Ibid., 2:215.

92. Ibid., 2:202.

93. On October 9, 1973, the court ruled in favor of giving "S," N's wife, custody of the child. On November 5, 1973, K made an appeal to the supreme court over this ruling. Ibid., 2:198.

94. Ibid., 2:195.

95. *Ribu*'s political ontology involves centrifugal and centripetal forces that constitute its conflictual core dynamic as a movement that moves both outward (toward society and others) and inward (reconstituting a subject's self-identity). This seemingly contradictory dynamic constitutes *ribu*'s fundamental tension as a collective and subjective political ontology constituted by the perpetual tension, collaboration, and desire of its subjects.

96. On Christmas day, fifty-five women converged on the Tokyo Haneda airport for a demonstration, shouting and denouncing the men at the airport who were headed to Seoul to participate in the Kisaeng tours. One of the pamphlets distributed at this event stated, "We women within this Japanese imperialist state will not allow the 'economic animal/sex animal' to go there. . . . 'Nippon Airlines,' 'Korean Airlines' stop this Kisaeng tourism immediately." "Haji o Shire: Kisen Meate no Kankōdan," Ribu Shinjuku Center pamphlet, December 25, 1973.

97. Miki, Saeki, and Mizoguchi, *Shiryō Nihon ūman ribu shi,* 2:252.

98. Interview with Mori Setsuko, Tokyo, February 5, 2003.

99. Many *ribu* women who were arrested, detained, and prosecuted for various extralegal guerrilla actions became self-employed because they were barred from obtaining jobs at larger companies or corporations due to their criminal records. However, like white political activists in the United States, these Japanese women's relatively privileged position enabled them to engage in such illegal actions without the additional fear of being racially/ethnically targeted by the state. In other words, these Japanese women, like their Japanese male counterparts, had relative ethnic/racial privilege unlike their *Zainichi* or *burakumin* counterparts.

100. Sanrizuka refers to the rebellion against the building of Narita airport, which became a symbol of the struggle of farmers and the many people who joined with them against the actions of an authoritarian state. For a rich account of the Sanrizuka struggle, see Apter and Nagayo, *Against the State.*

101. Interview with Asatori Sumie, Ishikawa City, Japan, March 21, 2007.

102. Ibid.

103. Editorial commentary in Miki, Saeki, and Mizoguchi, *Shiryō Nihon ūman ribu shi,* 2:346.

104. To support this "unmarried" mother to care for her child, the women at Three Points began a twenty-four-hour day care for children. In doing so, child rearing was treated as a collective effort rather than an individual mother's responsibility.

105. Miki, Saeki, and Mizoguchi, *Shiryō Nihon ūman ribu shi*, 2:352.

106. Hōkiboshi closed in 1980, but other *ribu* spaces in Shinjuku opened, such as the women's bar and restaurant, Oni no Ie, which operated until 2000.

107. Ishino and Wakabayashi, "Japan: Lesbian Activism," 95–102. Wakabayashi is also one of the founders of the Asian Lesbian Network.

108. Nishimura, *Onna-tachi no kyōdōtai*.

109. Interview with Yonezu, March 23, 2001.

110. Miki, Saeki, and Mizoguchi, *Shiryō Nihon ūman ribu shi*, 2:87–91.

111. *Ribu Shinjuku Sentā shiryō shūsei: panfuretto hen*, 275.

112. In July 1972, Kunihisa Kazuko, a *ribu* member, was arrested under the suspicion of aiding and concealing the leaders of the United Red Army. Miki, Saeki, and Mizoguchi, *Shiryō Nihon ūman ribu shi*, 2:54–55, 2:66, 2:81–87. In chapter 5, I address in detail the links between *ribu* and the United Red Army. Interviews with Tanaka Mitsu, October 24–25, 2000; interview with Saeki Yōko, September 16, 2002.

113. In 1972, the value of 300,000 yen was about one thousand U.S. dollars.

114. Namahara Reiko (roundtable participant), "Zadankai: ribu sen," 227.

115. Ibid., 211.

116. Yonezu Tomoko, "Watashi ni totte no *ribu* sen to wa," unpublished essay (1983); Endō Misako, "Ribu Shinjuku sentā no sōkatsu ni yosete," unpublished essay (1993). Cf. chapter 4, note 132.

117. Wakabayashi spent time at a feminist women's clinic in California, and her time in the United States nurtured her coming-out process.

118. Interview with Asatori Sumie, Ishikawa City, Japan, March 2007.

119. Shoshiren was founded in 1982 and is an abbreviation for Yūsei Hogo Hō Kaiaku Shoshi Renraku Kai.

120. In 1996, the term *eugenics* was changed to *botai* so that the new name is the Maternal Protection Law.

121. These collectives worked out of JOKI, a cooperative office for feminist groups in the Shinjuku district of Tokyo.

122. In 1985, Asatori started the publishing house Workshop for Women JO-JO to make more feminist information available. Since 1987, JO-JO has been publishing a feminist-Japanese women's history calendar on an annual basis. This calendar introduces Japanese women who, over the last two centuries, forged new roads inspiring other women. Asatori currently lives as part of a women's communal house in Chiba, which she built. Workshop for Women JO-JO is located on the lower floor of her house.

123. Since the 1990s, there has been a revival of the *ribu* camp *(gasshuku)* meetings. Every spring, veteran *ribu* activists, and occasionally younger-generation women, come together at various hot springs *(onsen)* throughout the country to exchange news and information about the local activism with which they are involved. I have attended three of these *ribu* retreats.

124. Inoue et al., *Iwanami joseigaku jiten*, 40. Secondary commentary on *ribu* has

almost uniformly described *ribu* as a past social movement of the 1970s, ignoring its many forms of continuity.

4. *Ribu* and Tanaka Mitsu

I thank Watanabe Fumie, Miki Sōko, Yonezu Tomoko, Muto Ichiyo, Wakabayashi Naeko, and Sayama Sachi for their comments regarding this chapter during the writing process. I am grateful to Erica Edwards for her generous advice and comments on chapter 4 regarding the problems of charismatic leadership. Unless otherwise indicated, all translations are my own.

1. Machino Michiko mentions this clothing detail about Tanaka when asked how she began her involvement with the Ribu Shinjuku Center. "Zadankai: ribu sen," in *Zenkyōtō kara ribu e*, 206. Cf. chapter 1, note 81.

2. Tanaka Mitsu, "Eros kaihō sengen," in Miki, Saeki, and Mizoguchi, *Shiryō Nihon ūman ribu shi,* 1:194–95. See my translation of this manifesto in Shigematsu, "Tanaka Mitsu and the Women's Liberation Movement in Japan," app. 1. Cf. chapter 1, note 81.

3. As a member of the Group of Fighting Women, Tanaka was involved in organizing most of *ribu*'s main events, such as the October 21, 1970, antiwar demonstration in Ginza; the November 14, 1970, meeting in Tokyo; the August 1971 *ribu* summer camp in Nagano; and the May 1972 Ribu Conference in Tokyo. These events were discussed in chapter 3. She was also one of the main writers for the *Ribu nyūsu konomichi hitosuji,* hereafter *Ribu News,* which was published and disseminated from the Ribu Shinjuku Center.

4. *Ribu Shinjuku Sentā shiryō shūsei: bira hen,* eds. Ribu Shinjuku Sentā Shiryō Hozon Kai (Tokyo: Inpakuto Shuppankai, 2008), 10, 16, 18, 25, 33. 39.

5. Most of the published photographs of the movement capture groups of *ribu* women; in contrast, Tanaka was often photographed by herself. Two professional photographers who followed the movement, Matsumoto Michiko and Fukushima Kikujiro, often focused their lenses on her, capturing dynamic moments of Tanaka's involvement during the early seventies that remain as still portraits over time. Fukushima was one of her boyfriends during the movement and thus was given privileged access to women-only spaces. In 1999, almost thirty years since *ribu*'s dawn, photos of Tanaka were reprinted in a retrospective *Year Book on Twentieth Century Men's and Women's Affairs*. It shows the young Tanaka leading a demonstration on Mother's Day, 1972, stylishly dressed in platform heels, carrying a banner that says, "Mother's day, What a laugh!" Another photo captures Tanaka's intentful gaze, with a caption stating that she was "the eye of *ribu*'s typhoon." *Shūkan Year Book Special Issue 10: nichi roku 20 seiki*—Akiyama Yōko, "Otoko to onna no jikenbōku," (Tokyo: Kōdansha, 1999), 24–25.

6. Akiyama, *Ribu shishi nōto,* 202.

7. Ibid., 195.

8. Ibid., 194–206. Akiyama concludes that it is not appropriate to consider Tanaka

as the "leader" *(shidōsha)* or "representative theorist" *(daihyōteki rironka)* of the movement but that she represented the era of *ribu* (205).

9. Muto, "The Birth of the Women's Liberation Movement," 163.

10. Interview with Akiyama Yōko, February 26, 2001.

11. Interview with Inoue Teruko, February 24, 2001. Cf. Epilogue, note 22.

12. The Japanese term commonly used to describe this role was *ribu no daihyō*.

13. Telephone conversation with Mizoguchi Ayeko, February 23, 2001.

14. Saeki Yōko, written response to interview questions, March 8, 2001.

15. In the course of my fieldwork, Tanaka described her role as *ribu*'s *"yobikake-nin"* (messenger). According to the 2000 edition of the *Kojien* dictionary, the actions of a *yobikake-nin* involve "explaining one's assertion, and taking action to seek out agreement. To use one's words to appeal to and move other people."

16. "Ūman ribu: 'dansei tengoku' ni jōriku," *Asahi Shinbun,* October 4, 1970, 24; "Otoko no ronri o kokuhatsu suru: ūman ribu no ben," *Asahi Shinbun,* Tokyo edition, October 6, 1970, 24; "'Matsu onna' kara dappi," *Asahi Shinbun,* morning edition, October 25, 1970; "Ūman ribu zadankai," *Asahi Jānaru: tokushū ūman ribu o arai naosu zadankai,* June 25, 1971, 16–22.

17. "'Matsu onna' kara dappi," 23. The *Asahi Shinbun* is one of the largest circulating daily newspapers, following the *Yomiuri,* along with *Mainichi Shinbun, Nihon Keizai Shinbun,* and *Sankei Shinbun.*

18. Max Weber's description of charismatic authority characterizes it as a "revolutionary force" (362). "Indeed, in its purest form charismatic authority may be said to exist only in the process of originating" (354). Max Weber, *The Theory of Social and Economic Organization,* trans. and ed. A. M. Henderson and Talcott Parsons (New York: Free Press, 1964). Christopher Adair-Toteff, "Max Weber's Charisma," in *Journal of Classical Sociology* 5, no. 2 (July 2005): 189–204. Adair-Toteff elaborates some of the potential weaknesses of charismatic authority as "extremely personal, it is highly irrational, it is very temporary, it is especially unusual" (191) and "dependent on the followers for recognition" (195).

19. *Ribu*'s antielitism has often been misrecognized as being anti-intellectual or antitheoretical. For example, Kanai Yoshiko describes how *ribu* had an "allergy to theory and logic." Kanai, "Ūman ribu tōjo kara 80 nendai ronsō made," in special issue, *Wakaritai anata no tame no feminizumu nyūmon bessatsu takarajima 85* (Tokyo: JICC Shuppan Kyōkai, 1988), 70–79. However, this interpretation fails to understand the political and historical significance of *ribu*'s resistance to theory for theory's sake. The women of *ribu* formed a class of organic intellectuals and purposely eschewed the identification of the "traditional intellectual" because of the condition of the sectarianism and dogmatism in the New Left, which violently battled over which sect possessed the correct revolutionary theory and tactics. This resistance to privileging theory for theory's sake also stemmed from *ribu*'s basic antielitist stance that in turn derived from the politics of Zenkyōtō, which sought to negate one's class privilege as part of the process of self-negation *(jikō hitei).*

20. Ueno Chizuko and Tanaka Mitsu, *Mitsu to Chizuko no konton ton karari* (Tokyo: Mokuseisha, 1987). Although Tanaka certainly thinks of herself as a recognized intellectual, to express her critical attitude toward the elitist trappings of the traditional or professional intellectual, she refers to herself as "closer to the people." For a period during the 1990s, Tanaka was especially vocal about what she regarded to be the elitism of feminists in Japan. In this published dialogue with Ueno Chizuko, who is arguably the most famous feminist scholar in Japan, Tanaka contrasts her position with Ueno's, saying, with a sarcastic bite, "If we say that you Ueno-san are an *intelli* (meaning an intellectual and educated person), I guess I am closer to the people, after all" (19). Tanaka also makes a point of referring to herself as the daughter of a fisherman to contrast herself with Ueno, whom she refers to as the daughter of a doctor (130). Since 2000, there has been an apparent rapproachment between these two iconic feminists and much more of an alliance between them.

21. Ibid., 10. The talk was titled "Watashi ga jidai datta ano goro," which was referred to in Tanaka's published dialogue with Ueno Chizuko.

22. Tanaka, *Doko ni iyou to riburian*, 264.

23. Weber describes charisma as "a certain quality of an individual personality, by virtue of which he is set apart from ordinary men and treated as endowed with supernatural, superhuman, or at least specifically exceptional powers or qualities. These are such as are not accessible to the ordinary person, but are regarded as of divine origin or as exemplary, and on the basis of them the individual concerned is treated as a leader." Weber, *The Theory of Social and Economic Organization*, 358–59.

24. The Japanese New Left emerged during the 1960s as a complex web of Marxist and communist offshoots critical of the establishment Left. The establishment Left comprised the Japanese Communist Party (JCP), the Japan Socialist Party (JSP), and Sohyō (the General Council of Trade Unions of Japan). The emergence and history of the New Left in Japan is addressed in detail in chapter 2. Tanaka's shift away from the radical politics of the early 1970s and her investment in healing and spiritualism becomes more pronounced in her later writings. Having followed the changes of Tanaka's work over a forty-year period, the following periodization roughly thematizes the changing emphasis of her writings:

1970–71	The theory of the liberation of sex
1972–75	Radical feminine ontology
1980s	Writing the body
1990s	Spirituality
2000–2010	Reflections and production of a master narrative about her role in *ribu*

Although in this chapter I focus mainly on her first period of writings (1970–75), I read her earliest works cognizant of these later changes.

25. The name of Tanaka's group was Betonamu Sensai Koji ni Ai o Okuru Kai (Sending Love to the Injured Orphans of the Vietnam War). In *Inochi no onna-tachi e,* Tanaka describes her politicization as occurring through processes of identifications; she speaks of her own sense of injury, due to an incident of sexual abuse that she

experienced as a young girl, as a means by which to identify with the injury of others. Her willingness and desire to identify with the other's victimization appears to be the path to her process of politicization. Tanaka's attention to the notion of the other within the self enabled her to use her introspective capacities as a source for her political discourse.

26. Iijima Aiko and her group are discussed in chapter 1. In an interview with Iijima, she described how she knew Tanaka during her process of intellectual formation, before she wrote her *ribu* manifestos. According to Iijima, she once received what she called a "love letter" from Tanaka. As a point of contrast, when I asked Tanaka about this love letter, Tanaka denied that it was a real love letter but stated that it was simply a "strategic" letter. Interview with Ijima Aiko, March 11, 2002. Thanks to Hama Retsuko for introducing me to Ijima Aiko.

27. Tanaka recommends this book in the pamphlet "Why Sexual Liberation," *Ribu Shinjuku Sentā shiryō shūsei: bira hen,* 37, 48. Wilhelm Reich's *The Sexual Revolution: Toward a Self-Governing Character Structure* (Die sexualitat im Kulturkamf) was translated into Japanese in 1969 by Nakao Hajime and published by Keisō Shobō. Reich (1897–1957) was an Austrian psychiatrist, a biophysicist, and a student of Sigmund Freud. His main thesis was that sexuality was "the center around which revolves the whole of social life as well as the inner life of the individual." He was a hero of student radicals of the 1960s, with their slogan "Make love, not war." For further discussion of Tanaka's use of and differences with Reich, see Shigematsu, "Tanaka Mitsu and the Women's Liberation Movement in Japan," chap. 3. Cf. chapter 3, note 8.

28. Tanaka, "Liberation from the Toilet (rev.)" (October 1970) reprinted in *Doko ni iyou to ribu rian,* 266.

29. Each of these intellectual traditions structure Tanaka's thought in different ways. For example, Marxism provides the materialist and structuralist basis for her analysis, which is informed by Reichian psychoanalysis, which adds a conceptual dimension of the symbolic analysis, a notion of the unconscious and the repressed. The black liberation movement provided the defiant model of taking one's own liberation into one's own hands, inspiring *ribu* to wake up from its "slave consciousness." However, like many other feminist and liberation movements, black liberation thought served as a reservoir of political legitimacy, as a model of liberation from oppression, to draw from and to mimic, without often entailing any substantive engagement or solidarity with black liberation but instead enacting an appropriation of black oppression for the purposes of shoring up one's own political capital.

30. Hélène Cixous writes, "When 'The Repressed' of their culture and their society come back, it is an explosive return, which is absolutely shattering, staggering, overturning, with a force never let loose before." Hélène Cixous and Catherine Clément, *The Newly Born Woman,* trans. Betsy Wing (Minneapolis: University of Minnesota Press, 1986).

31. Kanai Yoshiko, "Tanaka Mitsu to feminizumu: karada to erosu to ekurichūru feminin," *Risō: Tokushū feminizumu to tetsugaku*, no. 659 (1997), 2–19.

32. Cixous and Clément, *The Newly Born Woman*.

33. Tanaka, *Inochi no onna-tachi e*, 196.

34. Morizaki Kazue, *Tatakai to erosu* (Tokyo: Sanichi Shobo, 1970).

35. See my translation in Shigematsu, "Tanaka Mitsu and the Women's Liberation Movement in Japan," app. 3, 299.

36. The United Red Army (URA) events occurred from January to February 1972. They are discussed in chapter 5. This sect's internal discipline and surveillance measures resulted in the lynching of its members.

37. Tanaka Mitsu, "Shinsayoku to ribu: harakiri to junshi," in *Inochi no onna-tachi e*, 210. Shigematsu, "Tanaka Mitsu and the Women's Liberation Movement in Japan," app. 3, 300.

38. "Liberation from the Toilet (rev.)" in *Doko ni iyou to riburian*, 267.

39. Ibid.

40. Ibid.

41. According to Weber, the charismatic authority figure "repudiates the past" and "in this sense is a specifically revolutionary force." Weber, *The Theory of Social and Economic Organization*, 362.

42. Tanaka, "Shinsayoku to ribu," 210. Shigematsu, "Tanaka Mitsu and the Women's Liberation Movement in Japan," app. 3, 301.

43. Tanaka went so far as to say that for a woman in the New Left, "revolution" is a masculine synonym for a man. *Inoch no onna-tachi e*, 255. This statement very much follows from what Iijima Aiko has already stated, that "theory itself is a male." Iijima, "Onna ni totte sabetsu towa nanika," 1:47, 1:52. See chapter 1, cf. note 67.

44. Miki, Saeki, and Mizoguchi, *Shiryō Nihon ūman ribu shi*, 1:230–33.

45. As noted in chapter 1, *ribu* activists use the term *ie seidō* even when referring to the postwar family system. See chapter 1, cf. note 78.

46. "Liberation from the Toilet (rev.)," *Doko ni iyou to riburian*, 277.

47. Shigematsu, "Tanaka Mitsu and the Women's Liberation Movement in Japan," app. 3, 301.

48. See note 27.

49. Tanaka Mitsu, "Eros kaihō sengen," in Miki, Saeki, and Mizoguchi, *Shiryō Nihon ūman ribu shi*, 1:194–95. See my translation in Shigematsu, "Tanaka Mitsu and the Women's Liberation Movement in Japan," app. 1, 289–93.

50. See note 2. Akiyama, *Ribu shi shi nōto*, 195. Akiyama describes "Liberation from the Toilet" as a "historical pamphlet" that "should be called the declaration of Japan's *ribu* movement." Its striking expressions and dense content packed into its thirteen thousand characters express the power that was *ribu*.

51. Shigematsu, "Tanaka Mitsu and the Women's Liberation Movement in Japan," app. 2, 294–300.

52. Tanaka, "Liberation from the Toilet," in Miki, Saeki, and Mizoguchi, *Shiryō Nihon ūman ribu shi*, 1:205.

53. Tanaka, "Why Sexual Liberation." Shigematsu, "Tanaka Mitsu and the Women's Liberation Movement in Japan," app. 2, 294.

54. "In addition to the fact that women's sex is endowed with reproduction, women's sex is more powerful, for the reason it hides secretly within it essentially anarchist tendencies." Tanaka, *Doko ni iyou to riburian*, 270.

55. Tanaka's notion of eros also resonates with Audre Lorde's notion of the power of the erotic. See Audre Lorde, "The Uses of the Erotic: The Erotic as Power in *Sister Outsider: Essays and Speeches by Audre Lorde*" (Trumansburg, N.Y.: Crossing Press, 1984).

56. This emphasis on women's sex can be read as a pivotal point of entry in a connective series that will lead to a universalizable form of human liberation. In other words, Tanaka's conception of women's sex can be read as a first term in a symbolic chain of equivalence: women–sex–eros–desire. The liberation of woman–sex–eros also implies the liberation of human desire.

57. In the revised version of "Liberation from the Toilet," Tanaka writes, "Women have to form their own subjectivity in the midst of the tensions of the relation between the part and the totality." *Doko ni iyou to riburian*, 273.

58. Ibid., 273.

59. "Liberation from the Toilet," in Miki, Saeki, and Mizoguchi, *Shiryō Nihon ūman ribu shi*, 1:205.

60. Ibid., 205. Although Tanaka's early writings were critical of what she refers to here as a "nationalistic form of women's rights," she did not develop any sustained critique of the relationship between the United States and Japan, Japanese nationalism, or Japanese identity. The anti-imperialist theme in her work in the early 1970s is therefore arguably due to the influence of the New Left on her work.

61. Tanaka claimed that she only knows about the American women's liberation movement through information she has received through the mass media. "Liberation from the Toilet," reprinted in Miki, Saeki, and Mizoguchi, *Shiryō Nihon ūman ribu shi*, 1:205.

62. Ibid., 278.

63. Takeda Miyuki (roundtable participant), "Zadankai: ribu sen," 204–51. For some women, such as Takeda Miyuki, Tanaka was a love object who returned affection and care (237).

64. But for others, she was a person who had caused them much emotional pain. For several years after the dissolution of the center, some women stated that they did not want to see Tanaka again because they were too hurt through their experiences with Tanaka. Interview with Sayama Sachi, San Francisco, June 7, 2001. Interview with Hama Retsuko, March 6, 2001.

65. Miki, Saeki, and Mizoguchi, *Shiryō Nihon ūman ribu shi,* 1:278–79.

66. Although Tanaka was critical about privileging the abstract over the materiality of embodied practice, she nonetheless continually pursued abstract and open-ended philosophical questions. For Tanaka, questions such as What does it mean to be an *onna?* and Are we even able to live as *onna* in this society? were fundamental. Ibid., 1:397.

67. Ibid., 1:397. *Onna no hangyaku* is one of *ribu*'s enduring alternative media (*mini-komi*) magazines that Kuno Ayako, its editor, has continued to publish for forty years.

68. Chūpiren is introduced and discussed in chapter 3. Chūpiren was the women's group that advocated the use of the pill. Some *ribu* women considered the group a part of *ribu,* but others did not. In the early days of Chūpiren, the Group of Fighting Women organized with it against the revision of the Eugenic Protection Law. See, for the example, the pamphlet, "Iki iki kokoro wa nokoru," by Tanaka Mitsu, October 15, 1971, unpublished *ribu* documents from the archives of the Yokohama Women's Forum, compiled by Yonezu Tomoko.

69. Email interview correspondence with Sayama Sachi, August 16, 2010. Sayama writes about her visit to the *ribu* collective in Hokkaidō, saying it did not have the darkness and gloominess of the Ribu Shinjuku Center, where she lived and worked.

70. Some *ribu* women and other feminist activists have even described Tanaka as the *emperor of ribu (ribu no tenno),* which is suggestive of the degree of her dominance and influence. Interview with Sayama Sachi, June 7, 2001. At the outset of my fieldwork in 2000, Tomomi Yamaguchi also informed me that among feminist activists of Kōdōsuru Kai, Tanaka was known as the *tenno* (emperor) of *ribu.* Yamaguchi conducted ethnographic research on Kōdōsuru Kai (the group's full name is Kokusai Fujin-nen o Kikkate to Shite Kōdō o Okosu Onna-tachi no Kai), a major feminist activist group that began in 1975.

71. "Liberation from the Toilet (rev.)," 274. The concept of the "here-existing *onna*" is further elaborated in chapter 5.

72. Asakawa Mariko (roundtable participant), "Zadankai: ribu sen," 256. Miki, Saeki, and Mizoguchi, *Shiryō Nihon ūman ribu shi,* 1:209. Machino Michiko says that the group's first organizing center was Tanaka's newly built apartment in Hongo. Later they moved to the second floor of Hongo San-chō me. This tiny space would become one of the first organizing centers of the *ribu* movement in Tokyo. "Zadankai, ribu sen," 206.

73. Email correspondence with Sayama Sachi, July 12, 2010.

74. "Korekutibu ga genjyokyō o kirisaku—Gurūpu tatakau onna medaka korekutibu ni kesshu seyo!," in Miki, Saeki, and Mizoguchi, *Shiryō Nihon ūman ribu shi,* 1:233.

75. The formation of the Ribu Shinjuku Center is discussed in chapter 3. Sayama states that as Tanaka's power grew dominant within the Group of Fighting Women,

many other women members (seven or eight) quit one by one. By 1975, all the members had left the group except for Sayama. Interview with Sayama, June 7, 2001, San Francisco, California. Email interview correspondence, August 16, 2010.

76. Because Tanaka's concern was directed toward the debasement of heterosexual relations without questioning the coerciveness of compulsory heterosexuality, her notion of liberation remained within the confines of a heterosexual logic. For example, Tanaka writes, "Fundamentally that other human, for a man is a woman, and for woman is a man" ("Liberation from the Toilet (rev.)," 269). Tanaka departed from a premise that naturalizes heterosexuality insofar as she imagined a better form of heterosexual relations as a kind of restoration of a more natural state.

77. Tanaka, "Liberation from the Toilet (rev.)," 271.

78. In her early manifestos, Tanaka makes reference to "nature" *(shizen)*, or the lost naturalness of male/female relations, saying, "We forget that once upon a time there were people who lived a more raw existence." Ibid., 278.

79. Here I am referring to the formation of "political-lesbian feminists" as a distinct radical feminist position that emerged in the early 1970s in the United States. See Echols, *Daring to Be Bad*. See also Adrienne Rich's classic 1980 essay, "Compulsory Heterosexuality and Lesbian Existence," in *Blood, Bread and Poetry: Selected Prose, 1979–1985* (New York: W.W. Norton, 1994).

80. It should be made clear that a lesbian or queer positive culture was not yet in formation across leftist and women's movements and would later emerge within *ribu*. However, my point here is that Tanaka's strong heterosexual focus was a highly influential factor in determining the heterodominance of the movement.

81. For example, at the Ribu Shinjuku Center, a lesbian-identified activist ("M") was deeply hurt when she found out that some other *ribu* women had said they did not want to sleep beside her. Such homophobic expressions made by some women in the movement were not adequately criticized and addressed, and such conditions made M feel that she needed a respite from the movement.

82. Email correspondence with Yonezu Tomoko, August 22, 2010.

83. Fuyumi (first name only is used), "Onna no ai o habamu chūkinhō ni akanbe shiyō: onna zukina onna ga nande chūkinhō kangaeruka ni tsuite." Miki, Saeki, and Mizoguchi, *Shiryō Nihon ūman ribu shi*, 2:115. This group continued its reading group meetings for decades into the 1990s (116).

84. *Onna Erosu: tokushū: hankekkon o ikiru*, no. 2 (1974): 86–104, and no. 3 (1975): 80–92. Amano Michimi was a lesbian-identified woman who was also part of the Ribu Shinjuku Center. With only two years difference in their ages, she was closer in terms of life experience to Tanaka. However, she was allegedly pushed out of the commune by Tanaka because she resisted and refused to comply with Tanaka's directives. Email correspondence with James Welker, April 25–26, 2010. See also Welker, "Transfiguring the Female," which focuses on the relationship between *ribu* and the emergence of lesbian culture and politics.

85. Feminist scholar and *ribu* participant Inoue Teruko describes this book as the "monumental work that the *ribu* movement gave birth to." In framing this book as a collective creation, Inoue places the emphasis of authorship not on the individual Tanaka but on the movement. Inoue, *Joseigaku e no shōtai*, 4.

86. Tanaka Mitsu, "Ribu sen o ronzureba," *Ribu News*, Inaugural Issue, October 1, 1970, 7.

87. Ibid.

88. Ibid.

89. "Zadankai: ribu sen," 230.

90. Ibid., 236. This was confirmed by all the *ribu* women I interviewed. Tanaka's location in Tokyo—the center of the nation's media production network—and the combination of her verbal skills and charismatic personality added to her ability to engage with the mass media.

91. In my observations of Tanaka during my fieldwork from 1999 to 2001, her tendency was to publicly place and promote herself on stage. When I volunteered to help her "Okinawan music activism" from 2000 to 2001, which involved her organizing Okinawan musicians to perform in Tokyo, she routinely acted as the emcee at such events. However, due to the amount of time she spent on stage, on one occasion an Okinawan musician publicly criticized her from the stage for "talking too much" and acting like a *"yamatonchu,"* a critical slang term that refers to mainlander Japanese.

92. Because Tanaka maintained her own separate apartment, her earnings went to support her own expenses as well as toward the Shinjuku Center.

93. "Zadankai: ribu sen," 229.

94. Similar to the organizing principles of Beheiren and Zenkyōtō, *ribu* emphasized the importance of each woman doing whatever she could, wherever her help was needed, and did not require equal investments or sameness of participation. Ibid., 204–50. One of the younger members, Namahara, states that she remembers always doing the dishes, but other members disagreed with her memory, saying that different people were always doing the dishes (232–34).

95. Ibid., 236, 241.

96. Yonezu's key role as a *ribu* activist is discussed in chapter 3.

97. "Zadankai: ribu sen," 233.

98. In 1974, the women began to discuss the possibility of reducing the activities of the Shinjuku Center to allow the women to work more on their interpersonal relations. That same year, Tanaka proposed that they close the center and move to the United States. Endō, "Ribu Shinjuku Sentā no sōkatsu ni yosete."

99. During my years of research in *ūman ribu* (1999–2005), I did not hear about or encounter any women who quit the *ribu* movement because of Tanaka's style of leadership, but from 2009 to 2010, I heard of the accounts of women leaving the center because of Tanaka, although they stayed involved in the movement.

100. Interview with Sayama Sachi, via email correspondence, August 16, 2010.

101. Equality *(byōdō)* was not one of ribu's key concepts and rarely appears in *ribu*'s primary documents. However, the term *taitō* is used from time to time. The choice of terms is significant in that the first character in *byōdō* signifies "peace," or to subjugate, consume, or be suppressed, whereas the first character in *taitō* signifies the opposite, anti-, to counter or confront, and face to face.

102. "Zadankai: ribu sen," 231, 236.

103. Ibid., 232. Other *ribu* women from the center, such as Namahara Reiko and Machino Michiko, have also criticized how Tanaka treated them, saying that at times they felt they were doing too much work *for Tanaka* instead of for the sake of the movement. Namahara states that she "did not feel right" helping with work that went toward supplementing Tanaka's own living expenses. "I would try to avoid seeing Tanaka so that she would not ask me for help" (232). Machino Michiko also stated that while working at the center, she eventually refused to continue doing the typesetting for Tanaka's writings, because Tanaka would rewrite her texts so many times.

104. Ibid., 238. Yonezu Tomoko repeated this statement in an interview, March 23, 2001.

105. Ibid., 239. In this connection, Apter and Nagayo write, "Sect membership involves above all writing. Even rank and file members who are relatively inarticulate in their speech may be involved in writing and distributing leaflets, pamphlets and other materials. . . . The action of writing is important; the words themselves are evidence on the printed page that the revolution exists. They are performatives—expressions that are not factually correct or incorrect but rather by being uttered are aimed at having a consequence" (127). Apter and Nagayo, *Against the State*.

106. "Zadankai: ribu sen," 241–42.

107. Interview with Yonezu Tomoko, March 23, 2001. Tanaka one time complimented another woman's writing, saying that it had improved. However, the other women said that it had merely become more like Tanaka's. This anecdote points to how Tanaka's manner of encouraging other women to write became, at times, recognized more as a reflection of her ego than it was a practice of *ribu*'s politics.

108. Reading the writings of the women at the Shinjuku Center, it is possible to decipher and detect where Tanaka inserts herself into the text: suddenly a striking Tanaka-esque phrase or paragraphs appears, and Tanaka's key words and phrases are repeated throughout the texts.

109. Chapter 1 addresses in further detail Tanaka's political stance on *kogoroshi no onna* (women who killed their children). Chapter 5 elaborates Tanaka's philosophy of liberation and violence.

110. Tanaka, *Inochi no onna-tachi e*, 98–99.

111. According to Wakabayashi, they first planned to go to the United States, but once there, they decided to attend the conference. Conversation with Wakabayashi Naeko, September 15, 2002.

112. Tanaka writes about her experiences in Mexico in her second book, *Doko ni iyou to riburian*.

113. Yonezu, "Watashi ni totte no ribu sen to wa." This decision not to formalize a system of authority or decision making was characteristic of the political style that Ichiyo Muto describes as the neo–New Left, referring to Beheiren and Zenkyōtō. Muto and Inoue, "Beyond the New Left (Part 2)," 54–73.

114. As Takeda Miyuki stated, the Shinjuku Center did not conform to the same values as dominant society. It was not wealth, beauty, or family status that determined the power relations between the women, forms of cultural capital that might typically be applicable to a woman's status. What determined the hierarchy at the center was "the person who had the strongest opinions and spoke with the most authority" *(hatsugen ken)*. "Zadankai: ribu sen," 237. Tanaka could speak with authority and persuasion. She was outstanding as a theorist and writer. In this way, *ribu*'s hierarchy reflected and refracted the alternative, yet established, culture of the left.

115. The entanglement of unconscious desires, transferences, and projections between the women at the Shinjuku Center formed a complicated web that remained unarticulated and unexamined because of the circumstances and time pressures of life at the center. The conscious and unconscious desires for recognition and acceptance, "equality," and love were directed toward other *ribu* women. These desires infused and generated a false (unconscious) assumption that the other *ribu* women could fulfill one's own concept (or fantasy) of the "ideal *ribu* woman" who was without contradiction or excess. It presumed an "ideal *ribu* woman" who was fully liberated from the dominant ideologies that had constituted her. This assumption and these misdirected desires created a structure of inevitable disappointment and hurt, so much so that many women wanted to be liberated from the emotional/psychic pain of these relationships. According to Sayama Sachi's opinion, Tanaka was not so interested in this communal life with other women but in a politics directed toward making effective societal interventions. Even though Sayama was hurt by Tanaka, she still states that she is grateful for the opportunity to work with such a talented and strategic activist like Tanaka. Interview via email correspondence, August 16, 2010.

116. Tanaka, "Tanaka Mitsu Intabyū," with Kitahara Minori (Part 1), and Ueno Chizuko (Part 2), 320. In this published dialogue, Tanaka states that the women were "free to quit" the movement if they so desired, unlike what occurred in the URA. According to women involved in the Ribu Shinjuku Center, even though they had meetings after her return to Japan to revisit what had happened at the center, Tanaka was reluctant to work through the mistakes she had made during their time living together. Cf. notes 132 and 133.

117. Tanaka has often been described as someone with anarchistic tendencies. Arguably, a strain of anarchistic principles initially informed her politics and the organizing principles of *ribu*, particularly an antihierarchical principle. One of Tanaka's key concepts was a notion of "derangement and chaos" *(torimidashi),* which she saw as an integral and inevitable part of being *onna.* This notion of derangement and chaos, and Tanaka's proclivity toward anarchism, informed the movement's (provisional) organizing principles, and the conditions of its organizing preempted the formulation of

a more systematic movement theory *(undō ron)* to expand and nurture the movement. Tanaka's initial commitment to antihierarchical relationships and antistate politics are two examples of her basic anarchist stance.

118. Inoue, *Iwanami joseigaku jiten*, 40.

119. Ibid., 40. Tanaka Mitsu also contributes to this tendency by publicly stating that the center stayed open for about "one year" after she left. "Tanaka Mitsu intabyū," 316.

120. Secondary commentary on *ribu* has almost uniformly described *ribu* as a *past* social movement of the 1970s, ignoring its many forms of continuity. See, for example, Ehara Yumiko, "Japanese Feminism in the 1970s and 1980s," trans. Yanagida Eino and Paula Long, *U.S.-Japan Women's Journal*, no. 4 (1993): 50. This article is based on Ehara Yumiko, *Feminizumu Ronsō: 70 nendai kara 90 nendai e* (Tokyo: Keisō Shobō, 1990), 2–46. Sociological explanations that situate *ribu* within in a narrative of progress from *ribu* to feminism are problematic in that their method of measuring *ribu*'s successes and failures and its continuing transformations often tends to misunderstand the very fundamentals of *ribu*'s historical formation. Instead of describing this change in terms of a suppression and disavowal of radical politics, these narratives describe the development of liberal feminism according to a logic of advancement and progress.

121. In the film *Looking for Fumiko*, Tanaka states, "Daitai *ribu* to iu no wa, 'watashi no kaihō o kitei ni shiteiru no yo.'"

122. In 2009, Tanaka published an extended interview with Ueno Chizuko and Kitahara Minori, revisiting and renarrating her relationship with the URA in the early 1970s. Through this published dialogue, Tanaka effectively distances herself from any alliance or solidarity with the URA despite the supportive activities that she engaged in from 1972 to 1974 in relation to the women of the URA. See chapter 5 for more details. This is a notable example of her shift in political discourse over the last few decades.

123. Tanaka Mitsu, "Ide-san to *ūman ribu*," Lecture in Tokyo, April 15, 2000.

124. Lippit, "Seitō and the Literary Roots of Japanese Feminism"; Hiroko, *Hiratsuka Raicho and Early Japanese Feminism;* Bardsley, *The Blue Stockings of Japan.*

125. Ueno Chizuko and Tanaka Mitsu, *Mitsu to Chizuko no konton tonkarari*, 47.

126. For example, in *Ribu shishi nōto*, Akiyama Yōko writes that, Tanaka is, in her opinion, "strangely enough, a person who rarely make mistakes" *(myo ni machigae nai hito)* (202).

127. Here I am referring to her style of self-representation, such as her description that she "hears voices from the heavens," as the inspiration for her liberation manifesto rather than to her intellectual sources, such as Iijima Aiko or Wilhelm Reich.

128. In "Japanese Feminism in the 1970s and 1980s," Ehara Yumiko periodizes what she calls the "stages of feminism in terms of changes in the main figures of the feminist movement." She divides the "era of liberation" (1970–77) into three periods: "the emergence, 1970–1972; the period of specialization, which lasted until 1975; and

development, in both quality and quantity, from 1975–1977" (50). She describes 1978 to 1982 as the "Emergence of Women's Studies." She characterizes 1983 onward as "a new era of serious feminist debate" (53). This periodization has become the dominant narrative about the development of second wave feminism in Japan.

129. In her recently published dialogue with Ueno, Tanaka distances herself from the radicalism of communist and Marxist sects like the URA and reproduces a narrative about the immaturity of their politics, Tanaka, "Tanaka Mitsu intabyū," 290–307.

130. Tanaka, *Doko ni iyou to riburian.*

131. Tanaka Mitsu, "Sekai wa 'yaban' o matte iru," in *Zenkyōtō kara ribu e,* 252–56.

132. In December 1983, former members of the Ribu Shinjuku Center held a retreat to theorize among themselves what happened at the center. Those such as Tanaka Mitsu, Yonezu Tomoko, and Endō Misako participated. This retreat was called Ribu sentā no sōkatsu ni yosete. I thank Yonezu and Endō for sharing with me their unpublished writings about this event.

133. This statement is based on how the remaining women at the center were angered and indignant that Tanaka attempted to direct them how to run the center after her departure in 1975. Cf. note 103. Tanaka's public disparaging remarks about other *ribu* women at the center, referring to them as a "grains of sticky rice" that she could never become, has also offended them. Tanaka Mitsu, "Kurashi to kyoiku o tsunagu," *We* (March–April 1995). Tanaka Mitsu, "Sekai wa yaban o matteiru: watashi wa zadankai ni denainoha naze ka no maku," in *Zenkyōtō kara ribu e,* 252–58. Her refusal to take part in a published roundtable about life at the center, in which she was criticized, is also indicative of her unwillingness to engage with most of the women with whom she worked in the 1970s.

134. During my fieldwork, I was informed by *ribu* activists that Tanaka had, in recent years, threatened other *ribu* women against claiming collective authorship for *ribu* texts, demanding that they make no public claims about collaborative authorship.

5. *Ribu*'s Response to the United Red Army

1. My conception of political violence as an aporetic condition is informed by Jacques Derrida, *Aporias,* trans. Thomas Dutoit (Stanford, Calif.: Stanford University Press, 1993). Derrida writes, "If I may say, of the aporos or of the aporia: the difficult or the impracticable, here the impossible, passage, the refused, denied, or prohibited passage, indeed the nonpassage, which can in fact be something else, the event of a coming or of a future advent . . . I was then trying to move not against or out of the impasse but, in another way, according to another thinking of the aporia, one perhaps more enduring" (8–13).

2. For a few examples of these debates, see Randall Williams, *The Divided World: On Human Rights and Its Violence* (Minneapolis: University of Minnesota Press, 2010); Kimberly Hutchings, "Feminist Ethics and Political Violence," *International*

Politics 44, no. 1 (2007): 90–106; Allen Feldman, *Formations of Violence: The Narrative of the Body and Political Terror in Northern Ireland* (Chicago: University of Chicago Press, 1991).

3. Due to the nature of the Japanese Red Army activities, by the 1970s, this group was considered by many governments as a "terrorist group." According to the Japanese National Police Agency Report issued in 2003, "The Japanese Red Army (JRA) is an international terrorist organization that was established by a faction of an extremist group who committed felonious crimes, such as attacks on police stations, bank raids, and the like in Japan with the objective of revolutionizing the country based on Marxist-Leninist ideology, and to ultimately unify the world under communism." See National Police Agency Web site, accessed August 20, 2009, http://www.npa.go.jp/keibi/kokutero1/english/pdf/sec03.pdf.

4. This was a "group with ideological ties to a Maoist group that had been ousted from the Japan Communist Party." Steinhoff, "Three Women Who Loved the Left," 308–9.

5. The Revolutionary Left Faction acquired guns through a successful robbery of a gun shop but lacked money to carry on its activities. In the late 1960s, Nagata first became involved in the Marxist Leninist Faction (ML Ha) but eventually became a member of the Revolutionary Left Faction. In college Nagata studied pharmacy, but she quit her job as a pharmacist to become a full-time activist.

6. See Steinhoff, "Death by Defeatism." For two filmic renditions of these events, see *Jitsuroku Rengo Sekigun: Asama Sanso e no michi* [United Red Army], directed by Wakamatsu Koji (2007), and *Hikari no Ame (Rain of Light)*, directed by Banmei Takahashi (2001).

7. NHK Online, accessed August 15, 2008, http://www.nhk.or.jp/digital museum/nhk50years_en/history/p16/index.html.

8. Steinhoff, "Three Women Who Loved the Left," 311.

9. *Japan Times,* March 15, 1972, 2.

10. Miki, Saeki, and Mizoguchi, *Shiryō Nihon ūman ribu shi,* 1:410. Miki indicates in her column that she is writing about the Osaka editions of the *Asahi Shinbun;* however, the Tokyo editions also carried many of the same stories. For example, it also printed the roundtable that Miki critiques as well as the article that links the Group of Fighting Women with the Red Army.

11. Ibid., 1:410. Cf. note 30 regarding the term *onna*.

12. *Asahi Shinbun,* Tokyo edition, March 11, 1972, 22.

13. Ibid.; Miki, Saeki, and Mizoguchi, *Shiryō Nihon ūman ribu shi,* 1:409.

14. *Asahi Shinbun,* Tokyo edition, March 11, 1972, 22.

15. Miki, Saeki, and Mizoguchi, *Shiryō Nihon ūman ribu shi,* 1:344, 1:410, 1:412, 2:294.

16. Ibid., 2:81.

17. Such photographs have been reprinted decades later in magazines such as

Flash, February 22, 1992, p. 70. *Flash* is an entertainment magazine directed at male audiences.

18. *Asahi Shinbun*, March 14, 1972, 3.

19. Steinhoff, "Three Women Who Loved the Left," 311.

20. Ibid., 311. The two feature-length films about this incident, *Hikari no ame* and *The United Red Army*, also reinscribe this portrayal of Nagata.

21. Miki, Saeki, and Mizoguchi, *Shiryō Nihon ūman ribu shi*, 1:371.

22. The *ribu* women described the lynching as a catastrophe *(hakyoku)*.

23. Although this violence initially was directed against the riot police and other select politicians and police officials, such violence subsequently turned toward other leftist groups. See chapter 2.

24. Miki, Saeki, and Mizoguchi, *Shiryō Nihon ūman ribu shi*, 1:344.

25. This activist uses the pen name Kazu; she is also known as M.M. Ibid., 1:344–45.

26. Onna Kaihō Gakusei Sensen, "Ataratana onna no tatakai e mukete," in Miki, Saeki, and Mizoguchi, *Shiryō Nihon ūman ribu shi*, 1:371.

27. *Asahi Shinbun*, Tokyo evening edition, March 11, 1972, 23.

28. "Kunihisa-san o shien suru gawa kara," *Ribu News*, no. 1, October 1, 1972, 8, reprinted in *Ribu nyūsu konomichi hitosuji*, 8.

29. *Ribu* activists publicly used the terms "support activities" *(kyūen katsudo)* and *shien*, meaning support or back up, instead of solidarity *(rentai)* to describe their work around the women of the URA. *Kyūen katsudō* during this era was typically used for support activities for those under siege from the state. For example, *kyūen* referred to support work for those incarcerated by the state and for AWOL soldiers of the U.S. military who were being supported by Japanese to enable them to escape capture and flee the country. The Japanese term for solidarity *(rentai)* implies sharing the same political views and can be associated with the notion of "collective responsibility" *(rentai sekinin)*, so the use of the term "solidarity" in Japanese, compared to English, may require a greater degree of agreement and unity in terms of political philosophy and responsibility. I coined the phrase "critical solidarity" to indicate how the *ribu* women were critical of the philosophy of the URA yet still engaged in a wide range of supportive political actions that went beyond support and rescue. This critical solidarity entailed a profound kind of political identification originating from a feminist solidarity and desire that sought to identify as *onna* with other criminalized *onna*. In English, solidarity more appropriately captures the scope of support and complex affiliations *ribu* had with the URA, although not necessarily implying agreement on all things or a notion of shared responsibility. Finally, it should be noted that veteran *ribu* activists such as Yonezu Tomoko described their solidarity with *kogoroshi no onna* and the women of the URA as fundamentally the same thing. Cf. note 36.

30. As elaborated in chapter 1, *onna* is a word for women with sexualized and "lower-class" connotations that *ribu* deliberately adopted and politicized.

31. Miki, Saeki, and Mizoguchi, *Shiryō Nihon ūman ribu shi,* 1:344, 1:410, 1:412, 2:294.

32. "Zadankai: ribu sen," 222.

33. Ibid.

34. In *Inochi no onna-tachi e,* Tanaka posed the question to herself, "What was it that made her [Nagata] become that?" (222).

35. Miki, Saeki, and Mizoguchi, *Shiryō Nihon ūman ribu shi,* 1:344.

36. *Ribu* activist Yonezu Tomoko stated in an interview (July 12, 2009) that her stance toward *kogoroshi no onna* and the women of the URA was fundamentally the same *(kihonteki onaji)* stance of solidarity *(rentai),* indicating the discrepancy and slippage between how the *ribu* women publicly described their stance (as *kyūen* and *shien)* and how they conceived it politically.

37. M (pseudonym), "Sangatsu touron kai hōhoku—3.28 Rengo Sekigun no genjitsu to, atashi-tachi ribu wa . . . kyūatsu tono tatakai" [The Reality of the URA: Ribu's Fight against . . . the Suppression: Report on the March Discussion]. Miki, Saeki, and Mizoguchi, *Shiryō Nihon ūman ribu shi,* 1:355.

38. Interview with Yonezu Tomoko, Nakano, Tokyo, July 12, 2009.

39. Tanaka Mitsu, "Tanaka Mitsu, *1968* o warau" [Tanaka Mitsu laughs at *1968*], *Shūkan Kinyōbi,* no. 781 (December 25, 2009): 27; Tanaka, "Tanaka Mitsu intabyū."

40. See chapters 3 and 4 for a more detailed account of the establishment of the Ribu Shinjuku Center.

41. According to *Ribu News,* this woman is described as a member of the Group of Fighting Women. Over the years, *ribu* activists have distanced themselves from the supportive work they did for the women of the URA in the 1970s.

42. In "Zadankai: ribu sen," Kano Mikiyo, one of the moderators of the roundtable, refers to this woman and reveals her real name to be Kimura Hisako (222).

43. Miki, Saeki, and Mizoguchi, *Shiryō Nihon ūman ribu shi,* 1:346.

44. Kunihisa Kazuko, "Jitsuzoū to kyozoū no iyama de," in *Ribu News,* reprinted in *Ribu nyūsu konomichi hitosuji,* 8. The article states that her child who was at home with her is in junior high school.

45. For example, in November 1972, another *ribu* newsletter, *Red June (Akai Rokugatsu),* based in the Kantō area, published a follow-up article by Kunihisa. Different groups within the *ribu* movement thus demonstrated their support and concern for the women of the URA and women like Kunihisa who became associated with the URA.

46. "Kunihisa-san o shien suru gawa kara," reprinted in *Ribu nyūsu konomichi hitosuji,* 8.

47. Ibid.

48. Ibid.

49. This meeting was advertised as "Nagata Hiroko shien ni tsuite" and was the "first spring teach-in." *Ribu Shinjuku Sentā shiryō shūsei: bira hen,* 444. *Ribu*'s URA sup-

port group, Koto no Honshitsu ni Semaru Kai, was established in February 1973. This group's meetings were held at the Ribu Shinjuku Center and specifically addressed the women of the URA and Nagata Hiroko, indicative of *ribu*'s women-centered politics.

50. Ashura is the name of one of the guardian devas of Buddha, with the three faces and six hands. She is known as the Sun Goddess, but her other faces represent the deities of war.

51. This newsletter was referred to as the preparatory newsletter, printed just before the inaugural edition published in March 1973.

52. *Ribu Shinjuku Sentā shiryō shūsei: bira hen,* 447.

53. Ibid.; Miki, Saeki, and Mizoguchi, *Shiryō Nihon ūman ribu shi,* 2:82.

54. Ibid.

55. Ibid., 2:82–83.

56. Ibid., 2:86–87.

57. This article is written by a person using the name Nomura. *Ribu Shinjuku Sentā shiryō shūsei: bira hen,* 447.

58. Ibid.

59. Miki, Saeki, and Mizoguchi, *Shiryō Nihon ūman ribu shi,* 2:82–83.

60. Ibid., 2:83.

61. Ibid.; *Ribu Shinjuku Sentā shiryō shūsei: bira hen,* 448.

62. Interview with anonymous informant, Tokyo, February 7, 2003.

63. After going to the hearings or visiting the women of the URA in prison, the *ribu* women would be followed by the police. The *ribu* women often wore disguises to the court hearings and tried to lose the police who were following them by changing their clothes and hairstyles on the return trip. Several *ribu* activists mentioned these facts during my conversations with them.

64. The translation of the first part of the title, "To Women with Spirit" *(Inochi no onna-tachi e),* is by James Welker. See chapter 1, note 101.

65. Inoue, *Joseigaku e no shōtai,* 4.

66. When she returned to Japan after living in Mexico from 1975 to 1979, Tanaka published *Doko ni iyou to riburian,* which can be translated, "Wherever I go, I am ribu." In this second book, Tanaka (re)visits and elaborates her declaration "I am Nagata Hiroko" and uses this phrase as one of her chapter titles. She repeatedly revisits this issue in her extended interview with Ueno Chizuko, "Tanaka Mitsu Intabyū." I observed a distinct change in Tanaka's stance toward the URA from the time I conducted fieldwork from 1999 to 2001 to this time of writing in 2009. In her 2009 interviews and writings, she clearly distances herself from the URA, expressing much more explicit disdain for their politics, and does not acknowledge any form of solidarity with them. For example, her infantalization of the members of the URA in her 2009 interviews is noteworthy as a rhetorical device that distances her from these criminalized revolutionaries, which contrasts with her discourse in 1972, 1973, and 1983 *(Doko*

ni iyou to riburian). See also "Tanaka Mitsu, *1968* o warau." This article is a harsh critique of Oguma Eiji's massive two-volume history, *1968*, in which Oguma devotes a chapter to *ribu* with a focus on Tanaka Mitsu, called "Ribu to watashi."

67. See chapter 1, note 81.

68. Tanaka, *Inochi no onna-tachi e*, 153.

69. In her later thought and writings, post-1980s, Tanaka would turn more explicitly to Eastern notions of Taoism and *in/yo* (yin and yang). At this early stage in Tanaka's thinking, contradiction and tension constituted the basic condition of the subject.

70. Tanaka, *Inochi no onna-tachi e*, 30.

71. Feminist thinkers across a wide spectrum of feminist thought—from liberal thinkers such as Mary Wollstonecraft to Marxist feminists such as Nancy Hartsock and feminists such as Andrea Dworkin and Catherine Mackinnon—have tended to regard violence as categorically negative and undesirable and have asserted that its origin and expression is male or masculinist. In the *Encyclopedia of Feminism,* violence is described in the following terms: "The problem of male violence has continually been a feminist concern. Patriarchal authority is expressed and maintained through violence and the threat of violence." This terse description exemplifies what is often assumed to be a commonly held feminist view of violence that comprehends violence to be an expression of patriarchal power and a negative, harmful force. According to this standard explanation, feminism is concerned with violence that is gendered male, implying either that "male violence" is the problem or that violence is a problem endemic to maleness. It then follows that if violence is rendered male or masculine, men are presumed to have a proclivity toward violence. Paradigmatically, men are seen as the perpetrators of violence, rendering women as the (presumed nonviolent) victims of patriarchy. In fact, some feminist thinkers go so far as to argue that femininity and violence are antithetical and that women are therefore not predisposed to violence. Tanaka's theorization of violence provides a striking contrast with these kinds of standard(ized) feminist definitions of violence. Lisa Tuttle, ed., *Encyclopedia of Feminism* (New York: Facts on File Publications, 1986), 396.

72. Tanaka, *Inochi no onna-tachi e*, 146.

73. A dialectic of violence and counterviolence constituted the struggle for survival as integral to the conflict not only between the oppressor and the oppressed but also between different oppressed subjects, as a manifestation of their lived conditions within structural violence. In this connection, Tanaka cites Angela Davis, who offers an interpretation of the Hegelian master–slave dialectic. "The master always exists at the border of becoming a slave, and the slave exists at the border of becoming the master because she already possesses the power to become the master." Ibid., 146–47.

74. Kakumaru was a well-known New Left sect that engaged in *uchigeba* with other New Left sects, like Chūkaku. For further explanation of Kakumaru and the context of its formation, see chapter 2. Apter and Nagayo, *Against the State,* 121. See Frederick Wheeler for more about Kakumaru. Cf. chapter 2, note 1.

75. Tanaka analyzes how her fantasies of masculinity, power, and violence are intertwined to shape her desire and her affect of repulsion to the cowardly, weak, beaten men of Kakumaru who have lost the battle to the men of the Red Army.

76. Satoshi Ukai, "The Road to Hell Is Paved with Good Intentions: For a 'Critique of Terrorism' to Come," *positions: east asia cultures critique* 13, no. 1 (2005): 240.

77. Williams, *The Divided World*, 5. In this passage, Williams is discussing Nelson Mandela's explanation of the decision to "use violence to overthrow the racist South African State" (4).

78. Tanaka, "Liberation from the Toilet (rev.)," 277. In *Inochi no onna-tachi e,* Tanaka discusses the repetition of the same imperialist and structuralist sexual violence referring to the soldiers of the imperial army, who used the comfort women, and contemporary Japanese men. The latter comprise the new front line of the Japanese economic animal, the cliental of the sex industry that exploits third world Asian women (252).

79. Ibid., 183.

80. Ibid., 182.

81. Even though the *ribu* women remained in proximity to political sects that engaged in violent actions against the state (that the state would label as "terrorist"), their ultimate refusal to regularly utilize violent actions against the state ensured their continuity. *Ribu* women contested a limited definition of revolutionary that rendered violence toward others as necessary.

82. Tanaka, "Tanaka Mitsu intabyū," 302.

83. "Tanaka Mitsu, *1968* o warau," 27.

84. Nagata Hiroko, *Jūroku no bōhyō: hono to shi no seishun* [Sixteen Graves: The Spring of Fire and Death] (Tokyo: Sairyūsha, 1982), 48.

85. "Tanaka Mitsu, *1968* o warau," 28.

86. Nagata, *Jūroku no bōhyō*, 48–49.

87. "Tanaka Mitsu, *1968* o warau," 27.

88. Tanaka, *Inochi no onna-tachi e,* 209. See my translation in Shigematsu, "Tanaka Mitsu and the Women's Liberation Movement in Japan," app. 3, 299–300.

89. Tanaka, "Tanaka Mitsu Intabyū," 308.

90. Ibid., 307–8. Interview with anonymous informant, Tokyo, February 7, 2003.

91. Tanaka, "Tanaka Mitsu Intabyū," 308.

92. Shigematsu, "Tanaka Mitsu and the Women's Liberation Movement in Japan," app. 3, 299–300.

93. "Tanaka Mitsu, *1968* o warau," 29.

94. Ibid. While the rest of "Japan is quiet from fear," Tanaka wrote, "Nagata Hiroko is me / I am Nagata Hiroko."

95. Tanaka, *Doko ni iyou to riburian*, 60. She writes the same thing in *Inochi no onna-tachi e.*

96. Ibid.

97. Tanaka, *Inochi no onna-tachi e,* 257.

98. Ibid.

99. Tanaka, *Doko ni iyou to riburian,* 58.

100. Nagata, *Jūroku no bōhyō.*

101. Oguma, *1968,* vol. 2. Oguma also recounts this experience (545) and gives several examples of how such forms of sexual violence were not uncommon in the New Left, citing several examples. See chapter 17, 685–66.

102. Nagata, *Jūroku no bōhyō,* 70.

103. Steinhoff, "Death by Defeatism," 198.

104. Tanaka, *Doko ni iyou to riburian,* 60.

105. For Nagata, Kaneko embodied too much "femininity" to be an "authentic revolutionary." In her memoirs, Nagata describes how her party, the Revolutionary Left, ignored sexual love and emotions *(seiteki kanjō).* Nagata, *Jūroku no bōhyō,* 1:70.

106. Tanaka, *Doko ni iyou to riburian,* 60.

107. Ibid.

108. "Kunihisa-san o shien suru gawa kara," 6. Reprinted in *Ribu nyūsu konomichi hitosuji,* 14.

109. While it is important to consider the possible meaning of her spiritual role within the movement, the danger of overemphasizing this role can lead to Tanaka's reification and an avoidance of a critical engagement with the ways in which many women in the movement found her to be a domineering and problematic figure both during the 1970s and thereafter. See chapter 4 for more details about her contradictory function within the *ribu* movement.

110. Tanaka, "Tanaka Mitsu Intabyū," 303.

111. In her second book, *Doko ni iyou to riburian,* Tanaka writes about Nagata, using the sentence "Nagata Hiroko is me" as the title of one of her chapters (55). Tanaka's deployment of such rhetorical devices renders her actions, in my view, in a category beyond "support activities" and exemplified a distillation of *ribu*'s form of political identification and solidarity with the criminalized *onna.* Tanaka's rhetorical creativity has done much to bring her attention for her bravado and originality; however, beyond the early 1970s, she has not engaged in any form of substantive support work and has publicly renounced past solidarity with such radicalism represented by the URA.

112. Ibid., 55.

113. *Ribu Shinjuku Sentā shiryō shūsei: bira hen,* 544.

114. Tanaka, *Ribu News,* March 1, 1973, 6. This is restated in *Doko ni iyou to riburian,* 54.

115. Tanaka, *Doko ni iyou to riburian,* 57.

116. Tanaka places causality and difference at the level of the forces that impinge upon the body, such as diseases that enter and act upon the body, altering it in ways that are often unseen and uncontrollable. Tanaka claims that it was only a chance

(tama tama) factor of different diseases that may have kept her from going down the same road as Nagata. By arguing that the main factor that differentiated her and Nagata was the difference of the disease each of them had contracted, Tanaka radically reduces the relevance of individual will and agency as the decisive factor in determining one's path. She repeats this position on the significance of contingency in her 2009 interview, "Tanaka Mitsu Intabyū," 302.

117. Nagata's first death sentence was decided in 1982 and confirmed again in 1986. She appealed it, but it was finally reinstated by the Supreme Court in 1993. She died on February 5, 2011, at the Tokyo Detention Center.

Epilogue

1. Prior to its popularization, the term *feminisuto* (feminist) actually referred to men who were kind to women, or who acted in a gentlemanly fashion, such as those who held doors open for women. The fourth edition of Kenkyūsha's Japanese–English dictionary, for example, defines a *feminisuto* as "an adorer of women; a man who is unusually kind [obliging] to women; a gallant." *Kenkyūsha's New Japanese–English Dictionary,* 4th ed. (Tokyo: Kenkyusha, reprinted 1998), 243. Some of those involved in establishing the magazine *Feminisuto* were Atsumi Ikuko, Mizuta Noriko, Diane Simpson, Ohashi Terue, Catherine Broderick, and Ikegami Chizuko, among others. The aim of the magazine was twofold: to popularize the "correct usage" of the term *feminizumu* in Japan and to produce a bilingual Japanese–English magazine to disseminate knowledge of the conditions of Japanese women to other English-speaking women. In this context, the terms *feminizumu* and *feminisuto* had immediate associations with a group of highly educated, professional women invested in developing networks with other English-speaking feminists.

2. Ueno Chizuko is arguably the most widely known, prolific, and controversial feminist scholar in Japan. Ueno, who identifies as a feminist, has suggested that *ribu* implies a particular generation of women who shared the same historical experience during the 1970s. However, many women who did not participate in the *ribu* movement during the 1970s began to identify with and as *ribu* for the first time during the 1980s. These women deliberately chose to identify with and as *ribu* instead of *feminizumu,* stating that they denote a different kind of politics.

3. Interview with Inoue Teruko, February 24, 2001.

4. Ibid.

5. The English editions also advertised feminist academic journals such as *Feminist Studies* and *Signs.*

6. This issue was part of a group discussion at the first Nihon ūman ribu shi dokusho kai, September 14–15, 2002. This break with the producers of *Feminisuto* was narrated by Saeki Yōko and Miki Sōko who at the time were editors of *Onna Erosu* magazine, known as the official *ribu* journal.

7. Shigematsu, "Feminism and Media," 555–89.

8. The establishment of *joseigaku* (women's studies) began in the late 1970s with the founding of the International Society for Women's Studies (Kokusai joseigaku kai) in 1977 and the Women's Studies Association of Japan (Nihon joseigaku kenkyūkai). Since the 1990s, there has been a proliferation of feminist academic textual production in Japan that can be broadly categorized under the interdisciplinary field of women's studies.

9. Mioko Fujieda and Kumiko Fujimura-Fanselow, "Women's Studies: An Overview," in *Japanese Women: New Feminist Perspectives on the Past, Present and Future*, 158. Kazuko Watanabe, "Japanese Women's Studies," *Women's Studies Quarterly* 22, no. 3/4 (1994): 73–88.

10. For an example of recent debates regarding the institutionalization of women's studies, see *Joseigaku* 9 (2001).

11. Fujieda and Fujimura-Fanselow, "Women's Studies," 158.

12. As an influential founder of women's studies, Iwao Sumiko has written disparagingly of the *ribu* movement. Ehara Yumiko describes Iwao as an author who "define[d] the women's liberation movement as having a negative effect on the propagation of women's issues, arguing that the emergence of women's studies started with a rejection of that earlier movement and its spectacular arguments in favor of more *moderate ones* that related to one's way of living." Ehara, "Japanese Feminism in the 1970s and 1980s," 52. For example, Iwao effaces the contributions of the *ūman ribu* movement, saying that Japanese women have won "an astonishing degree of freedom and independence quietly and unobtrusively, largely without the fanfare of an organized women's movement or overt feminism." In making such statements, Iwao erases the significance of the struggles of women who have been disruptive and instead makes homogenizing claims about how Japanese women protest discrimination. Iwao Sumiko, *Japanese Women* (New York: Free Press, 1993).

13. The home page of the Women's Studies Association of Japan is at http://www.joseigakkai-jp.org/eng/index-e.html. Kokusai joseigakukai was founded in 1977. It was renamed Kokusai jendagaku-kai, the International Society for Gender Studies, in 1997. See http://www.isgs-japan.org.

14. Miki Sōko, "Ribu tamashi no nai joseigaku nante?" *Onna Erosu*, no. 11 (1978): 145–49.

15. Ibid., 147. cf. 12.

16. Miki has stated that one of the problems with the establishment of women's studies in Japan has been the lack of debates about methodology and the relationship of women's studies to the university system. Interview with Miki Sōko, September 15, 2002. Miki repeats her criticism of women's studies in Japan in the documentary *30 Years of Sisterhood US Tour (30 nen no sistāfuddo US tsuā)*, produced by Onna-tachi no rekishi purojekkuto, Urara Satoko, Seyama Noriko, and Yamagami Chieko (2006).

17. Inoue, *Joseigaku e no shōtai*, 9–10.

18. Inoue et al., *Iwanami joseigaku jiten,* 213.

19. Interview with Inoue Teruko, February 24, 2001.

20. Fujieda and Fujimura-Fanselow, "Women's Studies," 161.

21. See chapters 3 and 4 for more discussion about this dominant narrative. For example, Ehara Yumiko writes in the *Women's Studies Dictionary* that "the closing of the Ribu Shinjuku Center in 1975 is largely seen as the end *(shūen)* of Japan's *ūman ribu.*" Inoue et al., *Iwanami joseigaku jiten,* 40. The Ribu Center remained open until 1977, and three *ribu* activists, Mori Setsuko, Sayama Sachi, and Yonezu Tomoko, continued to live and work there and produce *ribu* literature from their press, Aida Kōbō, during the 1980s.

22. Yamada Eiko, "Sōkai shinpojiumu hōkoku: ima naze Matsui Yayori o kataru no ka," in *VAWW-Net Japan News,* September 15, 2009. In Yamada's report, she points out that feminist scholar Ōgoshi Aiko problematized how, since the onset of the twenty-first century, Japanese feminist scholars have been reevaluating *ūman ribu* by giving the spotlight to Tanaka Mitsu, but she questions why Matsui Yayori's work has not been given such attention. See also Yamaguchi Tomomi, "Feminizumu, Ribu, Shuryū joseigaku ni okeru 'ribu-Tanaka mitsu' sho no mondai" [Feminism, Ribu, Mainstream Women's Studies Problematic Representation Ribu-Tanaka Mitsu], on her blog *Feminisuto to no ronkō* (http://d.hatera.ne.jp/yamtom/20060717/1153118252).

23. I discuss this in chapter 3. This coalition was called the Liaison Group for the Implementation of the Resolution from the International Women's Year Conference in Japan (Kokusai Fujin-nen Renraku Kai). See Matsui's critique of this group in "The Women's Movement: Progress and Obstacles: Dialogue with Kitazawa Yōko, Matsui Yayori, and Yunomae Tomoko," in Bunch, *Voices from the Japanese Women's Movement,* 26–31.

24. Nakano Mami, "Ten Years under the Equal Employment Opportunity Law," in Bunch, *Voices from the Japanese Women's Movement,* 66. The enactment of the Equal Employment Opportunity Law *(Danjo Koyō Kikai Kintō Hō),* followed by the policy of Equal Participation of Men and Women *(Danjo Byodō Sankaku Shakai)* during the late 1990s, are examples of how *equality* became a key term in state feminist discourse and policy. Barbara Molony, "Japan's 1986 Equal Employment Opportunity Law and the Changing Discourse on Gender," *Signs* 20, no. 2 (1995): 268–302; Ueno Chizuko and Ozawa Mari, "Danjo Byōdō Sankaku shakai kihon no mezasu mono" in *Radikaruni katarebqa: Ueno Chizuko taidanshū=Radically Speaking,* ed. Ueno Chizuko (Tokyo: Heibon Sha, 2001), 10–92.

25. Matsui, "The Women's Movement," 37.

26. See "The Women's International War Crimes Tribunal on Japan's Military Sexual Slavery," http://www1.jca.apc.org/vaww-net-japan/english/womenstribunal2000/whatstribunal.html.

27. Both Ueno Chizuko and Tanaka Mitsu have written about these endeavors. Tanaka Mitsu, "Konna Nanumu no Hōmon Ki," *Impakushon* 107 (1998), and with

Suzuki Kunio, "'Nanumu no Ie' Jyōei bōgai jiken o tōshite kangaeru," *Kinema Junpō* 1198 (1996). Tanaka has also publicly narrated how she raised funds for the former comfort women. "Tanaka Mitsu ga kataru 'ribu,'" University of Tokyo, Gender Colloquium, December 5, 2000. In *Nationalism and Gender,* Ueno writes extensively about her position on the comfort women issue and her critique of the Asian Women's Fund. She also writes about how her attempts to form an alternative citizen's fund failed but coincided with the government's initiative and how this was criticized by other feminists as "fulfilling the will of the government" (183). Ueno Chizuko and Beverley Yamamoto, *Nationalism and Gender* (Melbourne, Australia: Trans Pacific Press, 2004). Ueno's feminist approach to the comfort women has been widely criticized by Kim Puja, Oka Mari, Hanasaki Kohei, Hee-Kang Kim, and others. See Hanasaki Kohei, "Decolonization and the Assumption of War Responsibility," in *Inter-Asia Cultural Studies Reader,* ed. Kuan-Hsing Chen and Cha Beng (New York: Routledge, 2007), 178–90. Ulrike Wöhr, "A Touchstone for Transnational Feminism: Discourses on Comfort Women in 1990s Japan," *Japanstudien* 16 (2004): 59–90.

28. Matsui stated this to critique to me during my fieldwork, and many *ribu* women were aware of this critique. Matsui describes herself as a cofounder of the *ribu translation* group, called Wolf (Urufu no Kai), but as I discuss in chapters 1 and 4, her view did not become hegemonic, as did Tanaka Mitsu's discourse, but became one emblematic strand of the movement. Many *ribu* women, including Tanaka, Saeki, and others, viewed Matsui Yayori's politics as different from *ribu*'s stance regarding prostitution and sex work. Some *ribu* women engaged in work in the sex industry, as hostesses, dancers, and sex workers, as an extension of their feminist politics.

29. A few examples are the Japan Network against Trafficking in Persons (JNATIP) and HELP Asian Women's Shelter in Tokyo. See http://www.humantrafficking.org/organizations/146 regarding the JNATIP. For further information about HELP, see http://www.humantrafficking.org/organizations/145.

30. While leftist and feminist icons perform a significant function in attracting and inspiring people, their ongoing political work and relationship to movements should be critically engaged with beyond a recognition of past accomplishments.

31. *Ribu* activists Miki, Saeki, and Mizoguchi also published their three-volume series *Shiryō Nihon ūman ribu shi,* which spans from 1969 to 1982. *Inpakushion, tokushū ribu nijūnen* [Impaction, Special Issue: Twenty Years of Ribu], no. 73: (Inpakuto Shuppankai, Tokyo, 1992); *Zenkyōtō Kara Ribu e;* Kanō, *Ribu to iu Kakumei.*

32. *Ripples of Change; Extreme Private Eros Love Song 1974,* directed by Hara Kazuo (Shisso Purodakushon, 1974).

33. *Ribu* activists organize annual weekend retreats at different hotsprings *(onsen)* around Japan, providing a support and information-sharing group for *ribu* activists and others who wish to join them.

34. In particular, I have greatly appreciated Miki Sōko, Saeki Yōko, Watanabe Fumie, and Yumi Doi's strong sense of feminist sisterhood and solidarity, which has

informed their generosity and kindness to me throughout the long and often difficult process of writing this book.

35. *30 Years of Sisterhood*.

36. This U.S. tour was also made into a documentary video produced by Yamagami, Seyama, and Urara, who are affiliated with the feminist video-making collective Onna-tachi no rekishi purojekuto (2006). This video offers a significant contribution by documenting how *30 Years of Sisterhood* was received at the University of Chicago; University of Iowa; Grinnelle College; Yale University; the Lesbian, Gay, Bisexual and Transgender Community Center and Bluestockings Bookstore in New York; Boston College; Michigan University; University of Illinois, Urbana-Champaign; and Washington University in St. Louis.

INDEX

abjection, 219n6

abolitionist feminist politics, 29, 209n114, 209n118

abortion: child killing linked to, 25, 26; and Eugenic Protection Law, 225n70; laws, Japan, 26–27, 208n108, 224n68; Ōhashi Yukako on, 208n109; politics of, 73; *ribu* stance on, 26, 74, 86, 88–89; state control of, 225n76. *See also* Eugenic Protection Law

Abu Ghraib: torture scandal, x, 190n6

activism: direct action, xix

Aida Fumi, 24

Aida Kōbō (*ribu* activist-run press), 102, 251n21

Ainu, xxiii, xxiv, 74

Aki Shobō, 73

Akiyama Yōko, xxvii, 104, 110, 174, 226n78, 229n8; on "Liberation from the Toilet," 233n50; on Tanaka, 240n126

Albright, Madeline, x, 190n2

Alliance of Fighting Women (*ribu* group), 85

Amano Michimi, 120, 236n84

Anpo protests, xxiii, 8, 33–38, 209n2, 212n30. *See also* Group of Fighting Women; New Left, Japanese; U.S.–Japan Mutual Cooperation and Security Treaty

anticommunism: and *onna,* 69–72; U.S. foreign policy, xxiii, 189n1

anti-imperialism, ix, xxv, 15, 19, 192n6; and capitalism, xvii; of Matsui, 176; of New Left, xxxi, 69; of *ribu,* xxi, 19, 47, 69, 71, 74, 86, 87–89, 93, 94–95, 177, 221n30; of student movements, 38, 39, 40; and United States, xxiii; of Vietnam antiwar movement, 47, 70. *See also* imperialism; New Left, Japanese; *ribu*

Antiwar Youth Committee (Hansen), 211n18

Aoshiba no Kai, 90–91, 99–101

area studies, xvii

Arima Makiko, 83, 224n54

Asahi Journal, 81, 222n32, 223n48

Asahi Shinbun, 10, 17, 92, 106, 145, 149, 194n20, 242n10

Asakawa Mariko, 119–20, 235n72

Asatori Sumie, 101–2, 228n122. *See also* Iwatsuki Sumie

Ashura, 155–56, 245n50

Asia-Japan Women's Resource Center, 193n11

Asian Women's Committee Who Fight Discrimination=Aggression, 14, 16, 203n60

Asian Women's Fund, 176, 252n27

Asian Women's Resource Center, 13, 26, 65, 67, 203n62

Beheiren, xxxi, 40–42, 52, 212n22; antihierarchical structure of, 41, 44, 84, 224n66, 237n94; direct action, emphasis on, 41, 46; as neo–New Left movement, 40; radicalization of, 212n30. *See also* New Left, Japanese

biopolitics: of nation-state, 6

black liberation, 60, 110; appropriation of, 232n29

Black Power, xxv

bodies, disabled, 79, 80, 90, 91, 219n6; and *ribu*, 67, 79, 90, 91, 99–101, 178, 219n5. *See also* Yonezu Tomoko

bodies, women: state control of, 73, 87, 88, 90, 92, 93; and subjectivity, xiii; violence against, 25–26

Brown, Wendy, 88

Buckley, Sandra, 200n34

Bund (communist student organization), 37, 38, 211n16

burakumin, 227n99

capitalism: and imperialism, xvii; and individualism, 93; and inequality, xvi; Japanese, 4; women, control of, 11, 28; and women's labor, 201n37

Chifuren (National Federation of Regional Women's Organizations), 9, 201n42; aims of, 10

childbirth: and nation, 225n69; politicization of, 21–22

Christian Temperance Union (Kirisutokyō Kyofukai), 12

Chūkaku (New Left sect), 38, 53, 57–59, 144, 211n16, 246n74; Miyaoka, repression of, 60

Chūpiren (neo-*ribu* group), 88, 118, 225n78, 226n79; on the pill, 235n68

Civil Codes, Meiji, 4–5, 6–7, 196n4; reformation of, 5

Cixous, Hélène, 110, 232n30

class: and race, xi; in *ribu*, xvi, 10, 47, 15, 114; sex as, 114; of Tanaka, 108, 227n99; in Zenkyōtō, 46, 230n19

Clinton, Hillary Rodham, x

Code Pink, 190n7

Cold War, 210n12; and imperialism, xxiii

comfort women, xxiii, 18, 175, 251n27; *ribu* identification with, 48, 49, 67, 176

Cominform (Communist Information Bureau), 210n12

Comintern (Communist International), 210n12

Committee of Asian Women (Ajia Fujin Kaigi), 12, 16, 202n50

Committee to Contact and Prepare for Women's Liberation (Josei Kaihō Junbi Renraku Kaigi), 18, 89, 219n7. *See also* Committee to Prepare for Women's Liberation

Committee to Prepare for Women's Liberation, 67, 72, 103; manifesto, 70, 71, 203n60. *See also* Committee to Contact and Prepare for Women's Liberation

Committee to Prevent the Revision of the Eugenic Protection Law, 90, 91

communes, 101, 102; JO-JO, 228n122; *ribu*, xx, xxx, 19–21, 22, 67, 84, 85, 86, 89–90, 99, 119, 223n51

contraception, 73, 102; the pill, 73, 88, 226n78, 226n79, 235n68; *ribu* activism on, 74, 86, 87, 88, 148. *See also* abortion

counterhegemonic practices, 68, 139; of

INDEX

257

ribu, xii, xxx, xxxii, 68, 169; Tanaka on, 159. *See also* hegemony
critical solidarity, xxxiii, 140, 152–53, 154–55, 169, 170; defined, 150, 243n29; with URA women, 86, 99–100, 139, 150–51, 153, 154, 156–57, 169, 178, 209n118, 243n29, 244n45, 244n49, 245n63. *See also ribu,* actions and initiatives

Davis, Angela, 110, 191n11, 246n73
de Beauvoir, Simone, 43, 213n43
"Declaration of the Liberation of Eros, The" (Tanaka), 67–68, 113, 219n8
decolonization, xxvi
democracy: Japanese, post–World War II, xv–xvi, 8–9, 13, 34, 35, 36–38, 39–40, 52, 201n43, 210n9, 210n10; U.S., xxiii, 189n1
Democratic Women's Association (Minshu Fujin Kyōkai), 8
Derrida, Jacques, 241n1
discourse, feminist, ix, xi, xviii, xx. *See also ribu,* discourse; Tanaka Mitsu, discourse
Documents of the History of Women's Lib in Japan, 12, 132, 202n52; editing of, 202n52
Doi Yumi, 178
Dworkin, Andrea, 246n71

Ehara Yumiko: on Japanese feminism, 131, 174–75, 240n128; on *ribu* women, 39, 102, 128, 212n24; on women's studies, 250n12
Ehrenreich, Barbara: on "naïve" feminism, x
Engels, Friedrich, 109
England, Lynndie, x
Enoki Misako, 118, 225n78, 226n79
epistemology: feminist, 158, 169; and violence, xiii, 28–29, 246n71

Equal Employment Opportunity Law (1986), 175
eros: liberation of, 103, 111, 113, 119, 133, 140, 157, 234n55; *ribu,* core concept of, 60–61, 65, 68, 78; in Witch Concerts, 97
ethnic minorities, Japanese, xxiii, 74. *See also* Ainu; *burakumin;* Okinawa; Okinawans; *Zainichi*
Eugenic Protection Law, 16, 21, 27, 101, 208n108, 208n109; abortion statutes, 225n70; Committee to Prevent the Revision of the Eugenic Protection Law, 90, 91; and Group of Fighting Women, 235n68; Maternal Protection Law, renamed, 228n120; *ribu* campaign, 84, 86, 87–91, 235n68. *See also* eugenics
eugenics, 67. *See also* Eugenic Protection Law
existentialism, 110
Extreme Private Eros (film), 177

family, Japanese: as foundation of society, xvii, 3, 89; government regulation of, 4; as male-centric system, xxi; and nationalism, xxx, 19; "one-wife-one-husband" system, xxx; patriarchal family model, 6; politicization of, 20; post–World War II, 6. *See also ie*
Federation of Women's Organizations (Fudanren), 12
feminism: and Abu Ghraib, 190n6; antiimperialist, 192n6; and epistemology of violence, xiii, 28–29, 246n71; eurocentrism in, xxx; European, 172; hegemonic, 190n3; and hegemony, x; and imperialism, ix; international, 78; liberal, x, xx, xxvi, 7, 29, 116, 131, 169, 240n120; militant forms of, xx; New Left, relation to, xx;

Pan-Asian, xix, 203n61, 203n62; radical, xv, xxvii; second wave, x, xi, xviii, xxvi, 88, 128, 175; socialist, xx; state, 175, 176; state violence, complicity with, xi, xiv; transnational, xvii, xviii, 49, 192n6, 218n2; U.S., xxv, 172, 175–76; and violence, ix–x, xii, xiv, 161, 169–70, 179, 246n71; violent female subjects, production of, x, xxx, 4, 26–27, 106, 246n71. *See also* feminism, Japanese; *feminizumu; ribu;* Tanaka Mitsu

feminism, Japanese, 171; first wave, 116, 130; as foreign concept, xxii, 194n24; organizations, 198n20; pre-Occupation, 5–6; radical, 15; second wave, xxix, 128, 131, 178, 195n36, 241n128; U.S. feminism, distinctions from, xxii. *See also* feminism; *feminizumu; ribu;* Tanaka Mitsu

Feminist Majority Foundation, ix

Feminisuto (magazine), 172, 249n6

feminizumu, 174, 249n1; academic connotations of, 171–72; defined, 171. *See also* feminism; feminism, Japanese; *ribu*

Firestone, Shulamith, 88, 225n77

foreign policy, U.S.: in Afghanistan, 189n1; and anticommunism, xxiii. *See also* Japan; Korean War (U.S.); Okinawa; U.S.–Japan Mutual Cooperation and Security Treaty; Vietnam War (U.S.)

Freeman, Jo, 196n38

From Woman to Women (*ribu* newsletter), 144–45

Front (New Left sect), 38

Fujieda Mioko, 110

fujin, xviii, 4, 14, 15–17, 18, 172, 205n74. *See also* women, Japanese: terms for

Fukushima Kikjiro, 229n5

Funamoto Emi, 129

gebabō, 50–51; Mori on, 51, 66–67; *ribu,* use of, 70; symbology of, 51, 52, 218n5; Tanaka on, 219n5

Gordon, Andrew, 7, 225n76

Gramsci, Antonio, 89

Group of Fighting Women (*ribu* group), 18, 23, 72, 75, 106, 149, 178; Eugenic Protection Law, struggle against, 235n68; founding, 103; Kunihisa Kazuko, 153–54, 228n112; Ribu Conference, 83, 85, 117, 223n51; *ribu* summer camps, 223n50; Tanaka, role of, 107, 117, 118–19, 125, 206n80, 219n8, 229n3, 235n75; URA, interactions with, 244n36. *See also ribu;* Tanaka Mitsu

Group of Women Who Fight the Sexism of the Mass Media, 81, 82

Gurūpu Kan (*ribu* group), 119–20

Gurūpu Tatakau Onna. See Group of Fighting Women

Hall, Stuart, 177

Hane, Mikiso: on Japanese feminism, 5–6, 198n13

Hara Kazuo, 177, 206n86

Hartsock, Nancy, 246n71

Hayaki Yasuko, 142

hegemony, xii–xiii, 89; Euro-American, xvi; and feminism, x, 131, 173, 190n3, 192n6, 192n11, 252n28; and state violence, 144, 169; of Tanaka's views, 118, 125

Higuchi Keiko, 83

Hiratsuka Raichō, xxii, 6, 78, 130, 197n13, 198n14, 221n29

Hōkiboshi, 97, 228n106

Ichiyo Muto: on *ribu*, xix, 44, 104, 218n103, 239n113

ie (family system), xxii, 5, 28, 29; and imperialism, 112; *ribu* critique of, 18, 74, 84, 89, 92–93, 97, 233n45; Tanaka on, 112, 220n22

Iijima Aiko, 11–18; Japanese imperialism, critique of, 16, 74; JSP, purged from, 202n50; Marxism, critique of, 15, 204n67; on mothers, 203n56; Mother's Convention, critique of, 12–13; *onna*, disidentification with, 16, 204n72; and Ōta Ryū, 202n49, 202n51; *ribu*, coalition work with, 16; *ribu*, disidentification with, 74; *ribu*, influence on, 71, 240n127; Ribu Conference discussion, 83; as *ribu* forerunner, 11–12, 14, 15; on sex discrimination, 14; on sex oppression, 204n70; Tanaka, distinctions from, 204n72; Tanaka, interactions with, 109, 232n26; theory as male domain, 15, 204n67, 232n43; Tokoro, influence on, 43, 214n45; women's liberation theory of, 14

imperialism: gendered violence of, 47, 48, 49; and liberty, ix; and nationalism, xxiii; neo-imperialism, ix, xiii; and women, discrimination against, 71

imperialism, Japanese, xiii, xv, xxi, xxiii, 4, 6, 13, 19, 37, 73; neo-imperialism, ix, xiii; role of family in, xvii, 3; struggle against, 39; women's complicity in, 15; Yasukuni Shrine, 203n55

imperialism, Japanese–U.S., 47, 71

imperialism, U.S., xvii, xxiii, xxv, 6, 47; women's complicity in, 15. *See also* anti-imperialism

individualism, xxvi, 93, 169

inheritance laws, Japan, 24–25, 207n100; Shimazu on, 207n100

Inoue Teruko, 16, 174–75, 237n85; on *feminizumu*, 171–72, 174; Tokoro, influence of, 43, 104, 213n43

International Antiwar Day (1970), 69; New Left protests, 39, 75, 215n77, 221n27, 222n34; *ribu* protest, 17, 69, 72, 75, 211n18, 211n22, 218n103, 221n27

International Society for Women's Studies, 173, 250n8

International Women's Day, 94

International Women's Year Conference, 131, 251n23

International Year of the Woman, 101, 126, 131

ippu-ippu seidō ("one-husband one-wife" system), 21

Itō Noe, 130

Iwao Sumiko, 173, 250n12

Iwatsuki Sumie, 57, 66, 74, 95–98, 129; Hōkiboshi, 97, 228n106; name change, 97; *ribu*, disidentification with, 95–96; Witch Concerts, 96. *See also* Asatori Sumie

Japan: and Cold War, colonial legacy of, xv, xxi; immigration laws, 14, 89, 109, 175; leftism in, xv; militarism, xxiii; and orientalism, xv–xvi; post–World War II politics, 4–5; relations with the West, xv; social movements in, xxiiv; U.S. occupation of, xxii–xxiii, 4, 5, 34, 87. *See also* United States: foreign policy of

Japanese Association of Travel Agencies (JATA), 94

Japanese Association to Protect Children (Nihon Kodomo o Mamoru Kai), 12

Japanese Communist Party (JCP), 7,
　12, 34, 37, 231n24; affiliated groups,
　202n53; hierarchical structure of, 37;
　Korean War, reaction to, 210n12
Japanese Red Army (JRA), 140, 144,
　149, 160, 242n3
Japan Socialist Party (JSP), 7, 12, 34, 37,
　202n50, 231n24
Japan Teachers Union, 12
josei, xviii, 4, 13, 16–17, 18, 44, 172,
　205n75, 205n79, 205n80, 221n24. *See
　also* women, Japanese: terms for

Kageyama Hiroko, 83
Kaihō (New Left sect), 39, 53, 211n16
Kakumaru (New Left sect), 38, 53, 59,
　144, 246n74
Kanai Yoshiko, 110
Kanba Michiko: killing of, 34–36, 58,
　210n9, 210n10, 211n15
Kaneko Fumiko, 198n13, 248n105
Kaneko Michiyo: murder of, 33, 61–62,
　141, 153, 164
Kanno Sugako, xxii, 6, 83, 198n13
Kano, Ayako, 194n24
Kano Masanao, 16, 205n75
Kano Mikiyo, 174–75, 244n40
Katō Yoshitaka, 141
Kawashima Tsuyoshi, 165–66
Kazuko Tanaka: on post–World War II
　women's labor, 9
Keisō Shobō, 219n8
Khor, Diana, 198n20
Kimura Hisako, 244n41
Kisaeng tourism, 72, 93–95, 227n96;
　ribu protests, 86
Kishida Toshiko, 5
Kiyoko Kinjo, 200n33
knowledge production, xvi, xxv;
　gendered, xxiv, 173, 175; racialized,
　xxiv; of *ribu,* xxvii, xxxiv, 177
Kōdōsuru kai, 235n70

kogoroshi no onna ("mothers who killed
　their children"), xxi, 23, 24, 207n92;
　mass media coverage of, 23, 207n95;
　ribu solidarity with, xxi, xxx, 4, 24,
　26, 27, 30, 31, 86, 89, 93, 148, 151,
　177, 207n97, 215n67, 238n109; sub-
　jectivity of, 26; Tama on, 23; Tanaka
　on, 25–26, 90, 128, 207n97, 238n109;
　violent system, as response to, 26–27;
　Yonezu on, 207n97, 243n29, 244n36
Kojima Kazuko, 141
Korean War (U.S.), xxiii, 13, 40; antiwar
　movement, 34
koseki seidō (family registration sys-
　tem), 6, 22, 24–25, 90, 198n16; *ribu*
　critique of, 20–23
K-san (Keiko) case, 91–93, 227n93;
　media coverage of, 91, 92, 96
Kunihisa Kazuko, 153–54, 228n112,
　244n44, 244n45
Kuno Ayako, 74, 78, 122, 196n2, 221n30,
　235n67

labor movements, 7
Labor Standards Act (1947), 9
Left, established Japanese: hierarchical
　structure of, 37, 38, 210n11. *See also*
　Japanese Communist Party; New
　Left, Japanese
lesbianism, 119, 218n3; political,
　236n79; and *ribu,* 68–69
lesbians, 101; activism, 68–69, 102,
　119–20, 132, 178, 220n14; and Ribu
　Shinjuku Center, 236n81, 236n84
Liberal Democratic Party (LDP), 88
liberalism: and counterviolence, xii; and
　individualism, 93
liberation, 106, 110, 113–15; genealogies
　of, xxvi; and subjectivity, 42
"Liberation from the Toilet" (Tanaka),
　18–19, 71, 103, 108–9, 111, 113,
　115–16, 119, 205n80, 220n22, 233n43

liberation of *onna,* xvi, xviii, 44, 68, 70, 73, 113
liberation of sex, 26, 68, 44, 86, 99, 103, 113–16, 119, 128
Lorde, Audre, 234n55
"Love Letter to My Mother" (Group of Fighting Women), 23
Luxembourg, Rosa, 39, 45

MacArthur, Douglas, 4
Machino Michiko, 119–20, 122, 229n1, 235n72
Mackie, Vera: on Japanese feminism, xxii, 5–6, 7
Mackinnon, Catherine, 246n71
male supremacy, xx
Mandela, Nelson, 247n77
Maoism, 242n4
Marcuse, Herbert, 220n14
martial arts, 30, 101, 102
Martin, Patricia Yancey, 198n20
Marx, Karl, 110
Marxism, xxix, 13, 110; Iijima on, 15, 204n67; and Japanese New Left, 38; limits of, 15; and *ribu,* xxi, 39, 89, 219n13, 221n27; Tanaka on, 111, 114, 232n29. *See also* Japanese Communist Party; New Left, Japanese
Marxist-Leninist Faction (ML Ha) (New Left sect), 140, 242n4, 242n5
Matsui Machiko: on *ribu,* xix, 176
Matsui Yayori, 74, 174, 176, 192n11, 223n53; anti-imperialism of, 176; Asian Women's Resource Center, 203n62; Pan-Asian solidarity of, 203n62; recognitions of, 251n22; *ribu,* critique of, 203n62, 252n28; *ribu,* disidentification with, 74; on U.S. feminism, 175–76
Matsumoto Michiko, 120, 229n5
Medaka (Piranha) Collective (*ribu* group), 126

Meiji era (1868–1912), 87, 111, 196n4, 197n10, 206n83, 208n108
men's *ribu,* 86
Metropolitan (*ribu* group), 77, 222n34, 235n69
Miki Sōko, xxviii, 66, 97, 200n29; critique of women's studies, 173; editing work, 202n52; on *Feminisuto,* 249n6; on K-san case, 93; liberation of sex and *onna,* 68; media coverage of URA, critique of, 144–45, 149, 242n10; on *ribu* camps, 77; on URA, 152
mini-komi (mini-communications): *ribu,* use by, xxviii, 78–79, 81, 96, 235n67. *See also ribu,* actions and initiatives
Mioko Fujieda: New Left, impact on, 53; on women's liberation movements, xxix
Mishima Yukio: *hara-kiri* of, 42, 52–53, 215n81; on University of Tokyo struggle, 217n82, 217n86
Miyaoka Maki, 57–60, 66, 215n66; on Marx, 217n92; sexism, critique of, 59
Mizoguchi Ayeko, 8–9, 78, 200n29; editing work, 202n52, 222n42; on Ribu Conference, 223n52; on Tanaka, 104; on URA, 152
Mizuno, Noriko, 196n4
modernity: and capitalism, ix; and gender, 5; as global process, xxii
Mohanty, Chandra, 190n3
Mona Lisa spray incident, 86, 99
Morioka Masahiro: on Tanaka, 208n112
Mori Setsuko, 24, 66, 97; Aida Kōbō, founding of, 102; on *gebabō,* 51, 66–67; Kisaeng tourism action, 94–95; as medium, 94; on *onna,* 68, 150; on radical inclusivity, 153; RSC, division of labor at, 86, 122; on sexual difference, 219n13; on

Tanaka, 125; Thought Group SEX, founding of, 67, 68, 122; on URA women, 150, 152

Mori Tsuneo, 140, 141, 142, 147, 148; media representations of, 145

Morizaki Kazue, 43, 110

motherhood: as identity, 3, 23; as nationalist ideology, 19–21; organizing around, 12; post–World War II, 12, 200n35, 206n82; *ribu* critique of, 19, 20; state regulation of, 20, 23, 25, 92, 93; and unmarried mothers, 20, 22; and violence, xxx, 3–4

Mother's Convention, 12, 202n53, 202n54; Iijima critique of, 12–13

Mukaiyama Shigenori, 142

Murakami Nobohiko, 5

Murakami Tomoko, 129

Nagata Hiroko, 140–42, 144, 146, 153–54; as "crazy woman," 148, 150; criminalization of, 151; death of, 168, 249n117; on Kaneko, 248n105; media representations of, 145, 148, 155, 167, 242n17; as nonexisting woman, 165, 166; ontology of, 167; published appeal of, 155; rape of, 165–66; *ribu* on, 148–49, 154–55; sexist discourse on, 148; Tanaka, contact with, 163–64; Tanaka on, 140, 157, 163, 164–68, 248n111, 248n116; trial of, 152–53, 155, 156

Namahara Reiko, 100, 150–51

Namekata Masatoki, 141, 218n105

Nanako Kurihara, 128–29

Narita Ryūichi, 5, 197n9

nationalism: and imperialism, xxiii, 49, 215n67, 234n60; Japanese, xxi, xxxiv; postnationalism, xvii

National Organization of Women (NOW), 44, 191n9, 225n74

national women's strike (1970), 194n20

neoliberalism, xxxiv, 176, 178

neo–New Left, 40, 77, 239n113

New Japanese Women's League, 198n23

New Japan Women's League (Shin Nihon Fujin Dōmei), 8

New Left, xv, xxiii, xxix. *See also* New Left, Japanese; New Left, U.S.

New Left, Japanese, xix, xxix, xxxi, xxxiii, 14, 193n16, 202n50; and anticapitalism, 54; and anti-imperialism, xxxi, 74, 112; direct action, emphasis on, 39, 70; gender dynamics in, 61; hierarchy in, 224n66; liberal democracy, break from, 9; and logic of productivity, 62; and Marxism, 38, 231n24; masculinism in, 31, 41, 45, 53, 55–56, 58, 151–52, 167; origins of, xxxi, 38–40; police, clashes with, 55, 56, 58; *ribu*, erasure of, 218n103; *ribu*, response to, xxviii; role of women in, 51; sectarianism, 77, 95, 142, 160, 169, 214n54, 243n23, 246n74; sects, 204n63, 241n129; self-destruction of, 33, 53, 57, 61, 62, 139, 144; sexism in, 57, 58–59; violence in, 53, 55, 140, 142, 153, 248n101. *See also* Chūkaku; Front; Japanese Red Army (JRA); Kaihō; Kakumaru; Marxist Leninist Faction (ML Ha); New Left; New Left, U.S.; *ribu*; United Red Army (URA)

New Left, U.S., 193n16

Nichibo (doctors organization), 91, 226n89

Nihon Fujin Kaigi, 12

Nihon Fujin Yukensha Domei (Japan League of Women Voters), 198n23

Nishimura Mitsuko: on *ribu* communes, 20

nongovernmental organizations (NGOs), 176, 252n29

Norgren, Tiana, 91

Ochiai Emiko, 205n78

Oda Makoto, 41, 212n27

Ōgoshi Aiko, 251n22

Oguma Eiji, 246n66, 248n101

Ōhashi Yukako, 208n109

Okinawa, 215n69; and *ribu,* 13, 216n68; sex workers in, 49, 216n69; U.S. occupation of, xxii–xxiii, 13, 40, 49, 215n69, 222n32

Okinawans: musicians, 237n91; New Left solidarity, 74

Oku Mumeo, 201n39

Oni no Ie, 228n106

onna, xxx; defined, xvi; discourse of, 4, 11; Iijima on, 16, 204n72; liberation of, xvi, xviii, 44, 68, 70, 73, 113; and logic of productivity, 55; ontology of, 115, 157; organizing of, 70; Orie on, xvi, 16, 192n4; as political subject, xxiv, 20–21, 50, 73, 205n80, 215n71; positionality of, 71; relations among, 123–24; as revolutionary subject, xxvi; *ribu,* core concept of, 65, 205n79; *ribu,* reclamation by, 16, 17, 18, 31; Sayama on, xvi; subjectivity of, 157–59; Tanaka on, 113, 115, 124, 150, 158, 159, 205n80; as term, 221n24; theory of, 221n27; as victim/accomplice, 72. *See also ribu,* discourse; Tanaka Mitsu, discourse

Onna and Child's Festival, 83

Onna Erosu (*ribu* journal), 61, 78, 104, 120, 173, 192n2, 194n21, 201n44, 249n6; circulation of, 201n44

onna kotoba (écriture féminine), 110

Onna no hangyaku (*ribu* newsletter), 235n67

Onna's Mutiny (*Onna no hangyaku*), 78, 117, 196n2

Onna's Thought (*Onna no shisō*), 22, 59

ontology: feminine, 30, 56, 71, 169–70; feminist, xxvii, 56; of *onna,* 115,

157; political, xxxi, 71, 72, 93, 102, 220n18, 227n95; Tanaka on, 115, 157; of violence, xiii, xiv. *See also ribu,* discourse; Tanaka Mitsu, discourse

"Organization to Come, The" (Tokoro), 42–43, 44

Orie Endo: on *onna,* xvi, 16, 192n4

orientalism, xv–xvi, xvii

Ōta Ryū, 12, 202n49, 202n51

otherness, xvii

Ōtsuka Setsuko, 141

Ozaki Michio, 141

Ōzawa Ryōko: Ribu Conference discussion, 83

Ozawa Yōko, 215n56

pacifism, 34

Pax Americana, xxiii, 40

philosophy: feminist, xxvii. *See also ribu,* discourse; Tanaka Mitsu, discourse

politics, feminist, ix, xii, 29; leftist, xix, xxiii; state, 70. *See also* New Left, Japanese; *ribu;* Tanaka Mitsu

Popular Front for the Liberation of Palestine (PFLP), 141

poverty, xi

prisons, x–xi; incarceration of women, 191n11

Protesting Sex Discrimination: The Contentions of Ūman Ribu, 73

psychoanalysis, 110

Public Peace Police Law, 5, 197n7

race: intersections with class, xi

radicalism: in United States and Japan, xii–xiii

Read, Jacinda, x

Regumi Studio, 97

Reich, Wilhelm, 109, 114, 219n8, 220n14, 232n29, 240n127

reverse-orientalism, 194n24

Revolutionary Left Faction, 140, 242n5, 248n105

ribu, ix, xii; anticapitalism of, 43, 72, 88–89; and anti-imperialism, xxi, 19, 47, 69, 71, 74, 86, 87–89, 93, 94–95, 177, 221n30; "death" of, 102, 128, 130, 131, 175, 240n119, 240n120, 251n21; and direct action, 70, 92; equality, idealization of, 123–24, 125, 238n101; feminist logic of, 151; historical significance of, xxv; identity politics of, 14, 204n63; law, defiance of, 41; legacy of, xxxiii, 171, 195n31; liberatory praxis of, 215n67; as living philosophy, 84; and Marxism, xxi, 39, 219n13; mass media, representation in, 79–83, 100, 173, 223n43; mass media, use of, xxviii, 81; men's liberation, 97, 98; and minority women, 178; ontology, feminine of, 30, 56, 71, 169–70; ontology, political, xxxi, 71, 72, 93, 102, 227n95; parliamentary democracy, distrust of, 39; retrospectives of, 177; and sex workers, 177; transnational identification of, xxi; URA, media conflation with, 149–50, 242n10; and violence, xiii–xiv, 4, 13, 30, 247n81; visibility, politics of, 79. *See also ribu,* actions and initiatives; *ribu,* discourse; *ribu,* genealogy of; *ribu,* internal composition; Ribu Shinjuku Center; Tanaka Mitsu

ribu, actions and initiatives: alternative media of, xxviii; communes, xx, xxx, 19–21, 22, 67, 84, 85, 86, 89–90, 99, 119, 223n51; constitutive centers, 84–87; criminalized women, identification with, xxx–xxxi, 27, 29, 94, 152, 154, 157, 215n67, 243n29,

248n111; disabled persons, solidarity with, 67, 79, 90, 91, 99–101, 178, 219n5; International Antiwar Day (1970), 17, 69, 72, 75, 211n18, 211n22, 218n103, 221n27; *kogoroshi no onna,* solidarity with, xxi, xxx, 4, 24, 26, 27, 30, 31, 86, 89, 93, 148, 151, 177, 207n97, 215n67, 238n109; Mother's Day march (1971), 23; parody, use of, 81–83; publications, 10, 78, 81, 85, 119, 120, 144, 148, 154, 155; retreats, 252n33; summer camps *(ribu gasshuku),* xxxii, 72, 75–79, 117, 163, 174, 221n30, 223n50, 228n123; Tokyo gathering (11/12/1972), 11, 72; URA, critique of, 150, 156; URA, support of, xxxiii, 83, 84, 228n112; URA women, critical solidarity with, 86, 99–100, 139, 150–51, 153, 154, 156–57, 169, 178, 209n118, 243n29, 244n45, 244n49, 245n63. *See also ribu; ribu,* discourse; *ribu,* internal composition; Ribu Shinjuku Center; Tanaka Mitsu

ribu, discourse, xvii, xx, 3–4, 10, 11; on abortion, xx, xxxii, 26, 73, 87–89, 90, 148, 178; anti-imperialist, 71, 87–88; and antiviolence, 30; capitalism, critique of, 11; and comfort women, 67; on contraception, 148; on criminalized women, 23–24, 27, 67, 154; eros in, 60–61, 68, 78; family, critique of, xvii, 3, 61; *ie,* critique of, 18, 74, 84, 89, 92–93, 97, 233n45; imperialism, Japanese women's complicity in, 47–50, 73, 161; on *jiko hitei,* 46–47, 62; killing of *onna,* 62; on logic of productivity, 61, 67; as "male" language, 206n84; marriage, rejection of, 4, 10; Marxism, critique of, 89, 221n27; on masculinity, 73;

mass media, critique of, 92, 149; men
as enemy, 83, 84; on motherhood, 19,
26, 73; on Nagata, 148, 154–55; on
neo-imperialism, Japanese, 195n27;
on New Left masculinism, 53, 56,
148–49, 150, 151–52; New Left
violence, critique of, 52, 84; relationality in, 60–61, 68, 113, 157, 179;
on repression of *onna*, 55, 205n79;
revolutionary female sacrifice,
rejection of, 52; self-criticism of, 48;
self-determination, 77; self-negation,
rejection of, 5; sex, politicization
of, 17, 19; on sexual desire, 11;
subjectivity of, 58; Tanaka, effect on,
124; theory, critique of, 89, 221n27,
230n19; universalizing tendencies of,
15; and unmarried mothers, xxxii,
19, 26, 66, 86, 92, 99, 148, 227n104;
URA purge, media coverage of, 144,
148–49; and U.S. blacks, 204n65;
violence, critical feminist approach
to, 72, 151, 139, 151, 162; as "woman
lib," xviii–xix. *See also* discourse,
feminist; *ribu;* Tanaka Mitsu,
discourse

ribu, genealogy of, xxi, xxxi, 3, 26, 33,
149; defined, xviii; emergence of,
65, 70, 148; *feminizumu,* distinctions from, xix, xxxiv, 171, 193n12;
leftist men, disidentification with,
60; as non-Western movement, xviii;
origins of, xxix, 3, 8, 12, 14, 53, 60,
128, 149; other Japanese feminist
movements, distinctions from, xxx,
xxxiv, 3–4, 7, 9, 23, 28, 30; other
leftist movements, relation to, xv,
xvi, xix, xxv, 149; as Pan-Asian
movement, 14, 15, 94, 192n11; as
post-Anpo generational movement,
39; as post–New Left movement,

8, 10, 39, 40, 149, 163; as radical
feminist movement xix–xxi, xxvii,
3, 7, 15, 29, 59, 115, 163; as second
wave feminism, xxix, 175, 195n36;
as social movement, xxxi; women's
lib, U.S. differences from, xxi–xxii,
xxx, 74, 177. *See also ribu,* actions
and initiatives; *ribu,* discourse; *ribu,*
internal composition; Tanaka Mitsu

ribu, internal composition: antihierarchical principles of, xvi, xxxii,
44, 75, 77, 85, 104, 123–24, 192n3,
230n19, 239n117; class in, xvi, 10,
47, 15, 114; collective leadership
of, 73; collective subjectivity of, 50,
62, 65, 71, 77, 93, 127, 156, 215n70,
215n71; constitutive centers, 84–87;
continuity of, 228n124; homophobia
in, 119; internal power struggles,
116–17; as marginal majority, xxiiv;
onna centered organization of, xxxi,
95, 96, 97, 150; radical inclusivity
of, 150, 152–57, 169; as "relative"
whites, xxiii; size of, 10, 192n2. *See
also ribu,* actions and initiatives;
Ribu Shinjuku Center; Tanaka Mitsu

Ribu Conference (1972), 72, 85, 117,
120, 148, 153, 223n51, 223n52;
Chūpiren involvement in, 226n78

Ribu News, 153, 154, 166, 168, 201n44,
224n60, 229n3, 244n4

Ribu Shinjuku Center (RSC), 30, 67,
84, 100, 119, 178, 224n63; activism,
90, 91; antihierarchical organization, 123–24, 127, 224n65; closing
of, 128; communal living at, 86,
120–21, 235n69, 239n115; division of
labor at, 122, 124, 237n94, 237n98,
238n103; establishment of, 85, 153,
223n50, 224n64; homophobia in,
236n81; 1983 retreat, 241n132;

as *onna*-centered collective, 126; power dynamics, 120, 121–23, 125, 239n114; printing press, 85, 86, 155; Tanaka, impact on, 120, 125–28, 133, 229n1, 235n75, 237n92, 237n98, 239n116; writing, role of, 238n105, 238n107, 238n108. *See also ribu*, actions and initiatives; Tanaka Mitsu

Rice, Condoleezza, x

Richie, Beth, 191n11

riot police, 39, 50–52, 55, 56, 215n72

Ripples of Change: Japanese Women's Search for Self (film), xxxii, 128, 177, 206n89

Ritchie, Andrea, 191n11

ryōsai kenbo ("good wife and wise mother" ideology), 6–7; post–World War II, 13; *ribu*, denunciation by, 9, 24; Uno on, 7

Saeki Yōko, xxviii, 22, 66, 78, 97, 104–5, 122, 145, 200n29; editing, 202n52, 215n66, 222n42; on *Feminisuto*, 172, 249n6; on *onna*'s thought, 50; on URA, 152

Saishu Satoru, 52

Saito Masami, 81

Sakaguchi Hiroshi, 153–54

Sanpa-Zengakuren, 211n16

Sanrizuka (farmers' rebellion), 40, 95, 212n26, 227n99, 227n100

Sartre, Jean Paul, 109

Sasaki-Uemura, Wesley, 37; on Anpo, 210n9

Sayama Sachi, xxviii, 16–17, 24, 119, 126; on *onna*, xvi; Ribu Shinjuku Center, 86, 224n63, 235n69, 235n75; on Tanaka, 239n115

Scarlet Letter (Himonji) (*ribu* group), 85

Seichō no Ie, 87–88, 208n112, 225n72

Seitō (Blue Stockings movement), 6, 130, 197n13

Seitō Journal, 78

Senda Yuki, 71, 198n20

sex discrimination, 116; colonialism, link to, 74; imperialism, link to, 74; and Mori, 66–67; as origin of oppression, xx–xxi, 15, 31

Sexual Revolution, The (Reich), 219n8, 232n27

Seyama Noriko, 177, 178

Shibokusa, 14, 203n63

Shigenobu Fusako, 141

Shimazu Yoshiko, 207n100

Shindō Ryuzaburo, 141

Shin Nihon Fujin no Kai (JCP group), 202n53

Shoshiren, 101, 228n119

shufu, 4, 9–10, 16, 17–18, 196n1, 205n74, 220n22. *See also* women, Japanese: terms for

Shufuren (Housewives Association), 9–10, 200n36, 200n37, 201n39; Tanaka on, 201n40

Shūkan Asahi, 69

Sievers, Sharon: on Japanese feminism, xxii, 5–6

Sixteen Graves (Nagata), 165

Smeal, Eleanor, 189n1

Smith, Andrea, 191n11

Sōhyō, 34, 231n24

Stahl, Lesley, 189n2

state violence, 34–37, 38, 144. *See also* bodies, women; riot police

Steinhoff, Patricia, 144, 148, 166, 212n23

student movements. *See* Zengakuren; Zenkyōtō student movement

subjectivity, collective, xxxi, 50, 156; contingency of, xxxiii, 140, 153, 157, 168–69, 249n116; of *kogoroshi no onna*, 26; of *onna*, 157–59; as political, 45; revolutionary, xxi; and revolutionary potential, xxvi; Tanaka on, xxxiii, 115, 124, 133, 157, 162–63,

234n57. *See also ribu,* discourse; subjectivity, feminist; Tanaka Mitsu, discourse

subjectivity, feminist, ix–x, xi, 106; and alternative media, xxviii; and violence, xxx, 4, 26–27, 106, 246n71. *See also ribu,* discourse; subjectivity; Tanaka Mitsu, discourse

Sudbury, Julia, 191n11

suffrage movements, xxx, 7; Japanese, xxx, 5

summer camps, *ribu,* xxxii, 72, 75–79; Hokkaidō, 77; Izu, 222n34, Shinnohei, 75

Takada Motomu: on Zenkyōtō, 52

Takamure Itsue, xxii, 6, 43; "women's theory" of, 214n45

Takeda Miyuki, 24, 117, 126, 234n63, 239n114; on child-rearing, 20

Tama Yasuko: on *kogoroshi no onna,* 23

Tanaka Kazuko, 174

Tanaka Mitsu, xxv, xxvii–xxix, 16, 66, 74, 97, 102, 103–35, 178; class status, 108, 227n99; comfort women, support of, 176, 247n78; criticism of, 117–18; feminist theory of, 4, 25; immigration law struggle, 109; intellectual influences, 109–10; liberal feminism, critique of, 116; liberation, theory of, 105–6, 115, 116, 118, 157, 158–59, 162, 169; periodization of, 231n24; philosophy of violence, 157–63; politicization of, 231n25; post-RSC, 130; rhetoric of, 110–11, 117; self-identification of, 108; as unmarried mother, 129; women's rights, critique of, 194n20. *See also* Group of Fighting Women; *ribu;* Ribu Shinjuku Center; Tanaka Mitsu, discourse; Tanaka Mitsu,

leadership; Tanaka Mitsu, relation to the New Left

Tanaka Mitsu, discourse, 110, 129, 240n122; on abortion, 25, 26, 28–29, 90, 128, 208n112; on abstraction, 235n66; on anarchy, 239n117; antiimperialism of, 234n60; on capitalism, women's complicity in, 220n22; on comfort women, 71, 161; on contingency, xxxiii, 140, 153, 157, 168–69, 249n116; on feminism, U.S., 234n60, 234n61; on "here-existing" *onna,* 158, 159, 166; heterodominance of, 119, 236n76, 236n78; on heterosexual desire, 160; on *ie,* 112, 220n22; on individualism, 159; on *kogoroshi no onna,* 25–26, 90, 128, 207n97, 238n109; on liberation of eros, 103, 111, 113, 119, 133, 140, 157, 234n55; on liberation of *onna,* 113; on liberation of sex, 26, 103, 113–16, 119, 128; on logic of productivity, 54, 56, 57, 91, 113, 120, 146, 214n45; on Marxism, 111, 114, 232n29; on Mishima, 53; on *onna,* 113, 115, 124, 205n80; on ontology, xxxiii; on relationality, 113, 115–16, 120–21, 140, 157, 159, 162, 164, 169; on revolution and violence, 168, 217n87; on *ribu,* politics of, 118; selfreflexive discourse of, 161; sex, as class, 114; sex, as site of oppression, 114; on Shufuren, 10; on subjectivity, xxxiii, 115, 124, 133, 157, 162–63, 234n57; on *torimidashi* (contradiction and disorder), 140, 157, 158, 169; on "The Totality," 114–15, 234n57; violence, theory of, 140, 158, 159–60, 161, 247n75, 247n78; on women and violence, 25–26, 27, 28, 128, 158, 160–62, 246n71, 246n73; on women's sex, 159, 234n54, 234n56.

See also discourse, feminist; *ribu,* discourse; Tanaka Mitsu; Tanaka Mitsu, leadership; Tanaka Mitsu, relation to the New Left

Tanaka Mitsu, leadership: antielitism of, 108, 231n20; authorship in *ribu,* 133, 241n134; as charismatic leader, 109, 130; contradictions of, 85, 125–28, 129, 134, 235n70, 236n84, 237n92, 237n99; criticism of, 117–18; editing, 124–25; as icon, xxvii–xxviii, xxxii, 78, 104–5, 106, 108, 113, 130–32, 133, 134, 175, 248n109, 251n22; mass media, use of, 106, 134; as medium, 106–8, 111, 132, 133, 166; as messenger of *ribu,* 133, 230n15; relationships with other *ribu* women, 234n63, 234n64; Ribu Conference discussion, 83, 221n29, 221n30; RSC, departure from, 126–27, 241n133; RSC, influence on, 86, 133; RSC, as spokesperson of, 121, 125–28, 237n90. *See also* Group of Fighting Women; *ribu;* Ribu Shinjuku Center; Tanaka Mitsu; Tanaka Mitsu, discourse; Tanaka Mitsu, relation to the New Left

Tanaka Mitsu, relation to the New Left, 109, 110, 112–13; on JRA purge, 164; on masculinism of New Left, 56, 57, 112, 118, 159, 233n43; on Nagata, 140, 157, 163, 164–68, 248n111; Nagata, identification with, 163, 167–68, 248n116; New Left, critique of, 112, 113, 157, 215n56; on sectarian violence, 160, 241n129; on URA, 111, 157, 164, 166, 168, 240n122, 245n66, 248n111. *See also* Group of Fighting Women; Tanaka Mitsu; Tanaka Mitsu, discourse; Tanaka Mitsu, leadership; United Red Army

Tatakau Onna Dōmei (*ribu* group), 85
Taylor, Verta, 17
Teraoka Koichi, 141
terrorism, 170
30 Years of Sisterhood (film), 177, 178, 218n5, 253n36
Thompson, Becky: on feminism, hegemonic, 190n3
Thought Group SEX (*ribu* group), 66, 72, 75, 85, 122; direct action, use of, 66; tactics, 66
Three Points Café, 96, 227n104
Tokoro Mitsuko, 33, 42, 213n33, 213n35, 213n43; feminine ontology of, 56; intellectual work of, 42–43, 213n38; on "male thought," 43; New Left, critique of, 54; as *ribu* forerunner, 42; science, critique of, 88; women's theory, call for, 43, 50, 214n45; Zenkyōtō, invisibility in, 51–52
Tokyo Komu-unu (*ribu* commune), 20, 21, 85, 99, 206n86
Tonomura, Hitomi, 5, 197n9, 197n10
To Women with Spirit: A Disorderly Theory of Women's Liberation (Tanaka), 25, 28, 111, 120, 157, 159–60, 164, 168, 208n101, 237n85
Toyama Mieko, 141, 218n105
translation: and otherness, xxvi; as political practice, xxiiv; "translational trouble," xviii, xxvi, 192n10
translocational politics, xxiv–xxv; theorization of, xxv–xxvii
transnationalism: critiques of, xvii

Ueno Chizuko, 128, 130, 174–75, 176, 231n20, 249n2; on "feminism" v. "women's movements," 198n20; on motherhood, 206n2; on orientalism, 194n24

Ukai Satoshi, 160
ūman ribu. See ribu
UN Decade for Women, 173, 175
United Red Army (Rengo Sekigun), xiii,
  xxxi, 170; Asama Sansō incident,
  142–43; feminization of, 145; hearings, 156; lynchings, 33, 61–62,
  141–42, 143, 167, 218n105, 233n36;
  media representations of, 139,
  142–43, 155; negation of desire, 62;
  New Left, downfall of, 139, 144; *ribu,*
  relation to, xxxiii, 240n122; *ribu* on,
  83; sectarian violence of, 53, 55, 142,
  153; *sōkatsu* of, 141; and state control, 156; Tanaka on, 111, 157, 164,
  166, 168, 240n122, 245n66, 248n111.
  See also Nagata Hiroko; New Left,
  Japanese; *ribu;* Tanaka Mitsu
United States: foreign policy of, x; Occupation of Japan, xxii–xxiii, 4, 5,
  34, 87
University of Tokyo struggle, 35, 37,
  42, 50, 51, 54, 109, 213n31, 213n35,
  217n82
Uno, Kathleen, 198n17, 200n35; on
  motherhood, 206n82; on *ryōsai
  kenbo,* 7
Urara Satoko, 178
U.S.–Japan Mutual Cooperation and
  Security Treaty (Anpo), xxiii, 8, 33,
  67, 199n26. *See also* Anpo protests

Vietnam War (U.S.), xxiii, 13, 40, 140,
  144; antiwar movement, xv, xxxi, 39,
  40, 45, 47, 70. *See also* imperialism;
  imperialism, U.S.
violence: feminist ethics of, 161, 169–70,
  179, 209n120; hegemonic, 169;
  against men of color, xii; and politics, xxvii; strategic methods of, 161;
  against women, xi; among women,

xii; women, complicity with, xii,
  18–19, 72, 161; and women's bodies,
  25–26
violence, political, 139, 241n1. *See also*
  violence; violence, sectarian
violence, sectarian, 38, 53, 54, 55, 59–60,
  95, 230n19, 243n23; Wheeler on, 53.
  See also New Left, Japanese; United
  Red Army
violence, state, xi, xxxiii, 139; and
  hegemony, xiii
Violence Against Women Act of 1994
  (VAWA), 191n9
Violence Against Women in
  War–Network Japan (VAWW-Net),
  176, 193n11, 203n62
Violent Crime Control and Law Enforcement Act of 1994, 191n9

Wakabayashi Naeko, 69, 86, 97, 102,
  124, 133, 238n111; lesbian activism
  of, 119, 121, 227n107, 228n117
Wakita Haruko, 5, 197n9
Walthall, Anne, 5, 197n9
war: impact on women and children, xi,
  191n12. *See also* Korean War (U.S.);
  Vietnam War (U.S.); World War II
"war of terror," ix, xii
war on terror, 190n7
Watanabe Fumie, xxviii, 205n79, 206n84
Weber, Max: on charismatic leaders,
  109, 111, 230n18, 231n23, 233n41
Weekly Check on the Mass Media (RSC
  zine), 81
Weil, Simone, 43, 213n43
Welker, James, 194n35, 208n101, 218n3,
  220n15
"What Is Discrimination for *Onna?*"
  (Iijima), 15, 16
Wheeler, Frederick, 53, 214n48
Whelehan, Imelda, xx, 193n16, 199n21

Whittier, Nancy, 17
"Why Sexual Liberation? Raising the
    Problem of Women's Liberation"
    (Tanaka), 114
Williams, Randall, 160–61, 247n77
Witch Concerts, xxxii, 96–99; as eros, 97
Wolf Group (ribu group), 71, 226n79,
    252n28
Wollstonecraft, Mary, 246n71
women: agency of, xii; criminaliza-
    tion of, 27, 28, 29, 92, 151, 154; and
    political violence, xiii, 13, 83, 151;
    and politics of violence, xiii, xxvii,
    4; and victimhood, xii, 13; violence
    among, 48
women, Japanese: disenfranchisement,
    197; and Japanese imperialism, xii,
    15, 47–49, 71; liberation movement
    of, xii; terms for, 4, 16–18, 44, 71,
    205n74, 205n79, 221; unequal pay
    of, 9; and violence, xi, xii, 26, 151,
    246n71
women, South Korean, 93–95
Women in Black, 190n7
Women's Committee of Sanrizuka, 14,
    203n63
Women's Democratic Club (Fujin
    Minshū Kurabu), 8, 12, 199n24
Women's International War Crimes
    Tribunal for the Trial of Japanese
    Military Sexual Slavery, 176
women's liberation: as Western concept,
    xxii, 5, 194n24
women's liberation movements: Japa-
    nese, post–World War II, 7–8; pre-
    ribu, 111; U.S., xxi, 95, 116, 174. See
    also feminism; feminism, Japanese,
    feminizumu; ribu
women's organizations, Japanese:
    government, ties to, 9, 10, 15;
    post–World War II, 13; during U.S.

Occupation, 7–8. See also individual
    groups
women's studies, xix, xxxiii–xxxiv, 78,
    104, 131, 134, 250n8; assimilation-
    ist tendencies of, 173; emergence
    of, 172–75; institutionalization of,
    174, 250n10; Miki on, 250n16; ribu,
    distancing from, 172–74; in United
    States, 173
Women's Studies Association of Japan,
    173, 250n8
Workshop for Women JO-JO, 228n122
World War II, 4; as interimperialist
    war, 4

Yamada Takeshi, 141
Yamagami Chieko, 177, 178
Yamaguchi, Tomomi, 178, 235n70,
    251n22
Yamakawa Kikue, 8
Yamamoto Junichi, 141
Yamamoto Yoshitaka, 50, 51, 52,
    213n35; on jiko-hitei, 46; on Tokoro
    Mitsuko's death, 42
Yamazaki Jun, 141
Yasko, Guy, 42; on self-criticism and
    self-denial, 215n62; on Tokoro, 52;
    on Zenkyōtō, 45–46, 213n35
Yasukuni Shrine, 202n55
Yoda, Tomiko, 192n10, 194n35
Yōko Matsuoka, 14
Yonezu Tomoko, xxviii, 24, 26, 66,
    79–81, 97–98, 122; on abortion, 90;
    Aida Kōbō, 102; disability, politics of,
    79, 80, 90, 91; on hierarchy in ribu,
    122; on kogoroshi no onna, 207n97,
    243n29, 244n36; on Kunihisa, 154; on
    lesbianism, 119–20; Mona Lisa spray
    incident, 99; on radical inclusivity,
    153; on sexual difference, 219n13;
    on Tanaka, 124, 244n36; Thought

Group SEX, founding of, 67; on URA hearings, 152–53, 243n29. *See also* bodies, disabled; *ribu*

Yoshimoto Taka'aki, 215n61

Yoshitaka Katō, 141

Zainichi (resident Koreans), 227n99; New Left solidarity with, 74

Zengakuren (student movement), 34, 59, 214n48; Miyaoka intervention, 59; post-1960 Anpo, 38

Zenkyōtō student movement, xxxi, 33, 42, 51, 109, 214n52, 215n72; antihierarchical structure of, 41, 44, 84, 224n66, 237n94; autonomy in, 45; citizenship, rejection of, 52, 215n79; class contradiction, 46, 230n19; debate, emphasis on, 43, 46, 73; formation of, 213n31, 213n35, 214n48; localism in, 45–46, 215n58; Mishima's death, impact, 53; as neo–New Left movement, 40; *ribu,* affinity with, 45; as *ribu* precursor, 43–45; riot police, clashes with, 50, 51, 52, 215n72; self-criticism *(jiko hihan)* in, 46, 50; self-denial *(jiko hitei)* in, 46, 50; size of, 43; subjectivity in, 46; Tokoro Mitsuko, death of, 42. *See also* New Left, Japanese; *ribu;* Tokoro Mitsuko

Zen-Nihon Fujin Renmei (All-Japan Women's Federation), 199n22

SETSU SHIGEMATSU is assistant professor of media and cultural studies at the University of California–Riverside. She is coeditor of *Militarized Currents: Toward a Decolonized Future in Asia and the Pacific* (Minnesota, 2010).